India's Experiment with Democracy

Celebrating
30 Years of Publishing
in India

Praise for *India's Experiment with Democracy*

'In his fascinating book, Dr Quraishi unpacks the challenges of conducting elections in India. Simultaneously insightful, critical and thought provoking, this book is an invaluable contribution to the literature on the working of Indian democracy.'

—Justice A.P. Shah, (retired) chief justice, Delhi High Court and chairman, Law Commission of India

'An excellent collection of essays reflecting the insight and expertise of the most intellectual, courageous and dedicated chief election commissioner India had in the twenty-first century!'

—Christophe Jaffrelot, professor, India Institute, King's College, London

'Free and fair elections are one remarkable contribution of indian democracy. This compilation … discusses all aspects in depth. Essential reading for all students of Indian politics and democracy.'

—Dr Deepak Gupta, former chairman, UPSC

'This volume contains invaluable insights into the many challenges facing India's electoral democracy today—from electoral integrity to reforms, from political funding to matters of inclusion. It also encapsulates the wisdom of a civil servant who never quite retired from serving the public and became one of the finest critiques and defenders of India's democracy.'

—Gilles Verniers, senior fellow, Centre for Policy Research

'This collection of Dr Quraishi's writings covers a very large canvas covering various aspects of elections which he himself believes "to be the foundation of our democracy". It provides deep insight into the functioning of our democracy.'

—Jagdeep Chhokar, co-founder, Association for Democratic Reforms (ADR)

'A must-read for those who care for democracy.'
—Kapil Sibal, senior advocate, Supreme Court of India

'Over the years, I've learnt a lot from Dr Quraishi's insightful essays and articles; in particular those about concerns to do with our electoral system and controversies connected with our population. I have no doubt you will be a lot better informed once you read them yourself.'
—Karan Thapar, veteran journalist and president, Infotainment TV

'This volume contains at least three elements. It is, first, a detailed examination of the world's most awe-inspiring secular miracle—the electoral process in India. Second, it is an inventory of the controversies shaping India's momentous emergence as one of the world's great powers, and the vexing challenge of protecting its pluralism on the road to development. Third, it is a much-needed defence of tolerant and reasoned public debate written by a wise man, whose lifelong commitment to integrity and public service will hopefully inspire a new generation of free Indian citizens.'
—Kevin Casas-Zamora, secretary-general of International Institute for Democracy and Electoral Assistance, Stockholm, and former vice-president of Costa Rica

'Dr Quraishi's enormous experience and encyclopaedic knowledge of elections and the electoral process are encapsulated, with remarkable insights, in this eminently readable collection of essays, a part of his monumental trilogy.'
—Justice Madan Lokur, (retired) judge, Supreme Court of India

'Dr Quraishi is one of India's most respected voices on election management, electoral reforms and the law. This collection of his writings serves as an indispensable primer for readers who value Indian democracy and care deeply about its future trajectory.'
—Milan Vaishnav, senior fellow and director, South Asia Program, Carnegie Endowment for International Peace, Washington, DC

'S.Y. Quraishi, a Midnight's Child-turned-bureaucrat, participated in the functioning of India's democracy over several decades. As India's Chief Election Commissioner, his job was to supervise regular, free and fair elections, an unimaginably complex job. This book is both a reportage and a collection of rare data he has gathered all along. It offers us splendid insights into India's resilience and the challenges it faces in the twenty-first century.'

—Mrinal Pande, former chief editor, *Hindustan*

'A confident democracy should celebrate successes but assess its own shortcomings too. This bold and expert book does both.'

—Mukulika Banerjee, associate professor, London School of Economics, and author of *Cultivating Democracy* and *Why India Votes?*

'Dr S.Y. Quraishi, my erstwhile colleague in the Election Commission of India (ECI), has a flair for writing and a way with words, and has been a prolific writer on matters of elections whether in India or abroad. This book is about his experience of elections in many countries where he has been an election observer and covers many topical issues related to elections in India. I recommend the book to researchers, students and avid watchers of the election scenario.'

—N. Gopalaswami, former Chief Election Commissioner of India, and president, Vivekananda Education Society

'This encyclopaedic assessment by Dr Quraishi offers sharp insights and a fresh perspective on the complex interplay between elections and democracy in India. Delightfully written, this book should be read by anyone interested in India's democratic past and future.'

—Pradeep Chhibber, professor of political science and Indo-American Community chair in India studies, University of California, Berkeley

'In a sharply polarized discourse, Dr S.Y. Quraishi's is a vital voice and his latest, *India's Experiment with Democracy*, is a must-read book. Informed by his formidable experience in public affairs—from heading local administration to steering the Election Commission of India—it helps enrich our understanding of change in contemporary India, the role of institutions, the challenges they face from within and outside, and the citizen's place in this. In the Editorial and Ideas pages of *The Indian Express,* where some of the chapters first appeared, Dr Quraishi has carved out a very special place. One where ideas illuminate without ignoring what lies in shadow. That's why his book is a trusted guide to how the world's largest democracy is re-imagining herself.'

—Raj Kamal Jha, chief editor, *The Indian Express*

'I believe this book will serve to inspire meaningful dialogue, ignite informed debates and guide us towards a brighter democratic future. I warmly commend this formidable volume, which I am confident will offer the reader a nuanced and compelling understanding of India's life through its elections.'

—Dr Shashi Tharoor, member of Parliament

'Dr Quraishi chronicles the reforms that the Election Commission has implemented over the years. The chapters mirror India's democratic triumphs and challenges. This book is a must-read resource for every civil service aspirant and journalist.'

—Shekhar Gupta, founder and editor-in-chief, *The Print*

'Former Chief Election Commissioner S.Y. Quraishi has distilled his vast experience and knowledge about elections in this timely volume on India's apex and state electoral landscape. This timely volume discusses India's electoral machinery at [the] centre and states and suggests how we might improve the voting system and address some deficiencies, including the Election Commission's crisis of credibility. One hopes that the message of this book is heeded by the powers that be. With its broad and authoritative scope, this is a volume for both specialist and lay public and is an essential read as India moves towards the 2024 general elections.'

—Shiv Shankar Menon, former foreign secretary, and
national security advisor, India

'No one decodes the election process better than former Chief Election Commissioner Dr S. Y. Quraishi. He succinctly captures the challenges and intricacies of modern democracies in ensuring free, fair and transparent elections. Highly recommended for civil-service aspirants, media persons and everyone interested in the fundamental principles of democracy and governance.'

—Ambassador Vikas Swarup

'Dr Quraishi is a walking encyclopaedia on elections. This volume contains his distilled wisdom and experience of decades, on upholding democratic traditions through error-free elections. The writing is easy to read, incredibly rich in content and provides comprehensive coverage. Every discerning citizen must acquaint himself with the clarity and depth of this account.'

—Vinod Rai, former Comptroller and Auditor General of India

India's Experiment *with* Democracy

THE LIFE OF A NATION THROUGH
ITS ELECTIONS

S.Y. QURAISHI

HarperCollins *Publishers* India

First published in India by HarperCollins *Publishers* 2023
4th Floor, Tower A, Building No. 10, DLF Cyber City,
DLF Phase II, Gurugram, Haryana – 122002
www.harpercollins.co.in

2 4 6 8 10 9 7 5 3 1

P-ISBN: 978-93-5699-364-8
E-ISBN: 978-93-5699-365-5

Typeset in 11/14.3 Bembo Std at
Manipal Technologies Limited, Manipal

Printed and bound at
Thomson Press (India) Ltd

To the many millions of students and civil-services aspirants, I fondly dedicate this book, so that they may strive to make India the greatest democracy in the world.

Contents

Introduction   xix

General Elections

1. On India's Electoral Democracy   3
2. The First General Election of India   7
3. Political Parties, the Constitution and the Election
   Commission   12
4. The 2019 General Election   22
5. National Voter's Day   25

The Role of Election Commission: Powers, Procedures and Politics

Critiquing the Election Commission of India

1. The Election Commission Must Act Tough   31
2. A Crisis of Credibility in EC   35
3. On EC's Neutrality   39

xii   Contents

4.   Will the Modi Government Give the EC More Power
So It Is Fully Independent?   43
5.   Main Issues and Debates on EC   48

On Symbols Act

1.   Lok Janshakti Party Split   53
2.   Samajwadi Party's Symbol War-I   57
3.   Samajwadi Party's Symbol War-II   60
4.   Shiv Sena Split 2022   63

Concerning Electronic Voting Machines

1.   Glitches Apart, EVMs Are Necessary   67
2.   EVM is Tamper-Proof   71
3.   Proving a Point on Audit Trial   75

On Model Code of Conduct

1.   Laws and Violations of MCC   79
2.   EC Needs Urgent Institutional Safeguards   83
3.   Moral Hold of Poll Code   86

State Elections

Bihar Elections

1.   The Corona Election   91
2.   Clearing the COVID Challenge for Elections   95

Maharashtra Elections

1.   Conducting Elections during a Pandemic   99
2.   Another Government Formation, Another Day We Watch
Political Morality Disappear   103

Contents   xiii

Chhattisgarh Elections

1.	Chhattisgarh 2014 By-Election Scam	109
2.	At Stake in the Chhattisgarh Scam	112
3.	The Chhattisgarh By-Election Scam Is a Wake-up Call	115

Electoral Reforms

Simultaneous Elections

1.	Pros and Cons of Simultaneous Elections	121
2.	One Nation, One Poll: One Good Idea, Some Hurdles	125
3.	Debates and Drawbacks of Simultaneous Elections	129

Criminalization in Elections

1.	Has the SC Missed a Chance to Keep Criminals Out of Polls?	133
2.	Court's Lost Chance for Tackling Criminalization	136
3.	Crime and Politics	140

Financing in Elections

1.	The Opaque Electoral Bonds	145
2.	Can Electoral Bonds Cleanse Political Funding?	149
3.	Electoral Bonds: Its Advantages and Issues	151
4.	Should Elections Be State-Funded?	155
5.	State Funding for Political Parties	158
6.	On Black Money in Elections	161

Media Regulations and Reforms

1.	TRP: How It Works, Issues and the Way Forward	165
2.	Laws and Regulations of TV Media	170
3.	Undermining Polls	174

4.   Myths and Realities of TV Media   178

ON DEMONETIZATION

1.   Demonetization and the Long-Pending Reforms   187
2.   The Consequences on Electoral Systems   191

MAIN REFORMS AND RECOMMENDATIONS

1.   Why India Needs to Change Its Electoral Voting System   199
2.   It is Time to Take Stock of Electoral Process   205
3.   A Time for Electoral Reform   209
4.   Main Issues and Debates on EC   213
5.   On the Freebies Debate   217
6.   Freebies in an Unequal Democracy   221
7.   Prisoners Must Get the Right to Vote   227
8.   The Migrants' Right to Vote   231
9.   NRIs' Proxy Voting Will Not Serve the Purpose   235
10. NOTA Option in RS Polls   241

International Elections

1.   Colombo Collective   245
2.   A Defining Moment for Colombo   250
3.   As Sri Lanka Prepares for Polls   253
4.   Insights From Sri Lanka   257
5.   What I Saw in Pakistan   261
6.   In Nepal, With Hope   265
7.   A UK Election in the Time of Terror   269
8.   Their Westminster, And Ours   273
9.   Myanmar, Under the World's Eye   277
10. How Biden Got Elected   281
11. Polls Apart   286
12. Nigeria's Difficult Democratic Journey   290

13. Kenya Elections, 2013   294
14. Mozambique Elections, 2014   300

Constitution and Indian Polity

DEFECTION AND HORSE-TRADING

1.   Controversy over Karnataka RS Polls   307
2.   Karnataka Horse-Trading   311
3.   When Defection Is a Mere Detour for an MLA   315

THE BAR, THE BENCH AND THE ELECTION COMMISSION: THE CUSTODIANS OF INDIAN DEMOCRACY

ON THE OFFICE OF PROFIT ISSUE

ON RAHUL GANDHI'S DISQUALIFICATION

THE GOVERNOR'S ROLE: MEDDLER OR STABILIZER?

ON THE SUPREME COURT VERDICT ON THE APPOINTMENT OF ELECTION COMMISSIONERS

LINKING VOTER ID TO AADHAR

THE J&K DELIMITATION REPORT

MODEL CODE VIOLATIONS IN MULTI-PHASE ELECTIONS

Gender and the State of Democracy

ON WOMEN AND TRANSGENDERS IN DEMOCRACY

1.   The Lawmakers We Need   355

2.　On the Status of Women in India　359

3.　A Democracy for Her　364

4.　Faith and Her Freedom　367

5.　This Women's Day, Enable Them to Get Fair Share of Electoral Power　371

6.　Beyond Binaries　376

EVALUATING DEMOCRACY

1.　Sixty-Seven Years Young　381

2.　India Remains a Flawed Democracy Despite Being an Electoral Wonder　385

3.　A Moderate Performance　390

4.　Ease of Democracy　394

5.　Issues and Solutions for Indian Democracy　498

6.　Elections in the Time of Cambridge Analytica　401

ON SOCIAL MEDIA AND DEMOCRACY

1.　The Age of Social Media　405

2.　Social Media in a Violent Democracy　411

3.　Accountability of Social Media Platforms　417

4.　Fake News: A Big Threat to Democracy　421

PORTRAITS

1.　The Unsung Organizer of India's First Election　425

2.　Goodbye, Mr Seshan　430

Religion and the Future of India

RELIGION AND SECULARISM

1.　On Politics of Hatred in India　435

2.　The Secular Constitution　439

Contents

xvii

INDIAN CHILDREN AND YOUTH

1.	Consequences of Divisive Politics on Children	445
2.	The Pollution of Young Minds	448
3.	The Duty of the Young	452
	Conclusion	455

ANNEXURE

LEGISLATIVE FRAMEWORK OF ELECTION LAW IN INDIA

1.	Constitution of India: The following Articles of the Constitution Provided the Framework for the Electoral System of India	463
2.	Representation of the People Act	469
3.	Tables	485
4.	Indian Elections at a Glance	487
	Bibliography	529
	Index	534
	Acknowledgements	551

Introduction

India and Me—A Journey Together

I WAS NOT BORN FREE. HOWEVER, MY BIRTH ON 11 JUNE 1947 ENSURED that I did not have to suffer the indignity, humiliation and frustration of living in a slave country for more than two months. Maybe I can take the credit of achieving what Mahatma Gandhi and his team could not in half a century!

Being one of the 'midnight children' of my country does give me a feeling of being special. I am conscious that my personal history coincides with the history of free India—the only difference being that while seventy-five years is a whole lifetime for an individual, for a country, it is just a beginning.

India is still going through the pangs of adolescence—the same identity crisis, the same anxiety. 'Am I still a child or an adult? Are we a developing or a developed country? Are we a socialist country of the poor or a developed country of the rich?'—like an adolescent desperate to shed its tag of the rich?' Like an adolescent desperate to shed its tag of being a child and identify with the grown-up world— the big boys!

For a developing country, the big boys are, of course, the developed Western countries. It is interesting to see how much we idealize—and idolize—them, even at the risk of shedding our own distinct historical and unique identity.

In my own official experience, when a debate questioning the reliability of our electronic voting machines (EVMs) was triggered by a small-time academic in Michigan a few years ago, I was tired of being asked how we had introduced this technology when *even* the US and Europe had not dared to do it. I was forced to remind them that our poor country gave equal voting rights to women and men in its very first shot at democracy in 1950, whereas it took the US 144 years and UK, the so-called mother of modern democracy, 100 years to do so.

We had a woman prime minister—and a powerful one at that—within nineteen years of democracy, whereas the US has not had a woman president in its 250 years of democracy. We had the first woman president of the Indian National Congress as early as 1925, while it took the UK 300 years before they chose Margaret Thatcher in 1979 as the first woman head of a national political party. Now, who has to learn from whom?

We don't have to learn everything from the West. We can teach them a thing or two. Prime Minister Modi has done well to push the United Nation (UN) to declare 21 June as the International Yoga Day. Similarly, it is nice to see the whole world celebrate International Day of Non-Violence to commemorate a historic Indian characteristic so effectively used by Mahatma Gandhi.

I was secretly amused and happy when an enterprising Indian businessman recently bought the notorious and now defunct East India Company! It seemed like history going full circle. History indeed has the bad habit of repeating itself. In the meantime, Indian-origin businessmen are taking the island country by storm.

While India gave the concept of the world being one family (*vasudhaiva kutumbakam*), the world has manifested this vision after 3,000 years through globalization. Whatever the positive impact of globalization, the negative forces are equally omnipresent. Racism abroad and casteism in India are in competition. The racist and the casteist are brothers separated at birth. Communal hostilities now have no boundaries. Forces of hatred are raising their ugly head. And technology has increased their destructive potential a million times.

Today we are becoming a violent and intolerant society. From road rage to lynch mobs, everyone has his own definition of rights and freedoms. We all think in terms of narrow caste, communal, parochial and political interests. This is threatening our identity as a nation. For short-terms gains, we are doing long-term damage to the idea of India.

This worries me. While the rest of the world can take care of itself, my idea of my India is under serious threat. The uniqueness of India is its 3,000-year-history of harmony and intermingling of the races. A good fallout of the constant inflow and intermingling was the birth of a composite culture which is India's abiding proud identity, its unique selling point (USP). Its pluralism is unparalleled. There is no doubt that India is the most diverse country in the world. The original megapolis. We have almost all the religions of the world, twenty-two official languages and 1,652 different recognized languages. Unity in diversity is our unique identity. I have often said that India is secular because the Hindus are secular. After the Partition of India on religious grounds, when Pakistan became an Islamic republic, India proudly chose to be a secular country with a unanimous vote in the Constituent Assembly, 83 per cent of which consisted of Hindus! Nobody would have batted an eyelid if we had chosen to be a Hindu country.

My worry is that this unique identity is under severe stress.

It is a great challenge for us to change this reality. It is imperative that we confront a series of pertinent questions to faithfully understand our contemporary dilemmas, dysfunctions and deliberations: what are the long-existing causes that have stealthily led us to the current moment? How may we, in other words, discern a history of the present? What foundational principles and priorities must be definitive to our ideas of nationhood, citizenship and democracy? How may we enliven our national discourse with a renewed spirit of reasoned inquiry, compassion and imaginative erudition? Most of the factors that are holding us back, like poor representation of women, massive illiteracy, criminalization of politics, and so on, are correctable. What we need are honest introspection and serious efforts. And, of course, political will.

It is the main intention of this book to pursue the compulsions and complications presented by the above questions and, in turn, present a holistic, reasoned and nuanced perspective of our nation's variegated crises, contestations and controversies. Ultimately, the underlying moral and political thrust of the book seeks to posit the virtues of reasoned argumentation, objective enquiry, secularism, civil liberty and compassion as indispensable features of a democracy. Therefore, it is hoped that this book speaks to both the immediate and the immemorial, the momentary and the momentous.

Questions and concerns in this regard are many, but I believe that India has a natural resilience. It accommodates all ideologies and philosophies. In the seven-and-a-half decades of its independent existence, the country indeed has made phenomenal progress. It has become a major military power, a major industrial, IT and economic power, and a space giant. India is now the fifth largest economy by GDP, recently overtaking the UK in terms of real GDP, and has the third-largest number of billionaires.

But the large disparities between the haves and the have-nots are pulling us back. We are ranked 132 in the Human Development Index (out of 187 countries). One in every three Indians lives below the poverty line. One in every four is still illiterate. We still have high infant and maternal mortality rates—far below even Sri Lanka's. More than half the population is malnourished. Drug abuse in some states has reached alarming proportions. Policies, programmes and funds for dealing with these issues are aplenty, but enormous corruption is preventing, percolation of the benefits to the people.

Furthermore, a quick look at the tables provided in the Annexure at the end of the book reveals some fascinating insights into the developments in our democracy, for instance, on issues such as political representation of Muslims and women, the various trends in voter turnouts, political financing and electoral expenditure.

India is home to over 200 million Muslims—which is more than the entire population of Bangladesh and Sri Lanka put together, or equivalent to three Frances. However, despite being such an important and significant part of India's population, our national record on political representation of Muslims in the Lok Sabha has been unsatisfactory. The reluctance of political parties to offer tickets to Muslim candidates cuts across all regional and national parties and is one of the biggest factors behind the community's under-representation. Between 1952 and 1977, when Muslims accounted for about 10 per cent of the population, only 5 per cent of all candidates nominated by the mainstream regional or national parties were Muslim.

Lack of Muslim representation is a crisis not of recent origin, but has, in fact, been a characteristic feature of our nation since the founding of the Republic. However, it must be said that the recent trends toward majoritarianism have greatly aggravated and amplified these trends. The lowest percentage of Muslim representation in India's history was registered in 2014, at a paltry 4.2 per cent. Even in the 2019 election, we must keep in mind that the Bharatiya Janta Party (BJP) had only *one* elected Muslim candidate, Saumitra Khan, among its 303 Lok Sabha members. In fact, Khan did not run on a BJP ticket, but later defected to the BJP from the Trinamool Congress on 9 January 2019.

Similarly, our national record on electoral representation of women has been deplorable, even though it has been improving over the years at a snail's pace. India, for instance, has fallen several places in the Inter-Parliamentary Union's global ranking of women's parliamentary presence, from 117th position after the 2014 election to 143rd as of January 2020, also reflecting the greater progress made by other countries in the intervening years. India, as of now, is currently behind Pakistan (106th, 20 per cent), Bangladesh (ninety-eighth, 21 per cent) and Nepal (forty-third, 33 per cent) and ahead of Sri Lanka (182nd, 5 per cent). In India, women still make up only 14.4 per cent of MPs in the lower house, the Lok Sabha. Furthermore, if it is to be assumed that candidates are fielded by political parties on the basis of their winnability, this record is all the more puzzling, because, as clear from Table C2 in the Annexure, the winnability of women contestants has always been higher than that of men ever since 1957.

But with regard to women's role in Indian elections, there is also some good news. The presence of women may be more powerfully felt as voters than as candidates. In 1962, voter turnout in India for men was 16 percentage points higher than for women (63 per cent for men, 47 per cent for women). Now, six decades later, in the 2019 Lok Sabha election, women's voter participation exceeded that of men for the first time, largely as a result of the Election Commission's voter education programme.

Table F3 in the Annexure also indicates a discernible trend in the patterns of electoral expenditure and, more broadly, of the growing role of money power in elections. The Election Commission of India (ECI), for instance, spent 6 paise per elector in the first general election of 1952, whereas in 2014, it spent nearly ₹42. This multi-fold increase in electoral expenditure by the ECI is also reflective of further trends in financing of political parties through other means, such as by wealthy corporates and private individuals. The 2019 general election, for instance, was the most expensive election ever held in the history of world democracies. According to a study, a mind-boggling $8 billion was spent, of which a little more than half was spent by the BJP. For comparison, the 2016 US Presidential election cost $6.5 billion.

Over the years, the Election Commission of India has been trying to check the role of money power in elections through a series of regulations and checks. However, the array of seizures of illegal money in the more recent times has only showed a bleaker picture, suggesting a growing insidious role of money power in elections. For instance, the total seizures in the 2017 Gujarat assembly election alone were ₹27.21 crore. This already worrying number in fact increased ten-fold as the total seizures stood at ₹290.24 crore in the 2022 election. Even the 2019 Lok Sabha election may be considered historic for the unprecedented worth and quantity of cash, drugs, liquor and freebies seized by election authorities during its course. Around ₹3,500 crore was seized—a staggering figure, for it amounts to nearly 90 per cent of the amount that the government officially spent in conducting the 2014 Lok Sabha election.

Furthermore, what also made the 2019 Lok Sabha election historic was that it was the first time when election to a parliamentary constituency was cancelled because there was rampant use of money power. On 16 April, the Election Commission of India announced that it decided to cancel the election to the Vellore Lok Sabha constituency in Tamil Nadu.

Given this extremely worrying context, we have to ponder upon and resolutely act towards overturning the electoral bonds scheme. This scheme not only exacerbates the lack of accountability and transparency in political financing, but also actively exposes the field of elections to corporate interests and electoral corruption. In fact, later in the book I have discussed in greater detail a range of issues that the electoral bonds schemes open up.

We are a country of young people, with more than 70 per cent of Indians being below thirty-five years of age. They have new aspirations, but their basic requirement is employment. The rate of unemployment is huge, and that contributes to youth disgruntlement, frustration and even criminalization. Our education system has failed us, producing a huge mass of unemployables. It is good that the government set up a commission to draft a New Education Policy whose recommendations have come under vast public scrutiny. Finally, the New Education Policy saw the light of day.

One fourth of our young people are adolescents (aged ten to nineteen), who have their peculiar problems. This is the time to give them education in life skills, including gender sensitization. Any suggestion of giving sex education to these ignorant young is viewed with shock and horror. While our curriculum insists on teaching them calculus or trigonometry, which most will hardly ever use in their lives, any suggestion of sex education—which all of them will need—is considered as blasphemous. Let's hope the New Education Policy addresses this appropriately.

Population issues have gone off the political radar altogether. As a result, India has already overtaken China to become the most populous country. One under-discussed contributory factor to population explosion is child marriage. One in every three marriages in India is illegal—the bride usually being below the legal age of marriage. Not a whimper is ever heard about this. Early marriage leads to early pregnancy, which creates health complications (maternal mortality, morbidity, weak and malnourished children, stunted growth) for adolescent girls not equipped physically and mentally to deal with it.

Crime and violence against women are a major issue. We never critically look at the gender attitude of our sons. No wonder we rank 135 in the Global Gender Gap and 122 in the Gender Inequality Index!

The moral authority of institutions of democracy and governance in the country is fast eroding. The three curses of casteism, communalism and corruption are putting democracy itself to the test. It is no surprise that the *Economist*'s annual Global Democracy Index classifies India as a flawed democracy, despite its great elections that Hillary Clinton once described as a gold standard.

The problems are enormous and real freedom will be when we banish these problems. The potential is huge. Our young human resource, vibrant economy and democratic culture can propel India to the first world if we keep our people together and unitedly focused. I suggest an employment mission, a national gender education drive, a new population policy, an integrated adolescent development programme in mission mode and a national reconciliation mission.

That was the story of India, my twin sibling, through seventy-five years of history. What happened to me?

I was born in a family of Islamic scholars and writers of great eminence. However, my father, Zubair, was the first generation to go in for modern education when he joined the famous St Stephen's ('mission') College. There was a kind of social uproar as this was considered a radical departure from tradition. He, however, proved to be a bridge between conservative Islam and modern thinking. A great lover of education, he spent his lifetime running an English grammar school, with German and Persian often included. His discourses on Islam were laced entirely with modern explanations and interpretations. His emphasis on the pursuit of knowledge had to be seen to be believed. It was touching to see him at the age of sixty go every day to Max Mueller Bhawan with his walking stick to attend German classes. Years later, I followed suit and the German grammar formulas he had evolved made me a hero when I topped. His grammar diary was borrowed by all my classmates, and someone decided to keep it as a souvenir—a loss I regret. Needless to say, he ensured we all got the best possible education despite our financial challenges. I pray for his soul.

My father's love for sports was almost legendary. He was a great swimmer, horse rider, archer and footballer. He was the goalkeeper of the St Stephen's College team and the founder of Delhi Football Association. He was a great orator. I wish some of it had rubbed off on me.

We grew up in the syncretic culture of the historic city of Delhi. The population then was a great mix of Hindus and Muslims, despite the trauma of the post-Partition riots. But later we saw, strangely and sadly, gradual polarization. The ensuing segregation portends danger for communal harmony.

The educational atmosphere in our home ensured that we only had teachers in our family and kinship. I was the first person ever to go for civil service, becoming the first Muslim IAS officer in old Delhi after Independence, provoking a *Hindustan Times* editorial. My younger sister followed in my footsteps to set a similar record for her gender.

Thanks to this liberal atmosphere, two of my brothers did well in theatre, and one of them played football for India and captained the St Stephens College football and Delhi University Athletics teams. I played in a Beat Group (while working as a lecturer) featuring Sharon Prabhakar, who rose to be a pop star while I joined the ranks of 'babus'! But not to lag behind, I founded a rock band while in the Indian Administrative Services (IAS) Academy, which has survived to this day!

Starting as a lecturer, I spent my lifetime in the IAS, where I had a range of experiences. Some of the memories I cherish are my pioneering power reforms under Chaudhary Bansi Lal and my work in my postings as director general of Doordarshan and the National AIDS Control Organisation (NACO). My appointment at the Election Commission gave me the enviable opportunity of presiding over the electoral management of the world's largest democracy.

Some final remarks then about this book. Given my long years of experience in Indian bureaucracy and governance serving in various roles, many of the topics that appear here reflect also my own priorities and passions. Therefore, readers may be disappointed if they expect an all-encompassing appraisal of the Indian condition here, as this book is limited to my particular expertise and interests. Likewise, the book also becomes an occasion to gather my rather disparate and persistent written output over the decades. Given the book's overall conception and ambition, I hope it acquires archival value.

The book itself is structured and divided along thematic lines, containing essays that have wide-ranging perspectives, critiques and commentaries, explainers, first-hand accounts of election observation across continents, opinion columns, lecture transcriptions, biographical portraits, and analytical and recommendatory articles.

The first sections of the book cover the multifarious and teeming realm of elections; my primary expertise, thematized as 'General Elections', 'Role of Election Commission: Powers, Procedures and Politics', 'State Elections', 'Electoral Reforms', and additionally, 'International Elections'. Thereon, a section entitled 'Constitution and the Indian Polity' attends to issues concerning legal reforms, Supreme Court debates and electoral issues that demand constitutional deliberation. The subsequent section entitled 'Gender and' addresses these major areas wherein the impacts and implications of these entities for the overall project of democracy is discussed. The section titled 'Portraits' presents reflections on two significant personalities in the life of our nation. The final section, titled 'Religion and the Future of India' deals with the dangers that threaten our nation's moral fabric and its values of secularism. Thereafter, I end the book with a series of essays on the role of the Indian youth and children, our nation's future, who will take forward our hopes and struggles for a stronger India.

Even though the book is quite hefty, we ensured to keep it completely reader-friendly. You may choose to read the essays in your preferred order. I have long benefitted from the many questions and conversations I have had with thousands of students and civil service aspirants. I hope this book has the lucidity and the wealth of information that can reward their many and persistent inquiries. Readers may notice some repetition of arguments and topics. In some cases, they chart the gradual progression of an issue over the course of its run. In others, it serves to reinforce the urgency felt at the time about the issue. Likewise, I would have reiterated some points in various publications and at various times in order to consistently advocate and push forth the respective recommendations.

However, apart from all these, one ought to concede the fact that this collection spans essays across and over two decades, and given the sheer breadth of time, it is only natural that there will be repetitions and reiterations. If we have chosen not to withdraw these recurrences, it is only in the hope of retaining the archival nature of this project.

Being the largest democracy is not good enough; my dream is for India to become the greatest democracy in the world too. I am optimistic. We are an intelligent and hardworking nation, and can achieve this. And we will. What we need is integrity, determination and, of course, harmony.

My dreams and struggles for a better and greater India are alive even now, persisting from those days, decades away, when I was still preparing to appear for the civil service examinations. And it is to such dreamers, students and young civil service aspirants that I dedicate this book. For all those concerned with the health and life of a democracy, I hope this book proves to be of interest.

General Elections

1

On India's Electoral Democracy

The vote is the most powerful instrument ever devised by man for breaking down injustice and destroying the terrible walls which imprison men because they are different from other men.

—Lyndon B. Johnson

REAL FREEDOM IS EXPERIENCED WHEN CITIZENS CAN SPEAK FREELY without fear. Democratic elections provide the platform for citizens to assert their civil and political rights by holding their elected representatives accountable. Elections may or may not ensure that a society will become socio-economically equitable, but they do provide a starting point for justice, equality and good governance. Hence, free, fair and representative elections are essential for consensus-driven development.

The value of the one vote for every adult has long been recognized by our people. The demand that every man and woman be given a voice in nation-building lay at the heart of our freedom struggle. The history of the demand for universal franchise in India goes back to the nineteenth century. The Constitution of India Bill (1895) was the first non-official attempt at drafting a Constitution, wherein it was declared that every citizen living within the territory of India had the right to take part in the affairs of the country and to be admitted to public office. The Nehru Report of 1928 reaffirmed this idea of progressive citizenship, as did numerous such reports and resolutions during the freedom struggle. The electoral process itself was far from a novelty to us, as we already had significant experience in running provincial governments as a result of the Acts of 1919 and 1935. What was lacking was sovereignty—a government of, for and by the people.

Hence, despite the doubts and fears coming from many quarters, the founders of post–Independence India adopted the system of universal adult suffrage, literally without any debate in the Constituent Assembly, thus reposing faith in the wisdom of the common Indian to elect his or her representative to the seat of power.

Needless to say, the socio-economic indicators were appalling when Independence came. It was a period when approximately 84 per cent of Indians were illiterate and an equal ratio languishing in poverty. The makers of our Constitution were fully aware of the long list of challenges facing this unfathomably diverse country, which was traumatized by the unspeakable horrors of Partition and plagued by a highly fragmented social structure of caste-based hierarchy. It may be recalled that the United Kingdom granted voting rights to women only in 1932, about 100 years after its first elections. The United States held its first presidential elections in 1789, but women voters had to wait for the nineteenth amendment to their Constitution in 1920 to be able to vote.

France and Italy gave women voting rights only in 1944 and 1945, respectively. But our Constitution ensured that the oppressed masses of India, both male and female, had already voted in many elections before Switzerland allowed its women to vote, in 1971, and Australia its Aborigines, in 1967.

The Indian Constitution was promulgated on 26 January 1950. But Article 324 of the Constitution, which created the Election Commission of India as a Constitutional body, was among the very few provisions that were given effect to a full two months earlier, on 26 November 1949. Interestingly, the ECI was established on 25 January 1950, a day before India became a republic. Over the past seven decades, the Election Commission has delivered sixteen elections to the Lok Sabha and over 400 elections to state legislative assemblies, thus facilitating peaceful and orderly transfer of power.

In the past seventy-one years, India has seen a deepening of democracy and respect for Constitutional morality. The lowering of the voting age from twenty-one to eighteen was an electoral reform of great significance. The heterogeneity of parties and the rise of coalition politics reflect a bouquet of diverse aspirations among the people and the innumerable positives of power-sharing and consensus-building.

The seventy-third and seventy-fourth amendments have enabled the realization of grassroots-level decision-making in our villages and urban local bodies, which embodies the true spirit of 'self-rule' as envisaged by our freedom fighters. The rise of political leaders belonging to the marginalized sections of the society, farmers, women and minorities, to head the national and state governments, as well as the upward trend of participation of women, tribal communities, and the urban and rural poor in the decision-making process can be traced to the untiring efforts of the ECI in conjunction with an increasingly proactive civil society.

A stunning example of the inclusive nature of Indian democracy and a source of great pride and satisfaction for it is that a country where 80 per cent of the population is Hindu has had four Muslim, one Sikh and two Dalit Presidents, including the current President Mr Ramnath Kovind.

Several Muslim vice-presidents and a Sikh prime minister have graced the top positions in our country. The largest democracy in the world is now ruled by a prime minister whose mother was a domestic help and who himself worked as a tea vendor to earn a living. There was also a time when four of the largest states (Uttar Pradesh, West Bengal, Tamil Nadu and Rajasthan) and Delhi, the national capital, were governed by women chief ministers. They all came to power through elections conducted by the Election Commission of India.

As India's democracy marches on, our immense economic, demographic and social potential continues to stun the world, and even us. The potential of democracy is unparalleled, as it accommodates diverse interests and aspirations. This is why Nobel laureate Amartya Sen has remarked that a country does not become fit for democracy, but becomes fit through democracy.

While there is so much to celebrate, it is also imperative to be mindful of some shortcomings in our system, which leave a lot of scope for improvement in our democratic mechanisms. Many electoral reforms are long-pending as a result of lack of political will or plain lethargy. Reform of the election campaign finance laws, keeping out criminals from politics and creation of a proper law for transparent Constitutional appointments to posts, such as that of the chief election commissioner, are just some of the many issues regarding which the ECI has repeatedly written to the government to address. Several important reforms have come through the intervention of the judiciary, which has always acted as a guardian angel of democracy. As the country moves forward, many old and new challenges are surfacing, calling for swift and decisive action.

As we approach the seventeenth Lok Sabha elections, it is useful to look back and appreciate our momentous achievements, while being mindful of our shortcomings over these adventurous seven decades.

This volume aims to do just that—celebrate seven decades of India's unique democratic experiment by compiling opinions on various aspects of the electoral process from eminent voices all around the world, who have proven their mettle in academia, social work, public service, industry, journalism and the cinema. It is an attempt to look at electoral democracy through different frames of reference—political, historical, social, economic, journalistic and administrative.

2

The First General Election of India

Democracy in India is a source of immense national pride and a cornerstone of this country's identity. It did not, however, have a smooth start. Immeasurable struggles and the indomitable will of India's nation builders and people combined to make the second most populous country in the world also the largest democracy in the world.

The first Indian election was held from 25 October 1951 to 21 February 1952, with an astronomical 17,32,12,343 registered voters, of whom 10,59,50,083 exercised their newly acquired voting right. The geographical vastness of India, which even today poses a formidable challenge, was deemed insurmountable in the 1950s by most observers and experts.

Interestingly, the backdrop of the 1952 election was as much strategic as it was political. While India became independent in 1947, it remained a dominion. A British governor general remained at the head of the Indian political system, greater in stature than the prime minister. As the Constitution, promulgated on 26 November 1949, came into effect on 26 January 1950, Prime Minister Jawaharlal Nehru was anxious to get the election underway as soon as possible.

Democracy and establishment of the will of the people were the main premises on which the struggle for Independence was waged, and without elections that premise would remain unfulfilled. The man this mammoth task was entrusted to was Sukumar Sen, an unsung hero of Indian democracy.

It was decided that the electoral process would be started as early as 1951. It was mandated that any Indian citizen twenty-one years of age and above, residing in a particular constituency for more than 180 days would be eligible to vote in that constituency. It is significant that as poor and backward as India was, it still gave its people, men and women, an equal vote, while it took the so-called greatest democracy, the US, 144 years and the UK 100 years to give equal voting rights to women after they became democracies.

In a country with massive illiteracy (84 per cent), with lakhs of residents missing key identification documents due to the turmoil of Partition, this was perhaps a significant challenge. But at the same time, the step was a befitting homage to the ideals of democracy and representation that had fuelled an independence struggle spanning over half a century. In the heralded democracies of the West, such as the US or the UK, elections are held with two or at best three competing political parties. In India, however, the first election saw fifty-three registered political parties (including fourteen national parties) competing for 489 seats in the lower house of parliament.

The Election Commission of India (ECI) was created as an independent, autonomous constitutional body. While introducing draft Article 289 (which later became Article 324 in the final Constitution) on 15 June 1949 in the Constituent Assembly, B.R. Ambedkar, chairman of the drafting committee, explained the rationale for an independent central and federal Election Commission. Thus, an independent Election Commission was constituted, vested with the superintendence, direction and control of preparing the electoral rolls and conducting elections to parliament, the state legislatures and the offices of the President and Vice President of India.

The first election of 1952 under Sukumar Sen was pivotal, because it set the standard for all subsequent elections. Sen started from scratch. There were no staff, permanent or temporary, no infrastructure, no training facilities, no institutional memory, as a large number of the staff who had conducted the 1944 assembly elections had either migrated out of the country or were killed in the Partition riots. Sen started with a blank slate.

The making of the first electoral roll

'An electoral roll on the basis of universal franchise prepared and maintained as accurately and as up-to-date as possible, was the plinth upon which the institutions of electoral democracy would rest.' Thus writes Ornit Shani, capturing the very essence of Indian democracy and the reason why she undertakes the task of exploring the 'greatest experiment in democratic human history'.

How India became Democratic is a never-told-before story of the first general election in India and the administrative efforts that went behind it. Shani has put in tremendous research—the archival materials that form the bedrock of this narrative were literally excavated by her from the basement of the Election Commission of India. Building on this rich material, the book tells a vivid and fascinating tale of how the first voters' list was drawn up by far-sighted bureaucrats even before the Election Commission of India was born and even before the 552 princely states were integrated into the newly formed country.

On attaining Independence, India was left an illiterate and poor nation with millions of refugees and masses of people without identification documents. To establish people's adulthood in the absence of any documents and to decide the fate of millions of refugees who had poured in was no mean task. The criteria for registration were simple. A person had to be a citizen and had to be residing in the place of registration for a minimum of 180 days. However, who was an 'Indian' or a 'citizen' was a very contested question at the time. And the surest way to become a citizen was to be enrolled on the voters' list. So, millions of refugees made it a point to enrol themselves as voters in order to ensure their democratic citizenship of India. Aware of the advantages that would come by being on the voters' list and consequently as citizens, Partition refugees strove for a place on the electoral rolls. To do so, they had to declare, at the time of registration, that they intended to permanently reside at the place where they were registering.

Thus, India's tryst with democracy, argues Shani, is not a tale of a top-down approach by a few elite bureaucrats. Democracy in India was the result of a struggle by the very people whose lives were at stake, as well as of the low- and middle-level bureaucrats who ensured that the democratic experiment was a huge success. Shani illustrates how every effort was made to include all sections of the society. For example, through letters and archival material, she demonstrates how vagrants in Mumbai, living in huts on municipal land without permission and paying no rent, were also included as citizens and thus registered on the electoral rolls.

Shani's book, however, is not a bureaucratic account of the mechanical process of the making of India's electoral rolls. It, in fact, is a fascinating tale of the 'democratic imagination' of the country. When many harp on the continuation of the colonial legacy in post-colonial India, this book is a tale about India breaking away from its colonial past and defying the colonial belief that it would be a misfit in adopting the concept of universal adult franchise. The colonial administration had, in fact, widely claimed that universal adult suffrage was 'administratively unmanageable' and 'impracticable at present'. However, unlike other British colonies with similar structures, which could not evolve into fully functioning democracies, India became an exception to the rule. The book is a testimony to the revolutionary thinking of our Constituent Assembly and brings to light the fact that Indians became voters before they became citizens, thanks to the far-sightedness of the officials involved.

For the first general election held in 1951, the 'complex preparatory work' had begun from September 1947. Unlike the current-day-perception of bureaucrats as an inefficient lot, this book portrays them in a whole new light, as champions of Indian democracy. B.N. Rau, S.N. Mukherjee, K.V. Padmanabhan, P.S. Subramanian—all members of the Constituent Assembly Secretariat (CAS)—are rightly described by Shani as the unsung heroes of Indian democracy. And it is due to the heroism of these officials that on the eve of the 1951 general election, 49 per cent of India's population (173 million citizens) was registered as voters—the largest in any country!

Shani's is a valuable addition to the scarce literature on the democratic enigma that is India. Any person wishing to understand the process of India's democratic transition must read her book.

3

Political Parties, the Constitution and the Election Commission

Acccoording to Thomas Carothers, the American political scientist, 'no workable form of democratic pluralism has been invented that operates without political parties'. Political parties, in our system of parliamentary government, form the link between the machinery of the mighty State and the common citizens. They are central to mobilizing public opinion, act as potent pressure groups and take legislative action when in power. Hence, despite all their flaws, we need political parties in a democracy.

Despite having one of the most detailed and lengthy constitutions in the history of the world, the Constitution of India, which came into force on 26 January 1950, did not contain a word about the formation, organization or functioning of political parties in our Westminster-style parliamentary system. This is far from unprecedented, as many constitutions in history, including that of the United States of America, do not mention political parties. George Washington warned against their 'insinuation' into the democratic system, and James Madison, one of the founding figures of America, called them 'factions', a term with a negative connotation. On the other hand, constitutions such as that of post-war Germany do mention political parties and, also, have laws in place to regulate them. In the German model of party regulation, for example, a specific law exists to make sure the ideals enlisted in Article 21 of their Constitution regarding political parties are realized.

One possible reason for this general Constitutional neglect of political parties in India can be found in the political situation that obtained in India at the time of Independence. The Indian National Congress was an umbrella organization, which accommodated a plethora of cultural, social, ethnic, linguistic and religious factions, differing in ideology and their vision of the future. With the situation changing rapidly, from a single dominant party system to a multi-party system in the years following 1947, political parties grew to become individual entities, something the Constituent Assembly might not have been able to predict. Another reason could be the preference for ordinary legislation.

As political parties are dynamic entities and the Indian Constitution is a broadly fixed document, the job was best left to the parliament to make a law on the subject. Regulation requires specifics, and a constitution can only guide in this direction rather than make relatively inflexible laws that would require repeated amendments.

Party systems in other countries

As mentioned earlier, there is no specific constitutional provision for political parties in most democracies. Sometimes, this is to protect their freedom of organization and functioning. For example, the Constitution of the Fifth Republic of France states that the national assembly cannot legislate to limit the free functioning of political parties. But in other cases, such as the German Constitution, political parties have been institutionalized by the inclusion of provisions such as the 5 per cent clause, which impede the formation of fringe parties.

This was done to deter the rise of fascist forces in that country. There are statutory provisions which have come later for regulation of political parties in many countries such as Spain, Portugal and Canada. Party reforms are long pending in countries such as the US, where there has been a two-party system for centuries. Party loyalties remain loose and the number of swing and independent voters are on the rise. As the American Constitution has aged considerably, there is no mention of political parties. The concept itself was only emerging in Britain when Americans wrote their Constitution. There is generally a high degree of factionalism within the modern political parties in federal polities such as the US, Australia and Canada. There is also class organization of parties, as seen in Australia. In Canada, the Centre remains relatively weak, unless it gets support from at least some regional parties.

The Election Commission's role

The Election Commission of India has played a central role in the story of evolution of political parties in India. The Commission came into existence a day before our first Republic Day, which goes on to show the importance of the Commission as one of the main pillars of post-Independence India. Article 324 provides it the crucial responsibility of supervising, directing and controlling the conduct of elections to the parliament and state assemblies, and also for the posts of President and Vice President. In *Mohinder Singh Gill vs. Chief Election Commissioner (1978)*, the Supreme Court observed that the Election Commission has been vested with 'comprehensive responsibilities', and that 'this responsibility (of conducting free and fair elections) may cover powers, duties and functions of many sorts, administrative or other, depending on the circumstances'.

The ECI is also entrusted with powers to ensure that a 'proper conducive atmosphere' is maintained for the conduct of elections, according *to Bhim Singh vs. the Election Commission (1996)*. It goes on to say that 'it can exercise any power which is necessary to achieve this objective even if the Conduct of Elections Act and the rules made thereunder do not confer such power specifically'. This, in principle, gives vast residuary powers to the Election Commission to act in unforeseen circumstances to ensure fair political representation and those powers have aided it through seven decades in formulating rules for the conduct of political parties. The ECI has played its role in recognizing the existence and role of political parties ever since the very first general election was held in 1951-52. Out of the twenty-nine political parties that claimed national status, fourteen were recognized as multi-state parties in July 1951.

Additionally, fifty-nine other parties were recognized as state parties. The Election Symbols (Reservation and Allotment) Order, 1968, was issued to enable the ECI to award symbols to candidates for facilitating their recognition by voters for the purpose of elections under the Conduct of Election Rules, 1961.

This was necessary to enable illiterate citizens to vote, the ratio of illiteracy in India at the time being as high as 84 per cent. Later, with the passage of the anti-defection amendment in 1985, political parties were formally recognized as part of the parliamentary process to deter candidates from changing their political allegiance after they had won an election. In 1989, the Election Commission of India got the authority to register political parties after insertion of Section 29(A) to the Representation of People Act, 1951.

There was an additional qualification required for their registration—all parties shall have a provision for a set of bye-laws/a party constitution, which unequivocally contained 'a specific provision that the association shall bear true faith and allegiance to the Constitution of India as by law established, and uphold the principles of socialism, secularism and democracy and the sovereignty, unity and integrity of India'. Recognition of a party at the state or the national level brings a lot of perks with it, including free air time on state-run television and radio—Doordarshan and All India Radio, respectively—at the time of elections, and free electoral rolls for its members. In the Supreme Court judgment in *Indian National Congress*

(I) vs. the Institute of Social Welfare & Ors. (2002), while the Election Commission has the power to register political parties, subject to specific criteria, it has no power to de-register them. There are many who argue that this power too should be given to the Election Commission, and many who argue against it.

Those who are against it are afraid that should the Election Commission exercise that power, it would amount to politicization of the Commission. In getting to decide whose conduct is not in accordance with the Constitutional spirit, it will be taking a political stand when it de-registers a party. Parties, at present, are by law de-recognized at the state and national levels on the basis of their poll performance—a minimum percentage of seats must be secured in each election—or their violation of the Model Code of Conduct.

A need for reform

Today, most political parties in India have become hotbeds of incompetence and dishonesty and exhibit a lack of internal democracy. The elected representatives' inaccessibility, due to which citizens do not get to interact with individual politicians, keeps them out of touch with the general aspirations of the people. The representatives claim to be defenders of the popular interest, but parties function in a very top-down manner, with some of their members wielding too much power when it comes to deciding who from the party gets to contest elections. Decision making is highly centralized because of the cult of personality or dynasticism. The voters who vote in the internal elections of political parties are nominated by influential people within the party ranks.

This is fundamentally undemocratic. As a result, the same candidates from a party keep entering the fray and mobility within the party ranks becomes extremely difficult. As Jagdeep Chhokar, one of the founding members of the Association for Democratic Reforms, has said, 'these [internal party elections] are sham elections'. All the prominent democracy and freedom indices in the world today use 'inner party democracy' for their rankings as a heavily weighted indicator for assessing the robustness of a democracy, and this is not without reason.

Unfortunately, the ECI has at present no jurisdiction to actually probe into the robustness of internal democracy at political parties in India. The Justice V.R. Krishna Iyer Committee in 1994 called for a law ensuring inner party democracy in all political parties and legal sanction audit and accounts.

The Law Commission in its seventeenth report, 'Reform of the Electoral Laws', stated clearly that a political party cannot be a 'dictatorship internally and democratic in its functioning outside'. Besides, it also proposed the institution of a separate commissioner to ensure that political parties were not promoting communalism and were not involved in any unconstitutional conduct.

In 2002, the National Committee to Review the Working of the Constitution recognized the need for regulation of party funds, both during election and non-election times, for auditing the accounts of political parties, which would then be open for general inspection. This was to be done so that measures could be taken to check the increasing casteism and communalism in elections, for strengthening of the anti-defection law and for restoration of morality in public life in general. Casteism, communalism and regionalism are blindly used for partisan interests without putting the country first and the result is increasing violence due to blind pandering to their vote base by political parties to win elections. Disclosure of financial statements is another area which needs reform, both from within and without. Financial disclosure by political parties would be in their own self-interest, as it leads to building of public confidence in a party and its candidates. The information deficit is bridged for the voter, who can now take informed decisions about whom to choose to best represent their interests in the corridors of power.

The ECI has taken some laudable initiatives in this direction by making it mandatory for candidates to disclose information about their educational qualifications and finances in an affidavit after a direction by the Supreme Court in 2002. Just one example of how resistant political parties are to any change in the status quo is their response to the Right to Information (RTI) Act and open audits. In 2006, the Association for Democratic Reforms filed an appeal with the Central Information Commission (CIC) to make political parties' income tax returns public.

Even for this, a two-year struggle had to be waged before the CIC decided, in 2008, that political parties would make public their income tax returns. In 2013, there was stiff resistance by political parties against the CIC declaring six national parties as 'public authorities', thereby bringing them under the ambit of Section 2(H) of the RTI Act. This was later dropped after there were threats that the RTI Act itself would be amended under Article 123(1), which deals with the ordinance-making power of the President.

These six national parties continue to operate in the same manner they did earlier. The expenditure incurred by political parties for propaganda work is not added to the prescribed ceiling for individual candidates running for elections. Hence, there is at present practically no cap on how much political parties can spend. The issue of electoral bonds is inescapable when talking about reforms related to the financing of political parties. The electoral bonds have actually encouraged crony capitalism. It is a regressive reform. Crores of rupees can be paid by companies, and one will not get to know which company has given money to which party.

The system is the complete opposite of transparent. The result of this reform is that capitalists will run the country, as they have probably been for years, but now in a more legalized way. Now, a company can donate 100 per cent of its profits to one political party, which will in turn make policy friendly to it. The same system is a cause of great resentment in other democracies, such as the US, and so we should not follow it.

I have time and again talked about state funding of political parties in India. That is because monitoring of political parties is easier than monitoring of money in elections. We cannot monitor the ways in which black money is put to use in bribing voters, in creating paid news and other forms of transgressions, though we have had some measure of success in this respect. As far back as in 1990, the Dinesh Goswami Committee suggested that limited state funding in kind should begin for recognized political parties.

In 1998, the Indrajit Gupta Committee on State Funding of Elections endorsed partial state funding of recognized political parties and their candidates in elections. This would level the playing field and give all parties an equal chance to compete in elections, which is central to a healthy democratic process. But it also acknowledged that independent candidates cannot be funded in this manner and that parties can be funded only in kind.

I suggest a common pool of funding, which is the model prevalent in many European countries. Here, the parties get a fixed amount against the number or percentage of votes polled in their favour in the last election. We could, for instance, agree that for every vote obtained, ₹100 be given. Why do I think this amount will suffice? In the last general election, 55 crore votes were cast. So, at the rate of ₹100 per vote, the amount disbursed to parties would amount to around ₹5,500 crore. Is this amount adequate? This amount roughly corresponds to the cumulative amount raised by all political parties in five years! This money can be distributed among the parties based on their poll performance and must be paid by cheque. Now, unless their disclosures are inaccurate, this system of common pool funding is in the parties' own economic self-interest. State funding of parties will also go a long way in reducing the massive costs incurred in election campaigning, which the Indrajit Gupta Committee also noted.

A study, 'Political Finance Regulations Around the World', by the International Institute for Democracy and Electoral Assistance, Stockholm (2012), conducted in 180 countries revealed that as many as seventy-one nations give state funds to political parties based on the number of votes they won in the previous election. This system is followed in 86 per cent of the countries in Europe, 71 per cent of the countries in Africa, 63 per cent of the countries in the Americas and 58 per cent of the countries in Asia. So, this system by no means is unprecedented. All we need is the political will to implement it. Another issue is that of tainted legislators. Section 8 of the Representation of People Act, 1951, bans convicted politicians from contesting elections. But those facing trial, no matter how serious the charges, are free to contest elections. The fielding of candidates is a function of their 'winnability' and so, all political parties seem to be united in their opposition to any legislation on this front. The Justice Kuldip Singh panel under the National Commission to Review the Working of the Constitution (NCRWC) 2001 had recommended the barring of candidates with criminal backgrounds or those facing criminal charges framed by a court from contesting any polls.

The past three Lok Sabhas have seen an increasing number of legislators with criminal backgrounds or with pending cases against them—124 in 2004, 162 in 2009 and 182 in 2014. A five-judge bench led by Chief Justice Dipak Misra, in a September 2018 verdict of the Supreme Court, said the court cannot play the role of parliament. Parliament is obliged to make a law on the matter, according to Article 102(1) of the Constitution, but that has not happened—and if history is any indication, it is highly unlikely to happen.

In this matter, the judiciary has also refused to aid the ECI, which has been crying hoarse for the past two decades in its fight against criminalization of politics. They will risk the ECI coming across as a politically motivated constitutional body. The methods of campaigning and reaching out to the voter base are getting technologically sophisticated, and the thin line between voter outreach and voter manipulation is frequently breached by political parties.

There needs to be regulation to ensure that the phenomenon of 'paid news' and 'fake news', as spread by biased news networks and social media, does not distort political outcomes. While the electoral rolls have been used over the years for voter outreach and there is nothing wrong with it, the increasing use of social media has raised serious concerns about breach of privacy. The Cambridge Analytica scandal is a recent case in point (refer to the chapter 'Elections in the Time of Cambridge Analytica').

The party cadre needs to be responsible and ethical in their voter outreach. It is high time that political parties in India are regulated. Many a lacunae in the regulations governing how political parties are formed, funded, audited and run needs to be plugged. In a democracy, those at the helm of political affairs cannot function like oligarchies. Many great models which have proved effective in countering criminality in politics are available throughout the world; they have increased accountability and decreased opacity in the system.

There has been a consistent trend of politicians moulding outcomes that are in their own favour by procedural misuse. This is the antithesis of a democracy, as both an idea and a system. Rather than attempting to dilute the existing laws and moulding the system to suit their own ends, political parties should exhibit a collective political will to set aside their individual interests and come together to legislate in the interest of our democracy.

4

The 2019 General Election

Gᴇɴᴇʀᴀʟ Eʟᴇᴄᴛɪᴏɴ 2019 ʜᴀs ꜰɪɴᴀʟʟʏ ᴄᴏᴍᴇ ᴛᴏ ᴀ ᴄʟᴏsᴇ, ʙᴜᴛ ɴᴏᴛ without raising fire and brimstone. Our elections, months before they are even announced, grab international attention and admiration. The reasons are simple—they are record-breaking and an unparalleled logistical challenge, which the Election Commission of India overcomes every five years with precision.

My association with the ECI, first as election commissioner (2006–2010) and then as chief election commissioner of India (2010–2012), has given me a vast diversity of experiences. Elections bring back mixed memories of rewarding struggles and the professional satisfaction that comes with doing one's constitutional duty well in ensuring free and fair polls.

When the election was announced, I was shuttling between London and Stockholm on work-cum-holiday. It was certainly an inopportune time to be missing in action from the country when the biggest election in world history was taking place. There was an unending stream of phone calls from television channels, news portals, newspapers and magazines requesting for my views and comments. Skype and iPad came in handy. However, even after expressing regrets to 90 per cent of the requests, I was quite a nuisance to my hosts. It was quite a relief to come back home in the middle of the long-drawn exercise.

The last two months have been a trying time for me to see the Election Commission under unprecedented attack. It was a constant and painful dilemma for me: whether to criticize the Commission, defend it, or keep quiet.

Then someone reminded me of the words of Plato, 'I will put down your silence as consent.' The immortal words of Martin Luther King, Jr. served to egg me on: 'Our lives begin to end the day we become silent about things that matter.' This motivated me to express my opinion, though reluctantly, but as constructively as I possibly could.

Ever since I demitted office, I have been a self-appointed spokesperson for the Commission, defending its every action that needed defending, in the absence of its own presence on social media. I refused at least a hundred requests by the media to comment on certain disturbing events that unfortunately became hallmarks of the 2019 election. On the few occasions that I was drawn into the debate, it was a struggle to phrase my opinion in a way that would not sound like an indictment of the institution that I was immensely proud to have been a part of. I noticed the same predicament on the faces of three former chief election commissioners who appeared on television.

I had earlier written that the suspension—by the government on recommendation of the ECI—of an IAS officer posted as an election observer in Odisha for checking the PM's helicopter was a missed opportunity to restore the Commission's declining credibility. It also didn't do well for PM's own image. After all, both these institutions have been under the public scanner and have received a lot of criticism for a number of incidents that have taken the centre stage in this election. In one stroke, the criticism against them would have come crumbling down and 'equality before law' would've been demonstrated. But, much to my disappointment, nothing of the sort happened. On the other hand, the Odisha Chief Minister Naveen Patnaik's dignified conduct when the authorities raided his chopper stood in sharp contrast.

This election was overwhelmed by the overarching influence of money power, hate speech, communalization of politics, abuse of social media and the unconstitutional conduct of politicians openly flouting the Model Code of Conduct. And whom did we find in the dock? Not the defaulting politicians but the Election Commission! Nothing could be more unfortunate. Reputations take years to build but moments to get demolished. I am afraid the events of this election will hang over the institution and haunt it for years to come.

Making our democracy itself fit for the twenty-first century will involve sweeping reforms concerning campaign finance, social media, inclusive political representation and depoliticization of constitutional appointments. Over forty reform proposals have remained pending for the past two decades, mainly because of political lethargy.

The 2019 election is yet another reminder that we are a flawed democracy in desperate need of reforms. My dream is for India to become the greatest and most successful democracy in the world. For that to become a reality, national interest must take precedence over petty political interests. My optimism has not waned, despite some unfortunate events that have unfolded recently. The reason is that despite our historic ups and downs, we have managed not only to survive, but thrive. One can only hope that the seventeenth Lok Sabha (elected in 2019) will truly aim to work for the people of this country and not disappoint the cause of progressive electoral reforms.

5

National Voter's Day

O N 25 JANUARY 2017, INDIA CELEBRATES ITS SIXTH NATIONAL Voters' Day. This is the biggest festival of democracy, next only to a general election in the country. Over 3 crore voters will get their identity cards at over 6 lakh booth-level functions all over the country. This number includes nearly 1 crore young people who have just turned eighteen.

The origin of National Voters' Day (NVD) is a story in itself. At a civil society meeting in Bhubaneswar late in September 2010, a young man in the audience got up and said, 'Eighteen years is an age that deserves to be celebrated. At least one day every year should be dedicated to eighteen-year-olds.' I thought it was a great idea—and NVD was born.

In a letter to the cabinet secretary 'informing' him of our plan to observe 25 January as NVD, I requested him to ask the ministries and state governments to extend the necessary cooperation. Three months later, with only a week left for the nationwide booth-level functions, a phone call from the cabinet secretary almost brought our plans crashing down. My 'proposal' was coming up before the cabinet and he asked whether we wanted a national holiday, and how much money we needed. Our answers saved the day: no, we did not want a national holiday; nor did we need a single rupee from the government. The cabinet secretary was, naturally, intrigued—8 lakh functions to be organized without any request for money! He had never seen such a proposal in his life.

Our secret was quite simple. Voter registration is a normal activity of the Election Commission of India (ECI), carried out through the year. All we did was to convert the staggered, sporadic activity into an 'event', using the normal budget. The first National Voters' Day was inaugurated by then President Pratibha Patil in the presence of thirty chief election commissioners from around the world. Some of them, including those from Pakistan and Bhutan, went back home and declared their own National Voters' Days.

After just four National Voters' Days, the 2014 general election was conducted with the addition of nearly 12 crore more voters than in 2009. This is like adding the entire population of South Africa and South Korea combined, or three Canadas, or four Australias, or ten Portugals, or twenty Finlands! National Voters' Day is the flagship event of another new programme of the EC—Systematic Voters' Education for Electoral Participation (SVEEP). This programme faced a few hiccups—some in the organization questioning whether 'educating' voters was the ECI's job, for example. For me, it indeed was. Low turnout had been the bane of our elections, raising questions about the legitimacy of our elected representatives. In this context, we considered voter education an imperative.

We had seen enormous public apathy, especially among the educated urban middle class, which not only abstained from voting, but also used to brag about this. Our challenge was to make not voting embarrassing. It didn't take long to achieve this. A 2010 campaign lampooning those who did not turn up to vote—'Pappu doesn't vote, aaha'—did the trick. It achieved a remarkable increase in voter turnout. A key strategy was to have brand ambassadors— headed by no less a person than former President A.P.J. Abdul Kalam. The youth, hitherto indifferent to or contemptuous of politics, started leading from the front. Twenty-five thousand campus ambassadors were appointed in universities and colleges. Schoolchildren became watchdogs of voter participation, coaxing apathetic parents to vote. All elections since 2010 have seen record turnouts. Election 2014 broke a six-decade record, with a 66.4 per cent turnout. In some states, this crossed 80 per cent. In half the states, women voters outnumbered men. Many have described this as a 'participation revolution'.

The inked finger became a symbol of right action—restaurants apparently started offering discounts, barbers giving free haircuts to those who turned up with inked fingers. ECI has now taken the movement to new heights. A grand voter fest (Matdaata Mahotsav) in Delhi last week attracted nearly 3 lakh citizens.

The best endorsement of ECI's proactive work on this front has come from Prime Minister Narendra Modi, who in his '*Mann Ki Baat*' said:

> Till a few years ago, we used to see that our Election Commission is working just as a regulator. But it has undergone a significant change in the past few years. Today, our EC is not a mere regulator anymore. It has instead become a facilitator, is more voter-friendly and voters are now at the centre of all its plans and thoughts.

What makes these remarks especially significant is that the ECI has consistently differed with Modi's advocacy of compulsory voting. Who says there is no freedom to differ in this country.

The Role of Election Commission: Powers, Procedures and Politics

1

The Election Commission Must Act Tough

THE 2019 GENERAL ELECTION WILL LONG BE REMEMBERED, NOT JUST for the transgressions of the top political leadership, but also for the Election Commission (EC) itself being put in the dock. The EC has repeatedly found itself at the receiving end of scathing attacks from the Opposition, the public, the media and the judiciary. This is unprecedented for what was until now the most trusted institution in the country.

Trust deficit

Indeed, the trust deficit between the ECI, the Opposition parties and the voters started with the EVM/voter-verified paper audit trail (VVPAT) saga. The EC was accused of being on the defensive rather than being communicative. On 8 April, in a letter to the President, a group of retired bureaucrats and diplomats expressed concerns over the ECI's 'weak-kneed conduct', and said the institution is 'suffering from a crisis of credibility today'.

The last two months have been a trying time for me as well. Ever since I demitted office in 2012, I have been a self-appointed spokesperson for the Election Commission, defending every action of the body that needed to be defended. I must have refused at least a hundred requests by the media to comment on the recent happenings. On the few occasions I was drawn into the debate, it was a painful struggle to find suitable words that would not sound like an indictment of the body of which I was proud to have been part of. I noticed the same predicament on the faces of two former chief election commissioners who appeared on television recently. Then I remembered the words of Martin Luther King, Jr: 'Our lives begin to end the day we become silent about things that matter.' And I remembered Plato: 'I will put down your silence as consent.'

It took repeated raps on the knuckles by the Supreme Court for the Election Commission to crack the whip. It is a pity that we needed the Supreme Court to remind the ECI of the powers it always had. Article 329 of the Constitution has barred courts from interfering in electoral matters after the election process has been set in motion. In a long chain of judgments, the Supreme Court has reiterated this provision and has restrained all courts from intervening in electoral matters. It is therefore significant that in the last couple of months, the apex court itself had to jump in to bring about a course correction. This is more serious than is realized at present.

On 15 April, a Supreme Court bench headed by the Chief Justice of India pulled up the ECI for not acting against hate speeches and statements that were on religious lines. The ECI reportedly told the apex court: 'We are toothless, we are powerless, we issue notices, then advisory and on repeated violation, we file complaint.' The Supreme Court was furious with this stand of ECI's.

The Supreme Court had made this observation in 1977:

> ... where these [the existing laws] are absent, and yet a
> situation has to be tackled, the Chief Election Commissioner
> has not to fold his hands and pray to God for divine inspiration

to enable him to exercise his functions and to perform his duties or to look to any external authority for the grant of powers to deal with the situation. He must lawfully exercise his power independently, in all matters relating to the conduct of elections, and see that the election process is completed properly, in a free and fair manner.

This has been the ECI's Bible.

After the ECI had not acted on complaints against Prime Minister Narendra Modi and BJP President Amit Shah for almost a month, the Supreme Court ordered it to do so before 6 May. It then promptly disposed of several complaints, giving the two leaders a clean chit in each case. Just as the EC was being written off as an impartial entity, we got the good news that at least one election commissioner had dissented on five decisions taken by the ECI—one giving a clean chit to Shah and four to Modi. He thought the Prime Minister had, in fact, invoked the armed forces in an election campaign, in violation of the ECI guidelines instructing politicians against doing so. His minority vote may not have changed the ECI verdict, but dissent is a healthy sign of objective deliberation and thus presents a ray of hope.

I can say from experience that the ECI has got away with many mistakes largely because of its credibility and people's trust in the institution. But this trust cannot be taken for granted. The moment there is a deficit of credibility, the problems begin.

Appointments and removals

The root of the problem lies in the flawed system of appointment of election commissioners. They are appointed unilaterally by the government of the day. There has been a demand for de-politicization of these appointments and to have them done through broad-based consultation, as it is in other countries. The uncertainty around their elevation, which is decided by a system based on seniority, makes the appointees vulnerable to government pressure. The government can control a defiant CEC through the majority voting power of the two election commissioners.

In its twenty-fifth report, the Law Commission of India recommended a collegium system for appointing election commissioners. Political stalwarts such as L.K. Advani and former CECs B.B. Tandon, N. Gopalaswami and I supported the idea, even when in office. But successive ruling dispensations have ducked the issue, not wanting to let go of their power. It is obvious that political and electoral interests take precedence over national interests.

A public interest litigation, asking for the collegium system to be adopted was also filed in the Supreme Court in 2018, which has been referred to a Constitution bench. I feel that on issues of such vital importance, even the Supreme Court, which I have always described as the guardian angel of democracy in India, has to act urgently. If democracy is derailed, the court's future too would be in jeopardy.

Apart from the manner of appointment of ECs, the provisions for their removal too needs correction. At present, only the CEC is protected from removal from office (except through impeachment). One has to remember that the Constitution enabled protection to the CEC as it was a one-man commission initially. This must now be extended to the other commissioners, who were added in 1993, as they collectively represent the Election Commission.

In the rich history of democratic India, all institutions of the state have come under pressure at one point or another. But the strength and credibility of an institution is tested by whether or not it buckles under political pressure.

It is unfortunate that the topic of debate is now the ECI rather than the political leaders and their appalling and unconstitutional conduct. Over forty electoral reforms have remained pending for two decades. While it seems futile to hope the political leadership will address them, it is imperative that the ECI asserts the ample authority it already possesses constitutionally. It has the full support of the Supreme Court. It must act tough. This is not merely a question of its discretionary powers, but of its constitutional duty. Governments come and go, but the reputation of the EC stays for good.

2

A Crisis of Credibility in EC

THE ELECTION COMMISSION OF INDIA IS A FORMIDABLE INSTITUTION which has led the world in electoral efficiency since its inception. But in the 2019 general election, it has come under the scanner like never before, in the wake of incidents involving breach of the Model Code of Conduct (MCC), particularly by the ruling party. On 8 April, in a letter to the president of India, a group of retired bureaucrats and diplomats, in the context of the recent incidents, expressed concern over the ECI's 'weak-kneed conduct' and the institution 'suffering from a crisis of credibility today'.

Points of concern

The letter described the Prime Minister's 27 March announcement of India's first anti-satellite (ASAT) test as a 'serious breach of propriety [which] amounts to giving unfair publicity to the party in power'. Questions were also raised over the launch of NaMo TV without a license, and about a biopic on the life of the prime minister, which was scheduled for release on 11 April, when elections commenced. The group also requested the EC to 'issue directions to withhold the release of all biopics and documentaries on any political personages through any media mechanism until the conclusion of the electoral process'. They asserted that such propaganda amounted to free publicity, and hence should be debited as election expenditure in the name of the candidate in question. They said the same standards should also apply to other such propaganda, an example being a web series titled *Modi: A Common Man's Journey*.

Other important issues highlighted in the letter included transfers of top officials, VVPAT audits, violations of the MCC by Rajasthan Governor Kalyan Singh (for which the group requested his removal on account of 'grave misdemeanour') and Uttar Pradesh Chief Minister Yogi Adityanath (in his speech, he referred to the armed forces as the army of Narendra Modi), and also corrosion of political discourse in general.

Needless to say, the questions being raised about the credibility of the ECI are a cause for worry. It is, however, not the first time that the conduct of the Commission has been questioned.

A flawed appointment system

To my mind, the genesis of the problem lies in the flawed system of appointment of election commissioners, who are appointed unilaterally by the government of the day. This debate can be settled once and for all by de-politicizing appointments, which must be done through broad-based consultation, as in some other countries.

In its twenty-fifth report, the Law Commission recommended a collegium, consisting of the Prime Minister, the leader of the Opposition and the chief justice of India, for appointment of the CEC and eCs. Political stalwarts such as L.K. Advani and former chief election commissioners, including B.B. Tandon, N. Gopalaswami and I, had supported the idea in the past, even when in office. But successive ruling dispensations have ducked the issue, not wanting to let go of their power. It is obvious that political and electoral interests take precedence over national interests.

A public interest litigation was also filed in the Supreme Court in late 2018 calling for a 'fair, just and transparent process of selection by constituting a neutral and independent Collegium/selection committee'. The matter has been referred to a Constitution bench. It's not a routine matter. On issues of such vital importance, even the Supreme Court—which I have always described as the guardian angel of democracy—has to act with utmost urgency. If democracy is derailed, the court's future too would be in jeopardy.

Besides the manner of appointment, the system for removal of election commissioners also needs correction. Only the chief election commissioner is protected from removal, except when it is by impeachment. The other two commissioners, who have equal voting power in the functioning of the Election Commission, can outvote the CEC ten times a day. The uncertainty of their elevation in the bureaucracy, decided as it is by a system that goes by seniority, makes them vulnerable to government pressure. The government can control a defiant CEC through the majority voting power of the two commissioners. One has to remember that the Constitution enabled protection to the CEC as it was a one-man commission initially. This must now be extended to the other commissioners, who were added in 1993, as they collectively represent the Election Commission.

Moving forward

The ECI's reputation also suffers when it is unable to tame recalcitrant political parties, especially the ruling party. This is because it has no power to de-register them even for the gravest of violations, despite being the registering authority for political parties under Section 29A of the Representation of the People Act, 1951. The EC has been seeking the power to de-register political parties, among the many other reforms that it has been asking for.

This reform was first suggested by the CEC in 1998 and reiterated several times. The EC also submitted an affidavit to the Supreme

Court last February, saying it wanted to be empowered 'to de-register a political party, particularly in view of its constitutional mandate'.

Elections are the bedrock of democracy, and the EC's credibility is central to democratic legitimacy. Hence, the guardian of elections itself needs urgent institutional safeguards to protect its autonomy. It is time that action is taken to depoliticize constitutional appointments and the EC empowered to de-register parties for electoral misconduct. It is a step needed towards restoring all-important public faith in the institution.

While these reforms may continue to be debated, nothing stops the EC from asserting the ample authority it already has under the Constitution and in being tough in discharging its duties. It's not at its discretion to be so but its constitutional mandate to be so. It did not need a reminder or a nudge from the Supreme Court.

3

On EC's Neutrality

ON THE MORNING OF 17 DECEMBER 2021, I WOKE UP TO A SHOCKING headline in the *Indian Express* that said the chief election commissioner and the two election commissioners were summoned by the Prime Minister's Office (PMO) to attend a meeting with the principal secretary to the PM.

My memory went back to 27 June 2006, when I received a call from Pulok Chatterji, principal secretary to the then Prime Minister Manmohan Singh, informing me that I was being considered for appointment as an election commissioner and asking if I would accept it. Postings in the government are not optional; you are just appointed. Why this question, then? The reason was made clear by Chatterji. I would have to resign from the IAS.

Why was my appointment as an election commissioner conditional on my resignation from the IAS? Therein lies the important constitutional principle of distancing the EC from the executive/ government. Importantly, a wall was built between me and the PM who had appointed me.

As a secretary to the government of India, I was at the mercy of the PM, but as an election commissioner, I was independent, neutral and distant from him. There was no question of his calling/summoning me to see him or with any request, let alone give me any direction or instruction. He could appoint me but could not order me or remove me because of the constitutional scheme of things. An independent Election Commission of India is a gift of the Constitution to the nation. Free, fair and credible elections are sine qua non of the ECI. The Supreme Court has repeatedly stressed this point, calling the Commission part of the basic structure of the Constitution.

The PMO's summoning or 'inviting' of not just the CEC but the full bench is in violation of the Constitution, irrespective of how important or urgent the issue is. Let alone the principal secretary to the PM, even on the part of the mighty PM it would be an unacceptable act. Can you imagine the principal secretary to the PM issuing such summons to the CJI, to come over with the full bench of the court and attend a meeting with him on judicial reforms? The secretary would be running for cover with a contempt of court case against him.

In my opinion, there is no difference between the neutrality and independence of the Supreme Court and of the ECI in this context. Both are independent constitutional authorities, deliberately separated from the executive. Forgetting the summoning of the CEC and eCs, the principal secretary to the PM cannot even call on the ECI without public knowledge of the meeting and what transpired in it. Politicians of all hues visit the ECI regularly with petitions, complaints or suggestions, but with full transparency. I never met any of them alone, insisting on the presence of my two colleagues. Transparency is the key word here, and perception of transparency is equally important.

Now, let us talk about the protocol in this matter, though that is secondary. The CEC is very high in the warrant of precedence—ninth—while the principal secretary to the PM is twenty-third. How can such a high-ranking constitutional functionary be summoned to attend a meeting with an officer, howsoever high and mighty? The law ministry, which advises the government on all legal and constitutional matters, should have known better than to convey that it was okay for the PMO to 'expect' the CEC/eCs to attend a meeting at the office.

I recall another event. One day, I got a call from Veerappa Moily, the then law minister: 'Mr Quraishi, you have been raising the issue of electoral reforms. Why don't you come for a cup of tea in my office so that we discuss them?' I was in a fix, but only for six seconds. My going there would have been in violation of the spirit of the Constitution. I declined the invite. Instead, I told the honourable minister, 'Sir, thank you for your kind offer but why don't you come over instead? I will introduce you to my brother commissioners and senior officers.' Gracious as he was, Moily came over the next day with four of his top officers. What was expected to be a short semi-courtesy meeting went on for over three hours. He asked whether we would like to join the ministry in hosting seven regional conferences to build a national consensus on electoral reforms. We readily agreed. When all the regional meetings were over, the law minister came over to the Election Commission a second time to discuss the arrangements for the final, national meeting.

Just as the reforms were materializing, Moily was shifted to another ministry and replaced by Salman Khurshid. I called up the PM to protest—just when Moily had built up a national consensus, you have transferred him, undoing all his and our work of six months, I told him. He said, 'Don't worry. Salman will carry forward this work. I will send him to you.' Note that the PM did not say, 'Go and meet him.'

Sure enough, Khurshid came over to the Commission's office within a week and reassured us about taking the reforms forward. It's a different matter that the proposal fizzled out. The important thing is that the Union law minister, who heads the ECI's administrative ministry and sanctions our budget, visited the ECI thrice in four months, in keeping with the spirit of the Constitution.

The initial reaction of horror and disgust on the part of the CEC and eCs at being called over to the PMO was most heartening, and I salute them. But why they got persuaded to attend the 'informal interaction' subsequently puzzles me. A meeting with the principal secretary to the PM, formal or informal, online or in the PMO or at the ECI office just before elections raises unnecessary suspicion. Who knows what was discussed. The election dates? Or something else?

This incident is a transgression that should not happen again. The arm's-length distance envisaged in the Constitution for interactions between certain institutions is sacrosanct. It should not only be maintained but also 'seen' to be maintained.

4

Will the Modi Government Give the EC More Power So It Is Fully Independent?

The Election Commission of India's suggestion for the power to punish entities for contempt of the Commission—on the lines of contempt of court—set the proverbial cat among the pigeons. As expected, it has drawn more flak and ridicule than support or sympathy.

The EC has sought to empower itself to punish anyone being 'disobedient and discourteous' towards its authority. It has cited examples of some countries whose election commissions have this power, directly or indirectly. The countries mentioned include the Philippines, Ghana, Liberia, Pakistan, Australia and Kenya. The proposal is to amend the Representation of the People Act, 1951, by insertion of Section 169A and to extend the provision of the Contempt of Courts Act, 1971 to the ECI and its commissioners.

The accompanying Explanation spells out contempt as 'wilful disobedience to any instructions, directions, order or opinion passed by the commission or wilful breach of an undertaking given to the commission'. Further, it includes any word or action that 'scandalises or lowers the authority of the commission'.

The EC has given three instances of wild allegations made against it: one, Delhi Chief Minister Arvind Kejriwal calling it 'Dhritarashtra', accusing it of blindly helping BJP's 'Duryodhana' win elections with the help of EVMs that he alleged had been tampered with; two, Manish Tewari of the Congress party accusing the EC of becoming an 'advocate of EVMs' and of trying to 'bulldoze the challenging political parties'; three, Kejriwal questioning the integrity of the ECI for doing everything to make BJP win.

The ECI was also immensely hurt when Kejriwal cast aspersions on two commissioners, A.K. Jyoti and O.P. Rawat, for being close to the BJP. This prompted Rawat, a perfect gentleman, to recuse himself from hearing all Aam Aadmi Party-related matters in the future.

I don't think the proposal is well considered. There is a basic difference between the ECI and the courts. The latter are never heard in public, even to defend their judgments, while the Commission is all over the media all the time. Even so, the power of the courts themselves is being increasingly questioned.

To be fair to the ECI, however, its anguish has to be understood in perspective. The ECI has over the years become the most trusted constitutional body in India. All political parties accept its neutrality and fairness, except in stray cases where a party or a leader has felt disgruntled when the Commission took action against it/him/her. Actually, some leaders, especially of the incumbent government, think the Commission should be harsh and stringent towards all others except themselves. Some leaders expect gratitude from commissioners for their appointment and take offence when the Commission does not oblige them—which is often.

The media was quick to attack the ECI's proposal. *DNA* commented, 'Participatory democracy is not built on authorities quick to take offence.' *The Hindu* called it 'unwarranted and poorly thought out', 'a travesty of our open and democratic system', 'harmful to free speech and criticism'. Making the ECI feel 'scandalised' or tending to 'lower its authority—is a vague and subjective provision that should have no place in contempt law'. To this extent, the criticism is unexceptionable. However, *The Hindu* goes on to add that there is 'no reason to believe that public confidence in the ECI will be shaken or its superintendence, direction and control over the election process undermined by criticism, however tendentious or calumnious it may be'. This certainly is not a correct assessment. Public trust that takes years to build can come crashing down even on commission of bona fide mistakes. The ECI has been delivering the biggest and most complex democratic exercise in the world because of people's trust in its fairness and neutrality. All surveys of the people's perceptions about institutions have rated the ECI highly. But if one is done today, I'm afraid the results will not be so rosy, as a lot of poison has been spewed on it in the wake of the EVM controversy by a swarming army of trolls of different hues, besides many political parties and a large section of the media.

Public comments on the proposal have been sharp: one hears or reads comments like 'gagging the mouth of democracy', 'contempt of democracy', 'dangerous weapon even against genuine charges', and 'a step towards dictatorship'.

Propaganda and rumour can set the country on fire, not just damage institutions. The perception of neutrality, independence and fairness on the part of the ECI has to be protected at all costs.

What is the solution?

The solution is two-fold: one, to make the ECI fully independent; and, two, to give it more disciplinary power over political parties.

For the EC to not only be truly independent but, also, be seen as independent, the system of appointment of election commissioners must change. The fact that the Commission is appointed by the government of the day makes the appointing authority feel like a proprietor who expects the appointee to toe the line set by it. Often, disgruntled elements point fingers at a commissioner as being favourable to the appointing party. It is ironic that perhaps the most powerful election commission in the world also has the most flawed system of appointment. Nowhere in the world does the government of the day unilaterally appoint the election commissioner. The appointment is always done by collegiums or after full parliamentary scrutiny/interview. In some countries, the candidates are interviewed on television for the nation to watch. Even in India, the judges of superior courts are appointed through a collegium system; and, not to mention appointments to constitutional bodies, even appointments to statutory bodies like the Central Vigilance Commission and the Central Information Commission are done in this manner. The Supreme Court has ordered the collegium system even for appointment of the director of the Central Bureau of Investigation—a government department.

When I was appointed election commissioner in 2006, a top aide of Prime Minister Manmohan Singh told me that my appointment by the government of the day may be its last, as the prime minister felt that it would be in the interest of the country to have a collegium for EC appointments, as demanded by Anna Hazare, among others. Why it did not happen, I do not know. Maybe sheer complacency, or procrastination or the desire of the government to not weaken its own powers. The present government is not being any different if it has a similar inclination. But then, when it is so critical of the omissions and commissions of its predecessors, why not undo another long-standing wrong? After all, it claims to be a party with a difference, one making a new beginning for India in myriad ways. Can it rise above narrow political/electoral considerations in the larger interest of the nation?

The second necessary reform for the independence of the ECI is to provide protection to the two commissioners from removal, except by impeachment, as provided by the Constitution for the chief election commissioner—the sole member at the time of the Commission's inception. They should not be made to feel like probationers trying to please the government. Appointment of the commissioners should be through a collegium, and elevation as CEC automatically by seniority, like for the post of chief justice of India.

The third reform should be to give the ECI the power to punish political parties (including de-registration of them) that commit major violations of their oath or indulge in wilful disobedience of lawful orders, like non-submission of accounts and audit reports, non-conduct of internal party elections, persistent violation of the MCC, etc.

Free and fair elections are part of the basic structure of the Constitution, and the ECI its cornerstone. Its independence and credibility must be guarded and strengthened, whatever it takes. I wish Prime Minister Narendra Modi's vision for a new India would include this essential reform.

5

Main Issues and Debates on EC

No election to a Rajya Sabha seat has ever generated so much heat as the one that concluded past midnight on 9 August 2017. People were glued to the television throughout the day and social media was abuzz with speculation. What made this election so special? Was it a media hype by the TV channels vying for TRPs, or were the issues involved really serious and unprecedented? But in the eye of this storm were indeed many interesting issues, ranging from the scourge of horse-trading to operation of the anti-defection law, the power and role of the Election Commission, NOTA, secrecy of the ballot, and the two questionable votes whose secrecy was violated.

The first act of horse-trading began with large-scale defections from the Congress. Six Congress MLAs joined the BJP, seven more defected later and one cross-voted. When the defection game began, the Congress transported forty-four of its remaining MLAs to the safety of Congress-ruled Bengaluru, where they camped at a luxury resort. The unfortunate practice of taking MLAs to secret places, often against their wishes, is nearly three decades old. Remember 'Aaya Ram Gaya Ram'? Given the money power in our political circles, it is almost impossible to prevent defections. Our legislators are notorious for their purchasability, and this has popularized the phrase 'horse-trading' in reportage on Indian politics. We have been seeing it with sickening regularity across the country. The figures mentioned for purchase of legislators are obscenely high, running into crores—maybe tens of crores.

The debate that ensued over the MLAs forced to holiday was interesting. The poachers were heard blaming the party that was trying to save its flock—a proverbial case of the pot calling the kettle black. The fact that none of the 'holidaymakers' defected proves the efficacy of this step of trapping them in a resort. The second issue was about the applicability of the anti-defection law. The law did operate in this case, when the six MLAs who defected to the BJP were unseated and disqualified from voting. However, the seven who crossed over could not be disqualified, as the anti-defection law operates only when the whip is violated as a part of legislative proceedings. An election is not part of these proceedings. It is noteworthy that defections become rampant anyway when the term of the house is coming to an end and the outgoing legislators have nothing much to lose. They suddenly discover some forgotten 'principles' or 'suffocation from the leadership style' of their erstwhile party.

Another issue that arose was NOTA, which has been in operation since January 2014 but was suddenly discovered by the Congress, which protested about it, even alleging mala fide intent on the part of the Election Commission. They took the matter to the Supreme Court, which rightly refused to stay the operation, questioning why the party had not raised it for three-and-a-half years. The court, however, will still decide on NOTA applicability in the peculiar case of these Rajya Sabha elections. The court's refusal to stay NOTA was rooted in the fact that Article 329 specifically prohibits any judicial interference in an election process that has been set in motion. And the Election Commission did invoke this Article in the court. I personally feel that the matter does need reconsideration, in view of the fact that elections to the posts of president and vice-president have been kept out of NOTA, and this has caused repeated confusion in their conduct, necessitating clarificatory notifications.

Secrecy of the ballot was another debated issue. The normal rule is that all votes in all elections are secret, and anyone who shows his vote gets his vote cancelled. There is, however, one exception—a Rajya Sabha election. To checkmate horse-trading, the election rules have provided that the voter in a Rajya Saba election will show his vote to an authorized representative of his party but to no one else (Rule 39, Code of Election Rules, 1961). In the Gujarat Rajya Sabha election case of 2014 mentioned earlier, two Congress MLAs showed their vote to rival BJP leaders to prove their new loyalty. The Congress lodged a protest with the Election Commission of India. The BJP said the protest was too late as the votes had already been put into the ballot box and could not be identified.

This was the time when the ECI came under the scanner of the public (read media). Social media buzzed with speculation. Questions were raised about the integrity of the commissioners, both BJP appointees. Both the involved parties launched an onslaught of delegations to the Election Commission. Many critics questioned the wisdom of the Commission seeing these delegations repeatedly, but I feel it was the right thing for it to do, as it must hear every conceivable point that may help it to decide a case with watertight credibility, and also in deference to the principle that justice should not only be done but appear to be done too.

Questions were raised by the BJP about the power of the Election Commission vis-à-vis that of the returning officer (RO). In response to public questions, I had tweeted that till the results of an election are announced the power of the Commission is total and exclusive, though after the result it is zero and shifts to the high courts. It is true that the RO has the ultimate power under the law, and that if he wanted to he could have started the counting and declared the results even if there was a blatant fraud. But to prevent such a possibility, as has happened in the past, the Election Commission sends an observer who can stop the counting and withhold the result till he and the Commission are fully satisfied. That's exactly what happened in this case.

An interesting question is: how were the disputed votes identified after they were already mixed up in the ballot box with all the others? Such a practical 'difficulty' can never be a reason to allow fraud to happen. Even one bogus vote is enough to 'vitiate' a poll, on the grounds of which the entire election in question can be countermanded. That's why the Election Commission rules provide a safeguard and a procedure to deal with such an eventuality. The impugned votes are identified from the unique number printed on the back of each ballot paper.

The ECI came out with flying colours. Contrary to speculation that both the commissioners, being appointees of the BJP (the CEC, in fact, was the former chief secretary of Narendra Modi when he was the chief minister of Gujarat), would be under pressure to rule in favour of the ruling party, they delivered a brilliant judgment. I would like to mention from my experience that there is a kind of aura that the office of the CEC has, and an institutional memory and framework that keep its conscience active. The Commission is also conscious of the judicial scrutiny it can be subjected to and its public image.

The contest was between the BJP and the Congress. But the winners are [Achal Kumar] Jyoti and [Om Prakash] Rawat. Proud of you, my friends.

1

Lok Janshakti Party Split

In June 2021, the sudden and dramatic developments in the Lok Janshakti Party (LJP) caused quite a storm in political circles, and I have been flooded with queries about the procedures involved and the role of the Election Commission in settling the dispute. The breaking away of the majority of the LJP parliamentary unit from Lok Sabha MP Chirag Paswan to form an independent group in the Lower House, had the full backing of the BJP as well as the Janata Dal (United), and will have far reaching consequences for the NDA equations in Bihar.

The Commission does not take suo motu cognizance of such cases. It comes into the picture only when one party approaches it with a claim of having majority. The Commission then starts proceedings, which are quasi-judicial in nature, under Section 15 of the Election Symbols (Reservation and Allotment) Order, 1968, by giving a notice to the other faction to provide its version of the matter in dispute. Both parties are asked to produce evidence in support of their claims, accompanied by affidavit I.

It is important to see what Section 15 of the Symbols Order lays down:

> When the Commission is satisfied on information in its possession, that there are rival sections or groups of a recognised political party, each of whom claims to be that party, the Commission may, after taking into account all the available facts and circumstances of the case … decide that one such rival section or group, or none of such rival sections or groups, of a recognised party, and the decision of the Commission shall be binding and on all such rivals sections or groups.

The Election Commission examines the claims and counterclaims of the two factions to determine which one has the majority. Those examined would include MPs, MLAs, MLCs and the party office bearers on the one hand, and the office-bearers of the party, on the other. The opposing factions often question and contest each other's supporter lists as inflated and containing many bogus signatures. Determining the genuineness of signatures is a time-consuming and often frustrating job. As lawyers get involved, the whole process normally takes four to five months.

A split in a political party is not a new phenomenon. There have been several cases in the past, with the opposing factions seeking recognition as the real party. The most important case has been that of the Indian National Congress, which split in 1969, leading to the formation of two parties—Congress(O) and Congress(I). Subsequently, the Indian National Congress split a second time in 1978, into Congress (Indira) and Congress (Tiwari). In the 1980s, in Tamil Nadu, the All India Anna Dravida Munnetra Kazhagam (AIADMK) split into two factions, one led by MGR's All India Anna Dravida Munnetra Kazhagam (AIADMK) the other by J. Jayalalithaa. Later, the Janata Dal went through a similar process, resulting in the JD(U) and JD(S) parties. In 2012, we had a similar situation in Uttarakhand, where the Uttarakhand Kranti Dal split, and in 2017 in UP, where the Samajwadi Party split just before the elections.

In all these cases, the Election Commission went through the above-mentioned process. The Commission looks at the strength of each group within the party and in the legislatures, applying the test of majority. Whenever the Commission could not determine the strength of rival groups based on the support they had within the party organization, it fell back on testing their majority among the party's elected MPs and MLAs.

Many of these cases have landed in the Supreme Court. The most significant case was that of the Indian National Congress (INC) in 1969, where the Supreme Court upheld the order of the ECI in its application of the test of majority (*Sadiq Ali vs. ECI, 1972*). It was a milestone judgment for the Election Commission, as the apex court upheld the constitutional validity of the Election Symbols (Reservation and Allotment) Order, 1968, giving an executive order the status of a subordinate legislation.

A three-judge Supreme Court bench, consisting of Justices H.R. Khanna, K.S. Hegde and A.N. Grover, clarified the purpose of paragraph 15 of the Symbols Order:

> The symbol is not a property to be divided between co-owners … And in case of a split, the Commission has been authorised to determine which of the rival groups or sections is the party entitled to the symbol. The Commission, in resolving this dispute, does not decide as to which group represents the party, but which group is that party …
>
> The Supreme Court has time and again upheld the test of majority in the Symbols Order to be a 'valuable and relevant test' to decide a dispute between rival groups within a 'democratic organization' like a recognized political party.

How did the Election Commission deal with such matters before the Symbols Order came into effect? Before 1968, the poll panel would issue notifications and executive orders under the Conduct of Election Rules, 1961. The most high-profile split of a party before 1968 was that of the Communist Party of India (CPI) in 1964. A breakaway group approached the Election Commission in December

1964, urging it to recognize them as the CPI (Marxist). They provided a list of MPs and MLAs from Andhra Pradesh, Kerala and West Bengal who supported them. The ECI recognized the faction as the CPI(M).

At that time, the Election Commission had no guidelines or precedents to fall back on. Using common sense, it gave its verdict through a notification. Not long thereafter, the Commission decided to frame guidelines and issued the Election Symbols Order 1968. In its very first case thereafter, it applied the test of majority in the Congress party split. The Supreme Court upheld this principle, which has been followed ever since. And it has never gone wrong.

This principle was followed up to 1997, when the Election Commission introduced a new rule under which while one faction which proved its majority got the party symbol and the other had to register itself as a separate party. The national- or state-party status of the new formation would be determined only on the basis of its performance in state or Central elections after its registration.

It has always been the practice of the Commission to give a detailed speaking order, which will stand judicial scrutiny. This is why its quasi-judicial or administrative orders almost always pass the judicial test. It will be interesting to see how the present case proceeds.

2

Samajwadi Party's Symbol War–I

IN JANUARY 2017, THE SUDDEN DRAMATIC DEVELOPMENTS IN THE Samajwadi Party in UP have thrown out of gear all the calculations of poll pundits for the upcoming state assembly elections.

I have been flooded with media queries about the implications of this development for the forthcoming elections and the role of the Election Commission in settling it. The Commission is not concerned with the mutual recrimination being played out in the media and the claims and counterclaims. It does not take suo motu action in such case, as it comes into the picture only when one party approaches it with its claim to being the original party.

The commission then starts quasi-judicial proceedings under Section 15 of The Election Symbols (Reservation and Allotment) Order, 1968, by giving notice to the other faction to give their version of the dispute. Both parties, obviously, claim that they are the real party. The Election Commission calls on both factions to produce evidence in support of their claims, along with affidavits.

Examination of claims and counterclaims

It will be useful to reproduce Section 15 of The Symbols Order, which runs as follows:

> When the Commission is satisfied on information in its position, that there are rival sections or groups of a recognised political party, each of whom claims to be that party, the Commission may, after taking into account all the available facts and circumstances of the case, and hearing such representatives of the sections or groups and other persons as desire to be heard, decide that one such rival section or group, or none of such arrival sections of groups, of a recognised party, and the decision of the Commission shall be binding and on all such rivals sections or groups.

Section 15 of The Election Symbols Order, 1968

The Election Commission will examine the claims and counterclaims to determine which faction has the majority. It will examine the MLAs, MLCs and the office bearers of the party. Our experience has been that both factions often question each other's lists as being inflated and containing many bogus signatures. Determining the genuineness of signatures becomes a ticklish job. Both parties will have to be given a hearing. The whole process can take three to five months.

Ad hoc symbols for warring factions

The question is, what happens if the dispute happens on the eve of an upcoming election, which is due within a few months? An interim arrangement has to be found. Since both parties will stake claim to the party name and symbol, the latter may be frozen, pending the Commission's judgment. In the meantime, the two factions will be given ad hoc names, like SP(X) and SP(Y), and an interim symbol will be allotted to each.

This is not a new phenomenon. There have been several cases in the past when a party split into two factions, and both sought recognition as the real party. The best-remembered case is that of the Indian National Congress, which split in 1969, leading to the formation of two parties—Congress (O) and Congress (I). In fact, the Indian National Congress split a second time in 1978, when Congress (Indira) and Congress (Tiwari) resulted.

In the 1980s, in Tamil Nadu, the AIADMK split into two factions, one led by the late Tamil Nadu Chief Minister M.G. Ramachandra's wife, Janaki, and the other by J. Jayalalithaa. Later, the Janata Dal went through similar process, becoming JD (U) and JD (S). Not long ago, before the 2012 state elections, there was a similar situation in Uttarakhand, where the Uttarakhand Kranti Dal split. The Election Commission went through the above-mentioned process in all these cases.

Test of majority

The Election Commission looks at two factors—the constitution of the party and the strength of each group, applying the test of majority. Many of these cases have finally landed in the Supreme Court. The most important judgment was in the case of the INC, where the Supreme Court upheld the order of the ECI, which had applied its test of majority.

In the case of UP, while the constitution of the Samajwadi Party and the actions taken under its purview will certainly be crucial criteria, the test of majority, which has already been upheld by the Supreme Court, will perhaps override it.

Since these are all quasi-judicial proceedings, it will certainly take four to five months for the case to be decided. Till then, an ad hoc arrangement for giving distinguishable names and symbols to the two factions seems to be the likely scenario.

3

Samajwadi Party's Symbol War-II

AFTER NEARLY TWO WEEKS OF DRAMATIC DEVELOPMENTS OVER THE split in the Samajwadi Party and the claims of the two factions, the Election Commission delivered its verdict in favour of Uttar Pradesh Chief Minister Akhilesh Yadav. One newspaper headline screamed: 'Election Commission gifts Samajwadi Party & cycle symbol to Akhilesh Yadav.' Some eyebrows were raised at Commission's disposal of the case in a record time of less than two weeks. Some even tried to look for motives. All that is the result of a great deal of distortion of facts and a lot of interpretation. We need to understand the law, its processes and practice, followed by the Commission's actions in the past. A split in a political party is a subject under the Election Symbols (Reservation and Allotment) Order, 1968, which gives the Election Commission exclusive power to decide on it. As per paragraph 15 of the Symbols Order, the Commission can decide in favour of any faction or freeze the symbol of the political party in question. The Commission has not 'gifted' the name of the party and its symbol to Akhilesh Yadav, but has only adjudicated in his favour.

The procedure the Election Commission followed was exactly the one it always had. Before 1968, the Commission issued notifications and executive orders under the Conduct of Election Rules 1961. The best-known split before the order was in 1964, when the Communist Party split and one faction approached the Commission to recognize it as the real party, but with a new name—Communist Party of India (Marxist).

The Commission did not have to wait long after the 1968 Symbols order. Within a year, there was a split in the Congress when the old guard, known as the Syndicate, expelled the then Prime Minister Indira Gandhi for not supporting the official candidate for president of India. Indira Gandhi did not claim ownership of the parent body, but got her group recognized as a new party, the Congress (R), while the other group was named Congress (O). Indira was given the symbol of 'cow and calf', while the latter was allowed to retain the pair of bullocks the original party had as its symbol (*Sadiq Ali vs. Election Commission of India, 1972*). The most significant aspect of this judgment is that the Supreme Court upheld paragraph 15 of the Symbols Order, deriving its authority from Article 324, which gives it a reservoir of powers on all matters relating to 'superintendence, direction and control of all elections'.

After 1971, the Indira faction was recognized as the real Congress and allowed to retain the cow-and-calf symbol. The Congress split again in 1978. On this occasion, the cow-and-calf symbol was frozen and Indira chose the 'hand' as the party symbol, the other faction opting for the charkha. In Tamil Nadu, after M.G. Ramachandran's death, two factions of the AIADMK emerged—one under his wife, Janaki, and the other under J. Jayalalithaa. The Election Commission refused to recognize either of the two factions and froze the party's two-leaves symbol. Later, the two factions merged under Jayalalithaa and the party got back the symbol. In 1994, Telugu Desam Party, under N. Chandrababu Naidu, was allowed to retain the cycle symbol. Thus, there are precedents where the original symbol was frozen or allotted to one faction, depending on the support they enjoyed. In all these cases, the Election Commission has applied the test of majority, which had been upheld by the Supreme Court as early as in 1972.

In the current case, the Commission found a clear majority with the Akhilesh faction, which had produced evidence of almost 90 per cent support both within the organization and in the legislatures.

Was the Election Commission's decision taken in haste, that too for some inexplicable reason? Not at all. The Election Commission is an efficient organization known for its impartiality and quick decision-making. What facilitated the quick decision was a virtual no-show by the parent group of the party, which provided absolutely no evidence, despite repeated reminders and after being given a lot of opportunities to do so. What helped the Akhilesh group was the prompt generation of evidence and its presentation, thanks to the secretary-general of Samajwadi Party Ram Gopal Yadav's enormous experience and knowledge of election laws. The 'anti-climax' of Mulayam Singh Yadav extending support to Akhilesh after the whole battle is also not unprecedented, as is clear from the above analysis. Parties have split and then remerged in the past too. Therefore, far from being frowned upon, the Election Commission deserves kudos for its smart and timely decision.

4

Shiv Sena Split 2022

On 27 September, a five-judge Constitution bench of the Supreme Court, headed by Justice D. Y. Chandrachud, allowed the Election Commission of India to decide on Maharashtra Chief Minister Eknath Shinde's petition staking claim to the 'real' Shiv Sena and the party symbol of bow and arrow. This was a reversal of its earlier order restraining the poll body from adjudicating on the matter, on a plea by the former Chief Minister Uddhav Thackeray.

The lawyers of the Thackeray camp had argued against the EC's involvement by citing that disputes regarding disqualification of the MLAs in question and the validity of Shinde's takeover are pending in court. The Shinde faction responded by saying that proceedings under the 10th Schedule had nothing to do with the current dispute before the ECI. Amidst these calls and arguments by the rival parties and legal counsels, I have been flooded with media queries about the role of the Election Commission in this incident.

It is important to note that the EC does not jump into such cases by taking suo motu cognizance, and comes into the picture only when a party approaches it with a claim. The Commission then starts proceedings under Section 15 of the Election Symbols (Reservation and Allotment) Order, 1968, which are quasi-judicial in nature. It goes by the 'rule of majority and numerical strength', starting with a notice to the other faction to give its version of the disputed event. Both parties are asked to produce evidence in support of their claims, accompanied by affidavits.

It will be useful to see what Section 15 of the Symbols Order lays down:

> When the Commission is satisfied on information in its possession, that there are rival sections or groups of a recognized political party, each of whom claims to be that party, the Commission may, after taking into account all the available facts and circumstances of the case … decide that one such rival section or group … is that recognized party, and the decision of the Commission shall be binding and on all such rivals sections or groups.

The EC examines the claims and counterclaims of the two factions to determine which one has the majority. This includes MPs, MLAs and MLCs on the one hand, and the office-bearers of the party, on the other. Both factions often question and contest the supporters' list of the other faction as inflated and as containing many bogus signatures. Determining the genuineness of signatures is time-consuming and often a frustrating job. Since lawyers are involved, the whole process can normally take four to five months.

In the very first judicial test of the Symbols Order, a three-judge Supreme Court Bench of Justices H.R. Khanna, K.S. Hegde and A.N. Grover clarified the purpose of paragraph 15 in these words:

> The symbol is not a property to be divided between co-owners. The allotment of a symbol to the candidates set up by a political party is a legal right. And in case of a split, the Commission has been authorised to determine which of the

rival groups or sections is the party entitled to the symbol. The Commission, in resolving this dispute, does not decide as to which group represents the party, but which group is that party.

The court upheld the constitutionality of the 'test of majority' in the Congress-split case (*Sadiq Ali vs. Election Commission of India, 1971*). This principle has been repeatedly upheld by several subsequent judgments.

A split in a political party is not a new phenomenon. There have been several cases in the past, with the disputing factions each seeking recognition as the real party. The most important case, which became the benchmark, is that of the Indian National Congress, mentioned above, which split in 1969 leading to the formation of two parties— the Congress (O) and Congress (I).

Subsequently, the Congress split a second time in 1978, when Congress (Indira) and Congress (Urs) were created. In the 1980s, in Tamil Nadu, the AIADMK split into two factions, one led by MGR's wife Janaki and the other by J. Jayalalithaa. Later, the Janata Dal went through a similar process, splitting into the JD(U) and JD(S). In 2012, we had a similar situation in Uttarakhand, where the Uttarakhand Kranti Dal split; and in UP in 2017, when the Samajwadi Party split just before the election.

In all these cases, the EC went through the above-mentioned process. The EC looks at the strength of each group in the party organization and in the legislatures, applying the test of majority.

The Supreme Court has, time and again, upheld the test of majority in the Symbols Order to be a 'valuable and relevant test' to decide a dispute between rival groups within a 'democratic organisation' like a recognized political party.

But what happens if an election is scheduled before the Election Commission is able to decide? In such situations, the name of the party and the symbol are both frozen, and the two factions are given temporary names, like Party A and Party B, and symbol A and symbol B. When the EC finally decides in favour of a faction, the other faction is allowed to register itself as a new party with a new symbol.

As for the current scenario, it remains to be seen how the case proceeds, and what political and constitutional resolution it will lead us towards. Till then, an ad hoc arrangement for giving distinguishable names to the two factions and ad hoc symbols to each seems to be the likely scenario.

1

Glitches Apart, EVMs Are Necessary

Reports of malfunctioning VVPATs in the recently concluded by-polls for parliament and state assemblies have once again raised questions about the credibility of EVMs. In what is being seen as a huge setback, re-polls had to take place in seventy-three booths in Kairana in UP, forty-three in Maharashtra and for one seat in Nagaland. Election Commission officials blamed the excessive heat for the malfunctioning of VVPATs, which is surprising because when trials were held for the machines, they were subjected to all kinds of weather conditions. From the coastal conditions in Kerala to the excessive heat in Jaisalmer and extreme winter in Leh, VVPATs have survived extreme weather conditions, and any kind of malfunctioning was duly noticed and rectified by the Election Commission. The manufacturers have some explaining to do.

Let me point out two things. Firstly, it was precisely to remove doubts regarding the EVMs that VVPAT machines were introduced—to provide voters with a means to verify that their vote was cast correctly and for the audit of stored electronic results. Using these machines, voters can review a physical ballot to confirm their electronic vote.

Secondly, it was the VVPAT machines that malfunctioned in the recent by-polls, and not the EVMs. While it is true that Election Commission officials should have replaced the machines within the stipulated time frame of half an hour, this incident is hardly any reason to question the validity of EVMs.

The issue of 'tamperability' of EVMs has been doing the rounds ever since they were first introduced. Every time a political party loses an election, it blames the machine. However, none of them has been able to prove their allegations against the credibility of EVMs, and neither do they apologize when they win the elections where the same EVMs have been used. All that this manages to do, however, is shake the trust of people in the system.

Many critics, giving the example of Germany, say that EVMs have been declared illegal by the German Supreme Court. I would, however, like to point out that the German court has not declared EVMs illegal because any fault was found with the technology, but because the German Constitution specifically mentions that voting needs to be transparent. Based on the Basic Law for the Federal Republic of Germany, and the principle that all essential steps in the elections are subject to public examinability, the court said: 'When electronic voting machines are deployed, it must be possible for the citizen to check the essential steps in the election act and in the ascertainment of the results reliably and without special expert knowledge.'

We must remember that our own Supreme Court had given a similar judgment twenty-seven years before its German counterpart, in 1982, saying that the Representation of the People Act mentions only ballot paper and not EVM.

The Representation of the People Act, 1951 was then amended to allow for electronic voting. The point was a legal one, and there was no question about the effectiveness of the technology, either in the case of Germany or India.

Critics often also cite the examples of a few European nations, including the Netherlands and Italy, who have withdrawn the machine. However, they fail to mention that all the machines in these two nations were made by the same Dutch company.

Like any machinery, EVMs are of different varieties and technologies. Failure of one does not imply faultiness in all the other. In fact, if EVMs were so prone to manipulation, we would have never seen a change of regime in the country!

EVMs make the election process transparent. Counting is more efficient, and the results can be declared within three to four hours of an election instead of the traditional thirty to forty hours, when votes were counted manually. Further, EVMs have also ended the problem of invalid votes. The machines are not connected to any external sources whatsoever; therefore, there is neither any danger of data leak nor of tampering. Along with their technical security, their custodial security along their journey from the factories to the polling booths is equally important. At no stage do the machines go into private hands. The Election Commission has to ensure that no lapse ever takes place on this account. The VVPAT machines further reinforce the credibility of the EVMs. By allowing for verification of their respective votes, it ensures that there is no scope for doubt in the minds of the voters. In fact, in 2013, the Supreme Court had appreciated the Election Commission's initiative to introduce VVPATs and had directed the government to provide adequate funds for it. The failure of the VVPATs, though unfortunate, should not shake the faith of the people in the Election Commission and in the Indian democracy. The re-polls were successfully conducted in the affected areas.

The Election Commission ensures free and fair elections in the country, an absolute must for a well-functioning democracy. In case of a machine failure, the Commission has to replace the machine within half an hour. In the instant case mentioned above, the Commission's failure to do so within the stipulated time frame shows that its preparedness fell short somewhere. The CEC was honest enough to admit that the Commission's 'inadequately trained staff' were responsible for the malfunctioning of VVPATs.

I am sanguine that a critical introspection of what went wrong and how it can be prevented in future must be under way at the Commission. I believe the Commission should be more communicative regarding EVMs and VVPATs, and constantly reassure the nation as to their legitimacy. It must immediately put to rest any doubts regarding the credibility of the machines. Technology is the future of India and not just of its democracy, and EVMs have made India a proud global leader.

2

EVM is Tamper-Proof

E{VER SINCE THE ELECTIONS IN UP AND PUNJAB IN 2017, MANY} political parties have been questioning the reliability of EVMs. Besides the BSP, the AAP has been the most vocal critic. The latter has demanded that the ensuing municipal elections in Delhi must be conducted using paper ballots.

The State Election Commission rejected the demand, saying that all arrangements had been made for elections using EVMs and it would be impossible to go back to paper ballots. Even the Delhi High Court rejected this demand. The AAP's attack on EVMs became louder after its poor performance in the municipal elections.

Are EVMs vulnerable?

On 9 May, a member of the AAP demonstrated in the Delhi Vidhan Sabha a prototype of the EVM on which the results could be manipulated by activating a hidden code. Obviously, this became a hot topic of debate in the media.

The main argument against this demonstration is that a prototype is not the actual machine which is used by the Election Commission. ECI-EVMs are subjected to several layers of security checks, including a strict custodial security check.

It has been impossible in the last twenty years for any political party or potential hacker to get hold of an the ECI-EVM, except once when an EVM was stolen from the collectorate of Mumbai to demonstrate that hacking was possible.

A video went viral on YouTube, appearing to be clinching evidence of the hackability of the ECI-EVM. The guy who demonstrated the 'hacking' was asked by the police to disclose how he got the EVM, which was stolen property. The hacker refused to answer them and spent a good ten days in police and judicial custody.

The fact that over two decades, only one out of nearly 20,00,000 machines could be taken out of custodial security only proves how difficult it is for anyone to get hold of a real ECI-EVM.

Three generations of EVMs since 1998

The modus operandi demonstrated in the Delhi assembly included the embedding of a secret code in the machine, which could be activated at any point in time, after which every vote would go to a particular party.

Initially, it wowed the audience, but they soon realized that this was an imitation machine and not the one used by the ECI. Therein lies the crucial difference.

EVMs have been in use since 1998. No government has lasted in power right through these two decades.

Political parties have won and lost elections at regular intervals. Governments have come and gone. If the machines were hackable, the government under which the machines were first introduced would not have lost elections at all. There have been regular regime changes. So far, three generations of EVMs have been made under different regimes.

The ECI dare

The ECI has convened a meeting of all the political parties on 12 May to discuss the issue of hackability of its EVMs. There is speculation that the ECI will throw an open challenge to hackers to come and prove their claims that the machines are vulnerable.

It was reported that the ECI would invite all hacker-challengers in the first week of May for this. This has not happened yet, and this delay is leading to public disaffection and giving rise to speculation and rumours, which need to be nipped in the bud. Hopefully, at the all-party meeting the ECI will spell out its programme for the so-called hackathon.

Four tiers of security

Meanwhile, it is important to remember that there are four levels of security that EVMs have.

1. **Technical safeguards:** The machines are made exclusively by two central public sector undertakings, Bharat Electronics Ltd (BEL) and Electronics Corporation of India Ltd (ECIL), which make high-security defence equipment. The software used is burnt on to a one-time programmable/masked chip so that it cannot be altered or tampered with. The machines are not networked either by wire or by anything wireless with any other machine or system, which rules out hacking.

2. **Fool-proof protective custody at ALL stages of transportation:** From the strong room to the polling stations, there are three levels of checks and three mock polls. Political party representatives are always present to witness and certify the entire process. Additionally, this is videographed.

3. **An independent Technical Advisory Committee** of five professors from the top Indian Institutes of Technology oversee the entire process.

4. **The functioning of the ECI–EVMs has been challenged** before several high courts, which, after examining technicians and computer experts, were satisfied as to the non-tamperability of the ECI-EVMs.

Judicial scrutiny

The highest judicial examination was done by the apex court (*Subramanian Swamy vs. ECI, 2013*). It was contended that in order to make EVMs completely tamper-proof and to ensure transparency, a VVPAT is essential. The ECI informed the Supreme Court that it was already working on the concept, and that its technical advisory committee had already approved the design for it on 26 May 2011, and a field test had been conducted in five climatic zones. The apex court appreciated the 'pragmatism and reasonable approach' of the ECI and commented: '… we appreciate the efforts and good gesture made by ECI in introducing the system'.

Coming to the conclusion that the paper trail is an 'indispensable requirement of free and fair elections', the court 'directed' the Government of India to provide the requisite funds for procurement of VVPAT machines. The court allowed the ECI to introduce the machines in phases, which is being done.

Procurement of VVPAT machines before 2019

Unfortunately, the government delayed the release of requisite funds. After eleven reminders, it finally sanctioned the funds in the May of 2017. The question is whether 16 lakh machines would be ready by the 2019 general elections. In the meantime, the ECI must start using VVPATs in all the forthcoming state elections, in addition to the machines already procured. Hopefully, with VVPATs, the controversy over EVMs will end for good.

Public faith and trust in the electoral system is paramount. It must not be allowed to be shaken by the political noise over EVMs.

3

Proving a Point on Audit Trial

As the campaign for the 2019 general election builds up, so too does the debate on EVMs and voter-verifiable paper audit trails (VVPATs). For example, as a result of a new development in March 2019 in the Nizamabad parliamentary constituency in Telangana, the Election Commission has been forced to conduct elections using ballot papers as there are 185 candidates in the fray. This exceeds the capacity of the EVM, which can cater to sixty-four candidates (sixty-three candidates and None of the Above, or NOTA, option). The Election Commission is now considering the use of special machines which can accommodate up to 384 candidates. These will use twenty-four ballot units connected in series. For this the Commission will have to buy at an enormous cost 26,820 ballot units, 2,240 control units and 2,600 VVPATs. I wonder whether it is possible to acquire so many machines with the required technical changes in the short time available.

In the past, in AP

The use of ballot papers to conduct elections after the introduction of EVMs in Indian elections is not new; they were used in the same state in 2010 in a near-comic situation.

In July 2010, the Telangana agitation was at its peak, and twelve MLAs of the Andhra Pradesh assembly had resigned and were contesting the by-elections. This coincided with the BJP-led anti-EVM campaign. After the Election Commission turned down the request of political parties to go back to paper ballots, the parties resorted to a smart ploy. The Telangana Rashtra Samithi (TRS) decided to field more than sixty-four independent candidates in each constituency. So, there were 114 nominations in Yellareddy (then in Nizamabad district) and 107 in Sircilla. Even after large-scale rejection of nominations, the number of candidates in six constituencies exceeded sixty-four. The Election Commission was forced to conduct elections in these constituencies by ballot paper. The other six were, of course, with the EVMs.

The Commission took it as a great opportunity to showcase the relative strength of the EVMs. While the EVM results were available in four hours, the ballot paper results took forty hours. Adding to this long-drawn process were thousands of invalid votes. The other issues were the economic and environmental costs of printing ballot sheets and the prolonged drudgery it meant for the polling staff. Ironically, the results from both systems across seats were similar.

How did the political parties respond then? A media report said the TRS opposed EVMs 'because it [had] reliable information that the Congress [would] try to manipulate the machines to win the polls'. The Telugu Desam Party President N. Chandrababu Naidu demanded that ballot papers be used in all twelve constituencies going to the polls. Bandaru Dattatreya, BJP president in then undivided Andhra Pradesh, said, 'We have been demanding that there should be a nationwide debate on EVMs. The TRS has used the right strategy.' A Congress spokesman said it was unfortunate that the parties had doubted the integrity of the Election Commission, forcing it to incur additional printing expenses. So, while the issue remains the same, the characters who rake it up are many.

It is pertinent to point out that the difference between the 2010 incident and this time (in terms of the number of candidates) is that a large number of farmers are contesting as independent candidates to highlight their problems. It has nothing to do with an anti-EVM movement.

Stringent trials

Since the last general election, there have been allegations of the BJP hacking EVMs. The Election Commission has repeatedly challenged the conspiracy theorists to come forward and demonstrate that EVMs can be hacked, but no party has accepted the challenge.

This debate should have ended in October 2010 when the EC called an all-party meeting, which unanimously recommended adoption of VVPATs, which was promptly accepted too. The two factories manufacturing EVMs were asked to develop VVPATs and an independent committee of professors from five Indian Institutes of Technology was requested to monitor the process.

There was a series of trials, followed by two full-day election simulations in five cities across India (with different climatic conditions) in 2011–12. Only after the VVPATs passed all the rigorous tests (climatic endurance and technology) were they deployed, initially in 20,000 polling booths. As manufacturing progressed, all constituencies were equipped with VVPATs. In 2013, the Supreme Court lauded the ECI's initiatives, directing the government to release adequate funds for procurement of VVPATs for all booths for the 2019 election. Since 2017, all elections have been held with VVPAT-attached EVMs. A total of 1,500 machines have been counted, as per the present norm of counting the slips generated by one VVPAT in each assembly constituency. Not a single mismatch has been detected.

Sorting things out

The only pending issue is that of VVPAT audits. As many as twenty-three Opposition parties have moved the Supreme Court demanding that half the total slips generated by VVPATs be tallied. A group of retired bureaucrats and diplomats has also written to the ECI regarding the sample size to ensure 99.9 per cent public satisfaction with VVPATs.

The ECI has submitted to the court that a three-member expert panel comprising members from the Indian Statistical Institute, the Chennai Mathematical Institute and the Central Statistics Office has endorsed the current practice of counting one VVPAT per assembly constituency, and that the sample size proposed by political parties would only serve to delay results by six days. The court judgment is expected soon.

I have also proposed an alternative. The top two runners-up in a constituency can choose any two VVPATs to be counted, as they have the highest stake in the results. This would serve to do away with a large sample, as only four machines per assembly would have to be counted to ensure public faith in the system. This would be analogous to the highly popular and successful umpire decision review system in cricket.

EVMs have made India a proud global leader in elections. After incorporating VVPATs, the system is now foolproof. After the expert panel report, the ECI's initiatives in this regard stand vindicated. It should now clinch the EVM debate and utilize the opportunity it obtained in the Nizamabad constituency to demonstrate the relative superiority of the EVM as the wonder machine of Indian democracy.

1

Laws and Violations of MCC

O N 8 FEBRUARY 2020, TWELVE DAYS OF CAMPAIGNING FOR ELECTIONS to the Delhi assembly have come to an end. Most Indians were no doubt waiting for the culmination of this campaign, in which the development debate was overshadowed by hate–mongering and outpouring of communal vitriol. The bone of contention remained Shaheen Bagh, a protest site that incited many of our politicians to make sinister comments like '*Desh ke gaddaron ko* …'; there were references to 'suicide bombers', and the incumbent chief minister was accused of being a terrorist. Such language should not be used in a private space, let alone in public forums.

After the flurry of such hate speeches, I have been flooded with queries about the nature of the Election Commission's response. I was asked whether the Model Code of Conduct is toothless or the Commission ineffective, and whether these offences are also under the purview of other laws of the land. My answer is that these offences violate not only the MCC, but also the Representation of the People Act, 1951 and Indian Penal Code, 1860.

Let's first understand the MCC. It is a set of behavioural guidelines for political parties and candidates for the peaceful conduct of elections, to prevent hate speech, malpractice, corruption and misuse of government machinery by the ruling party. Since it is not an act passed by parliament, the Code is not judicially enforceable. The action against a violator usually takes the form of advice, warning or censure. No punitive action can be taken against the offender. No wonder many consider the Code toothless. That, however, is not true. Its moral authority far outweighs its legal sanctity. Political leaders worth their salt are scared of inviting a notice for violation of the Code as it creates negative public opinion. Besides, unlike the legal processes, its impact is instant.

The legality of the Code has been judicially tested. Its first judicial acceptance came in 1997, when the Punjab and Haryana High Court gave the Election Commission power to enforce the Code. 'Such a code of conduct when it is seen that it does not violate any of the statutory provisions, can certainly be adopted by the Election Commission for the conduct of free and fair election, which should be pure as well,' the court said. The Supreme Court has repeatedly held that the Code must be enforced strictly.

The very first Section of the MCC lays down the following:

> Part I (1): 'No party or candidate shall include in any activity which may aggravate existing differences or create mutual hatred or cause tension between different castes and communities, religious or linguistic.'
> (2): '… Criticism of other parties or their workers based on unverified allegations or distortion shall be avoided.'

The Representation of the People Act, 1951, categorically defines the above two commissions as corrupt practices in Section 123 (3A) and Section 123 (4), respectively. With hate speech, the Act goes a step further and prescribes punitive measures in Section 125:

> Promoting enmity between classes in connection with election—Any person who in connection with an election

under this Act promotes or attempts to promote on grounds of religion, race, caste, community or language, feelings of enmity or hatred, between different classes of the citizens of India shall be punishable, with imprisonment for a term which may extend to three years, or with fine, or with both.

It is important to note that Section 153A of the Indian Penal Code has a similar provision:

Promoting enmity between different groups on ground of religion, race, place of birth, residence, language, etc., and doing acts prejudicial to maintenance of harmony. Whoever (a) by words … or otherwise, promotes or attempts to promote, on grounds of religion, race … caste or community or any other ground whatsoever, disharmony or feelings of enmity, hatred or ill-will between different religious groups or castes or communities, or (b) commits any act which is prejudicial to the maintenance of harmony between different religious … groups or castes or communities, and which disturbs or is likely to disturb the public tranquillity, or (c) … whatsoever causes or is likely to cause fear or alarm or a feeling of insecurity amongst members of such religious, racial, language or regional group or caste or community, shall be punished with imprisonment which may extend to three years, or with fine, or with both.

Now that we are well equipped with the provisions of the laws and the Model Code of Conduct, we must analyse the action taken by the Election Commission.

It must be appreciated that the Commission was prompt in its action against two leaders accused of hate speech. While it instantly, suo motu, deprived the two leaders, former West Delhi MP Parvesh Verma and Union Minister Anurag Thakur, of their star campaigner status, it also punished them with a gag order, using the ultimate weapon provided by Article 324. Moreover, the Commission categorically said it 'strongly condemned' the statements made by the two leaders. Parvesh Verma was slapped with a campaign ban because he said that the anti-CAA (Citizenship [Amendment] Act) NRC and -NRC (National Register of Citizen) protesters at Shaheen Bagh were capable of rape and murders, and for calling the Delhi CM Arvind Kejriwal a terrorist. Anurag Thakur was punished by the Commission for urging a crowd to chant the '*goli maaro*' ('gun down the traitors') slogan.

The Election Commission flexing its muscles outside the domain of the so-called 'toothless' MCC and invoking Article 324 is indeed a refreshing change. In earlier instances, it often had to let the culprits go with a mere 'warning, caution or censure'. In its notice to BJP leader Anurag Thakur, the Commission cited Sections 123 and 125 of the RP Act. What is baffling, however, is that if the Commission had found them guilty of offences deserving punishment, why did it stop short of filing FIRs against them?

Historically, the Election Commission has always taken simultaneous action under both the Model Code of Conduct and the other two provisions. While the MCC produces instant results, the penal provisions involve endless judicial processes. That the Commission did not take action against the offenders under the IPC encouraged the worthies like Parvesh Sahib Singh Verma to commit a repeat offence of indulging in a vitriolic diatribe against the Delhi CM, for which the Election Commission indicted him a second time within a week. That such small-time leaders repeatedly defy the Commission should be a matter of concern. The answer also lies with the Election Commission.

2

EC Needs Urgent Institutional Safeguards

THE ELECTION COMMISSION OF INDIA HAS MADE ITS MARK AS AN exemplary institution in electoral excellence ever since the first general election was held in 1952. But in 2019, it is coming under the scanner as it never has before.

A group of retired bureaucrats and diplomats has written a letter to the president of India dated 8 April 2019 terming the EC as 'weak-kneed' and 'suffering from a crisis of credibility'. The letter highlights the EC's 'pusillanimous' response to the prime minister's ASAT announcement, the Model Code of Conduct violations by Yogi Adityanath and Rajasthan Governor Kalyan Singh, the government's reluctance to undertake proper VVPAT audits, and corrosion of political discourse in general.

Though nowhere mentioned in the letter, legalization of the Model Code of Conduct is often proposed as a solution by many to 'empower' the Election Commission. This debate intensifies with every successive election. The case for legalization of the Code comes from those who either think it is toothless or, rather paradoxically, those who have been stung by it.

The reality is that the moral authority of the Code far outweighs its legal weight. Politicians realize that censures from the Election Commission invite negative public opinion. It is not without reason that the late Goa Chief Minister Manohar Parrikar said in May 2012 that he bows to the moral authority of the Model Code of Conduct, which should take precedence over his constitutional right. Censure under the Code has instant impact, unlike the long-drawn legal processes.

It is noteworthy that certain provisions of the Code already have statutory backing in laws such as the Indian Penal Code, 1860; the Representation of the People Act, 1951 and the Code of Criminal Procedure (CrPC), 1973. An action under the Model Code of Conduct does not preclude legal action under the relevant laws. The solution lies in strict enforcement of both the MCC and the legal provisions.

The MCC aside, the fresh questions being raised about the Election Commission's credibility are certainly worrying. Commission officials have been accused countless times in the past of being stooges of the government, but the present situation is certainly unprecedented. The genesis of the problem lies in the flawed system of appointment of the chief election commissioner (CEC) and election commissioners (EC), which is done unilaterally by the government of the day. This debate can be settled once and for all by depoliticizing EC appointments.

The Law Commission in its twenty-fifth report recommended a collegium, consisting of the PM, the leader of Opposition and the chief justice of India for appointment of the CEC and eCs. Political stalwarts such as L.K. Advani and former CECs, including B.B. Tandon, N. Gopalaswami and I, have supported the idea, even when we were in office. But successive governments have ignored the repeated calls for such a system.

In November 2018, a PIL was also filed in the Supreme Court, calling for a 'fair, just and transparent process of selection by constituting a neutral and independent collegium/selection committee'. On such a vital issue, the judiciary, which I have always described as the guardian angel of democracy, has to act urgently. Derailment of democracy and decline of public trust will lead to degradation in the credibility of all institutions, including the judiciary itself.

The system of removal of election commissioners also needs reform. Currently, only the CEC is protected from removal, except if it is by impeachment. The government can control a defiant CEC through the majority voting power of the two other commissioners, who have equal voting powers as the CEC. They have equal powers, but are vulnerable to government pressure because they do not enjoy the protection from removal as the CEC does.

Unsurprisingly, the Commission's reputation suffers when it is not able to tame recalcitrant political parties. This is especially true in the context of the ruling party. Despite being the registering authority for political parties under Section 29A of the RPA, 1951, the Commission has no power to de-register them for violations of the Model Code of Conduct or even for the gravest of violations of the oath taken by them at the time of their registration.

The Election Commission is the guardian of electoral democracy and needs urgent institutional safeguards to remain fiercely autonomous. It is time that action is taken—not for making the Model Code of Conduct into a law, which will actually be counterproductive, but for de-politicization of constitutional appointments, coupled with empowerment of the Election Commission to de-register political parties, which will deter grave electoral misconduct. This will lead to decision-making becoming quicker as well as more effective.

While these reforms are hotly debated, it is imperative that the Election Commission asserts the ample authority that it already has constitutionally. It must make tough decisions. It's not mere discretion that it is exercising, but a pious mandate.

3

Moral Hold of Poll Code

T HE 'GREAT INDIAN ELECTION' OF 2019 IS IN FULL SWING AND THE Model Code has taken centre stage. Reports of violations are coming in every day, with two cases involving Prime Minister Narendra Modi and one involving Uttar Pradesh Chief Minister Yogi Adityanath making the headlines.

So, what is the Model Code of Conduct? It is a set of behavioural guidelines for political parties and candidates for peaceful conduct of elections, equal opportunity for candidates in campaigning, right to peace for citizens and the decorum of the exercise. The guidelines also aim to prevent malpractices, corruption and misuse of government machinery by the ruling party, etc.

It is a voluntary code of self-discipline evolved by political parties and facilitated by the Election Commission. Since it is not an act passed by parliament, it's not judicially enforceable. The only action against a violator is in the form of advice, a warning or censure. No punitive action can be taken. No wonder many consider the Code toothless. That, however, is not true. Its moral authority far outweighs its legal sanctity. Political leaders are scared of inviting a notice for

86

violation of the Model Code of Conduct as it creates negative public opinion. Besides, unlike the legal processes, its impact is instant.

The legality of the Code has been judicially tested. Its first judicial acceptance came in 1997, when Punjab and Haryana High Court gave the Election Commission the power to enforce the Code from the day it came out with the election schedule to the day final results were announced. 'Such a code of conduct when it is seen that it does not violate any of the statutory provisions, can certainly be adopted by the Election Commission for the conduct of free and fair election, which should be pure as well,' the judgment said.

Four years later, the Supreme Court upheld this verdict, but said there should not be a gap of more than twenty-one days between the declaration of election dates and the poll notification.

There is a growing demand that the Code be made into a statute so that it is judicially enforceable. This demand is made by both those who think the Code is toothless and those stung by its force.

Political leaders view the code in many different ways. Two prominent examples come to mind.

During a by-election to Goa's Cortalim assembly constituency in May 2012, we heard that Chief Minister Manohar Parrikar was planning to induct his party candidate into his council of ministers. The Commission thought it would disturb the level playing field and 'advised' Parrikar to defer the move. An angry chief minister called me and argued that it was his constitutional right to induct any minister, any time.

I agreed that he had the full constitutional right to do so, but said it was EC's 'advice' that he put off the decision. To Parrikar's credit, he not only accepted the advice but also remarked that he 'bows to the moral authority of the model code of conduct', which should take precedence over his constitutional right. What a shining example of statesmanship!

In contrast, while campaigning for his wife, Law Minister Salman Khurshid announced that the Congress would double the reservation for minorities in government jobs. The BJP complained it was a serious Code breach. Khurshid's statement also invited condemnation from the media and civil society. Even the Election Commission was not spared, even after it censured the minister. Those who found Khurshid's announcement a breach of the Code thought the punishment was not adequate. Some went to the extent of calling it a fixed match. They missed the point that the Code is not a law, but just a code that asks for voluntary compliance, and that 'censure' is the most the EC can do.

What some thought was a toothless act stung the minister, as he stood convicted and punished by the 'censure' with no means of appeal against it.

Soon after, the parliamentary standing committee on personnel, public grievances, law and justice, sought to make the Code a part of the Representation of the People Act. But for many political analysts, it was a thinly disguised ploy to divest the Election Commission of its powers and transfer the code to the judicial domain. The move was dropped after the noise in media that followed.

Though short, the election period is charged and packed with incident. Legal battles over Code violations are bound to linger for years, rendering the judicial exercise futile. The Commission feels the effectiveness of the MCC lies in its instant impact. It works much like a fire brigade, dousing a fire immediately. It is important to remember that certain provisions of the Code are part of statutes such as the Indian Penal Code, 1860, Representation of the People Act, 1951, and Code of Criminal Procedure, 1973. Action under the Code does not preclude legal action under the relevant laws.

It is not without reason that the world looks at our unparalleled elections and unique election conduct code with wonder. It is not just a model code but a moral code. The Election Commission just needs to enforce it strictly. Since the party in power is often the biggest offender, the Commission must come down heavily and visibly on violations even if the highest leadership is involved.

State Elections

1

The Corona Election

Amid the clamour for postponing the impending Bihar assembly elections, the Election Commission of India has put its foot down and announced the timely conduct of elections to the 243-member legislative assembly, which is set to complete its tenure in November.

This is not the first time that the Election Commission would be holding polls during the coronavirus (or COVID-19) pandemic. After a few months of postponement, the Commission, quite successfully, from June onwards, administered the Rajya Sabha and legislative council elections in various states under strict COVID-specific guidelines.

We have seen how as many as thirty-four countries have conducted their national assembly or presidential elections while fighting the COVID-19 pandemic. The most successful examples have been those of South Korea and our immediate neighbour, Sri Lanka.

Taking its cue from other countries' management of elections, the Election Commission of India has come up with its own set of rules to be implemented during the Bihar elections. These include reduction in the number of electors per polling booth to 1,000 from the current 1,500; addition of 33,797 auxiliary polling stations to prevent overcrowding and COVID-sensitive capacity building for election officials. To avoid crowding at the counting centres, the counting tables have been reduced to seven per assembly constituency from fourteen, among other measures.

The Opposition parties' fear of poor voter turnout in the state elections due to the pandemic has been partly taken care of with the Election Commission's decision to extend the postal ballot option to senior citizens over the age of eighty, to COVID-positive patients, to persons with disabilities and to voters in essential services, along with its now famous Systematic Voter Education for Electoral Participation (SVEEP) programme and technological facilities to ensure voter education and mobilization. If implemented well, the Bihar election could record a satisfactory voter turnout, like in Sri Lanka, if not the highest, as reported in South Korea.

Even though speculation is rife that the Election Commission might allow physical campaigning with a limited number of people, the political parties in Bihar are mostly likely to resort to digital campaigning, after months of having protested against it. The ball was set rolling in this direction by the BJP back in June, when Home Minister Amit Shah addressed the people of Bihar in a virtual rally. Virtual rallies, besides social media, are going to be a dominant feature of digital campaigning. These rallies seem promising and innovative, and will keep the crowds at bay. Additionally, the bandwagon that follows a political leader visiting many different constituencies will come to a halt, reducing both campaign costs and COVID risks.

Can virtual rallies replace the door-to-door and large-scale physical campaigning that are the heart and soul of any democratic election? Not really. Virtual rallies have their own limitations, like inaccessibility, when it comes to addressing every nook and corner of rural, hilly and forest areas, what with internet penetration in Bihar being an abysmal 37 per cent. For online communication through smartphones, the situation is grimmer owing to low usage of smartphones in Bihar, which stands at just 27 per cent, and patchy mobile network even in the cities. Against this backdrop, with no expenditure ceiling for political parties, they will go for expensive communication devices like projection screens, among other things, to increase their voter reach.

This is why the issue of a level playing field for candidates is being raised by the Opposition parties. Such facilities are evidently going to be a costly affair and the richer political parties will have a gala time mobilizing voters, putting small regional/local parties at a disadvantage. Under the winner-takes-all voting system like ours, missing out even a single household could have a negative effect on a party's winning chances.

The problem of unequal opportunity also exists in the other mode of digital campaigning—social media. With the growing influence of social media, the generally technologically challenged political leaders and their parties have quickly adapted to this youthful platform—though the degree of adoption varies widely across political parties, depending on their financial position. During the Lok Sabha elections in 2019, the BJP reportedly spent the highest amount, ₹27 crore, on Google, Facebook and their sister platforms to place political ads, while the Congress was a distant second, spending ₹5.6 crore. Although this is not big at the national level, where thousands of crores of rupees are spent, one can guess how much the ruling party must have gained from investing more in ads than other parties to woo voters.

The Election Commission has another task in the realm of social media campaigning, other than funding of social media. This is to tackle fake news and hate propaganda. In both these areas, the Commission has been proactive. The recent example of its strict stance against hate propaganda came during the legislative assembly elections in Delhi, when the Commission ordered Twitter to take down a communal post by a BJP leader (Kapil Mishra) and followed it up by asking Delhi Police to file an FIR against him, setting a strong precedent. However, with the probability of physical campaigning being limited, the focus of all political parties and their candidates would be on the digital mode—resulting in social media platforms being flooded with problematic posts.

The EC could, however, consider relaxing its stringent norms for old, traditional methods like wall paintings, posters and flags. Maybe car, motorcycle and bicycle rallies maintaining proper distancing could be encouraged for deep and wide reach, but with restricted costs.

Even though there exists a Voluntary Code of Ethics, issued by the ECI in collaboration with social media platforms, allowing for direct engagement of the Commission and these platforms over problematic posts during election season, the recent revelations in the *Wall Street Journal* about Facebook have cast a shadow over the platform's neutrality. According to the report, on several occasions, Facebook India was averse to removing derogatory posts uploaded by the ruling party's leader. Against this backdrop, the implementation of a Voluntary Code of Ethics will be scrutinized and questioned by the Opposition parties.

The Bihar election could be an opportunity for the Election Commission to prove its efficiency once again to every sceptic out there. At a time when all the countries of the world are looking to each other for lessons, Bihar could provide a leading example of successful election management, and the ECI as a leading electoral management body.

2

Clearing the COVID Challenge for Elections

THE ELECTION TO THE BIHAR LEGISLATIVE ASSEMBLY WAS unprecedented in several ways. First, in view of the COVID-19 pandemic, there was apprehension as to whether the polls would be possible at all. Later, several political parties clamoured for postponement of the election.

The ECI, after initial doubts, was inspired by the successful electoral experiences of many countries, especially South Korea, which conducted its national elections in the midst of the pandemic with great success—and the highest-ever turnout. As many as thirty-four countries have conducted elections to their national assemblies or presidential posts while engaged in the battle against the novel coronavirus.

To leave nothing to chance, the ECI consulted its counterparts in several countries and asked them to share their experiences of conducting elections before deciding to overrule all objections and go ahead with the Bihar polls. It did well to test the ground with

Rajya Sabha polls as well as legislative council elections in various states under COVID-specific guidelines.

Equipped with such knowledge as well as its own experience, the ECI issued COVID guidelines in August for the Bihar assembly polls. Besides the usual norms related to sanitizing and social distancing, these guidelines included a reduction in the limit of electors per polling booth to 1,000 from the current 1,500 in order to prevent overcrowding.

The consequent addition of nearly 40,000 extra polling stations meant as many additional EVMs. To avoid crowding at the counting centres, the counting tables were reduced to seven per hall from fourteen.

Door-to-door canvassing was restricted to groups of five persons. Convoys of vehicles were to be spaced after every five vehicles instead of every ten. The number of participants at public meetings was to be restricted to the ceilings prescribed by the National Disaster Management Authority. Online facilities were provided for nominations, filing affidavits and making security deposits. The Opposition parties highlighted the possibility of voter turnout being low because of the pandemic. The ECI's answer to this was its decision to extend the postal ballot option to senior citizens over the age of eighty, to COVID-positive patients, to persons with disabilities and to voters employed in essential services, along with making use of its now famous Systematic Voter Education for Electoral Participation (SVEEP) programme. A satisfactory voter turnout proved the Commission right.

A concern raised by some parties was that digital campaigning, desirable to keep crowds at bay, would give the BJP an unfair advantage as the party has more technical and financial resources than the others. Another question was whether virtual rallies would replace door-to-door and large-scale physical campaigning, the soul of any democratic election. Virtual rallies have their own limitations, like inaccessibility, when it comes to reaching out to every nook and corner of rural, hilly and forest areas, especially because internet penetration in Bihar is as low as 37 per cent and smartphones are used by just 27 per cent of the state's population.

The BJP was, indeed, the leader when it came to virtual rallies. However, when the elections were actually announced, massive physical rallies were organized by most parties, causing serious concern to the ECI, which later came down heavily on violators.

The Commission faced other challenges too—fake news and hate propaganda. The ECI has been proactive in dealing with both. It had drafted a Voluntary Code of Ethics in collaboration with social media platforms, allowing it direct engagement with the platforms over problematic posts made during the election season.

The recent expose by the *Wall Street Journal* on Facebook's political leanings casts a shadow over the platform's neutrality. The report said that on several occasions Facebook India was averse to removing derogatory posts uploaded by the leaders of the ruling party. This brought the ECI under the lens, and it was accused of biased oversight regarding the conduct of political parties and social media platforms.

One unprecedented development on counting day was the ECI holding press conferences, not once or twice but four times, to answer all possible doubts and quell apprehensions and suspicions that arise when the margin of victory is low. In its very first briefing early afternoon on 10 November 2020, the Commission made it clear that because of the special COVID-related measures, counting would be slow and would go on very late into the night. Bihar's chief electoral officer said nearly 40 per cent extra polling booths had been put in place to prevent overcrowding. This meant an additional twenty to thirty minutes of counting for each of the extra 40,000 EVMs. The number of EVMs per counting table was also reduced, from fourteen to seven, as mentioned earlier. Consequently, the number of rounds of counting and results declarations increased by 40 to 50 per cent. But this clarification by the EC offices pre-empted rumours of fraud that normally fly thick and fast when there is any delay in the counting of votes.

A major issue was raised at around midnight on Tuesday about discrepancies in the winners' lists. Questions were also raised about the delay in declaration of results for about ten constituencies. On the former, the ECI has assured the complainants that each case will be investigated. Insofar as the delay in the announcement of results is concerned, demands for a recount of the postal ballots and for re-tabulation of the totals shown by each EVM are normal, and lead to some delay. When the margin of victory is less than the number of rejected postal ballots, a recount of votes is mandatory. A win by a margin of twelve votes in one constituency has been a topic of interest in this election, and it must remind us of the case of C.P. Joshi, once president of the Congress party in Rajasthan, who lost by just one vote in 2008 and accepted the verdict with dignity.

After facing some serious questions during the general election in 2019 that affected its image, the Bihar election was an opportunity for the ECI to prove its efficiency and even-handedness to every sceptic. At a time when all countries in the world are looking to each other for lessons, Bihar could be a leading example of successful election management—and the ECI of a leading election management agency.

1

Conducting Elections during a Pandemic

As Maharashtra struggled to tackle the COVID-19 pandemic, its people were staring at a unique problem. The deadlock between the governor of Maharashtra and Chief Minister Uddhav Thackeray looked like it would continue for a long time and cost Thackeray his post. But thanks to the intervention of the prime minister and prompt action by the Election Commission of India, the impending constitutional crisis has blown over in the state.

Averting a political crisis

Thackeray, who took oath as chief minister on 28 November 2019, has to become a member of the legislature within six months, that is, by 27 May. This would not have been a problem for him had the elections, scheduled to be held on 26 March, not been postponed indefinitely because of the pandemic. In postponing the elections, the ECI used its powers under Article 324 of the Constitution, along with Section 153 of the Representation of the People Act, 1951. A double application of Article 164(4) to extend this period for another six months was out of the question as the Supreme Court, in *S.R. Chaudhuri vs. State of Punjab and Ors (17 August 2001)*, had declared that it would tantamount subversion of the principle of representative government.

Consequently, the chief minister was left to take the nomination route. In pursuance of this, the state cabinet, headed by Deputy Chief Minister Ajit Pawar, submitted a proposal to the governor to nominate Thackeray to the legislative council. Article 171(3I), coupled with Article 171(5), empowers the governor to nominate an individual with 'special knowledge or practical experience' to the assembly. The governor, however, put the proposal in limbo for over a fortnight.

Given this situation, political analysts speculated as to whether Thackeray would knock on the door of the Supreme Court or follow the route Lalu Prasad took in Bihar in 1997 after being forced to resign following his conviction in a criminal case. Instead of seeing the end of his political career, he brought his wife, Rabri Devi, to replace him as chief minister. Analysts wondered if Thackeray would similarly hand over the reins of power to his son, an MLA.

However, better sense prevailed and the political leadership managed to avert a major crisis. The prime minister's intervention and the Election Commission's prompt action have averted a political impasse—polls to nine legislative council seats in Maharashtra will now be held on 21 May.

By deciding to hold elections during a pandemic, the Election Commission has taken up a big responsibility. Though only the 288 members of the Vidhan Sabha will be voting in this election, the Commission will have to ensure strict implementation of the health ministry's guidelines. Knowing the EC's capabilities and years of experience, this will be a cakewalk. South Korea just conducted its national election with 4.4 crore voters in the midst of the pandemic. It is a good source of inspiration for the Election Commission.

But a bigger concern for the EC will be the upcoming assembly elections in Bihar (which must be concluded by 29 November 2020),

West Bengal (30 May 2021), Assam (31 May 2021), Kerala (1 June 2021), Tamil Nadu (24 May 2021) and Puducherry (8 June 2021). Unlike the Rajya Sabha/legislative council elections, which can be postponed indefinitely, the EC can postpone elections to the Lok Sabha and state legislative assemblies for a period of only six months, the constitutionally defined limit between two sessions of the house/assembly (Article 85(1) and Article 174(1) of the Constitution, respectively).

For a further period of extension, the ball is in the executive's court. The executive will be faced with two possibilities. The first is the proviso to Article 172(1), whereby during a state of Emergency, an election can be postponed for one year, in addition to a period of six months after Emergency is lifted. The rider, however, is that a state of Emergency can be declared only if there is a threat to the security and sovereignty of the nation, not if there is an epidemic or a pandemic. The second option is to declare president's rule in the state in question, which is enabled by Article 356(1) of the Constitution. But its limits have been repeatedly defined by the Supreme Court.

Lessons from South Korea

Some experts say the COVID-19 pandemic could last for two years. Deferring elections for such a long time would be against the spirit of democracy and federalism, which are the basic components of the Constitution. As a result, holding elections seems to be the only way out. It is noteworthy that India will not be the only country to hold elections during this pandemic. According to the International Institute for Democracy and Electoral Assistance, nine countries have already held national elections and referendums during this public health crisis. Among them is South Korea, which, under strict guidelines, managed to pull off a near-perfect national election, recording the highest voter turnout of 66.2 per cent in twenty-eight years.

The EC could take into account the measures South Korea took to prepare a foolproof plan. South Korea disinfected polling centres, and mandated that voters practice physical distancing, wear gloves and masks and use hand sanitizer. Voters had their temperature checked on arrival at the booths. Those who had a temperature above 99.5 degrees Fahrenheit were sent to booths in secluded areas. Neither the interests of infected voters nor the interests of those suspected of having the virus were ignored: COVID-19-positive voters were allowed to mail their ballots while self-quarantined voters were allowed to vote after 6 p.m.

Unarguably, the population of states like Bihar (9.9 crore) is huge compared to that of South Korea (5.16 crore). The EC could adopt targeted measures for older voters who are more vulnerable to COVID-19. Options like proxy voting under a well-established legal framework, postal voting and mobile ballot boxes can be explored. The EC has a difficult task of sticking to its goal of 'No Voter Left Behind', while also ensuring that the elections do not turn into a public health nightmare.

The COVID-19 pandemic is a big threat to the established world order. It is quickly transforming fragile and vulnerable democracies into autocracies in the name of public safety. How India, a large and well-established democracy, responds to this crisis is the biggest challenge before it.

2

Another Government Formation, Another Day We Watch Political Morality Disappear

'Politics have no relation to morals.'
—Niccolo Machiavelli, the European Chanakya

WITH EACH PASSING INDIAN ELECTION, THE RELEVANCE OF THIS quote has made a comeback. Just last year, we witnessed a mockery of what is called 'democratic formation of government' in Karnataka. That situation has engulfed several states in the recent past: Arunachal Pradesh, Uttarakhand, Goa, Manipur, Nagaland, Rajasthan—and now Maharashtra. In Maharashtra, the dirty game of politics managed to involve the offices of the President and the Prime Minister besides the regular players, the governor and the unbiased umpire, the Supreme Court.

The events in Maharashtra have brought to the fore three issues of concern—the anti-defection law, post-poll alliances and the role of the governor.

Anti-defection law

'*Aaya Ram, Gaya Ram*—a popular term for fickle political loyalty, marked its beginning in the form of political defections in lieu of money and plum posts in 1967, when Congress MLA Gaya Lal defected thrice in fifteen days—including twice in just nine hours! With the rise of regional political parties and the shrinking of national parties' pan-India popularity, this became more rampant.

In order to nip this evil in the bud, the Rajiv Gandhi-led government introduced the anti-defection law, generally known as Tenth Schedule of the Constitution, in 1985 through the fifty-second amendment. As the name suggests, the law aimed to disqualify legislators from parliament/assembly if they voted against the party whip, abstained from voting or resigned from party membership.

However, this clause had a rider: if over one-third of the party in the legislature defected, then the defection would be deemed a 'merger' with the party the defectors joined, and would not lead to disqualification. When this failed to curb defections, the limit of one-third was amended to two-thirds of the party in the legislature with the ninety-first Constitutional amendment of 2003. Yet, the problem persists.

The law vested the power of disqualification of legislators in the speaker/chairman of the house and immunized their decision from judicial review. However, the clause on immunity was struck down by the Supreme Court as unconstitutional (*Kihoto Hollohan vs. Zachillhu and Others*, 1992) while upholding the discretionary power of the speaker/chairman of the house to decide on disqualifications. The Supreme Court held that the speaker performed as a tribunal under the anti-defection law, and therefore his decisions were subject to judicial review.

This judgment found resonance in the recent three-judge Supreme Court bench judgment (*Shrimanth Balasaheb Patel & Ors vs. Speaker Karnataka Legislative Assembly & Ors*, 2019), wherein it upheld the disqualification of seventeen rebel MLAs, but rejected the then Karnataka assembly speaker's order to restrict them from contesting till the end of the legislature's term in 2023.

Anti-defection law a piece of paper

Framed to act as a deterrent, the anti-defection law has been reduced to a piece of paper. Not only has it failed to stop 'horse-trading', it has also been unsuccessful in projecting the act of defection as something to be denounced. In the present times, as we have made peace with the immoral nature of politics, horse-trading has been accepted with open arms, with the use of popular references like '*Chanakya Niti*' to justify it.

Political ideology is now redundant and has been replaced with opportunism, and nothing stops MLAs/MPs from switching parties. As seen in Karnataka, despite their disqualification, the members find their way back to the assembly with a new party—and with loads of money to boot.

The four approaches to lure legislators to defect have been:

1. Promise of tickets to re-contest from their new party;
2. Offer of plum ministerial posts or chairmanship of lucrative corporations;
3. Offer of big sums of money to get them to abstain from participation in a trust vote; and
4. Offer of big sums of money to resign (turning the majority of their party on its head) and stay at home.

The total absence of loyalty to any ideology is on full display when MLAs/MPs are stuffed in private buses and locked in hotels to prevent them from getting poached. Who would have imagined poaching and horse-trading would metamorphose from the animal world to the political world.

Post-poll alliances

Another spectre haunting Indian politics is the post-poll alliances. Unlike pre-poll alliances, where citizens are mindful of the collaboration when they vote, post-poll alliances are viewed as a betrayal of the people's mandate and, ultimately, of democracy.

Maharashtrian voters experienced the rarest of rare situations: while they voted for or against a BJP—Shiv Sena alliance, they ended up with a strange combination of Shiv Sena–Congress–Nationalist Congress Party, called 'Maha Vikas Aghadi'. The alliance does raise eyebrows, for while the Congress and NCP have portrayed themselves as a secular front, the Shiv Sena follows a hard right-wing ideology. Despite having mutually agreed upon a common minimum programme, this alliance of strange bedfellows continues to be viewed as a display of political opportunism.

Is there indeed a solution to this? In a situation of fractured mandate, when no single party or pre-poll alliance obtains a majority, there are two possible options: mid-term polls or post-poll alliances. Mid-term polls would lead to huge expenditure and more communal polarization, and would still not guarantee a clear mandate. Against this backdrop, post-poll alliances present a safer bet.

Role of the governor

Fractured mandates have served opportunities to political parties to showcase their talent of twisting and turning the popular electoral mandate. And in this talent show, the judge is the governor. Constitutionally, governors were to act as a link between the state and Union governments. But, as history goes to show, they often become rubber stamps of the Centre. Their role has extended from the impromptu dissolution of elected governments to assenting to the arbitrary formation of governments.

Even though governors have discretionary powers, they are often accused of misusing them. The Sarkaria Commission, set up in 1983 to study the relationship between the Union and the states and the balance of power between them, went deep into this issue. While acknowledging the role of the governor, it laid down a priority list to be followed by the governor when there is a hung assembly:

1. Pre-poll alliance (it gave the highest priority to the pre-poll alliance);
2. Single–largest party (with the support of others);
3. Post-poll alliance (with all the parties in the alliance join the government); and
4. Post-poll alliance (with some joining the government and others supporting it from outside).

Acknowledging the importance of the people's vote, the Sarkaria Commission put post-poll alliances as the last resort. The Justice Punchhi Commission (2007) reiterated these recommendations.

The President and the PMO

A rather worrying development in the chain of events in Maharashtra politics was the involvement of the offices of the president and prime minister. In that political slugfest, they did not exactly cover themselves with glory.

Article 356 (providing for president's rule) was revoked in Maharashtra at 5.47 a.m. on 23 November 2019, based on the governor's recommendation. Ideally and usually, the governor's recommendation has to be approved by the Union cabinet. However, in this case a different approach was adopted: the government relied on Rule 12 of the Government of India (Transaction of Business) Rules, 1961, which allows the prime minister to dispense with cabinet approval.

One must question what prompted the government to adopt a rule meant to be used for war-time situations and for important legislations in this case, or why president's rule was revoked in the early hours of 23 November, when earlier the governor had swiftly advised for its application while refusing NCP's request for additional time?

The way forward

The time has come for our political class to act responsibly and take the following steps to dissipate the concerns mentioned above:

(1)   Anti-defection law: Defecting legislators must be banned from being appointed as ministers/chairmen of boards, etc., for six years and must not be allowed to re-contest elections for the same period. This still leaves one problem unresolved—which is payment of big sums of money to a legislator to resign and sit at home, reducing his original party to a minority, to the benefit of the rival party.

(2)   The discretionary powers of the governor must be done away with and a mechanism based on the Sarkaria Commission recommendations must be put in place. If there is a demand for abolition of the post of governor, the governors have no one to blame but themselves.

The country just observed Constitution Day. We must not allow today's politicians to distort the vision of our country's founders.

1

Chhattisgarh 2014 By-Election Scam

THE LEAD STORY IN THE *INDIAN EXPRESS* ON 30 DECEMBER 2015 about the dirty role of money in the Chhattisgarh by-election in 2014 makes for depressing reading. The candidate of the grand old national party, the INC, suddenly withdrew his nomination a day before the last day for withdrawal. He was of course expelled from the party for the treacherous act soon afterwards, but the story does not seem to have ended there. The event is despicable. But what adds to its gravity is the purported involvement of the incumbent chief minister (his family, to be precise) and a former chief minister and his sons. To what depths can politics fall!

The transcripts of the tapes do not clearly indicate the amounts involved—whether they were ₹7 lakh and ₹10 lakh, or ₹7 crore and ₹10 crore. While in the legalistic sense, this would make no difference, the figures are material for gauging the depth to which politics has fallen. It is inconceivable that a potentially winning candidate of a great party would indulge in a deception game in this serious matter and withdraw—that too for a measly ₹7 (or 10) lakh, when crores are being spent even in elections for the post of panchayat member. And if the figures are in crores, it shows what a high-stake game Indian elections have become.

In terms of economics, perhaps it is cheaper for a candidate to spend ₹10 crore to make a rival contender withdraw than to spend ₹20–30 crore on actually contesting the election—and this seems to have become the norm. One hopes that it does not become an election economics model too!

Money power in elections is the only unsolved problem in Indian elections, which, ironically, Senator Hillary Clinton recently described as the global 'gold standard'. In my book *An Undocumented Wonder – the Making of the Great Indian Election* published last year, I had listed forty modus operandi for cheating in elections that the Election Commission had come across. The list may have looked shockingly long and exhaustive at that time, but subsequent events have shown that it was only illustrative—a sample, if you will.

I have often said that money in elections has become the root cause of all corruption in the country. When a candidate spends crores of rupees in an election, he will not only recover this amount after he comes to power, but also ensure that he makes much more. This he collects by dubious and illegal means—cuts on government contracts, licences and quotas, extortion, etc. Bribes seem to be the most innocent means of making money in this list!

We have often seen candidates who make it a business to file their nominations and withdraw later in exchange for money from anyone who fears division of their votes. A senior leader of a political party once told me how several candidates who get money from the party (he mentioned ₹2.5 crore each at the time) for election expenses pocket most of it when they sense they have no chance of winning. After all, a bird in hand is worth two in the bush!

The present case, besides showing the dirty role of money in elections, also highlights the evil of infighting within parties. There are examples galore of leaders undercutting their own parties and sabotaging an emerging rival's chances of winning an election. This case smacks of that possibility too.

Now the question is, what can the Election Commission do in this case? Perhaps little. After the election results are announced, the EC becomes functus officio (having no further force or authority, having fulfilled one's functions, discharged from the office, or accomplished one's purpose). Post election results, its role is confined to receiving and examining the expenditure statements of candidates, which must be done within thirty to forty-five days of an election. The power then shifts to the high courts, which entertain election petitions on the prescribed grounds, including corrupt practices.

Can the high courts, therefore, do something? Again, the answer seems to be in the negative, as election petitions have to be filed within forty-five days of the end of polls. If indeed one was filed at the time and is now pending in a high court, it has to be examined whether corrupt practice was the charge. No new grounds can be added after the time limit for petitions. However, if a writ petition is filed, the high court can perhaps use its extraordinary jurisdiction and maybe order a CBI inquiry. Even income tax authorities can step in to investigate.

It is pertinent to mention here that the judiciary has been a guardian angel of the integrity of our electoral process. The Supreme Court order that every candidate file an affidavit listing his or her financial dealings and pending criminal cases against them has been a landmark in electoral transparency. Even if it has not rooted out corruption, at least it has become a matter of public debate.

In 2012, when the buying of votes for the Rajya Sabha elections had assumed scandalous proportions in Jharkhand, the Election Commission had countermanded elections to two seats after seizing over ₹2 crore in cash in a car belonging to a candidate. Before taking this unprecedented action, we debated what the response of the judiciary would be if the matter went to court.

We were a little wary that the court might accuse us of arbitrariness in linking the seized money to the election without 'conclusive' proof. This did not deter us from the call of our conscience. The matter did go to the Jharkhand High Court, which not only upheld our order but hailed it as 'the only step of great consequence taken by the election commission after independence of the country'. It even slapped a fine of ₹1 lakh on the petitioner candidate!

2

At Stake in the Chhattisgarh Scam

The *Indian Express* story about the dirty role money apparently played in a Chhattisgarh by-election in 2014 ('We have to go up to seven at least … he is expecting ten. We will bring him down … ', 30 December 2014) makes for depressing reading. The Congress candidate suddenly withdrew his nomination, just before the last day for withdrawal of nominations. Soon thereafter, he was expelled from the party. But the story does not seem to end there.

What adds to the gravity of an already despicable event is the purported involvement of an incumbent CM (his family, to be precise) and a former CM and his son. The transcripts do not clearly indicate the amounts involved. Are they ₹7 lakh and ₹10 lakh, or were the amounts referred to in crores? Legally, it makes no difference, but the figures are material for gauging the depth to which politics has fallen. It is inconceivable that a potentially winning candidate would indulge in this serious deception game and withdraw for a measly ₹7 (or 10) lakh when crores or rupees are being spent on the election of a panchayat member. And if the figure is ₹10 crore, it shows what a high-stakes game elections have become. Perhaps it is cheaper to spend ₹10 crore to make a rival contender fraudulently withdraw than to actually contest in the election and spend ₹20–30 crore.

Money power is the only unsolved problem in Indian elections, the root cause of all corruption. If a candidate spends crores of rupees on getting elected, he will collect a lot more once in office—through government contracts, issue of licences and quotas, by extortion, etc. We have often seen candidates file their nominations and then withdraw for money offered by anyone who fears a division of votes. A senior political leader once told me how several candidates who get money from his party (he mentioned ₹2.5 crore each) for campaigning pocket most of it if they sense they have no chance of winning.

The present case also highlights the evil of party infighting. There are examples galore of a leader undercutting his own party and making its candidates lose to sabotage an emerging rival. The case above seems to suggest that possibility too. What can the Election Commission do in such a case? Perhaps little. After the announcement of election results, the EC becomes functus officio—it has no further force or authority. Post results, its role is confined to receiving and examining the expenditure statements of candidates within thirty to forty-five days of the elections. The power then shifts to the high courts, which can entertain election petitions on certain grounds.

Can the high courts, then, do something? Probably not, as election petitions have to be filed within forty-five days of the election in question. If indeed an election petition has already been filed at the time and is now pending in a high court, one has to see if corrupt practice was a charge. No new grounds can be added after the time limit. However, if a writ petition is filed, the HC can, perhaps, use its extraordinary jurisdiction and order a CBI inquiry. Even the income tax authorities could step in to investigate.

The judiciary has been the guardian of the integrity of our electoral process. The Supreme Court order making it mandatory for candidates to file an affidavit as to her financial dealings and pending criminal cases is a landmark one. In 2012, when buying votes for winning Rajya Sabha elections had assumed scandalous proportions in Jharkhand, the Election Commission had countermanded elections to two seats after seizing over ₹2 crore in cash from a car belonging to a candidate. Before taking this unprecedented action, we discussed the possible response of the court. We were wary that the court could accuse us of arbitrariness in linking the seized money to the election without 'conclusive' proof. But this did not deter us. The matter did go to the Jharkhand High Court, which not only upheld our order but also hailed it as 'the only step of such great consequence taken by the Election Commission after Independence'. It even slapped a fine of ₹1 lakh on the petitioner candidate.

We now have a great opportunity for the concerned constitutional and state authorities to step in and make yet another attempt to stem the rot. Political parties themselves should debate the issue and consider the long-pending electoral reforms.

3

The Chhattisgarh By-Election Scam
Is a Wake-up Call

THE SAD SAGA OF CORRUPT PRACTICES TAKING PLACE DURING elections has played out in its ugliest form in the Antagarh (Chhattisgarh) by-election held in September 2014, as exposed by the *Indian Express*. The tapes of the purported conversations among the key players, including incumbent Chief Minister Raman Singh's family and a former chief minister, Ajit Jogi, and his son, show the depths to which our electoral politics has fallen.

The role of money in elections has assumed alarming proportions. Though this problem is not confined to India, the ingenuity of our politicians in devising new ways to use money in elections is becoming legendary. In my book *An Undocumented Wonder: The Making of the Great Indian Election,* I had listed forty different ways in which abuse of money power takes place in elections, but that now seems to be just the tip of the iceberg.

Election-time corruption is not an isolated phenomenon, but is the root cause of all corruption in the country. In our increasingly competitive, no-holds-barred elections, candidates and political parties spend crores of rupees to ensure victory, by hook or crook. When they spend crores, they must collect crores. The 'recovery' begins soon after elections. No donor gives money to a politician without entertaining hopes of getting some return. The quid pro quo is obvious—promise of lucrative government contracts, licences and favours of all kinds. Money from drug lords and crime mafia, perhaps even foreign money, finds its way into the election process as an 'investment'. The result: the cancer of corruption is eating into the vitals of our society and polity. For the citizens, nothing gets done without money.

Role of money power

Besides overspending and the bribing of voters, there are many other forms in which money plays its abusive role in elections. We have seen many candidates who have made it a profession to stand for election, only to subsequently withdraw for money from a rival who does not want anyone to cut into his or her votes.

Putting up bogus or dummy candidates to cut into rivals' votes (or to confuse the voter) is common. Sometimes, dummy candidates are put up to circumvent the expenditure ceiling for campaigning. The expenditure ceiling available to such candidates is used by the sponsoring candidate. The Election Commission has often caught dummy candidates carrying another party's election materials.

Now that these explosive tapes have surfaced, what can the Election Commission do? Actually, not very much, at least directly. After the announcement of election results, the Commission becomes functus officio. Having fulfilled its function and accomplished its purpose, it holds no further force or authority. The power shifts instead to the high courts, which only can entertain a complaint in the form of an election petition. Fortunately, in this case the petition of the losing candidate, Rupdhar Pudo, is still pending in the Bilaspur High Court. He has come out in the media to say he had filed a complaint at that time itself when other candidates withdrew making the same allegations.

Significantly, Rupdhar Pudo was the only candidate left in the fray when eleven of the thirteen candidates for the Antagarh seat, including the Congress candidate, Manturam Pawar, withdrew their nominations. Pudo has alleged that the personal secretary of the chief minister repeatedly tried to pressure him to withdraw his nomination—for any consideration he demanded. He had requested the high court to issue directions to set aside the election. The case is listed for 21 January for recording of evidence.

One would like to hope that court will take up this case with extraordinary seriousness, now that it has come into national focus. It is pertinent to mention that the Representation of the People Act, 1951, stipulates disposal of an election petition within six months. It's a pity that this is one law which remains on paper, and ironical that our otherwise brilliant judiciary falls short in cases such as this one. Instead of upholding this law, the court itself becomes a defaulter.

Let us consider here what Section 86(6) of the RPA actually says: 'The trial of an election petition *shall*, so far as is practicable consistently with the interests of justice in respect of the trial, *be continued from day to day until its conclusion*, unless the High Court finds the adjournment of the trial beyond the following day to be necessary for reasons to be recorded.'

And Section 86(7) goes on to reinforce the urgency thus: 'Every election petition *shall* be tried as expeditiously as possible and *endeavour shall be made to conclude the trial within six months* from the date on which the election petition is presented to the High Court for trial.'

Pudo also complained about the lack of action on the part of the Election Commission in his complaint. The Commission seems to have finally written to the chief secretary of Chhattisgarh on 31 December 2015 and to its own chief electoral officer, to get an inquiry conducted and to take the necessary action. Both can ask the police to file an FIR under various sub-sections of Section 171 of the Indian Penal Code.

This case amply attracts various provisions of Section 171 of the IPC, which I list below:

1. Section 171 A(b), which defines the right of a person to stand or withdraw as an electoral candidate as an 'electoral right'.
2. Section 171 B(i) and (ii), which deal with any offer or receiving of gratification in the exercise of an electoral right as an offence of bribery.
3. Section 171 E, which prescribes punishment for bribery, which is imprisonment of up to one year with or without fine.
4. Section 171 C(1) defines an attempt to interfere with the free exercise of any electoral right as undue influence at elections. This also carries similar imprisonment (as Sec. 171 F).
5. Section 171 H, which makes any illegal payment (over ₹10) by anyone punishable by a fine.
6. Sec 171 I, which holds failure to keep election accounts as an offence, punishable with a fine.

The scam is a wake-up call for the various parties involved to take the case to its logical conclusion. The parties are the Election Commission of India, the state government, the police and the high court. One hopes they live up to the people's expectations and seize the initiative. Public trust in constitutional institutions is too precious to be allowed to dissipate.

India's election system is highly regarded across the globe. It is ironical that only a fortnight ago, a regional conference of South Asian countries, represented by the participating nations' election commissions, political leaders, academics and civil society, passed what was proudly termed as the New Delhi Declaration of Guiding Principles for Regulating Political Finance in South Asia, 2015. Ugly incidents like the Chhattisgarh election scandal cast a shadow on the fair name that Indian elections have achieved worldwide. We must collectively protect that image. The country's political leadership has the greatest responsibility to adopt, without further delay, electoral reforms that can clean up our electoral system. These reforms have been pending for over two decades now.

Electoral Reforms

1

Pros and Cons of Simultaneous Elections

PRIME MINISTER NARENDRA MODI'S SUGGESTION THAT ELECTIONS to the Lok Sabha, Vidhan Sabhas and local bodies should be held simultaneously has brought to centre stage an issue that has been raised intermittently for years now. Earlier, L.K. Advani had made the same suggestion. In a May 2010 blog post, he advocated a fixed term for elected bodies and simultaneous elections. Leaders of several parties also raised the issue, leading to a parliament committee examining it. The idea is good in principle, but seems fraught with constitutional issues and administrative problems.

Let us first examine the reasons that have prompted this proposal—frequent elections bring to a standstill the normal functioning of the government and the life of the citizens, and bring heavy recurring costs.

It is true that normal work comes to a standstill to a considerable extent. Typically, elections to the Lok Sabha are spread over two and a half months. As soon as the Election Commission announces the poll dates, the MCC comes into operation. This means the government cannot announce any new schemes, make any new appointments, transfers or postings without Election Commission approval. Ministers get busy with election campaigns and the district administrative machinery gets totally focused on elections.

The second reason, costs, is a major issue. Election costs have risen enormously. They have two components—election management costs borne by the EC/government, and costs borne by the candidates and political parties. Though there are no exact estimates, one guesstimate puts the total cost of the conduct of elections at ₹4,500 crore. The bigger problem is the havoc played by the money power of the political parties and the contestants. Though the law prescribes a ceiling on election expenditure incurred by candidates, the fact is that it is violated with impunity. In my earlier book, I had documented forty ways of abuse of money power identified by us at the Commission and the steps taken to check them. But the politicians soon outsmarted us. Among other things, the money is now spent much before the Election Commission comes into the picture. The worst problem is that there is no cap on election expenditure incurred by political parties, which exploit this loophole to the hilt. The ceiling of ₹70 lakh per Lok Sabha candidate seems like peanuts when political parties spend ten or twenty times more to promote their candidates, which distorts the level playing field besides vitiating the spirit of free and fair elections.

Another consequence of frequent elections is the aggravation of vices like communalism, casteism, corruption (vote buying and fundraising) and crony capitalism. If the country is perpetually in election mode, there is no respite from these evils.

Frequent elections have some benefits too. One, politicians who tend to forget voters after the elections for five years have to return to them. This enhances accountability on their part and keeps them on their toes. Two, elections give a boost to the economy at the grassroots level, creating work opportunities for lakhs of people. Three, there are some environmental benefits also that flow out of the rigorous enforcement of public discipline, like strict measures against defacement of private and public property, noise and air pollution;

ban on plastics, etc. 'Let EC Raj continue', was one headline in a Punjab paper. And one national newspaper from the south carried letters to the editor for one whole week after the 2011 election in Tamil Nadu, expressing appreciation for the quality of life during the MCC days! Four, local and national issues do not get mixed up and distort priorities. In voters' minds, local issues overtake wider state and national issues.

Some suggest that at least the Vidhan Sabha and panchayat elections could be clubbed—which will ensure that the impact of a collapse of a panchayat or state government will be restricted to the state in question. But I doubt if subversion of the people's mandate at the panchayat level too can be taken lightly. Infringement of the people's right to choose their representatives for the sake of saving money or for administrative convenience, or 'to save party workers their time' (the immediate provocation for PM Modi's suggestion) cannot pass judicial muster.

Imagine a scenario in which the Lok Sabha gets dissolved (in thirteen days, as actually happened in 1998) and, for the sake of simultaneity, all the state assemblies with full or thin majorities are also dissolved. And then, imagine that in the resultant Lok Sabha elections the same party comes to power (as actually happened in 1999), but state assemblies go topsy-turvy!

Did the Constituent Assembly anticipate such a situation? Only partly. Initially, it considered a part-time Election Commission, thinking there would be no work for the Commission between two elections for five whole years. Eventually, as a concession to the remote possibility of elections happening in between, it provided for a single, full-time CEC. We did not have to wait for long to see the possibility of unforeseen elections becoming a harsh reality. In 1956, the Kerala Vidhan Sabha was dissolved, establishing a questionable trend that worsened with time.

In conclusion, if the reasons for the demand for simultaneous elections are accepted, let's look at what is possible. It's possible to reduce the duration of the election process—by conducting the elections in one phase. That requires making available to the EC five times the Central armed police forces that are currently provided to it for elections. Instead of 700–800 companies, the EC will then need 3,500 companies. Creation of a few extra battalions of various paramilitary forces will also give relief to the Central forces who are now extremely stretched and stressed, provide employment and contribute to better law enforcement in troubled areas.

The other possible and desirable action is to reduce the role of money power in elections. This requires two measures: Putting a cap on expenditure by political parties, and putting in place a system for state funding of political parties (not elections), with a simultaneous ban on all private, especially corporate, funds. Prime Minister Modi has the majority and the clout to get these reforms implemented.

2

One Nation, One Poll: One Good Idea, Some Hurdles

THE ISSUE OF CONDUCTING SIMULTANEOUS ELECTIONS HAS BEEN repeatedly raised by Prime Minister Narendra Modi over the last two years. The Indian economist and Indologist Bibek Debroy and former Officer on Special Duty for NITI Aayog, Kishore Arun Desai, in a paper addressed to NITI Aayog, had pointed out that apart from the 2014 general election, polls in about fifteen states were held between March 2014 and May 2016. In some cases, elections to state assemblies were announced within a month of conclusion of elections to other state assemblies. It is argued that if the country is always in electoral mode, it negatively impacts development activities in the states and at the national level.

In 2015, a parliamentary standing committee examined the issue and endorsed the suggestion. The EC also supported this in principle, subject to political consensus.

Exorbitant costs and prolonged disruption of development activities were the two main reasons cited. But I would like to add another reason: elections are when communalism, casteism, corruption and crony capitalism are at their peak. Frequent elections mean there is no respite from these evils at all.

Internationally, there are several countries which hold simultaneous elections. Sweden's county and municipal councils occur simultaneously with the general election every four years. In South Africa, elections to the national and provincial assemblies are held simultaneously in a five-year cycle, while in Belgium, elections to the federal parliament are normally held every five years, coinciding with the European (and, consequently, also regional) elections.

In the United States of America, simultaneous elections are a reality. In many states, a voter chooses not just the US president, but also twenty different contestants on a single ballot, including members of the US senate and the House of Representatives, the state senate, governor, state attorney general and even the Supreme Court judge.

In India, however, there are various reasons why simultaneous elections, even if desirable, are not feasible, at least in the near future. Being a federal republic, every state in India follows its own political course. What is one to do, for example, if a particular state witnesses an upturned majority after a few MLAs decide to shift 'loyalties'? How are simultaneous elections to be continued in such a scenario?

Or, as was the case in 1996, what happens if the Lok Sabha is dissolved within thirteen days of its formation? Do we also dissolve all the state assemblies? And what happens if one of the state assemblies is dissolved? Does the entire country go to the polls again? The idea sounds problematic and appears against the ethos of democracy as it undermines the people's choice. How can we dissolve state assemblies because of events happening outside the state (like the dissolution of parliament), when the assembly members have been democratically chosen by the people of the state?

Realizing these problems, NITI Aayog has proposed the holding of two elections in five years—elections to fourteen states to be held along with the Lok Sabha election in 2019 in the first phase, and elections to the remaining states to be held in October–November 2021. Once these elections are synchronized, then polls would be held in India once every two-and-a-half years.

This, however, seems to be a radical dilution of the original proposal to conduct elections at the national, state and panchayat levels at the same time.

With panchayat elections and its 30 lakh representatives now already out of the discussion and the bifurcation of the remaining two tiers of governance (4,120 MLAs and 543 MPs), what is left is a very watered-down version of the original proposal. It does not seem to be worth the effort in the face of serious questions being raised about the federal structure of the Constitution.

Further, frequent elections are not without their own benefits. Politicians are notorious for disappearing once an election is over. Frequent elections at least ensure that they 'show their face' to the people regularly. Election time results in the creation of work opportunities at the grassroots level. That's why people love elections. For the poor, this is the only power they have. Finally, separate elections at three tiers ensure that local, regional and national issues do not get mixed up.

Two recent developments have put a question mark on the authenticity of the proposal. First, Gujarat and Himachal Pradesh elections, which were always held simultaneously, could not be held together when political exigency decided otherwise. More recently, when the Karnataka elections were held in May 2018, sixteen by-elections were held three weeks later, prolonging the MCC period and the consequent disruption of normal development activities.

What moral authority is then left in the proposal?

Till simultaneous elections become a possibility, could we not look at alternative routes? The exorbitant cost of elections could be tackled by putting a cap on campaign expenditure by political parties. Collection of private funds, especially corporate, could be banned, to be replaced by state funding of political parties (not elections), based on the votes obtained by them in the latest elections.

To deal with the second major reason for the proposal—namely, prolonged disruption of normal development activities—we could look at the possibility of reducing the duration of elections from the current two to three months to thirty-three days by making available more Central police forces.

Simultaneous elections are a far-reaching electoral reform, which can only be implemented by a political consensus. It is good that the prime minister has called for a national debate to evolve a national consensus through the Law Commission.

3

Debates and Drawbacks of Simultaneous Elections

Nот even a month after the world's largest election in history, the debate around 'one nation, one election' has been resurrected. Prime Minister Narendra Modi, who has flagged the issue for the last five years, has called for a meeting on the subject with leaders of other political parties on 19 June 2019.

The 2014 manifesto of the ruling BJP said: 'The BJP will seek, through consultation with other parties, to evolve a method of holding Assembly and Lok Sabha elections simultaneously. Apart from reducing election expenses for both political parties and Government, this will ensure certain stability for State Governments.'

Indian elections, where the sun never sets

In an interview with a news channel in January 2018, the Prime Minister had rightly highlighted the disadvantages of the country being in constant election mode. 'One election finishes, the second starts,' he said. He argued that simultaneous parliamentary, assembly, civic and panchayat polls once every five years and completed within a month or so would save the country money, resources and manpower. This waste of resources, he pointed out, happened on account of a large section of the security forces, bureaucracy and political machinery having to be mobilized for up to 200 days in the year on account of frequent elections.

The BJP's 2019 manifesto also mentions it will work towards simultaneous parliament, state assembly and local body elections to 'ensure efficient utilization of government resources and security forces and … effective policy planning'. It goes on to say that the party 'will try to build consensus on this issue with all parties'. It is in this spirit of reform and consensus building that the prime minister has revived the debate, calling an all-party meeting for discussions on 19 June 2019.

The re-elected chief minister of Odisha, Naveen Patnaik, has already welcomed the idea. On 15 June, he said that frequent elections affect the development climate, and hence it would be better to have simultaneous elections in the country.

The Law Commission had recommended simultaneous elections to the Lok Sabha, Vidhan Sabhas and local bodies as far back as in 1999. BJP's L.K. Advani had also supported the idea back in 2010, in an eloquent blog post. The matter was examined by a parliamentary standing committee in December 2015 and was also referred to the Election Commission of India. Both supported it in principle.

Genuine concerns

The concerns raised are indeed genuine and worth debating. First, it is becoming more and more difficult to contest in elections. The 2019 general election was the most expensive on record—a whopping ₹60,000 crore was reportedly spent on the whole exercise. Given that there is no cap on the expenditure incurred by political parties, they spend obscene amounts of money in every election. It is argued that simultaneous elections would help reduce this cost.

Second, frequent elections hamper the normal functioning of the government and disrupt civic life. This happens because the Model Code of Conduct (MCC) comes into operation as soon as the EC announces election dates. This means the government cannot announce any new schemes during this period, resulting in what is often referred to as policy paralysis. The government cannot make any new appointments or transfer officials. The government's entire manpower is involved in the conduct of elections.

I would also like to add that elections are the time when communalism, casteism and corruption are at their peak. Frequent elections mean there is no respite from these evils at all. This has directly resulted in the souring of the political discourse, something that was on full display during the 2019 general election.

From the point of view of the Election Commission, simultaneous elections make perfect sense because the voters for all three tiers are the same; the polling booths are the same and the staff/security the same too. The suggestion of 'one nation, one election' seems logical.

The hurdles

However, there are some hurdles in the way of implementing the idea. First, how will 'one nation, one election' work in case of premature dissolution of the Lok Sabha, for instance, as happened in late 1990s, when the house was dissolved long before its term of five years was over? In such an eventuality, would we also dissolve all the state assemblies? Similarly, what happens when one of the state assemblies is dissolved? Will the entire country go to the polls again? This sounds unworkable, both in theory and in practice, for a democracy.

Second, as for implementation of government schemes during the MCC period, only new schemes are stopped as these could tantamount to enticing/bribing voters on the eve of elections. All ongoing programmes go on unhindered. Even new announcements that are of urgent public interest can be made with the prior approval of the Election Commission.

Additionally, frequent elections are not so bad when it comes to accountability, after all. They ensure that politicians turn up in front of their voters regularly. Creation of work opportunities at the grassroots level is another big upside. The most important consideration is undoubtedly the federal spirit, which, inter alia, requires that local and national issues are not mixed up.

Now, as the debate has been rekindled, wider deliberation on the need for a range of reforms must be considered. I have two alternative suggestions for what measures may be put in place till there is political consensus on the issue.

First, the problem of uncontrolled campaign expenditure can be remedied by introducing a cap on the election expenditure incurred by political parties. State funding of political parties based on their poll performance is also a suggestion worth considering. Collection of private and corporate funds may be banned.

Second, as I have suggested elsewhere, the poll duration can be reduced from the current two to three months to about thirty-three to thirty-five days if more Central armed police forces can be provided. The problems associated with a multi-phased election have been compounded by the list of issues growing with every election. Violence, social media-related transgressions and issues related to enforcement of the MCC, which are unavoidable in a staggered election, will vanish if the election is conducted in a single day. All that needs to be done is to raise more battalions of security forces. This will also help in job creation.

A healthy debate

To conclude, it is undeniable that simultaneous elections would be a far-reaching electoral reform. If it is to be implemented, there needs to be a solid political consensus and an agenda of comprehensive electoral reforms to supplement it. The pros and cons need to be appropriately assessed and the practical alternatives sincerely considered. It is good that the government continues to encourage debate on the subject rather than forcibly pushing its views through.

1

Has the SC Missed a Chance to Keep Criminals Out of Polls?

THE 25 SEPTEMBER 2018 VERDICT OF THE SUPREME COURT ON criminalization of politics left much to be desired. The Election Commission, frustrated by its own helplessness in the matter, has been crying hoarse to the government, political parties and the apex court for help in stemming the corrupt influences on our legislatures. The court's verdict essentially passed on the responsibility to the Commission itself.

The court also said it cannot play the role of parliament. But parliament, regardless of which coalition parties are in power, has not been playing its own legitimate role. According to Article 102(1) of the Constitution, parliament is obliged to make a law on the matter. But if history is any indicator, there is a slim chance, if any, that legislative action will follow the Supreme Court judgment.

What the court directed

The directions given by the Supreme Court are welcome, but there are some practical issues. For instance, the apex court has instructed political parties to carry on their websites information on candidates who have criminal antecedents. But how many voters are capable of accessing these websites? Also, both the candidate and the political party are required to publicize this information. Why would they actively publicize anything that goes against their own interests?

The Election Commission has also been asked to publicize information on the background of electoral candidates. The Commission already displays on its website the details provided by the candidates in their affidavits. The only difference if there is criminality on the part of the candidate is that these details are to be given in bold. Any additional 'warning' indicated by the EC will create problems for it, such as allegations of subjectivity, bias and partiality against it.

Section 8 of the Representation of the People Act, 1951, bans convicted politicians from contesting. However, those facing trial, no matter how serious the charges, are free to contest.

In fact, political parties appear to be competing with each other to field candidates with criminal records, as their 'winnability' has been proven to be higher than that of regular candidates. The past three Lok Sabhas have seen an increasing number of legislators with criminal backgrounds—128 in 2004, 162 in 2009 and 184 in 2014.

The ECI proposal to bar candidates accused of offences punishable with at least five years' imprisonment from contesting elections after charges are framed against them by a court has been opposed by many parties. Their opposition is on two grounds: ruling politicians will misuse this against the Opposition; and the law of the land assumes everyone to be innocent till proved guilty or convicted.

ECI safeguards

The ECI safeguards in this regard are crystal clear. First, all criminal cases will not invite a ban on the accused; only those concerned with heinous offences like rape, dacoity, murder and kidnapping will. Second, the case should be registered at least six months before the elections. Third, a court must have framed charges against the candidate.

Further assertions regarding a candidate being 'innocent until proven guilty' are debatable. After all, there are about 2.7 lakh prisoners in jails still under trial, and hence, innocent. Yet, they are denied fundamental rights, like the right to liberty, freedom of movement, freedom of pursuing one's chosen occupation and right to dignity. May I remind the reader that contesting elections is a statutory right, not even a fundamental right?

The Supreme Court verdict has arrived as a huge disappointment when seen in the context of the need for untainted parliamentarians in the country. Judicial activism has saved this country many times when the executive and the legislature were not willing to do their job. We know from history that the legislature has not moved on this front. An activist measure from the judiciary in this case too would have been welcome.

The order is in line with the principles of natural justice and separation of powers between the judiciary and the parliament.

2

Court's Lost Chance for Tackling Criminalization

On Tuesday, 25 September 2018, the Supreme Court delivered its much-awaited pronouncement on the petitions asking it to bar politicians facing heinous criminal charges—like rape, murder and kidnapping—from contesting elections. A five-judge bench led by Chief Justice of India Dipak Misra said the court cannot play the role of parliament. The CJI did express concern over the issue of criminals participating in politics; something needed to be done urgently in this respect and society is helpless when it comes to stemming the phenomena, he said. But the judgment left much to be desired.

I am disappointed, but not surprised. I have, time and again, called the judiciary the guardian angel of democracy in general, and of the Election Commission in particular. But this time, the SC has passed the buck to the Commission, even though the latter has been crying hoarse for the apex court to come to its aid for the past two decades. Parliament is obliged to make a law on the matter, according to Article 102(1) of the Constitution, but if history is anything to go by, that is unlikely to happen.

The bench pronounced that it is not in a position to enable disqualification of candidates who face criminal charges. It has, however, provided a slew of directions to curb criminals from entering the legislature. First, while filing their nominations, electoral candidates must declare if there are pending criminal cases against them in court. Second, political parties are also responsible for putting up the details of criminal cases filed against their candidates on their websites. Third, parliament must legislate on the matter to ensure that candidates with criminal antecedents do not enter public life or become lawmakers. Fourth, while filling their nomination forms, candidates must declare their criminal past and the cases pending against them in bold letters. Lastly, political parties should publicize the background of their candidates via electronic media and issue declarations.

The recommendations, though welcome, involve some practical problems. Parliament, regardless of who is in power, has always been reluctant to legislate on the issue. Voters do not generally read the websites of political parties. The recommendation regarding publicization of the criminal background of candidates by political parties sounds counter-intuitive. Why would they actively publicize anything that goes against their interests?

Section 8 of the Representation of the People Act, 1951, bans convicted politicians from standing for elections. But those facing trial, no matter how serious the charges, are free to contest elections. A law to bar candidates charged for heinous crimes will require broad consensus across the party lines, and that seems highly unlikely. The fielding of candidates is not based on their moral standing, but on their 'winnability'. At present, far from denying tickets to criminals, all parties seem to compete with each other in the number of criminals they field. The past three Lok Sabhas have seen an increasing number of legislators with a criminal background or with pending criminal cases against them—124 in 2004, 162 in 2009 and 182 in 2014. The political parties are united in their opposition to any law that would debar perpetrators of heinous offences during the pendency of their cases. They hold that this could lead to false cases being filed against candidates. This assertion is partly valid. However, the Election Commission's proposal provides for safeguards against this. First, not all criminal cases will invite a ban on the candidates in question; only those involving heinous offences will. Second, the cases should be registered at least six months before the elections. Third, the court must have framed charges against the candidates.

Opponents of the Commission's proposal time and again point out that electoral candidates and legislators are deemed 'innocent until proven guilty'. One wonders what they have to say about the 2.7 lakh undertrials, not yet convicted and hence innocent, who are currently locked up in jails in India as per the National Crimes Record Bureau.

Four fundamental rights stand suspended for these undertrials—liberty, freedom of movement, freedom to pursue one's occupation of choice and right to dignity. If the rights of those undertrials can be suspended within the ambit of the law, what is the sanctity of the candidates' right to contest elections, which is after all only a statutory right and not a fundamental right?

Attorney General K.K. Venugopal had submitted that fast-track courts to try the charges against electoral candidates were 'the only solution'. It is surprising that the court has not said a word on this, though the issue is entirely in its domain. Fast-tracking has been the accepted norm. There are many categories of special courts, such as CBI courts, consumer courts and, more recently, fast-track courts for rape cases; so there are special categories for the purpose of adjudication and nobody has called this discriminatory. The Representation of the People Act also recognizes this in principle, requiring the high courts to decide on election petitions within six months. The conventional courts take many years to decide on election petitions. It is not a deficiency of the law that accounts for all this, but neglect by the judiciary of its statutory obligation.

The government had promptly offered its full support for implementation of the March 2014 Supreme Court judgment, in which the court had accepted the urgent need to cleanse politics and directed all the subordinate courts to give their verdicts on cases involving legislators within a year, or give reasons for not doing so to the chief justices of their high courts. Progress in this matter has not been reviewed.

The verdict given on 25 September seems a missed opportunity for the Supreme Court, especially when seen in light of the nation's fight for free, fair and clean elections. Judicial activism has been at the root of some of the most ground-breaking reforms in India's democratic history. In this case, the court crossing the *Lakshman rekha* would have been both welcome and justified. The doctrine of separation of powers between the executive, the judiciary and parliament has to be seen in light of the need for checks and balances. When the executive and the legislature are unwilling to do their job, the judiciary must step in on behalf of the citizens. It remains to be seen whether parliamentarians will the show political will to heed the apex court's advice and aid fulfilment of the nation's dream for a corruption-free India.

3

Crime and Politics

ON 10 AUGUST 2021, THE SUPREME COURT MADE A NEW MOVE IN its bid to call into question the rising tide of politicians with criminal records contesting elections. The judgment came in response to a plea of contempt filed by advocate Brajesh Singh against political parties flouting the court's orders on disclosure of the criminal antecedents of candidates in the 2020 Bihar Assembly elections. 'The nation continues to wait and is losing patience,' the apex court has gone on record to say.

The court has imposed fines of ₹1 lakh each on the BJP, the Congress and the JD(U), among others, for failing to comply with its orders regarding complete disclosure of their candidates' criminal history. The CPI(M) and the Nationalist Congress Party were fined ₹5 lakh each for complete failure to comply with any of its mandates.

Growing participation by members with criminal backgrounds has been a constant theme in Indian politics. According to the Association for Democratic Reforms (ADR), 233 MPs in the current Lok Sabha are facing criminal charges, up from 187 in 2014, 162 in 2009 and 128 in 2004.

The current orders of the SC have put fresh onus on the Election Commission to do something concrete—for example, create a phone app to display the detailed criminal history of every contesting candidate. There should also be a separate cell in the ECI to monitor compliance by the political parties of the orders, and any breach should be brought to the attention of the Supreme Court without delay.

While seeking to strengthen the Election Commission to combat the issue is a welcome step, the Supreme Court remains sceptical about the legislature taking concrete steps to solve the problem. This scepticism is not unwarranted. Political parties in India have always been notoriously reluctant to introduce changes to prevent the entry of criminals into the legislature, and the excuses they have given for doing so have remained nearly unchanged since Independence.

The Supreme Court has, however, stopped short of drastic steps to combat this problem. It has rejected the suggestion of senior advocate and amicus curiae K.V. Viswanathan to direct the Election Commission to bar political parties that fail to comply with the court directives by using its authority derived from Clause 16A of the Election Symbols Order. This step, the Supreme Court reasons, would be going too far and infiltrating the domain of the legislature.

The legislature has been very slow in addressing this issue, and political parties remain extremely reluctant to change their ways, citing two major excuses. 'Winnability' of candidates is the first reason. The logic that a candidate with criminal charges will do good for the people of a constituency is dubious at best. The winnability explanation is an attempt by parties to absolve themselves of all blame for encouragement of criminals in politics and put the onus of sending a candidate charged with a crime to parliament solely on the voter. This is unacceptable.

The other reason offered by political parties is summarized by the maxim of Indian law, which is that any accused is innocent until proven guilty. Most candidates accused of crime, Indian political party spokespeople maintain, are victims of 'vendetta politics'. While there is some merit to this argument, I have pointed out the fallacy of its application in this matter multiple times. There were 4.78 lakh prisoners (as of December 2019), of whom 3.30 lakh were under trial, i.e., not yet proven guilty. Yet, their fundamental rights—right to liberty, freedom of movement, freedom to pursue their occupation of choice and right to dignity—are curbed completely.

I have posed this question on various fora where honourable judges and eminent jurists were present. Nobody has ever explained this paradox to me. Besides, the Supreme Court had annulled the appointment of a central vigilance commissioner on the grounds that a criminal case was pending against him. These blatant double standards are a clear violation of Article 14, which guarantees to all citizens equality before the law. Even a peon cannot be appointed if a minor criminal case is pending against him. But a person charge-sheeted for murder or rape can become a legislator and even a minister.

To add insult to injury, an 'innocent' undertrial cannot vote, but a man charge-sheeted for murder can even contest an election from jail.

The ECI has suggested some safeguards against vendetta politics, which results in framing of false charges against candidates. First, only offences that carry punishment of imprisonment of at least five years are to be considered. The case in question against the candidate should have been filed at least six months before the scheduled elections for it to be considered. And, finally, a competent court must have framed the charges.

An alternative solution would be to try cases against political candidates in fast-track courts. The Supreme Court had sent a directive to this effect as far back as in 2014, directing that cases against political candidates must be completed within a year, failing which the matter should be reported to the chief justices of the respective high courts. This is a matter entirely in the judicial domain. We have heard nothing about implementation of this order. Why has the apex court lost sight of it?

The Supreme Court's anguish and limited proactiveness at least provide a semblance of hope.

Your Lordships, in the face of your apparent helplessness to circumvent the maxim of 'innocent till proven guilty', may I humbly submit that the release of 3.30 lakh 'innocent' undertrials be considered forthwith, to uphold Article 14—equality of all before the law? Here, you don't have to beg and plead with the legislature and the executive. This is entirely in your domain. Please admit this as my PIL.

1

The Opaque Electoral Bonds

THE FINANCE MINISTRY HAS LAUNCHED ITS QUARTERLY WINDOW FOR the sale of electoral bonds which will remain open from 1 April to 10 April 2021. This comes after the Supreme Court refused to stay the scheme last week. During the hearing, the apex court, however, flagged a new issue—the possibility of misuse of money received by political parties for activities like funding terror or violent protests—and asked the Centre whether it has any control on the end use of the money. I wish the court had mentioned another important and new area of dubious expenditure—purchase of MLAs after elections to overturn the public mandate.

The bench was hearing a plea by the Association for Democratic Reforms (ADR), which was seeking a stay on fresh sale of electoral bonds while its petition challenging the electoral bonds scheme was pending.

The issue has been hanging fire since February 2017 when, in his budget speech, Finance Minister Arun Jaitley made two profound statements: one, without transparency of political funding, free and fair elections are not possible; and two, despite seventy years of concern we have failed to achieve the transparency required. After these momentous statements, one expected that the issue would be resolved. However, what he announced was the opposite of the desire he expressed.

Electoral bonds were born. And transparency died. Till then, every transaction of more than ₹20,000 in the context of elections was reported to the Election Commission. Now, even ₹20 crore or ₹200 crore could be donated anonymously. The reason given was that the donors want secrecy.

Why would donors want secrecy? To hide return favours like contracts, licences and bank loans, with which some of them may abscond to foreign lands? For seven decades, corporations have been donating to all parties in India, and often the same donors fund rival parties. Did any ruling party ever harass a donor who donated to its rivals? Did the current ruling party do so? If not, the excuse that donors want secrecy is phoney. It is clearly a case of private interests in conflict with the public interest of transparency.

Importantly, both the RBI and ECI, standing up to their mandates, had registered their strong protest against the electoral bonds scheme. The ECI, in a letter to the ministry of law and justice, warned that electoral bonds, combined with the preceding legislative amendments, would encourage large sums in illegal donations. It would lead to the mushrooming of shell companies to funnel black money into the political system through these bearer bonds.

However, the ECI counsel in April 2021 submitted that the commission supports electoral bonds. 'Without electoral bonds, we will go back to the earlier cash system, which was unaccounted. Bonds is one step forward, as all transactions are through banking channels,' he said. This is exactly the government line. Is this change of stand surprising?

The introduction of electoral bonds through the budget was not an isolated act. The Finance Act 2017 introduced amendments in the Reserve Bank of India Act, Companies Act, Income Tax Act, Representation of the People Act and Foreign Contribution Regulations Act to make way for electoral bonds.

There were three serious changes which did not receive the deserved attention. First, the limit of 7.5 per cent of profits which a company could donate was not just increased but completely done away with by amending Section 182 of the Companies Act, 2013. Thus, a company can donate 100 per cent of its profits to a political party. Even a loss-making company could make political donations. This is a sure step to legitimize and legalize crony capitalism. Companies can now virtually run the government, as we can see happening.

There was more to follow. Section 29B of the Representation of the People Act, 1951 prohibits political parties from accepting any contribution from a 'foreign source'. Moreover, Section 3 of the 2010 Foreign Contribution (Regulation) Act bars candidates, legislative members, political parties and party office holders from accepting foreign contributions. In 2014, when the Delhi High Court found that the Congress and BJP had accepted foreign funds in violation of the FCRA 1976, the BJP government passed a retroactive amendment through a 2016 finance bill, which repealed the 1976 Act and replaced it with the modified 2010 statute.

If any foreign country is financing our elections, it will now be a protected secret. We have seen how foreign interference in other countries' elections is a reality. Even a superpower such as the US could not protect itself from this transgression, that too from its declared enemy number one. This is a serious concern, indeed a blot, on any democracy's electoral system.

The Supreme Court's concern about the possibility of misuse of funds is very pertinent. We need transparency, both about the source of income and its expenditure. The Election Commission has been demanding that a law be passed to make political parties liable to get their accounts audited by an auditor from a panel suggested by the Comptroller and Auditor General (CAG) or the Election Commission, and not by their party cardholders, who only whitewash the accounts.

I think the best way forward is simple—don't abolish electoral bonds if you don't want to, just disclose the identities of the donors and the recipients. This is something the government could do in thirty seconds. Since it is futile to expect the government to do it, the Supreme Court could have easily ordered this and clinched the issue. One wishes the highest court of the land would consider this case as one of national importance and show some urgency.

Let's not forget that it was the same Supreme Court which had done great service in 2002–03 for the cause of transparency when it made it compulsory for electoral candidates to declare their financial dealings and criminal cases while filing their nominations. When the government tried to dilute the judgment by an enactment, the court even declared the law ultra vires. Is it wrong to expect the same judicial standards in other cases too?

Another alternative is to do away with collection of private funds altogether and replace it with public funding of political parties. This is not likely to amount to more than ₹10,000 crore every five years, if we were to go by the collection made by all the parties cumulatively. It's a small price to pay for democracy.

Another feasible option is to establish a national election fund to which all donations could be directed. This would take care of the imaginary fear of political reprisal against the donors. Income tax rebates would make it an attractive proposition. The money from the fund could then be allocated to political parties on the basis of their electoral performance.

Let's end by reminding the finance minister of her predecessor's opening statement in the 2017 Budget speech, that 'without transparency of political funding, free and fair elections are not possible'.

2

Can Electoral Bonds Cleanse Political Funding?

ONE OF THE MOST SIGNIFICANT FEATURES OF THE UNION BUDGET 2017 was the intention expressed by the finance minister to increase transparency in electoral funding. When it was presented in March, it seemed like a good beginning towards cleansing politics of money power. At that time, the finance minister had strongly acknowledged that a transparent method of funding political parties was vital to the system of free and fair elections. He also expressed concern that even seventy years after Independence, the country had not been able to evolve one. He said political parties continue to receive most of their funds through anonymous donations, which are made in cash. The finance minister categorically stated: 'An effort, therefore, is required to be made to cleanse the system of political funding in India.'

The most significant proposal was to issue electoral bonds which donors could purchase from authorized banks. These bonds would be redeemable only in the designated account of a registered party within a short time of their issuance, which the finance minister specified as three to four weeks. This would stop cash payments, which are subject to abuse. Currently, all donations above ₹20,000 are disclosed by political parties to the Election Commission.

Questions were raised as to whether the donations made through bonds would also be disclosed to the Election Commission. Under Section 182 of the Companies Act, no political donation can be made by a company unless its board of directors passes a resolution authorizing it. The minutes of a board meeting of a listed company being in the public domain, it's hoped that donations made through these bonds will be transparent. The full operational details, however, will be known only after the scheme is framed by the government of India.

Today what has raised alarm is a last-minute amendment in the Finance Bill, made quietly, removing the cap of 7.5 per cent of the average of the last three years' profit that a company can donate to a political party. Experts are questioning this move, especially when the identity of the recipient of the donations will be kept a secret.

The finance minister, in his reply to a Rajya Sabha debate, assured the House that all concerns will be addressed in the Electoral Bonds Scheme, which is being formulated. He invited suggestions from everyone, assuring them that their concerns will be addressed.

The government putting transparency of political funding high on its agenda is most welcome. But its own actions must be fully transparent too. The ideal solution would be to set up a national electoral fund to which all donors can openly contribute, without expressing any preference for any political party. The money in this fund could then be allocated to all registered political parties in proportion to the votes obtained by them. This will also address the donors' concerns about secrecy.

Once public funding of political parties is ensured, private donations made directly to political parties must be totally banned. And, since public funds will be involved, there must be an annual audit of the donations by the comptroller and auditor general of India or by an auditor approved by it. This will be the most decisive action electoral reform that the country needs.

3

Electoral Bonds: Its Advantages and Issues

AN INVESTIGATION BY THE *QUINT* HAS RECENTLY REVEALED THAT electoral bonds have a hidden alphanumeric number printed on them, which is not visible to the naked eye. The *Quint* bought two electoral bonds of ₹1,000 each and sent them to a forensic lab, which found that these bonds had serial numbers on them, which could only be seen under UV light. This exposé has resulted in questions being raised about the motives behind the introduction of electoral bonds—a step which has not found many supporters since the very beginning.

The current government has been advocating greater transparency in political funding in India. The finance minister (FM), in the 2017 Union budget speech, had proposed the introduction of electoral bonds as a measure to ensure clean political funding in India. Such a step was considered necessary to stop the cash donations being made to political parties.

With this background, the FM announced the Electoral Bonds Scheme in a Press Information Bureau release on 2 January 2018.

Electoral bonds, which are interest-free banking instruments, can be bought only from specified branches of State Bank of India in multiples of ₹1,000, ₹1 lakh, ₹10 lakh or ₹1 crore.

The life of the electoral bond is fifteen days, and it can be encashed only by registered political parties through a designated bank account. The electoral bonds are available for purchase for a period of ten days each in the months of January, April, July and October, as specified by the government. Additionally, a thirty-day period will be specified by the Central government in the year of a general election.

Advantages of the electoral bond scheme

The FM had argued that electoral bonds were essential to change the existing system of political funding and move towards a more transparent system. Political funding has so far been based on donations, big and small, corporate and private, and are made by both cheque or cash, besides the political parties' revenues on investments and properties.

These donations, coming from a range of sources—including political workers, party sympathizers, small businesspersons and large industrialists—were mostly anonymous and their source was never revealed. This resulted in 'unclean' money (read black money) entering the system, making the whole process non-transparent.

The FM believes that electoral bonds will be the beginning of political reforms in the country, as all parties will have to operate through banks. The aim is to root out the current system of anonymous cash donations made to political parties, which leads to generation of black money in the economy.

The issue with electoral bonds

As I have pointed out earlier, one major problem with electoral bonds is that under the scheme, the names of the donor and the receiver are not revealed. Electoral bonds aim to conceal the identity of the donor.

The rationale given is that many a time people wish to donate to political parties anonymously to guard against reprisal or harassment from others to whom they have not donated or have donated less.

I think the real reason could be that the donors do not want the return favours (quid pro quo) bestowed by governments in the form of contracts, licences, loans, etc., to become public. It's a clear case of the private interest of donors being in conflict with the public interest of transparency. In such a scenario, electoral bonds will serve the opposite purpose of what they were introduced for in the first place. Instead of making electoral funding more transparent, the process will become way more opaque and information will be blacked out from the public.

'Heavy bias in favour of ruling party'

The recent revelation by the investigation team of the *Quint* has raised even more important questions regarding the other major issue with electoral bonds—its heavy bias in favour of the ruling party. The ruling party may easily be able to find out which corporation has bought electoral bonds.

With the recent disclosure that electoral bonds in fact have serial numbers printed on them, which are not visible to the naked eye, the government's misuse of the information seems a very real possibility. Entities buying electoral bonds need to furnish their KYC (know your customer) details, which are recorded before the sale of the bonds.

The recipients can only encash these bonds at select SBI branches. The serial number of the bond, matched with the KYC details, will clearly reveal who donated how much money and to whom. While it is true that even bank notes have serial numbers on them, why is the number on electoral bonds hidden from the people and is only discoverable in a forensic lab?

Slyness should not the option of a government that wishes for transparency. Its every move has to be in the public domain—except, of course, in defence and security matters.

While the government is claiming that it wants to move towards transparent political funding in India, the truth is that in the last year it has in fact introduced new laws which seems to be taking the electoral system in the opposite direction. Through the Finance Bill, 2017, the government scrapped the ceiling that had until then restricted corporate firms from donating more than 7.5 percent of their average three-year profits to political parties.

This effectively meant that corporations can now legally exist with the sole purpose of funding political parties. The recent amendment to the Foreign Contribution (Regulation) Act (FCRA), 2010, also exempts political parties from scrutiny of the foreign funds received by them. The amendment, making it legal for political parties to receive funding from foreign donors—that too with forty-two years' retrospective effect—has made the electoral funding system in India more opaque than ever before. Secret numbers on electoral bonds compound the opacity manifold.

Transparent political funding is a must for a successful Indian democracy. For this purpose it is essential that the government be accountable to its citizens, respond to whatever concerns they may have and provide them answers. It is essential that the government clarifies these latest findings by the *Quint* so as to ensure that its credibility remains intact.

4

Should Elections Be State-Funded?

To CHECK CORRUPTION IN ELECTIONS, IT IS NECESSARY TO CONSIDER public funding of political parties—though certainly not public funding of elections. It is important to understand the distinction between state funding of elections and state funding of political parties, and why I am a votary of the latter. It is impossible to keep tabs on the money spent in elections. That is why I have consistently opposed state funding of elections. The issue here is one of black money and not white money. We cannot monitor how black money is put to use in bribing voters, for paid news and other forms of transgressions, though we have been able to have some measure of success in this.

Funding parties post-election

To give you an example: for Vidhan Sabha elections, there is a ceiling of ₹28 lakh for each candidate, but we all know how that is breached, as we are aware of how money is spent in contesting these elections. We also know that politics cannot be run without money. So, I suggest that it is easier to monitor the funding of political parties, which is a far more realistic goal than seeking state funding of elections. Political parties can be funded post-elections, based on their actual performance. We could arrive at some calculations based on their performance. We could, for instance, agree that ₹100 be given to a political party for every vote obtained by it. Since the number of votes polled cannot be fudged, reimbursement based on polled votes would be accurate. As we know, the number of votes secured by each candidate, the actual votes cast, cannot be contested at all. So, if a candidate gets one vote, I will say, he or she be given ₹100, and the candidate will have no cause for complaint as the amount is based on his or her electoral performance. No serious candidate, regardless of the number of votes cast in his favour, will bear a grudge against this system.

In the last general election, 55 crore votes were cast. So, at the rate of ₹100 per vote, the amount would work out to ₹5,500 crore. Is this adequate? I'd say yes. This roughly corresponds to the amount raised by all political parties together in five years. This money can be distributed among the parties based on their poll performance and must be paid by cheque. No extortion. No bribes. No quid pro quo. Also, all private donations can be totally banned if we follow this system. And the party accounts will be subject to audit by the comptroller and auditor general.

As for why the public should pay for political parties, one easy answer is, if you want honesty and transparency in governance, this is a small price to pay. Hypothetically, a few thousand crores of rupees of public money is peanuts compared to the end result of ensuring transparency in elections.

If that is not acceptable, we should create a national election fund to which corporates and others can be asked to donate. Business houses can make donations to the parties they are beholden to. Don't tax the public then, and allow only corporate houses donate to the National Election Fund.

A study, 'Political Finance Regulations Around the World', by the International Institute for Democracy and Electoral Assistance,

Stockholm (2012), shows that seventy-one of the 180 countries studied have the facility of state funds for political parties based on the votes they obtained. This includes 86 per cent of the countries in Europe, 71 per cent in Africa, 63 per cent in the Americas and 58 per cent in Asia. If it works well in so many countries, there is no reason why it cannot be implemented in India.

5

State Funding for Political Parties

L ET US FIRST TURN OUR ATTENTION TO THE TIMELINE OF EVENTS since 2014 when Narendra Modi came to power. First, as was mentioned in the BJP manifesto, came the prime minister's call for simultaneous elections, in view of the repeated overwhelming costs (besides disturbance of normal life). Then came the surprise announcement of demonetization on 8 November 2016, with the stated objective of rooting out the monster of black money from the economy. This would have surely hit the parties that were getting ready to move sackfuls of black money to be distributed among voters going to the polls in the next six months. Then came his direction to all his party legislators to disclose all their bank transactions from 8 November 2016. I thought all this constituted the first positive step towards bringing about financial transparency among politicians. The prime minister repeated this call to his party workers on 7 January 2017. He was beginning with his own party, and this sent out a good signal.

The most explicit development is the PM's expression of concern about the need for electoral reforms, which he made in his address to his party MPs on the eve of the winter session of parliament in 2016.

The focus on a cashless economy, even if it is an afterthought, also has a bearing on political parties. When even a rickshaw-puller or vegetable seller is told to stop cash transactions, the exemption of donations to political parties below ₹20,000 in cash from having to be disclosed must be dispensed with straightaway. This will take care of non-transparency in 80 per cent of political funding, which all political parties show as cash donations.

The Election Commission of India has been deeply concerned about the use of black money in elections. While its recommendations for reforms have been falling on deaf ears, it itself took some proactive measures, including the setting up of a full-fledged expenditure monitoring division headed by an income tax commissioner in 2010. It led to some landmark achievements, including seizure of hundreds of crores of rupees, the unseating and disqualification of a sitting MLA in UP for improper declaration of election expenses and paid news in 2011, and the countermanding of two elections to the Rajya Sabha in Jharkhand in 2012 to stop 'horse-trading', which had become rampant many a Rajya Sabha election. In 2017, the EC took the unprecedented step of cancelling elections to two Tamil Nadu assembly seats—namely, Aravakurichi and Thanjavur.

It seems the time is ripe for addressing the long-standing concern about electoral reforms. The prime minister should immediately review all the proposals of the Election Commission in this regard.

What are the reforms that we are demanding? I recapitulate below just the electoral finance reforms:

- Prescribe a ceiling for political parties' expenditure, as has been done for electoral candidates.
- Consider state funding of political parties (not elections) with independent audit, and a complete ban on private donations.
- Set up an independent national election fund where all tax-free donations could be made.
- Enforce internal democracy and transparency in the working of the political parties and bring them under RTI.

- Accept the Election Commission proposal to legally empower it to cancel elections where credible evidence of abuse of money is found.
- Debar persons against whom cases of heinous offences are pending in courts from contesting elections.
- Empower the Election Commission to deregister those political parties that haven't contested any election for ten years and have still benefited from tax exemptions.
- Make paid news an electoral office with two years' imprisonment, by declaring it a 'corrupt practice' (Section 100 of the Representation of the People Act) and 'undue influence' (Sec 123(2)).

Prime Minister Narendra Modi is a person of strong will. He must take his initiatives to their logical conclusion.

6

On Black Money in Elections

A SERIES OF NEW AND DRAMATIC DEVELOPMENTS HAS BROUGHT TO centre stage the long-discussed—and long-evaded—subject of electoral reforms.

It all started in 2015 with the prime minister calling for the need for simultaneous elections in view of the overwhelming costs and disturbance to normal life it entailed. As the debate on this issue was still heating up, he came up with the surprise announcement of demonetization of currency notes of ₹1,000 and ₹500 denominations. While his stated objective was to root out the monster of black money from the economy, many critics saw in it an attempt to turn into junk the sackfuls of currency notes with the Opposition parties. I, for one, find it a great move as far as the role of black money in elections is concerned.

All political parties use black money to finance their campaigns and to bribe voters. Earlier, the bribing of voters used to happen just a few days before an election, but ever since the ECI put together expenditure-control mechanisms in 2010, followed by a crackdown on unaccounted money as soon as the Model Code came into play, political parties changed their strategy and advanced their voter-enticement activities by a few weeks. Since elections to five state assemblies are round the corner, this is the time when the money would have been moving.

Some subsequent developments, even if not originally intended, also have a bearing on electoral reforms. After the demonetization exercise threw up huge logistical challenges, the government's campaigns to promote e-banking, e-wallet, etc., have made everyone familiar with these payment mechanisms. This, again, is a positive development. When even a rickshaw-puller or vegetable seller is told to stop cash transactions, exempting payments under ₹20,000 to political parties from the 'by cheque only' regulation must also be dispensed with straightaway. This will take care of the non-transparency of 80 per cent of political funding, which all political parties have shown as cash donations. This amounts to an average of ₹1,000 crore per year.

The third development is the PM's directive to his party legislators to disclose all their bank transactions since 8 November 2016. Many questions were raised at this. My reaction is that instead of criticizing it and suggesting what the PM could have done better, why not welcome it as the first positive step towards financial transparency for politicians? Another great move of the government is the act it passed to curb benami property deals and the subsequent crackdown on such deals. This should also have a salutary effect on the role of black money in elections.

In the context of these developments, one report came as a shock. This was the law ministry rejecting the ECI's proposal to give it permanent legal powers to countermand polls on credible evidence of the use of black money.

The ECI has been deeply concerned about the use of black money in elections. It has repeatedly written to the government for the last two decades, suggesting electoral reforms to curb the menace. On its part, the ECI has been doing its best. The setting up of the expenditure monitoring division in 2010 in the commission was a milestone in its efforts to challenge the abuse of money in elections.

Stringent guidelines and their strict enforcement led to the seizure of hundreds of crores of rupees, and put some fear of God in the hearts of the profligate politicians. Our proactive steps led to some landmark achievements, including the unseating and disqualification of a sitting MLA in UP, Umlesh Yadav, for improper declaration of election expenses and paid news. Another was the countermanding of two elections to the Rajya Sabha in Jharkhand in 2012, putting to a stop the 'horse-trading' that had become rampant in many a Rajya Sabha election. The Jharkhand High Court upheld this as the most decisive step taken against corruption and even fined the petitioner ₹1 lakh. In 2016, the ECI took the unprecedented step of cancelling elections to two Tamil Nadu assembly seats, Aravakurichi and Thanjavur.

In this context, the government's rejection a week ago—the second in two months—of the ECI's proposal to give it permanent powers to cancel elections on credible evidence of abuse of money was indeed a surprise, as it goes against the prime minister's avowed war against black money. My charitable interpretation is that this rejection has actually been made about without the knowledge of the PM. I am sanguine that if the ECI now refers the case back to the law ministry, it would not have the moral authority to reject it.

The most explicit development is the PM's expression of concern in his address to the party MPs on the eve of the winter session of Parliament in 2016 about the need for electoral reform. It seems the time is ripe for it. He should immediately review all the proposals of the ECI.

What reforms are we looking for? I recapitulate below, briefly, just the political finance reforms: One, prescribe a cap on election expenditure for political parties, as has been done for electoral candidates. Two, consider state funding of political parties (not elections), which will be independently audited, and a complete ban on private donations. Three, enforce internal democracy and transparency in the working of political parties. Bring them under the RTI Act. Four, set up an independent national election fund to which all tax-free donations could be made. It could be operated by the ECI or any other independent body.

Five, accept the ECI's proposal to legally empower it to cancel elections where credible evidence of abuse of money has been found. Six, debar persons against whom cases of heinous offences are pending in courts from contesting elections. Seven, empower the ECI to deregister those political parties which have not contested any election for ten years and yet benefit from tax exemptions. Eight, make paid news an electoral offence with two years' imprisonment by declaring it a 'corrupt practice' (Section 100, RPA) and an 'undue influence' (Sec 123(2)).

In December 2015, the ECI had organized a conference of South Asian Association for Regional Cooperation (SAARC) countries in collaboration with the International Institute of Democracy and Electoral Assistance-IDEA on the scourge of money power in elections. The conference adopted a historic New Delhi Declaration, laying down the guiding principles for transparency in electoral financing. Member countries of the region and IDEA are trying to get this declaration widely accepted. India, considered as having the gold standard of elections, has a moral responsibility to lead from the front. Over to you, Prime Minister!

1

TRP: How It Works, Issues and the Way Forward

THE TRP (TELEVISION RATING POINT) SCANDAL UNEARTHED BY THE Mumbai police on Thursday, 8 October 2020, which has shocked the nation, actually goes back nearly twenty years. As the director general of Doordarshan (DD) in 2002-03, I had encountered the racket, which was rampant and was working against the national broadcaster. Even though thirty-five out of the top fifty programmes watched in all TV homes (Terrestrial and Cable & Satellite [C&S]) were Doordarshan's, television audience measurement (TAM) did not show even a single DD programme as featuring among the first fifty in the C&S homes category. When DD National's prime-time news share was 92 per cent, a private channel which described itself as '*sab se tez*', with just a 4 per cent share, was declared as the number one channel by TAM.

When our suspicions grew, I started investigating how the TRP system works. Very few may remember that initially there were two rating agencies—TAM and INTAM. Both were coming out with data almost diametrically opposed to each other, causing great confusion. Soon enough, TAM acquired INTAM in 2001. This was nothing short of monopoly. But TAM coined a clever term—'single currency'—to idealize its monopoly, which even the so-called experts at Doordarshan happily lapped up. This killed the possibility of real audience figures coming out.

Curious to know how TAM works, I decided to get a 'people-meter' installed on my office television. I observed that connecting the meter involved removing the back cover of the TV and soldering two wires from the meter on to the tuner of the television. Why would anyone allow such tinkering with his TV set, losing its warranty, I wondered.

The data card was collected twice a week by a worker from AC Nielsen, an American information, data and market-measurement firm. I asked him whether any payment is made to the households where the meters are installed. At first, he denied it. Later, when I had befriended him over tea and samosas, he came out with the truth and revealed that the households are given incentives, in kind, like a pressure cooker or a dining set. The cat was out of the bag!

To dive deep into the issue, it is important to understand how the people-meter works. This is a set-top box with a remote control, where specific buttons are assigned to each member of the family. Every member who watches a particular programme has to press the assigned button and when they go out of the room, they have to press the button again. Who would have the patience to follow this drill throughout the day? Except the poor, who are paid—as little as ₹400 per month to keep the bribing channel on throughout the day—as was discovered in Mumbai.

Another odd thing was that there were only about 2,000 meters measuring the audience, and this figure was being extrapolated for the country's population of 1 billion. Even the number of cities where the meters were installed was as few as a dozen. The demand was repeatedly raised that the number of cities and meters installed should be increased.

There was once a news item revealing the addresses where the meters were installed. The embarrassed company (AC Nielsen) that set up the meters apologized for this leak and promised to ensure complete secrecy. But the game was out.

The then CEO of Prasar Bharati, K.S. Sarma, moved by my agitation, organized a meeting with the top ten advertisers in the country in Mumbai, along with a representative from AC Nielsen. Both parties presented their case. In the mid-2000s, the TV ad spend was about ₹8,000 crore. It is now ₹27,000 crore. I asked them why they were they not scrutinizing the audience figures to ensure that their money goes to the right channels. Their reply was astonishing: When we advertise, we have to go by some figures, and since TAM is the only figure available, we have no option. I asked them whether bogus figures do not bother them at all. All I got was blank looks. They also had no idea as to how the data was actually collected—they had never seen a people-meter. I asked the advertisers if they would volunteer to instal a meter in their homes in the national interest. This too obviously drew a blank.

We also learnt that a top international TV network, famous for its highly viewed serials, had common ownership with the (grand)parent organization of the research agency. This conflict of interest also did not seem to bother anyone.

The controversy continued to simmer till it was raised in Parliament in 2008. TAM was repeatedly accused of installing an inadequate number of 'people meters' and of corruption. NDTV even sued TAM and Nielsen, a global TV rating agency, for billions of dollars, for allegedly manipulating viewership data in India. The then information and broadcasting minister, Priya Ranjan Dasmunshi, said the TRP mechanism in India is not only faulty, but is a 'game between stock exchange and company. This mechanism should be looked into and more transparency introduced in the system'.

In 2008, the ministry of information and broadcasting (MIB) asked the Telecom Regulatory Authority of India (TRAI) to frame policy guidelines for rating agencies. TRAI recommended an approach of self-regulation through the setting up of an industry-led body, the Broadcast Audience Research Council (BARC).

A committee constituted by the MIB under the chairmanship of Amit Mitra, then secretary general of the Federation of Indian Chambers of Commerce and Industry (FICCI), made extensive recommendations for a transparent and credible self-regulatory mechanism for BARC to follow.

Though BARC came into existence in July 2010, it did not make any progress for three years. The MIB notified Policy Guidelines for Television Rating Agencies in India in January 2014 and accredited BARC on 28 July 2015 to carry out television ratings in India. TAM exited TV viewership measurement on 29 February 2016. Since then, BARC has been the sole provider of TV rating services in India on a commercial basis. At present, BARC has 40,000 sample TV households in their measurement universe (2019) out of 15.35 crore TV households, divided almost equally between urban and rural areas.

BARC hired a research agency called Hansa to implement the project. Hansa Research is one of the largest consumer insight companies in the world, operating in seventy-seven countries. In April 2018, Hansa had registered a police complaint after a leak of BARC data by an employee in Gwalior, who was booked. Reportedly, this is not the first time the company has approached the police against one of its own employees.

What is the way forward?

With the huge penetration of direct-to-home (DTH) television, the situation has drastically changed. The set-top box can now be tweaked to record which channel is being actually watched (if this has already not already been done clandestinely). This will certainly raise the question of viewer privacy, for which a solution like encryption can surely be found.

As of 31 December 2019, there were 6.99 crore active, paying DTH subscribers. Besides, there are free DTH services offered by DD, which has 5 crore subscribers—25 per cent of all homes. Even if a fraction of these subscribers are adapted as audience monitors, it will be a huge number and will provide foolproof data—better than the small sample of 40,000 people meters with a history of manipulation.

The manipulation does not involve just financial fraud, but a bigger crime of fraud on the people's right to know the truth, which the media is morally and legally bound to provide, instead of fake news and manufactured hate narratives.

2

Laws and Regulations of TV Media

T HE SUPREME COURT ON 19 NOVEMBER 2020 CAME DOWN HEAVILY on a TV channel that was intent on broadcasting hate-filled news programmes. The court underlined the need for laying down clear guidelines for the media on hate speech and effective implementation of them. This has brought to centre stage, once again, the debate on the need for media regulation, and the scope and extent to which it can be done.

The government has made several attempts in the past to regulate the media, but all such attempts came crashing down in the wake of public outcry against it. The last such attempt was in April 2018, when the MIB issued a circular stipulating that it would suspend or permanently cancel the accreditation granted to journalists found to have 'created and/or propagated' fake news. The next fifteen hours witnessed a huge furore against the circular, culminating in the I&B ministry revoking it.

It is undeniable that television has become the most powerful segment of the media, wielding unprecedented influence over the minds of the people. TV channels have the power to set the country afire with their hateful discourse, which some of them have become notorious for. Everyone can see that freedom of speech is being blatantly abused on a daily basis.

Unbridled power is always dangerous. Some checks and regulations are obviously required. What are the possible forms of such regulations? They are government regulation, self-regulation and independent regulation.

Government regulations are, of course, not desirable, as they could interfere with the freedom of speech and expression enshrined in the Constitution (Article 19), though it is pertinent to remember that the same Article also provides for 'reasonable restrictions' on this freedom.

Currently, the government is not without its own regulatory policies: provisions in the Cable Television Network Rules of 1994, the Cable Television Networks (Regulation) Act of 1995, and the Policy Guidelines for Uplinking of Television Channels from India of 2000, give it the power to block transmission and re-transmission of any channel in the country. How effective or fair this is a matter for critical examination.

The second alternative—self-regulation—though ideal, is easier said than done, and continues to be a pipe dream, at least in India.

That brings us to the third and most desirable option—independent regulation. Who will set up the independent regulator? If the government does it, the whole world will be ready to pounce on it. A great responsibility has fallen on the Supreme Court, an opportunity that it must not miss.

Incidentally, a fourth model has accidentally evolved—self-cum-independent regulation. The News Broadcasters Association (NBA), which was set up in 2008, in turn set up the National Broadcasting Standards Authority (NBSA), with the legendary former Chief Justice of India J.S. Verma as its chairman. He agreed to chair this body on the express condition that this would be an independent body and that he would brook no interference from the parent body—the NBA—a condition which the NBA has always honoured. The NBSA consists of four representatives from among media editors and an equal number of independent members of eminence, besides the chairman. I was an independent member for nearly seven years and can vouch for the total non-interference on the part of the parent body, despite several orders going against its members. It imposed heavy cash fines on recalcitrant channels and, more significantly, forced them to telecast a public apology at prime time, often for several days. The channels seemed more scared of this humiliation than of the cash fines.

There was only one occasion when, upset with a series of hostile orders, the fuming association came calling. It took just five minutes of tough- speak from us for them to back off.

The NBA is a private association of news broadcasters (twenty-five in number, comprising sixty-five news and current affairs channels, when I left in 2019); its objectives were to 'foster high standards, ethics and practices in news broadcasting' and take action against defaulters.

In the first ten years, the NBSA has considered and dealt with 2,669 complaints and issued seventy-four judgments/orders. Its role has already been acknowledged by the MIB and the Election Commission, which, by the way, has been referring complaints to them. However, I must admit we often felt exasperated that despite our best efforts we could not discipline some of the channels spewing venom day in and day out.

The NBSA did suffer from some serious shortcomings. First, its writ extended only to its members, which was limited because NBSA membership was voluntary. Those who were unhappy with a verdict found it easy to walk out. I always thought the government should step in to provide this unique model with statutory backing, extending the jurisdiction of the regulatory body to non-members too, besides empowering it to take punitive action, like suspension and cancellation of licences.

Here, the UK offers a good example in the form of OfCom (Office of Communications)—the government-approved regulatory and competition authority for the broadcasting, telecommunications and postal industries. Like the NBA, OfCom is support by fees from the industry itself. However, unlike the NBA—and this is what makes a substantial difference—it is created by an act of parliament. This implies that OfCom is given authority by the British parliament, is answerable to it and has been given legitimacy. Not long ago, in February 2020, the UK government announced that it intended Ofcom to have a greater role in internet regulation to protect users from 'harmful and illegal' content.

The government has pointed out to the Supreme Court the disastrous role social media is playing in tearing apart the social fabric of the nation and the need to tackle it before it does television. This seems to be a red herring to divert the attention of the Supreme Court. I do not think it is an either-or situation. Both forms of media are destroying social harmony in the country, often in tandem. Both need to be dealt with decisively and urgently.

To both preserve the independence of the media, whose role in a democracy is indispensable, as well as to regulate it, there are several possible indigenous models. One model is to empower the NBSA with statutory backing and more stringent powers, and to extend its writ to all news channels. The other model could be a Supreme Court-appointed monitoring panel—like the one it set up in 1998 to monitor encroachments in Delhi, which worked very effectively till the members became too old and the court appeared to have just forgot about them after appointing them. The Press Council model is an equal failure, spineless and toothless, despite a retired Supreme Judge heading it. The fourth model is like the Election Commission—a constitutionally-appointed body which was empowered by the Supreme Court in 2002 as a regulator to enforce the Model Code of Conduct evolved by the political parties voluntarily for self-discipline.

Whichever model it chooses, the Supreme Court must not fall prey to the diversionary tactics of vested interests. It should also see this case as an opportunity to change the image of inaction and insensitivity it has unfortunately acquired during the last couple of years.

Lordships, you are the country's last hope. You can be the country's saviours. Please do not put the issue on the back-burner while the country is afire.

3

Undermining Polls

EVERY ELECTION SEASON, WE FIND TELEVISION CHANNELS FLOODED with opinion polls. Critics have often questioned their authenticity. All the political parties too have opposed these polls and have demanded for their ban—except when they are shown as winning. The media, on the other hand, invariably opposes the idea of banning opinion polls as seat forecasts attract prime-time viewership.

In most democracies, opinion and exit polls are common during elections. However, restrictions have been imposed on them in many countries, and they may not be conducted for a certain period—varying from as little as two days to as many as twenty-one days—before the actual polls. Canada, France, Italy, Poland, Turkey, Argentina, Brazil and Colombia, to name a few examples, have such restrictions in place. The opposition to the ban in India is mainly on the ground that freedom of speech and expression is granted by the Constitution (Article 19). What is conveniently forgotten is that this freedom is not absolute and that the same Article allows for 'reasonable restrictions' on it. The Indian Penal Code and the Representation of the People Act, 1951, do contain certain restrictions too in this respect.

While the Constitution allows for reasonable restrictions on freedom of expression, its mandate to the ECI for free and fair elections is absolute. The Supreme Court, in a series of judgments, has emphasized this requirement: 'Democracy cannot survive without free and fair elections' (*Union of India vs. ADR,* 2003); 'Free and fair elections is the basic structure of the Constitution' (*PUCL vs. Union of India,* 2003; NOTA judgment, 2013); 'The heart of the parliamentary system is free and fair elections' (*Mohinder Singh Gill vs. CEC of India,* 1977).

Why does the ECI feel that opinion polls interfere with free and fair elections? Having seen 'paid news' in action, it is apprehensive about some opinion polls being sponsored, motivated and biased. Also, almost all such polls are non-transparent, providing little information on the methodology they use. With such infirmities, many 'polls' amount to disinformation that can result in 'undue influence', which is an 'electoral offence' under IPC Section 171 (C). Spreading of disinformation is a 'corrupt practice' under Section 123 (2) of the RPA.

The demand for a ban on opinion polls is not new. At two all-party meetings called by the Election Commission in 1997 and 2004, there was unanimous demand for a ban on them. The difference of opinion was only as to whether the ban should apply from the date of announcement of the poll schedule or the date of notification of the schedule. In 1998, the ECI issued guidelines for this, which were challenged in the Supreme Court. A five-judge Constitution Bench asked the ECI how it would enforce these decisions in the absence of a law. Realizing its weakness in this regard, the ECI withdrew the guidelines until such time as a law could be made. Unfortunately, this left the constitutionality of the issue undecided.

The matter resurfaced in 2008, when many political parties came to the ECI demanding the banning of opinion and exit polls. The ECI advised them to raise the matter in parliament, as it required legislative amendment. The ECI even vetted a draft of the proposed amendment. Surprisingly, parliament banned exit polls but not opinion polls (126A, RPA). It is not clear why the parties, which were unanimous in demanding a ban on both opinion and exit polls, did not ban such polls in parliament in their entirety.

In 2013, the debate on banning opinion polls was revived when the law ministry advised the ECI to once again seek the views of all the political parties. Fifteen political parties responded, and all but one (BJP) supported a ban. It was interesting to watch the debate on the subject in the media. All the participants—media, pollsters and jurists—were heard supporting opinion polls, yet admitting to the presence of serious flaws in them.

The ECI and the political parties are not alone in doubting the integrity of opinion polls. The Press Council of India says:

> This has become necessary to emphasise today, since the print media is sought to be exploited by interested individuals or groups to misguide and mislead the unwary voters by subtle and not so subtle propaganda on casteist, religious and ethnic basis as well as by the use of sophisticated means like the alleged poll surveys …

In early 2014, a sting operation by a television news channel caused quite a stir. As many as eleven polling companies were caught red-handed fraudulently manipulating surveys. These polling agencies were willing to manipulate the margin of error, the victory margins of candidates, the seat projections for a party, or hide negative findings about a party. Unfortunately, this exposé did not receive the attention it deserved.

What is the way forward? Ideally, an independent regulator, like the British Polling Council, would be a viable option. All agencies doing such polls must disclose the sponsor of the polls for scrutiny, besides the sample size, methodology, time frame, quality of training of research staff, etc. India could set up its own professional body on the same lines. After the Bihar 2015 election, six leading agencies had spoken about the possibility of starting a self-regulatory body, to be called the Indian Polling Council. Six years later, there has been no progress.

A related issue is exit polls, which were banned by an amendment to the RPA in 2008, making both conduct of the polls and dissemination of their results illegal. However, the media has regularly flouted the law by 'conducting' exit polls on poll days, though airing the results only after the closure of polls on the last day.

Surprisingly, the ECI continues to overlook this violation. In fact, an ECI order allows dissemination of exit poll results half an hour after the end of polling on the last poll day. It makes no mention of the ban on conduct of the poll itself, which is expressly prohibited by the law. Thus, ECI's guidelines stand opposed to the provision of the law. This is creating confusion.

4

Myths and Realities of TV Media

WITH THE EXPONENTIAL INCREASE IN TELEVISION VIEWERSHIP during the ten years between 2004 and 2014, election coverage in the country is now on a quantitatively different scale as compared to the early 1990s, when only a few periodicals would publish findings from election surveys. Today, most news channels telecast multiple rounds of opinion polls, even for assembly elections.

Many political scientists, activists and even a few journalists have voiced their concern about these polls. All the political parties have opposed these polls and even demanded a ban on them—except, of course, when they are shown as winning! The media, on the other hand, invariably opposes the idea of a ban, as seat forecasts and pre-poll surveys continue to attract prime-time viewership. The ECI invariably finds itself in the middle of the debate, between these two contrasting positions.

Opinion polls by themselves, like all research, are an extremely useful exercise, especially when conducted by social scientists and policymakers to gather insights into what people think about policies and programmes and their expectations from the state. Research is an essential marketing tool to learn about consumer needs, preferences, their knowledge, attitudes and practices. Marketing companies spend crores to understand consumers' minds so that they can position their products and brands for wider acceptance. Election-related polls, on the other hand, have only one objective—to provide information about who is likely to win in an election. In most cases, there is no other concern, academic or otherwise.

The ECI opposes the conduct and telecast of opinion polls because, in part, it strongly suspects their integrity. Having dealt first-hand with the ugly reality of 'paid news', it is aware that a dubious poll can spread massive misinformation among voters. This, in the ECI's view, potentially ends up affecting the choice of many voters, especially those who carry bandwagon tendencies or are likely to vote strategically. The prime responsibility of the ECI is to conduct free and fair elections, and for that it should be able to restrict any activity that could potentially hinder the fairness of the election process.

Before taking the discussion forward, let us look at how public opinion came to be recognized as a force. The importance of public opinion has been commented upon by a variety of writers and thinkers over the last five centuries. William Shakespeare called public opinion the 'mistress of success', and Blaise Pascal, a French mathematician and thinker of the seventeenth century, thought it was 'the queen of the world'. John Locke in his treatise, 'An Essay Concerning Human Understanding', said man was subject to three laws: divine law, civil law and, most importantly, law of opinion or reputation. Public opinion acquired tremendous political importance in the nineteenth century with improving literacy and increasing circulation of mass media. Governments also recognized the importance of managing and directing public opinion.

As public opinion plays an important role in the political sphere, particularly in voting behaviour, special-interest groups often sought to impact election outcomes. German social theorist Jürgen Habermas observed that opinion, in Western democracies, is highly susceptible to manipulation by the elite. And the media are an important player in this. The formation of public opinion starts with 'agenda setting' and 'framing'. Agenda setting dictates what is newsworthy and how and when a news item will be reported. Framing is when a story or piece of news is portrayed in a particular way and is meant to sway the consumers' attitude one way or the other. In recent years, mass media utilize a wide variety of advertising techniques to get their message out and influence public opinion.

There are good reasons to believe that attempts at similar manipulation of public information also occurs in India. For example, in the case of election forecasting, a channel may conduct a study merely to build a positive or negative perception about a political party. It may hide important findings or alter them to suit a particular party's political interests. To prevent this, it may be better to introduce a ban on exit polls and pre-poll surveys close to elections.

In most democracies, opinion and exit polls are common at the time of elections. However, restrictions are also imposed on many of them, and they may not be conducted for a certain period of time—varying from two days to twenty-one days, depending on the country. Canada, France, Italy, Poland, Turkey, Argentina, Brazil, Colombia, to name a few, have these restrictions. The opposition in India to banning these polls is mainly on the ground that freedom of speech and expression is granted by the Constitution of India (Article 19). What is conveniently forgotten is that this freedom is not absolute, and a subsequent section of the same Article allows for 'reasonable restrictions'. The Indian Penal Code, and even the Representation of the People Act, 1951, do not allow for absolute freedom and impose certain restrictions on citizens.2 Exit polls were banned in 2008 by an amendment to the RPA, and this has not been challenged in court.

While the Constitution allows for reasonable restrictions on freedom of expression, the mandate of the ECI to ensure free and fair election is absolute. There can be no compromise or dilution of this mandate. The Supreme Court, in a series of judgments, has emphasized this requirement: 'Democracy cannot survive without free and fair elections' (*Union of India vs. ADR, 2003*); 'Free and fair elections is the basic structure of the Constitution' (*PUCL vs. Union of India, 2003; NOTA judgment*); 'The heart of the parliamentary system is free and fair elections' (*Mohinder Singh Gill vs. CEC of India, 1977*). No one can argue that free and fair elections must be subjected to some restrictions. It is a non-negotiable requirement. Every election has to be completely free and fair.

Why does the ECI feel that opinion and exit polls will interfere with free and fair elections? Having seen 'paid news' in action, it realizes that some opinion polls may be sponsored, motivated and biased. Also, almost all these polls are non-transparent, providing limited information on the methodology they use. With such infirmities, many 'polls' amount to disinformation designed to cause 'undue influence', which is an 'electoral offence' under the Indian Penal Code and a 'corrupt practice' under Section 123 of the RPA. Thus, the ECI is responsible for ensuring that no survey agency is allowed to release such important information without due checks.

The demand for a ban on opinion polls is not new and has to be understood in perspective. There was unanimous agreement on this at two all-party meetings called by the Election Commission in 1997 and 2004. The difference of opinion was only as to whether the ban should apply from the announcement of the poll schedule or from the date of notification of polls. In 1998, the ECI issued guidelines, which were challenged in the Supreme Court. A five-judge Constitution bench asked the ECI how it would enforce a ban on opinion polls in the absence of a law to that effect. Realizing this, the ECI withdrew its guidelines, which were to be kept in abeyance until such time as a law was made. Unfortunately, this left the constitutionality issue of the matter undecided.

This finally went to parliament in 2008, which banned exit polls but not opinion polls (126A, RPA). Soon thereafter, the political parties came back to the ECI once again complaining about opinion polls! It is not clear why the parties, which were unanimous in demanding a ban on both opinion and exit polls, did not pass a decision to this effect in parliament, confining the ban only to the conduct and dissemination of exit polls.

Incidentally, despite a clear ban on exit polls, the media have regularly flouted the law by conducting exit polls on poll days, though they air the results only after the closure of polls on the last day. They conveniently forget that not just dissemination of results, but even conducting exit polls is illegal. This vitiates the fairness of the actual poll. Political parties, to swing opinion in their favour, systematically leak findings from exit polls in a phased election. It is surprising that the ECI has turned a blind eye to this violation. In fact, the ECI order imposing the ban allows dissemination of exit poll results only half an hour after the end of polling on the last poll day. It makes no mention of the ban on the conduct of the poll, which is expressly prohibited by the law itself. Nevertheless, the ECI has been able to control the problem of surveys being published in the middle of multi-phase elections and thus influencing voters.

In 2013, the debate on the banning of opinion polls resumed as the law ministry advised the ECI to once again seek the view of all political parties. Fifteen political parties responded, and all but one, the BJP, supported the banning of opinion polls. Contending that a ban could be a potential violation of freedom of expression, enshrined under Article 19 of the Constitution, parties like the Congress, AIADMK and TMC expressed their disapproval of the lack of transparency and dubious methodology used by most of the pollsters conducting the opinion polls.

It was interesting to watch the debate on the subject in the media. All the participants—media, pollsters and jurists—were heard supporting opinion polls, yet admitting to the presence of serious flaws in them. They referred to the rogue pollsters as 'unprofessional' and 'not serious types'; others remarked that psephology is 'no exact science', and that 'after all, researchers are human'. One participant even went on to say that the rogue polls were meant to only influence the morale of the party workers. No one gave an unqualified certificate to the opinion polls. The bottom line of the pollsters and media using them was: 'my poll was right, all others' were dubious'. Obviously, the ECI was concerned about the dubious ones.

The arguments of the jurists in the television debates were also noteworthy. 'By what law can the ECI take action?' 'Defy the order,' one of them exhorted. Well, the ECI was certainly not ordering anything against the law. It had only suggested to the government to make a law. 'The citizens have freedom of expression,' said another pre-eminent jurist. Yes, the Constitution does grant freedom of expression, but does it grant freedom to spread disinformation or to cheat? The Supreme Court, in the *M.S. Gill and Anr vs. Union Territory, 2013*, has remarked: 'One-sided information, disinformation, misinformation and non-information all create an uninformed citizenry, which make democracy a farce.'

An interesting part of the debate was the refrain, 'The opinion polls do not make any *significant* difference to voters' choice.' Now, what is a 'significant' difference? Even a *single* voter, cheated into believing that X is winning and thus falling in line to vote for X (because of the bandwagon effect) is bad enough. I would like to remind the readers of the case of the Congress leader, C.P. Joshi, who lost the Rajasthan assembly election in 2008 by a single vote! It was widely believed that he would have become the chief minister if he had not lost his own seat. Multiple single-vote victory margins and two tied verdicts, eventually decided by a draw of lots, should suffice for those who talk about 'significant difference'! It is the prime objective of the Election Commission to ensure that each voter is able to exercise choice without any fear of a social backlash.

One might ask, if opinion polls make no 'significant' difference to public opinion, why do them at all? What purpose do they serve, except to provide some entertainment on the media? But opposition to opinion polls goes much further than this dim view about the significance or usefulness of opinion polls. Many people, as well as political parties and the Election Commission find the integrity of opinion polls questionable. The Press Council of India, a statutory media regulatory body with a predominance of media owners, says:

This has become necessary to emphasize today, since the print media is sought to be exploited by interested individuals or groups to misguide and mislead the unwary voters by subtle and not so subtle propaganda on casteist, religious and ethnic basis as well as by the use of sophisticated means like the alleged poll surveys.

Also, though it may appear paradoxical in this context, the ECI is one of the biggest proponents of freedom of expression. The entire election exercise is about free expression. A vote is the expression of opinion given by a citizen in a totally free and fair manner. Anything that interferes with freedom of expression has to be put down with a heavy hand. Even the Supreme Court has emphasized the right to vote, or to not vote, as a part of freedom of expression (NOTA judgment). Similarly, its order that candidates must submit affidavits listing their financial details and declaring all the criminal cases pending against them was meant to enable voters to exercise their freedom to elect their representatives as an informed choice.

Criticism of public broadcast of election forecasts should not be misconstrued as criticism of survey research. The ECI itself conducts mass surveys for improving its SVEEP (systematic voters' education and electoral participation) programme and for evaluating the performance of its voter-awareness initiatives. All state assembly and national elections since 2010 have been preceded by KABP (knowledge, attitude, behaviour and practice) surveys to understand what dissuades electors from voting, why many do not seek to register themselves on the electoral rolls, etc. The insights gained have helped the ECI develop strategies for voter education and facilitation. Unlike opinion polls for election forecasting, our surveys are essentially driven by a positive agenda of gaining insights for our voter education campaigns.

In early 2014, a sting operation by a television news channel, News Express, caused quite a stir. As many as eleven polling companies were caught red-handed fraudulently manipulating the findings of their opinion poll surveys. It was pathetic to see their owners and executives trying to impress potential (decoy) clients with their ingenious modus operandi. It is good that two news channels,

Times Now and Headlines Today, suspended their contracts with the agencies to establish that they were not party to the malpractice, but their victims. These polling agencies were willing to manipulate the margin of error, the victory margin of candidates, seat projections for a party or hide negative findings. A few agencies even offered to field dummy candidates to improve the prospects of victory for their clients.

This shocking, but not surprising, exposé was a watershed moment, spurring political parties to demand the banning of opinion polls before elections. Most media outlets, both TV and print, immediately protested this demand, calling it a violation of freedom of expression by quoting Article 19 ad nauseum. The perspective was totally lost.

Interestingly, these worthies forgot all about the sting operation itself. Not a word was uttered about the fraud that had been going on in the name of opinion polls. There was no comment on the modus operandi that the fraud perpetrators revealed or on its magnitude and consequences, forget talk on strategies to prevent it in the future.

What, then, is the way forward? Opinion polls would be fine only if their integrity was beyond doubt. What can be done to ensure that? Ideally, an independent regulator would be a viable option. The regulator would establish standards of professional integrity and accreditation of the polling agencies. All polling agencies that wish to conduct surveys must make their operational details—like sample size, methodology, time frame, quality of training of research staff—available for scrutiny. Earlier, one of the country's foremost psephologists had criticized the polling industry in India for not following the highest standards of professional and rigorous polling, and for their lack of transparency in not revealing their methodological details.

A model for professional and ethical rules that market researchers should follow already exists with the European Society for Opinion and Market Research (ESOMAR), a membership organization representing the interests of the market research profession at an international level. More than 4,900 members and sixty national market research associations worldwide have adopted its rules.

In collaboration with the International Chamber of Commerce, ESOMAR established the ICC/ESOMAR International Code on Market and Social Research. All individual members agree to abide by these standards while conducting market research. The Code has also been adopted or endorsed by more than sixty-five national associations worldwide.

Another international professional association of researchers in the fields of communication and survey research is the World Association for Public Opinion Research (WAPOR). Established in 1947 as the World Congress on Public Opinion Research, it became the sole non-government consultant organization to UNESCO in the field of polling. Over time, WAPOR's membership has grown and become more international. By 2012, the association had over 600 members from research institutes and universities in over sixty countries on six continents.

The ESOMAR and WAPOR Guidelines on Opinion Polls and Published Surveys set out the responsibilities of researchers for conducting opinion polls in a professional and ethical way. These guidelines highlight the information that researchers and those publishing survey data must make available to enable the public and other stakeholders to evaluate the results. It provides guidance on different types of opinion polls, including exit polls and online polls.

India could easily join these organizations or set up its own professional body on the same lines. This is one reform that needs to be considered without further delay. After the Bihar 2015 election, when some of the pollsters faced flak for wrongly predicting an NDA victory, six leading agencies had spoken about the possibility of starting a self-regulatory body—to be named the Indian Polling Council.5 More than six months and one election cycle has passed since, but there seems to be no progress on this front. One wonders whether this could be attributed to the absence of seriousness among the stakeholders about increasing transparency and improving the quality of election-related polling.

1

Demonetization and the Long-Pending Reforms

THE DEMONETIZATION OF CURRENCY NOTES OF DENOMINATIONS OF ₹1,000 and ₹500 (in 2016) rattled the nation. Experts are divided on whether this government decision will curb corruption in the country. The actual impact will be seen after some time.

Meanwhile, I have been flooded with questions about the impact of this drastic step on elections, particularly in view of the impending polls in five states—Uttar Pradesh, Punjab, Uttarakhand, Puducherry and Goa.

An electoral democracy cannot function without political financing. It costs to reach out to voters and funds must be raised to meet this expenditure. To ensure a level playing field for the contestants, the law prescribes a ceiling on expenditure, to be fixed periodically. The objective is to limit the 'pernicious influence' of big money in controlling the democratic process. But violations have been rampant, which made the redoubtable Justice J.S. Verma to comment that the prescription of a ceiling on expenditure by an electoral candidate is a mere eyewash.

Over the years, the role of money power in elections has gone from bad to worse. All political parties have been expressing concern, verbally, without taking any action on the reforms proposed by the Election Commission of India. Instead, political parties and candidates have devised ingenious ways of distributing cash and liquor.

The ECI has been deeply concerned about the use of money to bribe voters ahead of polls. In my inaugural press conference on taking over as the chief election commissioner (CEC), I had given myself two challenges—curbing abuse of money and dealing with voter apathy. Two new divisions were created to address these issues seriously. Both met with tremendous success—one achieving the highest-ever voter turnouts ever since, and the other unearthing crores of rupees and goods, including liquor. Our proactive steps led to some landmark achievements, including the unseating and disqualification of a sitting MLA in UP and the countermanding of two Rajya Sabha elections in Jharkhand.

This year, in an unprecedented step, the ECI was forced to cancel elections to two Tamil Nadu assembly seats, Aravakurichi and Thanjavur, for the uncontrolled use of money. The poll panel then wrote to the government seeking permanent legal powers to countermand polls on credible evidence of the use of black money.

That we are notorious for cash-for-votes being a regular feature in our elections was conveyed by US diplomatic cables, and was leaked by WikiLeaks. A cable quoted a confidant of a union minister from Tamil Nadu distributing up to ₹5,000 per voter in a by-election in 2009. After his victory, the politician announced that his formula was a sure winner. This notorious 'Thirumangalam formula' became our biggest challenge.

Unaccounted cash amounting to ₹300 crore was seized by the commission during the 2014 election. Cash seizures across all assembly elections since 2014 have been at an all-time high. Bihar, for instance, registered the highest seizure of cash (₹19 crore) during the assembly polls in 2015. In Tamil Nadu, in 2016, the figure crossed ₹100 crore.

Money power and its pernicious effects on electoral outcomes universally affect all countries, not just India. Several conferences in the last few of years have sought to address the issue. A conference of SAARC countries on 'Regulating Campaign Finance: Ensuring Free and Fair Elections' was organized by the Forum of Election Management Bodies of South Asia (FEMBoSA) in November 2014, at Kathmandu in Nepal.

The culmination of these deliberations was a regional conference held jointly by the international IDEA and ECI in New Delhi in December 2015. 'The Money in Politics and its effects on Peoples' Representations' was the theme. Based on the collective wisdom and shared experience of the participants, the conference unanimously adopted a resolution christened 'New Delhi Declaration on Political Finance Regulation', laying down nine 'overarching principles' and an equal number of implementation guidelines.

Ever since the ECI started coming down hard on black money in polls, candidates and parties have started distributing money early, much before the ECI enforces the MCC.

The demonetization has come at the right time, just ahead of five state elections. Parties and candidates who were ready with their bonanza for distribution will not know what to do with that money now. Even fake money from across the borders will be hit. However, politicians are ingenious. In my book *An Undocumented Wonder: The Making of the Great Indian Election*, I had documented forty methods of illegal distribution of funds political parties use to seduce voters. Many more have been invented since.

My fear is that a money-laundering industry will mushroom with the complicity of bank officials. The government must watch out for the omnipresent touts and colluding bank officials. This advice is based on our experience. Once during the Uttar Pradesh Elections in April 2012, our IT vigilance team intercepted a vehicle carrying over ₹2 crore. We were told that the money was for refilling an ATM. So we let it off with an apology. The next day, another of our teams caught a vehicle with double the amount, and a third vehicle carrying ₹11 crore was apprehended. In both these cases, the explanation was the same as earlier. We investigated and found that the vans were not accompanied by an armed guard and did not follow other security protocols. I immediately spoke to RBI governor D. Subbarao, who was shocked to hear of this mode of money laundering.

Money in elections is the mother of all corruption. The more politicians spend, the more they will need to collect it back by all means, fair or foul. As much as 80 per cent of political funds (in hundreds of crores) comes from undisclosed sources. This opacity is not acceptable. I hope the time for long-pending electoral reforms has finally come.

2

The Consequences on Electoral Systems

THE DEMONETIZATION OF ₹1,000- AND ₹500-DENOMINATION NOTES has triggered an unprecedented debate on black money and corruption in the political arena. It is good that, at last, a long-avoided subject is becoming the focus of serious attention. It is important to understand why the matter is of great essence and consequence.

Systemic Corruption

Rampant abuse of money power in elections is the mother of all corruption in the country. When candidates and political parties spend crores of rupees on election campaigns, they have to generate enough funds by hook or by crook when they come to power. The 'collection drive' that follows inevitably leads to a politician-bureaucracy nexus.

When the two most important instruments of governance join hands in this unholy alliance, corruption spreads in all directions, horizontally and vertically, and seeps into every sphere of life. The lowest functionaries, like a constable or a patwari, confronted while in the act of taking bribes, have a stock answer: '*Ooper tak dena hai*' (we have to pay up to the top). Who is the highest 'ooper wala' is not spelt out, but refers to the minister or higher.

State funding of polls

It is not that political leaders have not expressed concern about how polls are funded. However, in the absence of serious discussion among them on this topic, it seems their concern is mere lip service. The problem has been discussed in parliamentary debates, and committees have been constituted, but the only refrain we hear is that there should be state funding of elections.

The most famous of the committees was the one set up in 1999, headed by Indrajit Gupta. It consisted of many political stalwarts, like Dr Manmohan Singh. The committee recommended only partial state funding of elections, and even that was conditional upon parties establishing genuine inner-party democracy—which no party likes.

The 255th report of the Law Commission of India (March 2015) also brought into focus the urgent need for the overdue electoral reforms.

Transparency in donations

It is a fact that a democracy cannot function without politicians having the funds to contest elections. However, money cannot be allowed to dominate the process to such an extent that only the rich can contest and hijack the political system.

The law, therefore, prescribes a ceiling on expenditure for electoral candidates—though, strangely, not for political parties. The absence of a ceiling on electoral expenditure for political parties negates the whole logic of any ceiling on electoral expenditure and creates conditions for financial indiscipline. To outdo their rivals, all parties spend thousands of crores of rupees. In the 2014 general election, the amount spent on campaigns was estimated at a staggering ₹30,000 crore.

Where does this money come from? The sources could be corporate funds, small donations, sale of coupons and membership fees, besides earnings from interest on deposits, and rental and revenue income. There is no transparency as to the source of most donations made to political parties or their candidates. As much as 75–80 per cent of these funds are shown as cash donations, and their source is not disclosed. This is a serious matter. It may consist of foreign money or money donated by the crime, drug or real estate mafia.

Parties ignore ECI demands

The Election Commission has been demanding for over twenty years that there should be complete transparency when it comes to the source of funds obtained by political parties and their expenditure. It wants a law prescribing an annual audit of political parties by an independent auditor from a panel provided by the ECI, instead of by an in-house auditor who only does a job of whitewashing. The audited accounts must be put up on the website of every party for all to see.

In 2013, the Aam Aadmi Party, by suo motu deciding to put all its fund receipts on its website, had created a healthy precedent worth emulating. It will be worthwhile to look at this model closely and understand its working.

Other political parties, unfortunately, have not bothered to consider the Election Commission's demands seriously. Governments have come and gone, pushing the proposal under the carpet. And it is not political parties alone who refuse to disclose their sources of income; corporate houses donating to them also prefer anonymity. A Confederation of India Industry report in 2012 had demanded that political donations be kept secret. The confederation reasoned that if the competing parties get to know what they have given to their rivals, they would either be flooded with similar requests or face vindictiveness. The real reason, however, is that neither the political parties nor the corporates would like their quid pro quo arrangements to be exposed.

Election trust fund

Unfortunately, the image of the political class in India is abysmal, which is very unfortunate for democracy. Not all politicians are corrupt. India has become a major power in the world, thanks to its many great statesmen and political leaders.

In both public and political discourse, state funding of elections has often been mentioned as the panacea for fighting corruption. State funding would obviously be limited to the legal ceiling on such expenditure. Thus, even if entire legally permissible expenditure (₹70 lakh for Lok Sabha candidate per election and ₹28 lakh for Vidhan Sabha candidate per election) is state funded, how will it stop the illegal expenditure, which is fifty to hundred times these limits? It's not the white money but the black that we want to root out.

The best way out is to implement state funding of political parties, not state funding of elections. This is based on a study of the experience of countries worldwide.

In the general election to the Lok Sabha in 2014, nearly 55 crore votes were cast. If the state were to pay the party ₹50 for every vote obtained, this would add up to ₹2,750 crore. An equal amount can be paid to political parties based on the parties' performance in the Vidhan Sabha elections. This will make for a total liability of ₹5,500 crore over a five-year period. This will roughly correspond to the fund collection of all political parties put together. Private and corporate donations, which are at the root of the problem, can then be totally banned.

State funding will free political parties from dependence on the corporate houses, who like to run the government by proxy. The amount of state funding proposed is so small that it can easily be accommodated in the national budget. But, if necessary, an 'election trust fund' could be created, to which corporates may be asked to make transparent donations. The fund could be administered by an independent trust or by the Election Commission. Allocation of funds will be based on the actual performance of political parties in an election. The operational details can easily be worked out if the proposal is approved in principle.

Independent auditor

The accounts of the political parties will then have to be audited by an independent auditor from an Election Commission–approved panel or by the CAG itself. A study, 'Political Finance Regulations Around the World', by the International Institute of Democracy and Electoral Assistance (IDEA), Stockholm (2012), showed that this system is working well in over seventy countries of the world, including most countries of Europe. There is no reason why it will not work in India.

The NDA government has an adequate mandate and a powerful leadership that can make it happen. The current situation may be a godsend. We should not let it slip.

1

Why India Needs to Change Its Electoral Voting System

THE BEST ELECTORAL SYSTEM IS THE ONE THAT STRAIGHTFORWARDLY and most accurately reflects the preferences of voters,' the legal scholar Donald Horowitz noted in his 2003 seminal essay on electoral systems, *Electoral Systems: A Primer for Decision Makers*. But there is no definite answer as to which system fits that bill. India and the United Kingdom follow the Westminster electoral model, in which the voters elect their representatives to the Lok Sabha and the House of Commons, respectively. The voting procedure as well as the election of candidates is based on the first-past-the-post (FPTP) system—electors vote for one candidate among all those contesting the elections from one constituency. The candidate with the highest number of votes, irrespective of the margin of victory or percentage of votes polled, is declared the winner.

In recent years (since 2010), both countries have questioned the merits of the FPTP procedure. In 2011, the UK conducted a referendum on whether to retain the voting system—68 per cent voted in its favour. (However, the voter turnout for the referendum was only 41 per cent, which means a majority did not participate in the decision-making process.) In India, too, the FPTP system is under scrutiny this year. On 22 April 2017, the Parliamentary Standing Committee on Personnel, Public Grievances, Law and Justice—headed by Anand Sharma, a Congress member of parliament in the Rajya Sabha—issued a press release announcing an examination of the issue of electoral reforms and alternative voting systems. In late August, the *Indian Express* reported that the committee had sent a questionnaire on electoral reforms to all parties and to the Election Commission. According to the news report, the questionnaire stated that 'apprehensions are now being raised that in recent years the FPTP system is not the best suited' to India.

The FPTP has several advantages, because of which it is considered to be the simplest electoral system. The first advantage is clarity—it is an easy system to understand, the choices for the voters are clear, and the counting is also simple and straightforward. As soon as the votes are counted, the winner is immediately evident. The system also guarantees one representative for each constituency, who is accountable to his electorate, which is not necessarily the case in other voting systems. A third advantage is that candidates get to know their relative support in the constituency, unlike in other systems where electors vote for a party and not for individual candidates.

In a country such as India, with nearly 1 billion voters, the ease of administering voting in this system almost makes it the most viable model to follow. For a long time, I was a strong advocate of the first-past-the-post system because I believed it to be the most efficient in the Indian context. However, I felt compelled to reconsider my position after the 2014 general election, in which the Bahujan Samaj Party—which was the third-largest party in terms of the national vote share, securing 20 per cent of the votes in Uttar Pradesh and 4.2 per cent at the national level—did not get a single seat in the Lok Sabha. On the other hand, parties with lower vote shares won a considerable number of seats—for instance, despite winning only 3.9 per cent of the votes, the Trinamool Congress won thirty-four seats. The following year, a similar phenomenon occurred in the UK—the UK Independence Party obtained only one seat in the general election despite being the third-largest party in terms of vote share, with nearly 13 per cent of the total votes being cast in its favour. Such results are possible in the FPTP system because a candidate is elected solely on the basis of whether she receives the highest number of votes, and not on the basis of the proportion of votes polled by her.

It is increasingly becoming clear that the first-past-the-post system of voting is fraught with serious problems. In the 2014 Lok Sabha election (according to the report by EC the same year), despite the 'Modi wave', only 37 per cent of the elected candidates, or 201 MPs, obtained a majority of the votes in their constituencies. In the 2009 elections, only 22 percent, or 120 MLAs, had secured a majority of the votes. At the legislative assembly level, across all states, an average of 44.5 percent of the MLAs secured more than 50 percent of the vote share in their constituencies.

These instances reflect the main shortcoming of the FPTP system—the lack of legitimacy of political parties that are voted to a majority of the seats by a minority of the voters. In India's electoral history, the Congress party's P.K. Khanna recorded the victory with the lowest-ever vote share in 1967, getting elected to the Shahjahanpur constituency in Uttar Pradesh with just 15.6 per cent of the vote. Even in the Congress wave in the 1984 general election after the assassination of Indira Gandhi, the party could not get a majority of the votes, despite winning a historic 404 of 533 seats, or 75 percent of the seats, in the Lok Sabha. The party only received 49.1 per cent of the vote. In such a scenario, the will of the actual majority of voters is substituted by the will of a minority of voters.

Another consequence of the winner-takes-all nature of the FPTP system is that it rewards parties which target and treat preferentially specific segments of the electorate, or 'vote banks', rather than the majority of electors. The system thus rewards divisive electoral strategies and encourages parties to field tainted candidates.

One way to address these concerns regarding this voting system would be to hold a run-off election—a second round of elections between the two candidates with the highest number of votes, which is followed in the French presidential elections. However, it is not feasible to conduct two rounds of voting in India, owing to the magnitude and complexity of the exercise required. Imagine going back to militancy-affected areas for a second time within a month; one election itself in these areas is subject to grave risk to lives—of the voters, polling staff and security forces.

In order to overcome the shortcomings of the first-past-the-post system, some critics advocate the proportional representation (PR) system of voting. In the PR system, every party gets a share of seats proportional to the share of votes it secures.

The PR system has many variants, such as the open-list and closed-list systems. In these, each voter is invited to indicate a preference or a ranking of several candidates from a list submitted by every party. Then, after the polls, each party is granted seats in proportion to the number of votes it receives. The candidates within each party's list are then elected in accordance with the percentage of votes polled by the party. For instance, if a party obtains a 15 per cent vote share and elections are being conducted for 200 seats, the top 30 candidates—or 15 per cent of the total number of seats—will be elected. As a result, the constituencies under the list system are multi-member—multiple candidates will be elected from one constituency, with the number of seats per constituency allotted according to the demography or other physical characteristics of the constituency. However, the system requires all candidates to be nominated by a political party and does not allow for independent candidates.

In the open-list variant of the system, voters can choose to not only vote for a party but also to rank candidates within that party's declared list of candidates. In the closed-list variant, voters opt for the party as a whole rather than vote for specific candidates.

However, the proportional-representation voting system presents some issues too. The system might make it difficult for parties to form the government, because the party with the maximum number of votes rarely obtains more than 30–35 per cent of the vote share. As a result, the dominant party would likely have to form a coalition with other large parties. In Indian politics, even under the current system, this has been necessary for the last twenty-five years.

Another concern is that under the list system, the parties determine which candidates are elected by placing them at the top of their lists. The system thus guarantees that influential party members get easily elected. In such a system, candidates would perhaps focus on wooing their party leaders instead of the voters. This could also reinforce various forms of capture of election tickets by the elite. At the whims of the party leadership, tickets could be issued to family members or to particular party leaders, or to candidates on the basis of their caste, linguistic or religious community.

Owing to the underlying problems in both the FPTP and the PR systems of voting, a mixed model that combines the advantages of both is worth consideration. Different variants of the mixed method are followed in several countries, including Germany and Nepal. While these mixed models, too, may present problems of implementation in the Indian political and geographical context, variations of these mixed voting systems may be the most suitable alternatives to the FPTP system for India.

In 1949, Germany adopted one such a method, known as the mixed-member proportional system of voting. Its parliament has 299 constituencies and 598 seats. On polling day, every voter casts two votes—one for a candidate in his or her constituency and the other for a party. Candidate wins are determined by the FPTP system; 299 seats are thus filled by the voters directly electing candidates, who have won the largest number of votes in their constituencies. The aim of the first vote is to enable voters to personally know their representative. The second vote allows the elector to vote for a party. It is this vote that determines the power of parties in the parliament. Based on this, the remaining 299 seats in the parliament are filled by parties in proportion to the votes secured by them in the second round of votes. This is how the 598 representatives of the Bundestag—the lower house of the German parliament, are determined. For instance, if a party wins twenty seats under the FPTP system and gets a 10 per cent vote share in the second round of voting, it is given 40 seats from the remaining 299—ensuring that it has 60 seats, or 10 per cent, of the total of 598 seats.

The German model, which accommodates both directly elected candidates to constituencies and parliamentary representation for political parties based on their vote share, also has its disadvantages. The chief among these is that any party that does not win either a 5 per cent vote share or three of 299 FPTP seats does not enter parliament. As a result, the choice of voters who voted for such candidates or parties is completely ignored.

Adopting this system in India would require either halving the number of constituencies or doubling the size of the Lok Sabha. The former is not feasible in India's political context, given that the ratio of constituencies to voters in India is already vastly disproportionate to that of other countries. For instance, the House of Commons comprises 650 MPs, and the Lok Sabha 543—a British MP represents an average of 72,000 electors, whereas an Indian MP represents 15 lakh. Halving the constituencies would imply that one elected candidate would represent 30 lakh electors, which would further limit voter accessibility to the MP and accountability between the MP and her constituency.

In India, increasing the strength of the Lok Sabha has been proposed in the past. Former President Pranab Mukherjee raised the issue at a seminar on economic reforms and electoral issues in April 2017, and various parliamentarians have previously suggested increasing the strength of the Lok Sabha by 181 seats—or one-third of its current strength—to introduce reservation for women in the house. In fact, a great advantage of this system is the opportunity it provides to introduce reservation for women in parliament, by reserving a quota for women on the list of candidates to be elected by the proportional representation system. My conversations with members of multiple political parties have indicated that their opposition to reservation of seats for women is largely due to their unwillingness to give up their existing Lok Sabha seats. The issue has seen no political will or traction—I am personally aware that the reasons for this include roadblocks by parliamentarians citing issues such as lack of seating space in the Lok Sabha.

A mixed system is also being adopted in Nepal—the model, which will be implemented in the upcoming election in November and December 2017, is known as the parallel system. Unlike the mixed-member proportional (MMP) system, the parallel system sees voters effectively participate in two separate elections for a single chamber using two different systems. There are two different ballot papers, one each for the FPTP and PR voting systems, whereas in Germany there is one ballot paper with a separate column for each system. Of the 275 members in Nepal's House of Representatives—its counterpart to the Lok Sabha—165 are elected through the FPTP system and 110 through the PR system. But, unlike the MMP system, the proportion of seats allotted under the PR system is a ratio of the number reserved for the PR system, 110 in this case, and a proportion of the entire 275 seats. Therefore, the results of one election have little or no impact on the results of the other. Adopting such a model in India would once again require a change in the strength of parliament, or in the demarcation of constituencies.

A 2017 report by the International Institute for Democracy and Electoral Assistance noted that the PR system is the most popular in the world, with eighty-three countries following it. According to its website, International IDEA is an intergovernmental organization that supports sustainable democracy worldwide. The report notes that the PR system is especially popular in Europe, where thirty-four countries—nearly 67 per cent—have adopted it. The FPTP system comes second in popularity, with sixty-one countries across the world employing it. The parallel system is the third-most popular one, and is followed in twenty-one countries.

What will it take to make the largest democracy of the world also the greatest? Of the various systems, the PR system seems to offer the best possibilities—which is also why it is the most popular system in the world. However, the proportional representation systems lack a certain level of clarity—after all, an alternative system should also aim to provide a distinct choice of candidate to a voter, which is achieved under the first-past-the-post system. To accommodate for this, India could invent its own mixed model to fit its political and cultural specificities. A dose of proportional representation would avoid the complete sidelining of important political forces. It would also push parties to collaborate in coalitions and alliances, rather than enable them to convert a minority of votes into a majority of seats.

What matters most is that electoral systems ensure reflection of the will of the voters and the legitimacy of the leaders. To this end, perhaps the strength of the Lok Sabha could be doubled and the German model without its threshold considered—the logistics of seating capacity cannot be allowed to come in the way of a more democratic and efficient voting system. Or the Nepali model from closer home too could work—the elections later this year could provide an opportunity for us to observe how it works.

With the flaws in the FPTP system increasingly becoming exposed, the time to look at alternative models has come. Now that the parliamentary committee has set in motion this serious debate, one hopes that the electoral system itself will be taken up as a key reform. Moreover, considering that Prime Minister Narendra Modi has pressed electoral reforms as a priority political agenda—addressing issues such as transparency in political funding and simultaneous elections to the Lok Sabha and state legislative assembles—he should not miss this opportunity to reform the electoral system itself.

2

It is Time to Take Stock of Electoral Process

THE BIGGEST ELECTION IN THE WORLD, THE 2019 INDIAN GENERAL election, has finally come to a successful end, for which the three election commissioners and their 1.2 crore staff deserve appreciation. Unfortunately, what deserved to be remembered as a subject of national pride became mired in several controversies. At the top of the list was the unprecedented attack on the Election Commission, which was accused of being soft on the top leadership of the BJP for its repeated violations of the Model Code of Conduct (MCC).

How long, elections?

Questions were also raised about the prolonged election spread over seven phases. The Election Commission has always maintained that the most pressing concern is voter security. All the political parties demand deployment of Central armed police forces, but the forces' limited availability necessitates multi-phase elections as there are not enough forces for security deployment everywhere at the same time. If the numbers of these forces were adequate, the Election Commission could have all the voting done in a single day. After all, in staggered elections, the MCC is difficult to operationalize in this age of social media. This is a trade-off the Election Commission is fully aware of. The cost-benefit analysis of multi-phase versus short-phase elections in the face of new challenges can be done afresh.

The highlight of 2019 was the highest-ever voter turnout in a general election so far (67.11 per cent) in the country, even though there was a lower turnout than usual in many constituencies, possibly because of oppressive weather, and varied turnouts across phases. However, the overall higher voter turnout proves that the EC's voter education programme (systematic voters' education and electoral participation) is effective.

The three 'M's

In this election, the role of money power was alarming. It is becoming more and more expensive to contest elections, and the problem of black money is very much alive. Even before the first phase had started, it was evident that Indian democracy is overwhelmed by the overarching role of money, media and mafia.

The Election Commission seized crores' worth of money, liquor and drugs. As of 24 May, money, drugs/narcotics, liquor, precious metals and freebies worth an estimated ₹3,475.76 crore were seized. The corresponding figure in 2014 was ₹1,200 crore. According to ECI data, Tamil Nadu (₹952 crore), Gujarat (₹553.76 crore), Delhi (₹430.39 crore), Punjab (₹286.41 crore) and Andhra Pradesh (₹232.02 crore) were the top five states/Union Territories that accounted for the total seizures. A cause for worry is that drugs/narcotics formed a large part of the seizures as well, with Gujarat topping the list (almost ₹524.35 crore).

Code violations and counting

Personally, what was most painful was to witness the Election Commission repeatedly come under the scanner for its delayed and often perfunctory actions on violations of the MCC. Once lauded for its conduct of free and fair elections, held with precision and integrity in the world's largest democracy, this time it was criticized, both nationally and internationally.

The check conducted of the prime minister's helicopter in Odisha on 16 April should have been used by the EC to demonstrate its commitment to equality of all before the law. But it chose a different course of action.

The EC was also questioned for its stand on the sample size used for its VVPAT verification. Its line was that tallying the VVPAT paper slips with the EVM counts—one per assembly constituency—was based on a scientific methodology and endorsed by the Indian Statistical Institute. But the Opposition parties went to the Supreme Court, which advised the Election Commission to raise the mandatory random counting to five VVPATs per assembly segment, laying emphasis on 'better voter confidence and credibility of electoral process'. The court believed this would ensure the 'greatest degree of accuracy and satisfaction'. Rather than going on the defensive, the EC should have discussed this issue with political parties with an open mind.

As the election progressed, the Opposition made two more demands: The random counting must be done on five machines and, in case of even one mismatch in an assembly segment, all the machines in the segment must be checked. The EC examined these proposals, only to reject them as being unfeasible.

The top court's repeated interventions (as many as six) also have long-term implications, given that Article 329 of the Constitution bars courts from interfering in electoral matters after the election process has been set in motion. But the court had to intervene repeatedly for course correction. The Supreme Court expressed displeasure over the Election Commission's stand on 15 April, when it submitted that it was 'toothless' and 'powerless' to act on hate speeches. When the court set the Commission a deadline of 6 May to act on this, the latter took strong and unprecedented action against some political leaders, debarring them from campaigning for up to three days by invoking Article 324. This was laudable, but when it came to acting on complaints against the prime minister and the BJP president, it reacted differently, giving the two leaders 'clean chits', thus casting a shadow on its own reputation for fearless independence.

Much later, it was shown that at least one election commissioner had dissented in five out of the eleven Election Commission decisions concerning violations of the MCC during the election. In the absence of unanimity, decisions can be taken by a majority vote, and this dissenting member's views did not change the verdict. But dissent is good news for a constitutional body as it is a healthy sign of objective deliberation and democratic functioning. The member's demand for his dissenting note to be made public was worthy of positive consideration.

Course correction

The ascendant role of money power, paid and fake news, communal polarization and hate rhetoric pose a serious challenge to the very foundations of our electoral system. As soon as the dust settles, India must introspect over these issues and find answers. A democracy is only as credible as the strength of the institutions fundamental to its legitimacy. I have hope that the seventeenth Lok Sabha will take it upon itself to reform the electoral process and enable the world's largest democracy to become the world's greatest too.

3

A Time for Electoral Reform

A WIDE RANGE OF ELECTORAL REFORM PROPOSALS HAS BEEN PENDING with the government, several of them for over two decades. Successive governments have evaded them, claiming lack of consensus in the matter. The consideration of three reforms—common electoral rolls for Vidhan Sabha and panchayat elections, extension of the qualifying date for registration of new young voters, and linking of Aadhaar with electoral rolls—by the Union cabinet on 15 December is, therefore, significant. Subsequently, on Tuesday, 28 March 2017, the Rajya Sabha passed the Election Laws (Amendment) Bill, which seeks to link the electoral rolls with the Aadhaar database. The Lok Sabha had passed the bill on Monday.

Currently, separate electoral rolls are maintained for elections to the Lok Sabha, Vidhan Sabha and local government bodies (panchayats or municipal). For years, the ECI has been advocating a common electoral roll for all elections—I remember discussing this at the annual joint meeting of the ECI and State Election Commissions (SEC) in 2011, where many state election commissioners had the same opinion.

There are two types of election management bodies in the country—the ECI, which conducts the Lok Sabha and Vidhan Sabha elections; and the SECs, which conduct the panchayat and municipal elections. The SECs have the option of either adopting the electoral rolls created by the ECI or preparing such rolls on their own. Most prefer to use the rolls prepared by the ECI. Some states, however, develop their rolls independently. These are Uttar Pradesh, Uttarakhand, Madhya Pradesh, Kerala, Odisha, Assam, Arunachal Pradesh, Nagaland and the Union Territory of Jammu and Kashmir.

The process for making electoral rolls is laid down in the Registration of Electors Rules, 1960. The primary unit taken into consideration for preparation of electoral rolls is the assembly constituency. Several such constituencies are aggregated to make a Lok Sabha constituency, or broken down into municipal or panchayat wards.

Considering that the voter for all three tiers of elected bodies is the same, why is it that she finds her name missing from one of the rolls, mostly the panchayat rolls? This is particularly surprising when the officials responsible for making both these rolls are the same. A common electoral roll is thus a logical solution. A common experience has been the stuffing of bogus voters in the panchayat/municipal rolls. This perhaps happens because membership to the panchayat has become extremely lucrative since the they started getting crores as funds after the Panchayati Raj Institution (PRI) Act, 1993. Corrupt practices are proportionately higher in PRI polls.

The process of making electoral rolls requires manpower from all governmental departments. A major chunk of the work falls on school teachers. Their involvement in non-teaching work takes its toll on them. A common electoral roll will obviate the need for deploying them repeatedly, besides saving enormous costs. The only difference between the PRI and Vidhan Sabha rolls is that the former has information about the ward in which the voter lives. The enumerator (usually the booth-level officer) knows the ward number of each home. All she needs to do is to write it down in an additional column, which will be masked for the state legislature elections and unmasked for PRI elections, which are conducted ward-wise.

The ECI and SECs can issue joint instructions for preparation of the common rolls. The roll-making machinery stays the same. Since different elections are held at different times, the rolls must always be ready. And they should be made every year. Pilot studies may be conducted in random constituencies to identify the discrepancies between the two sets of rolls and the reasons for them.

The second cabinet decision was about the eligibility date for new voters. According to Section 14(b) of the RPA, 1950, only those who have turned eighteen on or before 1 January of the running year are to be registered. This implies that all those who turn eighteen between 2 January and 31 December of a year must wait till the next year. This technicality results in the exclusion of a large section of eighteen-year-olds in every election.

The ECI has been expressing concern over these issues for some time. It had sent memorandums to the government about common electoral rolls in 1999 and 2004. It had also sent a letter to the law ministry on 4 November 2013 recommending issue of voter cards to individuals on their eighteenth birthday, ideally, or updating of the voter rolls every month or quarter. The current government has begun addressing these issues, which is undoubtedly a progressive step.

On 13 August 2016, the PMO called a meeting to discuss ways to create a common electoral roll. The SECs derive their powers to supervise local body elections from Articles 243K and 243ZA of the Constitution. Amendments to these articles to make compulsory a common electoral roll for all elections in the country was discussed at the meeting. Second, all state governments would have to change their electoral laws to adopt the ECI electoral rolls for local elections. A committee of the ministry of law and justice under Sushil Kumar Modi has proposed quarterly cut-off dates for voter registration—1 January, 1 April, 1 July and 1 October.

The proposal to link electoral rolls with Aadhaar was first mooted by the ECI in 2015, but work on it had to be stopped when the Supreme Court ruled that Aadhaar cannot be used except voluntarily for beneficiary-oriented schemes. In my view, the linking will help identify 'duplicate' voters—something the ECI has been desperately attempting for years to do using various 'de-duplication' software, but with limited success. But how will this 'voluntary' linking be implemented? Will 90 crore voters have to be asked individually?

Any progress in addressing the vexed issue of electoral reform—even in a piecemeal manner—is welcome. The time has come, however, for the government to consider the forty-plus pending proposals, instead of selectively going in for politically motivated reforms like simultaneous elections and electoral bonds.

4

Main Issues and Debates on EC

ON 3 JULY 2019, A SHORT DISCUSSION IN THE RAJYA SABHA ON electoral reforms attracted my attention. It was initiated by Trinamool Congress (TMC) MP Derek O'Brien, with the backing of as many as fourteen Opposition parties. I have been extremely passionate and vocal about electoral reforms throughout my years in office as well as after, and it was heartening to see political parties across the ideological divide trying to push the subject of how to make elections freer, fairer and more representative.

The TMC MP touched on six major themes—the appointment system for selection of election commissioners and chief election commissioner (CEC); money power; electronic voting machines (EVMs); conduct of simultaneous elections; the role of social media (which O'Brien called 'cheat India platforms'); and lastly, the use of government data and surrogate advertisements to target certain sections of voters.

Appointment process

On the issue of the election commissioner appointment process, O'Brien quoted B.R. Ambedkar's statement to the Constituent

Assembly, that 'the tenure can't be made a fixed and secure tenure if there is no provision in the Constitution to prevent a fool or a naive or a person who is likely to be under the thumb of the executive'.

The demand for revisiting the issue was supported by the Communist Party of India (CPI), the Communist Party of India-Marxist (CPI-M), the Dravida Munnetra Kazhagam (DMK) and the Bahujan Samaj Party (BSP), all of whom demanded the introduction of a collegium system for the same. As regards the chronic problem of the crippling influence of money power, O'Brien cited various reports and documents—a 1962 private member's bill by Atal Bihari Vajpayee; the Goswami Committee report on electoral reforms (1990); and the Indrajit Gupta Committee report on state funding of elections (1998). Congress MP Kapil Sibal, citing an independent think tank report on poll expenditure released in June 2019, discussed at length the regressive impact of amending the Foreign Contribution (Regulation) Act (FCRA) and removing the 7.5 per cent-of-profits cap on corporate donations.

Congress MP Rajeev Gowda termed electoral bonds 'a farce' and gave a proposal for state funding (of political parties), based on either a national electoral fund or the number of votes obtained by the respective parties. He also proposed crowdfunding in the form of small donations. He said the current election expenditure cap for candidates is unrealistic and should either be raised or removed to encourage transparency.

The Biju Janata Dal (BJD) supported capping the expenditure of political parties in accordance with a 1975 judgement of the Supreme Court on Section 77 of the Representation of the People Act (RPA), 1951. The Samajwadi Party (SP) suggested that expenditure on private planes, etc., should be added to the candidates' accounts and not to those of the party. The banning of corporate donations was passionately advocated by the CPI and the CPI(M).

The old issue of returning to ballot papers was raised by several parties. A TMC member said, 'when technology doesn't guarantee perfection, you have to question technology'. On the other hand, the BJD, the Janata Dal (United) and the BJP asserted that EVMs have reduced election-related violence in states like Bihar and Uttar Pradesh. The BJD said that to strengthen public faith in the voter-verified paper audit trails, five machines should be counted right at the beginning during an election. The BSP added that postal ballots should be scanned before counting so as to increase transparency.

On simultaneous elections

Many BJP MPs highlighted issues linked to electoral fatigue, expenditure and governance, and also cited reports of the Law Commission and NITI Aayog to push for simultaneous elections.

Vinay Sahasrabuddhe of the BJP said Prime Minister Narendra Modi's proposal should be seen with an open mind and made a suggestion that it should be understood as a call for a minimum-duration cycle of elections, rather than as a call for 'one nation one election'.

But the TMC said the solution lay in consulting constitutional experts and publishing a white paper for more deliberation. Simultaneous elections were vehemently opposed by CPI MP D. Raja, who called them 'unconstitutional and unrealistic'. Quoting Ambedkar, he said accountability should hold precedence over stability. Internal democracy within political parties was also mentioned by a couple of speakers. The BJD suggested that an independent regulator should be mandated to supervise and ensure inner-party democracy.

For improving the representativeness of election winners, a demand for a proportional representation system was put forth by the DMK, the CPI and the CPI(M). The DMK cited the example of the BSP's performance in the 2014 Lok Sabha election, when the party got a vote share of nearly 20 per cent in Uttar Pradesh but zero seats. A number of MPs argued for a mixed system, where there was provision for both first-past-the-post and proportional representation systems.

The important issue of the 'fidelity' of electoral rolls was raised by the YSR Congress Party (YSRCP). The idea of a common electoral roll for all the three tiers of democracy in the country was supported by the BJP and the SP.

For remedying the 'ruling party advantage' in elections, SP MP Ram Gopal Yadav made a radical suggestion that all MPs/MLAs should resign six months before elections and that a national government should be formed at the Centre. He said states going in for elections should be ruled by the governor, who would have to follow the binding advice of a three-member high court advisory board.

Advocacy over the years

I have long been an advocate of a number of these reform recommendations. Some proposals that I have elaborated upon in detail through the years include reduction of the number of phases in which elections are conducted by raising more security forces; depoliticization of constitutional appointments by appointing election commissioners through a broad-based collegium; state funding of political parties by means of a national electoral fund on the basis of the number of votes obtained; capping of the election expenditure of political parties; giving the Election Commission of India (ECI) powers to de-register recalcitrant political parties; inclusion of the proportional representation system; and revisiting of the Information Technology Act to strengthen social media regulations.

Hence, the parliamentary debate was music to my ears. But Indian politics has been suffering from a wide gap between thought and action. Governments should also rise above their obsession with immediate electoral gains and think of long-term national interests. The TMC MP was right in saying that parliament must not only urgently 'debate and deliberate but also legislate' on electoral reforms. The time has come to find and enact concrete solutions in this realm in the national interest. Having heard a number of practical and constructive proposals raised in the Rajya Sabha last week, I remain hopeful that parliament will take it upon itself to enable the world's largest democracy to become the world's greatest too.

5

On the Freebies Debate

EVERY ELECTION SEASON, THE RAIN OF FREEBIES BEGINS. THE REAL monsoon may fail, but this monsoon never does. The people are suddenly swamped by a flood of promises. Suddenly, political parties of all ideologies remember the poor aam aadmi whose needs and aspirations must be met urgently. Whether it's women, youth, scheduled castes/scheduled tribes, minorities, slum dwellers or residents of unauthorized colonies, they all become important. Their needs and desires are rediscovered. The promises are wide-ranging—free power and water, cheap foodgrain, televisions, washing machines, pressure cookers, farm loans, school uniforms and books, and, to keep pace with the twenty-first century, laptops and smartphones.

The promises can be divided into two kinds: those made before the announcement of elections and those after, when the Model Code of Conduct of the Election Commission of India comes into play. Promises made before the announcement of elections are the privilege of the ruling parties, who belatedly remember the commitments they had made before the previous election, but had forgotten conveniently. These may include subsidies, price cuts, reservations, new schemes, etc. The parties are in a hurry to make such announcements before the Code kicks in. It does not seem to matter what damage the populist schemes would do to the economy of the country or the state in question. The intelligentsia and economists start debating bad economics versus good politics. The verdict, however, is decided by the voters.

Promises of the second kind are the ones announced by parties through their election manifesto, released before or after elections have been announced. These did not attract the Model Code of Conduct till recently. The ₹2-kilo rice, free TVs, laptops, bicycles, etc., have all happened through this device. Ideally, the manifestoes should be announced immediately after the announcement of the poll schedule by the Election Commission. But the parties tend to wait till the very end so that they can out-promise their rivals. After the first manifesto is out, fierce debate follows, about the legality or propriety of the promises in it, besides the feasibility of their implementation. The Election Commission is flooded with requests to declare them illegal.

The fact is, manifestos are perfectly legal even if their promises are unrealistic and irresponsible. The Election Commission had no power to question them. The matter had gone to the Supreme Court, which too found itself faced with a great dilemma. In its judgment of 5 July 2013, it accepted that manifesto promises cannot be construed as 'corrupt practices' under the Representation of the People Act, though they do 'influence' the people and 'shake the roots of free and fair elections'. It directed the Election Commission to frame guidelines with regard to the content of manifestoes, in consultation with all the recognized political parties.

In their meeting with the ECI, most of the political parties, as expected, vehemently opposed any regulation of election manifesto content, arguing that in a democracy it is their 'right and duty' towards voters to make offers and promises through their manifestoes. Agreeing with this in principle, the ECI, however, mentioned the 'undesirable impact' of manifestoes. In deference to the Supreme Court directions, the ECI issued guidelines for political parties to state their rationale for the promises made in their manifestos, and the ways and means by which they would meet the financial requirements for them. These guidelines were added to the Model Code of Conduct as Part VIII.

On 23 August 2016, the AIADMK was 'censured' and also held guilty for not providing a rationale for and the ways and means by which it would meet the financial requirements for a whole range of poll promises in its manifesto for the Tamil Nadu assembly election in 2016. This was held a violation of the guidelines for election manifestoes contained in Part VIII of the Model Code of Conduct. Subsequently, in a reply to the notice, the party provided the Election Commission the rationale for its promises and also the ways and means by which it would implement them. It was 'advised' to be careful in future. The manifesto being a perfectly legal and legitimate democratic instrument, it is all the more important that rival parties expose the deceit of any party whose manifesto promises are unrealistic or absurd. Even if the common voter does not understand that the promises are un-implementable, he will indeed remember what promises were made in the last election and have not been fulfilled. Voters are now seen to be constantly rewarding good governance and punishing non-delivery of the same.

Why do electoral candidates suffer memory loss and forget their promises after an election, but their minds becoming fertile with bright ideas for new schemes only around the next election, is a moot question. Voters, gullible though they are, have come to understand this pattern. Opposition parties and the ever-alert media keep reminding them of forgotten or broken pledges. A contrarian view, however, is that promises like cheap food grain and free items of utility have done considerable good. The ₹1-kg rice scheme, introduced in Tamil Nadu in 2009, has ensured that starvation deaths do not happen any more. Some necessities/comforts of life, which people could only dream about earlier, now sometimes reach them. The distribution of free bicycles in Bihar has improved enrolment and retention of girls in schools. Loan waivers for farmers have prevented many suicides. Employment guarantee schemes have brought visible relief to the rural poor (but scarcity of domestic help for the urban rich!).

The new reality is that with all the parties offering the same or similar freebies, the expected political advantage to any one party from promising freebies gets neutralized. Whichever party the people vote for, the voters will end up getting a similar package.

Ever since he took office, Prime Minister Narendra Modi flagged the need for simultaneous elections—conducting simultaneously national, state and panchayat elections—on several occasions. The reasons he gave were the disruption they cause in the normal working of the government and the enormous cost of elections to political parties and the government. One could add one more reason for this demand—too many elections mean too many populist promises that affect the economy.

6

Freebies in an Unequal Democracy

THE TIME OF ELECTIONS IN INDIA IS USUALLY A TIME OF ENTICING promises and elaborate offers, when all the politicians are suddenly and touchingly concerned about the everyday plight of the common citizen. From urban slum dwellers to displaced tribals, from women and minorities to unemployed youth—neglected and ignored for well over four-and-a-half years—they are suddenly made subjects of urgent discussion for all sorts of alleviation programmes. Free electricity and water, cheaper food grains and fuels, free bicycles, phones, laptops and slim wads of cash appear on the usual menu of offerings. The voters, we are eloquently reminded, are the pillars of democracy, and who could disagree?

But is this fanciful, excessive and often misleading vein of promise-making indistinguishable from state-led provision of basic goods in a rights-based, welfarist apparatus? Secondly, must there be intervention by the judiciary or the ECI to tackle this issue of freebies?

221

The true interventionist

The recent debates sparked by the prime minister's comments on what he termed 'revdi culture' has once again reignited the significance of the above two questions. Let us first address the second question.

The promises made by political parties, often driven by short-term electoral calculations, can be divided into two types: promises made before elections are announced and promises made after. These promises are made by both the ruling and Opposition parties, with the ruling party having a distinct advantage as it controls the treasury. The parties are also in a rush to make their promises before the EC announces the Model Code of Conduct.

The second type of promises are the ones made through the manifestos, after elections have been announced. The government cannot announce new schemes after announcement of the poll dates because of the MCC. The promises made in the manifestos, however, do not attract the code. This is also why the ECI has no powers to question manifestos as they are perfectly legal, however infeasible their promises may seem.

Even the Supreme Court, in its judgment dated 5 July 2013, has accepted that manifesto promises cannot be construed as 'corrupt practices' under the RPA. However, it conceded that they do 'influence the people and shake the roots of free and fair elections'. It further directed the ECI to frame guidelines with regard to the content of manifestos in consultation with all the recognized political parties. In their meeting with the Election Commission, most of the political parties argued that in a healthy democratic polity, it is their 'right and duty' towards the voters to make promises through their manifestos. Agreeing with this in principle, the ECI, however, underlined its 'undesirable impact'.

In my opinion, neither the ECI nor the Supreme Court can get involved in this perfectly legal and legitimate democratic instrument. Even if the promises are unrealistic or absurd, it is for the rival parties to expose this. Furthermore, the voters do remember what promises have been fulfilled and what have not. They are now seen constantly rewarding good governance and punishing non-delivery.

Moreover, as matters of economic policy lie in the hands of the elected representatives, neither the ECI nor the Supreme Court must intervene in the purely political domain of a legislative government. It is ultimately for the voter to judge the economic and fiscal implications of freebie policies. The voter—and not the Supreme Court or the EC—therefore, will be the true interventionist to resolve the fate of freebies.

Having said this, there are, however, greater and broader issues at stake in the debates surrounding 'revdi culture', and they cannot be ignored because they present a troubling picture of the state of our democracy. We must now turn to the first question.

Welfarism vs. freebies

As several commentators have pointed out, the prime minister's remarks about 'revdi culture' betray not so much a concern for the health and discipline of our electoral process as his implicit denial of the legitimacy of welfarism itself, and more specifically his denial of state-led welfarism as a suitable model of development. In order, therefore, for us to take stock of these complexities, we must first briefly turn to the broader picture.

Oxfam's 2022 annual report on inequality in India has many troubling, stark revelations about our country's patterns of wealth accumulation and its governance structures. During the pandemic, when the country saw record levels of unemployment—urban unemployment climbing to as high as 15 per cent—when food insecurity worsened with stressed or non-existent public-provision programmes, when disastrous dips in growth rates turned up negative numbers, and when an overall increase in poverty was registered, with 84 per cent of the population suffering declined incomes, the count of dollar billionaires in India shot up by 39 per cent, to 142, and the richest even managed to double their already bloated wealth. It has been revealed that the wealth of the ten richest in India can fully fund the schooling and higher education of all the children in our country for twenty-five years. A mere additional 1 percentage point in tax on the richest ninety-eight billionaire Indian families can finance Ayushman Bharat, the world's largest health insurance scheme, for more than seven years.

What lessons, therefore, may we draw from a country where the number of poor doubled to 134 million simultaneously as its dollar billionaires' wealth doubled? Where the richest ninety-eight of them have the same wealth as its 56 crore citizens or the bottom 40 per cent of the population, and where the richest 1 per cent have amassed 51.5 per cent of the total wealth while the bottom 60 per cent of the population a mere 5 per cent? While we assess this dire economic situation, let us also briefly look at the social situation.

The former chief justice of India, N.V. Ramana, has recently said that there is 'diminishing' space for the Opposition, that the mutual respect between the Union government and the Opposition is dwindling. He also lamented the state of the media, whom he blamed for 'running kangaroo courts', expressing 'biased views' and running 'agenda-driven debates'. In the 2022 UN Human Development Index, India ranks 131, behind countries such as Iraq, Libya, Saudi Arabia and Mexico. The World Press Freedom Index ranked India at 150 out of 180 countries, just above Russia (155) and Pakistan (157). And Twitter's latest transparency report confirms India made more 'legal' demands than any other nation to remove content posted by verified journalists and news outlets during July–December 2021.

All of these indications clearly suggest a picture of a nation that is becoming more fractious and unequal, increasingly prone to a politics of division. I propose that we must take into consideration this broader milieu when grasping the implications of the jibe about 'revdi culture'.

Recently, Arvind Kejriwal, chief minister of Delhi, accused the Union government of hypocrisy when he pointed out that provisions to poor beneficiaries are termed 'revdi' while state-sponsored support measures for the rich are called 'incentives'. In September 2019, before the COVID-19 pandemic, the Narendra Modi government had slashed corporate tax rates for domestic manufacturers from 30 per cent to 22 per cent, and for new manufacturing companies from 25 per cent to 15 per cent, provided they do not claim any exemptions. The government took thirty-six hours to implement this decision with the help of Rule 12, which empowers the prime minister to take a decision and get the cabinet's ratification later. The Oxfam report states that these corporate cuts resulted in a loss of ₹1.5 lakh crore to the exchequer, contributing to an increase in the nation's fiscal deficit. For the first time in twelve years, income tax paid by individuals and Hindu Undivided Families amounted to more than corporate taxes paid by companies on the profits they make.

Further, the Oxfam India report highlighted that the government managed to compensate the shortfall in direct taxes (income tax, corporate tax and capital gains tax) by increasing indirect taxes (goods and services tax, excise duty, customs duty and VAT) during the pandemic. This directly led to a rise in fuel prices, driving up the prices of essential commodities such as foodgrains, which impact the poor more than the wealthy.

State policies, including the abolition of a wealth tax in 2016, steep cuts in corporate levies and an increase in indirect taxation, are among the factors that helped make the rich richer while the national minimum wage has remained at ₹178 a day since 2020. Reduced federal funding to local administrations amid growing privatization in the health and education sectors have further boosted inequalities. Meanwhile, our nation is home to a quarter of the world's undernourished people, according to the World Food Programme.

Given this overall socio-economic context, it is important that we reaffirm the value and necessity of our welfare programmes, and the urgent need to expand them. To provide its citizens with food, employment and education are the most fundamental responsibilities of a democratic state.

The so-called 'freebie' promises like cheap foodgrains and free items of utility have actually done considerable good to further the dream of democracy. Starvation deaths don't happen anymore, with rice having been made available at ₹1–2 per kg. Distribution of bicycles improved enrolment and retention of girls in schools in Bihar. Cheaper electricity and water was lapped up by Delhi voters. Employment guarantee schemes have brought visible relief to the rural poor.

Finally, I firmly believe that our nation will become a greater democracy if we redirect our concerned attention from revdi and freebies to rights and freedoms.

7

Prisoners Must Get the Right to Vote

O N 5 SEPTEMBER, THE ELECTION COMMISSION OF INDIA (ECI) sent a proposal to the law ministry expressing its keenness to expand the ambit of postal ballots to allow non-government employees on election duty to vote. These include people working in the areas of transport, aviation, shipping, medical and fire services, journalists involved in the coverage of elections, besides the aged and physically challenged. To quote the letter, 'It is necessary to explore all avenues to enable exercise of franchise by all eligible voters.'

This is a welcome proposal, consistent with the Commission's motto of 'no voter left behind'. In this context, I would like to highlight another section of the population which is in need of the same intervention—the 4.3 lakh prisoners languishing in Indian jails and considered by law as 'ineligible' to vote.

In May, a public interest litigation (PIL) was filed in the Delhi High Court challenging the constitutionality of Section 62(5) of the Representation of the People (RP) Act, which states:

No person shall vote at any election if he is confined in a prison, whether under a sentence of imprisonment or

> transportation or otherwise, or is in the lawful custody of the
> police: Provided that nothing in this sub-section shall apply
> to a person subjected to preventive detention under any law
> for the time being in force.

It keeps convicts, undertrials and those in temporary police custody on the same pedestal, violating the cornerstone principle of the criminal justice system: 'Innocent until proven guilty'. As a result, even the undertrials, i.e., 68 per cent of the prisoners, do not have the right to vote.

I see another legal anomaly: how can anyone be punished (denied the voting right and be deprived of the fundamental rights of liberty, freedom of movement, freedom of occupation and right to dignity) without conviction? What makes it even more unpalatable is the fact that those in jail can contest elections.

The law ministry's stand all these years has been that the right to vote is a statutory right created under the Act, and therefore subject to reasonable restrictions. But in *PUCL & Ors vs. Union of India (2013)*, voting has been defined as a medium of expression. As a result, it is protected under the fundamental right of freedom of expression—Article 19(1)(a)—enshrined in the Constitution. Robbing prisoners of their right to vote, while they retain their status as citizens, renders them as second class. It amounts to 'civic death' of the individual.

Guilty or marginalized?

A study of the composition of prison population reveals a stark positive correlation with their level of disadvantage. An overwhelming 65.8 per cent of convicts and 65.5 per cent of undertrials belong to the OBC, Dalit and Adivasi categories. Muslims comprise 15.8 per cent and 20.9 per cent of convicts and undertrials, respectively. There seems to be no incentive to legislate in their interest. It is no wonder that prison reforms have not seen the light of day.

As a result, jails are a hub of unspeakable suffering, riddled with overcrowding and unnatural deaths. For prisoners, the right to choose their representatives can usher in prison reforms faster than any other intervention. Additionally, humane conditions of living are an essential prerequisite for rehabilitative justice.

International trends

In 1999, South Africa's constitutional court, while ruling on the subject, stated, 'The universality of the franchise is important not only for nationhood and democracy. The vote of each and every citizen is a badge of dignity and personhood. Quite literally it says that everybody counts.'

In some countries, retention of prisoner's franchise serves as the basis of their status as citizens. For example, in France, Costa Rica, South Africa and Australia, a person does not automatically lose his right to vote when he is incarcerated.

The argument that voting is not just a symbol of representative democracy, but also a way for citizens to voice their problems, has been underlined in the majority judgment on prisoner disenfranchisement legislation by Canada's highest court. It said that denial of the right to vote, even in the case of the longest-serving sentence, is unjustified; it is a right that is 'fundamental to our democracy and the rule of law and cannot be lightly set aside'.

Around the world, countries are accepting this idea: Bernie Sanders, one of the candidates in the recent US presidential elections, is pitching for prisoners' right to vote. Countries like Israel, Japan and Sweden let prisoners vote, subject to varying degrees, i.e., felony disenfranchisement is conditional and not absolute. Germany encourages its prisoners, except for the ones engaged in electoral crimes, to participate in the electoral process. Hong Kong has lifted the ban on the right to vote for prisoners.

The European Court of Human Rights (ECHR) has delivered judgments in support of prisoner enfranchisement, asking the UK to amend its laws to abide by the judgment. As per the ECHR, 'Barring prisoners from voting may harm rehabilitation work since participating in elections may encourage them to become law–abiding and responsible citizens.'

Towards solutions

Since prisoners come from a wide range of constituencies, polling booths are not feasible. A simple solution is postal ballots, which is being proposed by the EC for other sections of voters.

According to Section 20 (8) of the RP Act, those using this facility at present include members of the armed forces, paramilitary forces and those serving abroad in our diplomatic missions, besides electionsstaff on duty outside their constituencies. This provision is proposed to be extended to all non–resident Indians (NRIs). It can simply be extended to other sections of the population (as proposed by EC), including prisoners, by amending Section 60 of the RP Act, 1951 and the Conduct of Election Rules, 1961.

The Commission's proposal is yet another step in its consistent efforts over decades aimed towards inclusive elections. Hence, it does not serve well to discriminate against prisoners living in miserable conditions, which are unlikely to change unless they the prisoners are empowered with the right to vote.

I hope the Election Commission and the law ministry will consider extending this facility to prisoners too to ensure that the fundamental right to equality is upheld in the true spirit of democracy and 'no voter is left behind'.

8

The Migrants' Right to Vote

ONE OF THE SIGNIFICANT FEATURES OF INDIA'S ELECTORAL RECORD has been its progressive betterment on two major counts—in registering eligible citizens as electors and in achieving increased participation of electors in voting. While only 17 per cent of eligible citizens were registered and 45 per cent of them turned out to vote in 1951 during India's first general election, in India's latest general election in 2019, over 91 per cent of its eligible citizens were registered, with 67 per cent of them coming out to vote, which is the highest voter turnout in the nation's history.

It is, however, worrying that a third of the eligible voters, a whopping 30 crore, do not vote. Among the many reasons, including urban apathy and geographical constraints, a prominent one is the inability of domestic migrants to vote, for different reasons.

In January 2023, the Election Commission announced that it is ready to pilot remote voting for domestic migrants, so they don't have to travel back to their home states to vote.

In its statement, the commission said that it has developed a prototype for a Multi-Constituency Remote Electronic Voting

Machine (RVM) that can handle multiple constituencies from a single remote polling booth.

The ECI invited representatives from all recognized national and state political parties to discuss the legal, administrative and statutory changes to resolve the issue. The discussion took place in the presence of a technical expert committee. It is important to recall that the last major decision on the voting system was the introduction in 2010 of the VVPAT, with the consensus of all political parties.

The consensus approach is imperative, not only to keep intact the democratic heritage of the Commission but also to help further entrench the popular trust it enjoys and its institutional integrity, which in recent times have been noticed to be in peril.

The Constitution guarantees every citizen freedom of movement and freedom to reside in any part of the country. However, migrant workers, especially circular or short-term migrants, constituting tens of millions of citizens, are some of the least represented groups in the ballot. The issue of disenfranchisement faced by migrant workers is not one arising out of deliberate denial of the right to vote, but from lack of access to vote. The Supreme Court, in a series of cases, has conclusively interpreted freedom to access the vote as within the ambit of Article 19(1)(a).

According to the 2011 Census, the number of internal migrants stands at 45 crore, a 45 per cent surge from the 2001 Census count. Among them, 26 per cent are inter-district migrants (11.7 crore) from within the same state, while 12 per cent of them (5.4 crore) are inter-state migrants. Both official and independent experts admit that this number is underestimated. Short-term and circular migration could itself make for 6–6.5 crore migrant workers and, if their family members are included, the number could approach 10 crore. Half of them would be inter-state migrants.

The root cause of the migrant voters' issue is that the individual's inalienable right to vote is conditioned by a rather strict residency qualification. As a consequence, it tends to disenfranchise the migrant population. In the survey report, 'Political Inclusion of Seasonal

Migrant Workers in India: Perceptions, Realities and Challenges' by Aajeevika Bureau, it was found that 'close to 60 per cent of respondents had missed voting in elections at least once because they were away from home seeking livelihood options'.

Most migrant voters have voter cards for their home constituency—78 per cent, according to a 2012 study. Most cannot commute to their home states on polling day. One survey shows that only 48 per cent of migrants voted in the 2009 Lok Sabha elections, when the national average was 59.7 per cent. These patterns have stayed consistent. In the 2019 Lok Sabha polls, major sender states such as Bihar and UP had among the lowest voter turnout rates, at 57.33 per cent and 59.21 per cent, respectively, while the national average was 67.4 per cent.

Although electoral laws allow people to register at their place of 'ordinary residence', most face difficulties in getting proof of residence. Moreover, many migrant voters may not be as intensively involved in the political affairs and interests in their host locations as they are in their home locations. There is a clear trade-off. Not registering at the host location will lead to a lack of interest among political parties in providing facilities to them. The law should provide migrants with the option to choose their place for voter registration.

What is the way out?

Section 60(c) of the Representation of the People Act, 1951, empowers the Election Commission of India, in consultation with the government, to notify 'classes' of voters who are unable to vote in person at their constituencies owing to their physical or social circumstances. Once notified, the voters are eligible to use the electronically transmitted postal ballot system (ETPB system).

In the 2019 general election, the ETPB system was accessed by 18 lakh defence personnel across the country. In 2019, in the backdrop of a public interest litigation before the Supreme Court, a bill was floated to extend similar remote voting to over 1 crore adult NRIs in order to 'boost their participation in nation-building'. In the 2019 Lok Sabha election, more than 28 lakh votes were received via postal ballot. In the existing system, remote voting within the constituency by voting via postal ballot is available to senior citizens, people with disabilities and COVID-affected personnel. Postal-ballot voting from outside the constituency is available only to service voters, persons on election duty and persons on preventive detention.

The Indian migrant worker too deserves the secured right to have access to vote through some mechanism.

The Election Commission has proposed the use of remote voting for migrant workers, wherein a modified version of the existing model of M3 EVMs will be placed at remote polling stations. In fact, Electronic Corporation of India Ltd. has already developed a prototype of a multi-constituency remote EVM (RVM)—a modified version of the existing EVM which can handle seventy-two constituencies in a single remote polling booth. The technical details will be available only after the crucial demonstration.

I hope the meeting proves to be a turning point in resolving the migrant voting issue once and for all. The task is daunting. Getting political parties to agree on the use of a 'remote' machine is a tall order, in view of the persisting questions even about the existing standalone EVMs.

I wish the ECI success in its stated objective of 'finding a technological solution which is credible, accessible and acceptable to all stakeholders'. Acceptable—that's the keyword that must be respected.

9

NRIs' Proxy Voting Will Not Serve the Purpose

A LARGE NUMBER OF INDIAN CITIZENS LIVE ABROAD—STUDYING, working, or for other reasons. Until recently, these non-resident Indians (NRIs) were not registered to vote here as the law held that only an 'ordinarily resident' citizen within the territorial limits of a constituency was eligible to be registered as a voter. On 3 August 2017, the government approved changes in the electoral laws allowing NRIs to cast their vote in assembly and Lok Sabha elections from overseas through a proxy, with one caveat—the proxy could be appointed for only one poll. Until now, only armed forces personnel were allowed to appoint proxies—they could appoint any adult living in the constituency in question as permanent proxies for all polls. Approximately 1 crore Indians are settled abroad, of whom about 60 lakh are adults and are eligible to vote.

The idea of NRI voting goes back to 2013, when a sizeable group of Indians launched an initiative called the Bharatiya Pravasi Diwas. When their demand to vote in Indian elections snowballed, then Prime Minister Manmohan Singh, in his address to the eighth

Bharatiya Pravasi Diwas in 2010, said NRIs would be able to vote from the following year.

His announcement came out of the blue for the Election Commission. The operational difficulties in making this possible had neither been studied nor discussed. Just the thought of registering lakhs of voters and making arrangements for them to cast their vote in Indian embassies and consulates across the world was unnerving—not just for us at the Election Commission, but for the external affairs ministry too.

To implement this promise, the Representation of the People Act, 1950, was amended—the amendment coming into force on 10 February 2011, with a new section, Section 20A. This section made special provisions for all citizens of India residing outside the country to enrol themselves as electors, provided they had not acquired citizenship of any other country and were otherwise eligible to be registered as Indian voters.

With great trepidation, the Election Commission took up the challenge.

Elections to Kerala, Tamil Nadu and three other states were due within a month at that time. Only NRIs from Kerala registered—about 8,500—and half of them came to Kerala to vote too. One NRI even contested the polls. The response in the other states, however, was less than desirable.

Proxy voting

The issue of proxy voting for NRIs came up in a public interest litigation in the Supreme Court in 2014. The Supreme Court asked the Election Commission to initiate a committee to examine the proposal, following which the Committee for Exploring Feasibility of Alternative Options for Voting by Overseas Electors was set up. The Election Commission looked at existing systems across the world and shortlisted four possible ones: voting in embassies, online voting, postal or e-postal ballot and proxy voting.

The commission then discussed the issue with all the political parties. Based on the committee report, the BJP was of the view that voting through proxy could be considered as there would be no logistical problems involved. The BSP, the Communist Party of India and the Congress were not in favour of proxy voting, as they said it could never be guaranteed that the proxy voter would vote as per the wishes of the actual voter. They also pointed out that proxy voting suffered from the inherent problem of 'trust deficiency' and violated the principles of 'secrecy of voting' and 'free and fair elections'.

The committee observed that the proxy-voting facility would be a 'convenient, efficacious and doable method' of providing voting facilities to overseas electors. Since proxies could be appointed at any point in time, the issues of time constraints, the logistical problem of voting at the embassies and the related issue of seeking the host country's permission, were completely eliminated. The load on the returning officers and the election machinery would also be considerably less.

The committee ruled out the first two possibilities—voting at the embassies and online voting—for logistical and technical reasons. It zeroed in on the last two—postal ballots and proxy voting. The committee concluded that a proxy-voting facility would operationally be the most simple and viable option for facilitating voting for overseas electors. Regarding the issue of trustworthiness of the proxy, was which raised by political parties, it was important to note that this issue was also applicable in the case of voters in the services who appoint proxies. It is expected that a person will appoint a proxy only when he or she has trust in the proxy.

The Supreme Court then asked the government to examine the proposals of the committee. On 3 August 2017, the government approved changes to the law to allow NRIs to vote through proxies.

The committee had recommended that proxy voting be considered as an option to be provided to overseas electors under the following conditions:

1. One person can act as a proxy for only one overseas elector.
2. Only a person already enrolled in the same constituency in which the overseas elector is enrolled can be appointed as a proxy for an overseas elector.

3. The appointment of a proxy shall be valid till the time it is revoked by the elector, who can then make a fresh appointment of proxy.

The government, however, modified the proposal to allow for appointment of a one-time proxy for each election.

Arguments against proxy voting

However, many have raised arguments against allowing NRIs to vote through proxies.

The basic argument in favour of allowing overseas residents to vote is that citizens have a democratic right to choose their legislators, wherever in the world they are. But those against the initiative argue that proxy voting threatens the very core of democracy. Arguing against it, eminent German political scientists Dieter Nohlen and Florian Grotz have said:

> … the notion of external voting … goes against one of the classic requirements … namely the residency inside the state territory. Furthermore the implementation of external voting poses heavy technical administrative problems that might interfere with other crucial features of universal franchise, mainly the principle of free elections.

The arguments against the broader issue of voting rights for citizens living abroad are more numerous and strong.

1. The fundamental right to equality is the prime argument. How can we give the special privilege of distance voting to some people who have migrated abroad when there are many times more domestic migrants who also seek distance-voting rights? It is patently discriminatory. If a person from Bihar moves to Delhi or Mumbai in search of a job or education, he loses his right to choose his legislator in his village, but if he goes to London, he will be entitled to the special privilege of voting for his legislator

of choice. Remember that the right to vote is not a fundamental right, whereas the right to equality is.

2.   There are strict regulations, including the Model Code, for campaigning. Bribery and inducements given to voters are strictly kept in check. These are impossible to implement abroad.

3.   There can be no guarantee that NRI voters will exercise their vote in a free and fair manner, as there can be no check on the coercion or inducements they may be subjected to or offered by their employers and supervisors, for example. Remember, a majority of Indian migrants overseas are poor workers, often at the mercy of their employers, who even take their passports into custody.

4.   There is no guarantee that votes would not be sold to the so-called proxy. Nor is it certain that the proxy will vote as per the wishes of the main voter. Secrecy of vote, of course, goes out the window.

The committee even recommended the safer alternative of e-postal ballots (sending ballots by email and receiving them back by post). It had also recommended first doing a pilot study for this and extending it only 'if found feasible, practicable and meeting the objectives of free and fair and elections'. Remember, a free and fair election is non-negotiable and is the basic structure of the Constitution, as repeatedly asserted by the Supreme Court.

Asserting the right to free and fair elections

The following are some of the Supreme Court judgments asserting citizens' right to free and fair elections:

1.   *Union vs. ADR*, 2003, where the court said, 'Democracy cannot survive without free and fair elections.'

2.   *Mohinder Singh Gill vs. Chief Election Commissioner of India*, 1977, where the court said, 'It needs little argument to hold that the heart of the parliamentary system is free and fair election.'

3.   *SC 2013 PUCL vs. Union (NOTA)*, where the court said, 'Free and fair election is the basic structure of the constitution.'

It is also important to remember that many election commission officials, including former chief election commissioners T.S. Krishnamurthy and N. Gopalaswami, have raised doubts about proxy voting.

Krishnamurthy has made the following points:

1. Blanket provision for proxy voting is 'not desirable'. It should be tried out 'on a limited scale to see what is the fallout'.
2. Better to first try very selectively for persons with disabilities and the ailing.
3. It will alter the voting patterns in states with large NRI populations.

Gopalaswami is even stronger in his observations:

1. NRI voting is 'something which is uncalled for'. Why not provide distance voting for migrants who have to return to villages to vote, losing their wages?
2. 'It's a beehive which will sting you.'
3. There seems to be a greater emphasis on NRIs instead of improving voting facilities for soldiers.

I strongly endorse these views. Besides, the arguments of the Election Committee-appointed committee about the resultant inconvenience and workload for the returning officers in handling e-postal ballots is not acceptable. A few hundred extra postal ballots will not make them collapse under the weight of the extra work involved.

The Election Commission has always tread with caution. Every reform was first tested in a small territory before it was scaled up. Reckless adventurism in as sensitive a matter as elections is fraught with serious consequences.

The matter will now come up in parliament. I hope parliament will consider this matter keeping in mind the long-term national interest instead of possible short-term political gains.

10

NOTA Option in RS Polls

THE HIGH-INTENSITY DRAMA THAT WAS WITNESSED ON 6 AUGUST 2017 in the Gujarat Vidhan Sabha has raised many questions regarding the anti-defection law, NOTA, secrecy of the ballot, and the power and role of the Election Commission in Indian democracy.

The practice of horse-trading and the purchasing of legislators has been plaguing our democracy for some time now. The current case came to light when the Congress shipped its MLAs in Gujarat to a resort in Karnataka to prevent poaching of its members by the BJP. On 6 August, two Congress MLAs voted for the BJP candidate in the elections to the Rajya Sabha. They further violated Rule 39 of the Code of Election Rules, 1961, by showing their ballot paper to the BJP agent.

The Election Commission, which is responsible for conducting elections to the Rajya Sabha under Article 324 of the Constitution, took a bold step against the culprits and gave a commendable judgment that went against the BJP. Amid speculation about the integrity of the Commission by certain sections of the media, given the fact that two of the commissioners were appointed by the BJP and the CEC was the former chief secretary of Gujarat under Narendra Modi when he was chief minister of the state, the judgment proves once again the independence and separation of the Election Commission from the political establishment, underscoring its importance in ensuring the smooth functioning of Indian democracy.

Another issue that came up was that of NOTA. The Congress conveniently raised the issue with the Supreme Court three-and-a-half years after its introduction in Rajya Sabha elections, to suit its convenience. I must, however, say that I feel this issue needs some reconsideration, as elections to the offices of president and vice president have been kept out of NOTA.

It may be worthwhile to recall a major horse-trading event the Election Commission encountered in March 2012, when I was the CEC. There were reports of blatant abuse of money power in elections for two Rajya Sabha seats in Jharkhand. When the Election Commission enforcement team caught a vehicle of a candidate carrying over ₹2 crore in cash, we decided to take the unprecedented step of countermanding the elections.

I was pleasantly surprised when I heard BJP leader Arun Jaitley comment that though the Commission's decision had hit one of his own party candidates, it was a most appropriate decision.

Even senior BJP leader L.K. Advani wrote a blog—'Kudos to SY Quraishi'—for a decision that struck at horse-trading like never before. I'm sure the leadership will take a similar view in this case and commend the decision of the Election Commission.

International Elections

1

Colombo Collective

ON 16 NOVEMBER 2019, SRI LANKA CONCLUDED ITS SIXTH presidential election, which was as dramatic as it was a landmark. The elections were held in a country with an authoritarian regime that had abolished all independent commissions, including the Election Commission. The polls were conducted by a government official designated as the commissioner of elections, with no power or control over the election poll bureaucracy and the police. However, it must be noted here that the Election Commission was abolished as an independent commission, but was retained as a government body.

I observed these polls rather closely as the head of a twenty-three-member observer delegation from the Association of Asian Election Authorities (AAEA), comprising eleven of the member countries, from Mongolia to the Maldives and from Korea to Kazakhstan. The Commonwealth Observer Group, led by former president of Guyana Bharrat Jagdeo, and a delegation from the Forum of the Management Bodies of South Asia (FEMBoSA) also monitored the poll, apart from several indigenous civil society groups.

The invitation sent out by the commissioner of elections to multiple observer groups was the first sign of a credible election. Commissioner

Mahinda Deshapriya seemed assured that his poll machinery, including the police, would pull off a free and fair election, despite the commissioner's inherent lack of powers. The Opposition parties also seemed to have confidence in his fairness, which was reassuring.

The proactive involvement of three major civil society organizations, the People's Action for Free and Fair Elections (PAFFREL), the Campaign for Free and Fair Elections (CaFFE) and the Centre for Monitoring Electoral Violence (CMEV) was a good barometer of civic freedom. They were vocal and aggressive while constantly analysing the situation and campaign trends, including complaints of violence, intimidation of voters and abuse of state machinery. A constant refrain was that the army had been blatantly used to intimidate voters to keep them from going to vote—it had set up 400 to 500 roadblocks. There were also allegations of discrimination directed at the police, which apparently registered cases against the Opposition and not against the ruling party, and at the government's distribution of food items in the name of flood relief.

However, the election commission and the police made sure that no intimidation would be allowed on polling day. We dispatched observers to all corners of the island. I travelled more than 1,200 km over four days, covering almost all of the former war zone in the north. I did not see a single roadblock by the army. Nor did anyone else from our team. So, were the allegations of intimidation false or exaggerated? Or did the presence of high-profile observers act as a deterrent to what had been happening earlier? The way the chief election commissioner pleaded with me to travel extensively in the northern area and deploy the most observers there pointed to the latter. The commissioner later confirmed this.

The fact that nearly all the officers posted in those districts were Tamil seemed proof enough that no intimidation of Tamil minorities would be possible, and neither was it intended. Our conversations with them reaffirmed our comfort with the poll machinery. In India, we have seen how the ruling parties try to instal loyalists in critical posts, particularly those of district magistrate and superintendent of police, ahead of elections.

Voter enthusiasm was high. As many as 81.52 per cent of the 150 lakh eligible persons voted. The operation was managed, as in India, by the bureaucracy, and about 2 lakh officials were deployed, besides 72,000 police and security personnel.

The defeat of President Mahinda Rajapaksa and the victory of Maithripala Sirisena were swift and dramatic developments. Till a couple of months ago, Rajapaksa was so much in command that he was reported to have said that he would be contesting against himself in a shadow-boxing match at the polls. Then, suddenly, he was hit by the proverbial bolt from the blue. Out of nowhere, his close aide and minister for health, also a Buddhist and from a rural area, defected and was declared the common candidate of the entire Opposition.

The challenge grew stronger by the day, and the results seemed inevitable. The incumbent president just could not recover from the shock of the secret plan of the Opposition. We were told that they had used communication tools like Viber and WhatsApp, technologies the ruling regime could not penetrate, despite every Opposition leader having been under surveillance.

We also heard that the president had decided to go for a mid-term poll, a full two years and two months before the end of his tenure, on the advice of his astrologer. The calculation, reportedly, was that if he won he would first complete his remaining term (allowed by the recently amended Constitution) and then take charge for the new six-year term. That old proverb, 'a bird in hand is better than two in the bush', would never have been proved so right.

Rajapaksa was banking on a fractured Opposition, especially a deeply divided United National Party. But the idea of a common Opposition candidate, though mooted over a year ago, snowballed once the election was announced. A stream of defections followed. According to the *Daily News*, itself an overnight turncoat newspaper, the support of the Tamil National Alliance and the Sri Lanka Muslim

Congress turned the Opposition into the broadest political coalition in Sri Lanka to date, cutting across party, ethnic and religious boundaries. Tamils constitute 15 per cent, Muslims 10 per cent and Christians 6 per cent of the coalition, and their unity proved to be the decisive factor.

The genesis of the rise of the dictatorial Rajapaksa—and his eventual downfall—lay in the infamous eighteenth amendment to the Constitution, dating back to October 2010, which gave him total power over all organs of governance, including the judiciary, and ended the limit of two tenures for the president. Particularly, the unique provision that he could seek the people's mandate before the end of the term and yet complete the existing term before starting the new one proved to be his undoing. Everyone was angered by the extension he gave himself. It was compounded by the blatant nepotism he practised, as his three brothers, his sons and his nephews controlled every crucial department in the government. Along with the large-scale corruption charges, these discontents far outweighed the nation's gratitude to Rajapaksa for the 'war' victory of 2009.

The peaceful transition of power initially surprised everyone. Contrary to widespread speculation, the change of guard was quick and peaceful. The way Rajapaksa accepted the verdict even before all the votes had been counted, and left the presidential residence and office, looked extremely dignified. There are whispers, however, that other 'possible options' had been contemplated, but he got no support from the key players. The spokesman of the new president has called it a coup attempt that will be investigated. The new president took his oath of office within six hours.

A very touching personal moment for me, and India, was when Mahinda Deshapriya, chairman of Election Commission, announced the results in the presence of the incoming president and prime minister holding my book, *An Undocumented Wonder: the Making of the Great Indian Election*, and quoting Gopal Gandhi—'Among the many great things that India has, three are most important: the Taj Mahal, Mahatma Gandhi and an electoral democracy.' Deshapriya prayed that the Indian model would be emulated in Sri Lanka and pleaded for the constitutional powers his Indian counterparts had.

Tailpiece: The country is abuzz with speculation about the future of the 'royal' astrologer. Many other astrologers have gone into overdrive to find the answer.

2

A Defining Moment for Colombo

S RI L ANKA GOES TO THE POLLS TODAY, 17 A UGUST 2015, TO ELECT ITS new parliament. The election is considered extremely significant, as it may decide the course of the 8 January revolution that led to the overthrow of the authoritarian president, Mahinda Rajapaksa.

Sri Lanka has a history of electoral violence, dating back to its twenty-six years of civil war from 1983 to 2009. True to tradition, seventy-seven violent incidents as of 3 August have already been reported by the watchdog, PAFFREL. Besides, there are 600-plus cases of electoral law violations, of which, significantly, over 100 relate to abuse of state power and resources, including misuse of public-sector employees.

During the ten years of Rajapaksa's presidency, the Tamil insurgency was crushed. The final stages were brutal and thousands died. The deaths were neither acknowledged nor investigated. This made Rajapaksa increasingly authoritarian, with no concern for reconciling with the Tamil minority. The treatment of Muslims and Christians was no different.

A group of rehabilitated former LTTE cadre has decided to contest independently, after the Tamil National Alliance (TNA) denied them nominations. The TNA spokesman explained to the media that the reason they were denied nominations was because of their suspected links with intelligence agencies, which they felt would hinder a political solution to the Tamil problem. The cadre claimed they would not campaign against the TNA, but contest under their independent party, Crusaders for Democracy.

President Maithripala Sirisena, who had sprung the biggest surprise by revolting against Rajapaksa, seems to excel in surprises. Everyone was taken aback when he ordered parliamentary elections eight months before schedule—'imposing it', as the Sri Lanka Guardian commented, 'on the people of Sri Lanka who do not want it'. Then he sprang a bigger surprise by allowing his bête noire, Rajapaksa to run for parliament. The nomination of Rajapaksa as the candidate of the United People's Freedom Alliance (UPFA) coalition has angered millions of voters and activists who had supported Sirisena in January. Although he has declined to name Rajapaksa as the prime ministerial hopeful, Rajapaksa loyalists are optimistic that he might be considered for prime ministership since he is still popular among the majority Sinhalese. If he becomes the PM, it will be for Rajapaksa, as the BBC described, an 'uneasy cohabitation with the man who unseated him'.

There are various theories on Sirisena's flip-flops. The most charitable one is that he has been a true soldier of the Sri Lanka Freedom Party (SLFP) throughout his career. He didn't want the SLFP to split under his watch. After his shock defeat, Rajapaksa had, in a surprise move, decided to support Sirisena to avoid splitting the SLFP. His farsightedness seems to have been rewarded. A large faction has continued to be loyal to him. Also, the SLFP cannot bear the prospect of being defeated by the United National Party (UNP). Sirisena was desperate to prevent a UNP landslide. Sirisena's own explanation is that he had no control over the UPFA nomination. Many consider this explanation wishy-washy.

Spiritual leader Sobitha Thero, the architect of the project to bring the opposition forces in Sri Lanka under a common umbrella, was the most vocal critic of Sirisena. 'You are fighting to try and protect your party, but the rest of us will have to battle to save our lives,' he said to Sirisena. Political analyst Sarath Wijesooriya said: 'Has Maithripala paved the path to put 62 lakh people six feet under?'

There may be more to the early election than meets the eye. Sirisena needs parliamentary support to push through his promised reforms, including limits on the powers of the executive presidency.

The timing is also important. The UN Human Rights Council is expected to release a report in September on human rights abuses that happened during the final phase of the civil war in 2009. The report could affect Rajapaksa's attempt to whip up nationalist sentiment to stage a comeback. A survey showed 27.5 per cent support for him, against 40 per cent for PM Ranil Wickremesinghe. This does not seem an impossible margin to bridge, considering that the ruling coalition is divided. Some feel Sri Lanka's six-month honeymoon with democracy may be over. For them, the counter-revolution has begun. Others feel this prophecy of doom may not actually come true.

But why is the outcome of the election in Sri Lanka important for the region and the world? According to US Admiral Dennis C. Blair, former director of National Intelligence, Sri Lanka is becoming the key transportation hub for South and South-east Asia. Rajapaksa had taken the country into the arms of China, which raised serious geopolitical concerns not only for the US but also—in fact, more so—for India. Both countries will be watching the course of events with bated breath.

3

As Sri Lanka Prepares for Polls

On 16 November 2019, Sri Lanka went to the polls to elect its new president. I was privileged to be a part of a pre-election assessment mission mounted jointly by the Republican Party and the Democratic Party of the United States through their independent institutes, the International Republican Institute (IRI) and National Democratic Institute (NDI).

Sri Lanka has a population of 2.2 crore, of whom 1.6 crore are registered voters. They will vote at 12,845 polling stations. Counting will be done at 1,500 counting centres. The president has to get a clear majority (50 per cent plus one vote). There is a preferential voting system, where every voter can make their second and third preferences known, which most voters rarely do. If no one gets 50 per cent as the voters' first choice, the second and third preference votes have to be counted. There is no run-off election. After the counting of all three preferences, if necessary, the candidate with the highest number of votes wins.

Every stakeholder we questioned vouched for the integrity of the Commission, which became a constitutional body only in 2018, and expressed full faith in its ability to conduct a free, fair and credible election. In fact, since the 2015 election, the chief election commissioner, Mahinda Deshapriya, has been no less than a national icon.

Whether the youth would participate was a common concern. There are nearly 3,00,000 first-time voters, and the general opinion was that there would be a sense of apathy among them. The reasons given for this were the youth's disillusionment with the performance of the government and lack of issues of interest to them.

The absence of a campaign finance regulation was also mentioned by almost every stakeholder. Enormous abuse of money power was a common concern. Some people even mentioned foreign money playing a role.

We had an interesting conversation with the former president, Mahinda Rajapaksa, where he complained of being a victim of the Opposition. He had complete faith in the Election Commission, despite accusing it of delaying the provincial elections 'under pressure of the government'. He made an interesting disclosure: one of the three commissioners often goes against the majority, and even goes to court sometimes.

Referring to the Easter terror attack, on 21 April 2019, in which three churches and three luxury hotels were bombed leading to the death of 269 people, he said the government had detailed information on it from the Government of India, 'including the names and telephone numbers' of the perpetrators, but the concerned agencies had not acted on it. He made it clear that it was an act of some Muslim extremists, but that it cannot be attributed to Islam. When asked whether he expects any foreign interference, he replied with a wink saying, 'hope it won't happen again'. It may be recalled that in the 2015 election, he had publicly attributed his defeat to Indian intelligence agencies.

We also met the prime minister, Ranil Wickremesinghe, who complained of low voter interest, attributing it to the general disenchantment with the political leaders and their unfulfilled promises. This was surprising to hear from an incumbent PM, and reflects the bitter dissensions within the ruling coalition. He also observed that the youth were not enthusiastic, as they see 'no big issue'. He also said there is a large number of 'floating voters', who can play a decisive role in the election. He made an interesting observation—that in 2015, then President Rajapaksa had everything, 'including sun and the moon', and yet he lost the election because of these voters. According to Wickremesinghe, 'it is certain that no one will get 50 per cent votes (leading to the counting of second and third preference votes)'. Significantly, he also mentioned the possible role of foreign money in the election.

He admitted that India had provided very specific intelligence about the Easter terror attack and lamented that 'we didn't follow up'. He expressed concern that Muslims are being vilified. He said he did not anticipate much violence during the polls. Another important ruling political leader (not a Muslim), however, said that terror is being used as a weapon to harass a community which is facing many human rights violations.

Women seem to have a very insignificant presence on the electoral scene. This is despite the fact that Sri Lanka gave the world its first elected woman president. Although women dominate the education scene, with 74 per cent of Sri Lankan students being female (and 20 per cent of its faculty), and with 25 per cent reservation for women at the provincial level, the political role of women at the national level has been confined to those from political families.

Everyone we met—from political leaders and civil society members to NGOs—complained about the spinelessness and partiality of the media, largely because most of the media are owned by political parties. There is zero self-regulation. Some called the media the 'washing machine' of the state. The most scathing comment was made by a journalist: 'SL is the worst country in the world for media prostitution!' (Does the comment ring a bell? Some consolation, this).

We met a very senior Tamil leader who said there was general voter apathy among the Tamils. However, when Gota Rajapaksa's candidacy was announced, the apathy disappeared. It is important to note that in 2015, it was the Tamil and Muslim vote that helped dislodge Rajapaksa's brother, President Mahinda Rajapaksa.

The Tamil leader lamented that 10 per cent of the Tamil political prisoners have not yet been released, one-third of the land belonging to the Tamils that had been seized has not been returned and, worse, none of the 20,000-plus Tamil individuals who had 'disappeared' have been found. He said Tamils are 'sick and tired' of voting for the 'lesser of the two evils'.

The same leader also said there was strong anti-Muslim feeling among the Tamils and feared that some violence was being planned by them against the Muslims, especially in the east, to prevent them from voting. He emphasized the need for the two communities to come together and hoped that 'close to the elections they would have to work together'.

SL elections always invite great world attention. The country is liberal in inviting international observers. Most importantly, its own civil society observers from the two main NGOs—People's Action for Free and Fair Elections (PAFFREL) and Centre for Monitoring Electoral Violence (CMEV)—have unrestricted access to the entire electoral process. They depute their observers to almost 80 per cent of the polling stations. Their monitoring and certification carries a lot of weight as well. In a meeting with them, they expressed satisfaction with the arrangements and hoped the elections, like in 2015, would be free, fair and credible.

Finally, the camaraderie and coordination between the representatives of the NDI and IRI was a treat to observe. One wishes to see such bonhomie between our two national parties too.

4

Insights From Sri Lanka

AFTER SUCCESSFULLY CONTAINING THE SPREAD OF COVID-19, SRI Lanka is set to hold parliamentary elections on 5 August 2020. The elections will be held for 196 legislative seats, along with elections to twenty-nine seats that are proportionally distributed among the political parties based on their national vote share.

In line with the nineteenth amendment to the country's Constitution, which mandated completion of a minimum term of four-and-a-half years for the parliament to avoid arbitrary dissolution of it by the president, President Gotabaya Rajapaksa dissolved parliament and called for general elections as soon as this time period was completed. Opposition parties and civil society groups filed several petitions in the Supreme Court against his decision. The court rejected the petitions, and elections were scheduled for 25 April 2020. But the COVID-19 pandemic forced Sri Lanka's Election Commission to postpone the elections to 20 June—two weeks past the completion of three months, the time period provided in Article 70(5) of the country's Constitution, which mandates that a newly elected parliament must meet within three months of proclamation of its dissolution by the president. Despite an uproar against the suspected Constitutional crisis, the Election Commission, considering the entailing health risks due to the pandemic, postponed the elections to 5 August.

To prevent the upcoming elections from becoming a public health hazard, the Election Commission has been holding mock elections. Additionally, the Sri Lankan government has issued health guidelines that include limiting the number of people engaged in door-to-door campaigning to five. Only 300 participants are allowed to attend meetings—which can be increased to 500 if a party leader is attending. All participants at a meeting are to maintain a 1-metre distance from each other and judiciously use hand sanitizers, masks and gloves. This is, however, a watered-down version of the guidelines suggested by the ministry of health (MoH). The MoH guidelines also called for the numbers of people at polling booths to be kept to a minimum, with separate entry and exit points, provision of PPE kits to election officers at polling booths and in quarantine centres, and permitting voters running a temperature to visit the polling stations towards the end of the voting process.

Though the Election Commission here has been increasingly wary of the pandemic situation unfolding in the country, it has chosen not to extend the provision of postal voting to sections vulnerable to COVID-19. Like in earlier elections, postal voting has been limited to public officials assigned to electoral duty. This is contrary to the practice in several countries that are holding elections during the pandemic. Even India, which offered the provision only to armed forces and senior citizens above the age of eighty, has allowed people infected with COVID-19 or in home quarantine to avail of this option in the Bihar elections.

Provision of absentee ballots ensures less crowding at polling centres, which in turn reduces the risk of voters and election staff contracting the virus. In addition, it will ensure maximum participation in polling. For instance, South Korea, with the help of postal voting and staggered voter timings, recorded its highest voter turnout of 66.2 per cent in twenty-eight years in its recent national elections. Similarly, Poland provided the options of both in-person voting and postal voting in the presidential elections, and witnessed its record voter turnout (64.5 per cent) in the first round since 1995.

Besides crowd control at voting centres, Sri Lanka's Election Commission faces several other implementation problems. With the pandemic, the campaigning has shifted to online platforms. Although this is a safer campaigning option, election management bodies across the world have consistently struggled to rein in fake news, hate speech and targeted political advertisements on online platforms. For Sri Lanka, in particular, the absence of campaign finance laws will further exacerbate the problem. Moreover, due to their restricted contact with voters, political parties are likely to use their affiliations with private media to float biased news without any inhibition because of the Election Commission's inability to monitor the online space.

The Election Commission would also have to keep in check its expenses. It is not a secret that every electoral management body is financially challenged, which is further compounded with the additional responsibilities of stocking safety equipment, increased polling staff and centres in view of the pandemic. Sri Lanka awaits an impending recession. With limited funds at its disposal, its Election Commission has to conduct a fool-proof election.

For successfully managing the COVID-19 pandemic, the incumbent Prime Minister Mahinda Rajapaksa, has a better chance in the parliamentary election. A majority in parliament will help President Gotabaya push through a constitutional amendment to strengthen his powers. The brothers' 'commitment' to public health was evident when their party, the Sri Lanka Podujana Peramuna, cancelled their campaigns, citing the sudden spike in the number of COVID-19 patients. This decision has earned them some brownie points among the voters.

The poll outcome, coming as it will against the backdrop of India–China tensions, will be closely watched in New Delhi. During the presidential term of Mahinda Rajapaksa, Sri Lanka had grown closer to China. Now, under President Gotabaya Rajapaksa, Colombo is rethinking the East Container Terminal project since India has kept Sri Lanka's request for a debt freeze hanging. With China increasing its presence in the neighbourhood, India would want to forgo its unpopular, masculine, 'big brother' attitude and foster its position as a gentle helping hand to Sri Lanka.

In the end, the elections in Sri Lanka will be of particular interest to the Election Commission of India, which is preparing itself for the Bihar assembly polls and is drawing lessons from countries that have conducted elections during the pandemic. So far, South Korea has been the template. Sri Lanka may provide some more insights.

5

What I Saw in Pakistan

THE GENERAL ELECTION IN PAKISTAN IS BEING DESCRIBED AS A milestone in the democratic history of the country. This is only the second transition from one full-term civilian government to another, and the first under the new Election Law, 2018. I got a great opportunity to observe the event from a ringside seat as a member of the Commonwealth Election Observers Group. The fifteen-member group, headed by Abdulsalami Abubakar, former head of state of Nigeria, spent twelve days in the country, observing the events leading up to the election, the polling and counting day, and the declaration of the results over three days.

The group met delegations from the leading political parties, civil society and the media to understand the pre-electoral environment, which was reported to point to a not-too-fair election. We were told of massive pre-poll 'rigging'. Mainly, three things were cited: the forcing of certain party leaders to return their tickets; muzzling of the media, and misuse of the army and judiciary in favour of a particular party. It is difficult to understand how the changing loyalties of political leaders can be described as rigging—such political engineering is common in the subcontinent where turncoats and horse-trading are household terms.

Some media representatives said that after a lot of subtle and overt intimidation, many have decided on self-censorship as a wiser option. The hold of the army on institutions like the judiciary, the National Accountability Bureau, the media, etc., was a common refrain. We were told that naming the army was taboo, full of risks. Therefore, alternative expressions or euphemisms had been evolved, like 'establishment', 'the powers that be', 'khalai makhlooq (people from outer space)', 'angels' and even 'agriculture department'.

People who questioned the impartiality of the military and the judiciary cited the timing of court cases against certain political leaders and candidates. The media were allegedly prevented from fully covering certain issues like the rights of minorities and the role of state institutions. For the poll-day arrangements, questions were focused on the large-scale deployment of the army. Concerns were raised about the order to deploy soldiers inside the polling stations. We, therefore, decided to focus special attention on these concerns.

We observed that candidates from across parties and independents too were able to campaign freely and peacefully. Maybe we arrived too late, by which time the games had already been played. The overall security situation was tense, especially in Khyber Pakhtunkhwa (KPK) and Balochistan, where terrorist attacks in the preceding weeks had claimed more than 170 lives, including those of three candidates. However, the parties were able to organize their rallies freely, as per Election Rules, 2017. A lot of negative and abusive campaigning was initially reported, but after the Election Commission of Pakistan's (ECP) stern action under its model code, most people fell in line.

We found the electoral system quite robust, with a substantially reformed legal framework consisting of the Constitution of Pakistan, the Elections Act, 2017, and Election Rules, 2017, which has led to a greater autonomy of the ECP—including financial autonomy, the power to make rules and punish for contempt, and to de-register or de-list an existing political party. Officials deputed for election duty have now been brought under the ECP's disciplinary control.

Some legal reforms for enhancing women voters' participation are noteworthy. The ECP can declare an election null and void if less than 10 per cent of the women in a constituency have voted.

This has had a salutary effect in those frontier regions where women were traditionally not allowed to vote. At least 5 per cent of the candidates nominated by each party for the general seats in the National Assembly must be women. There are 70 seats in the National Assembly (272 members) which are filled by political parties' nominees according to the number of seats won. (Incidentally, ten seats in the National Assembly are reserved for minorities.) Special campaigns by the National Database and Registration Authority (NADRA), political parties and civil society have helped increase the enrolment of women as voters. Separate polling stations for women, run entirely by women, also encouraged turnout.

Polling day passed off peacefully, much to everyone's relief. There was a 53 per cent turnout, significantly higher than the 48 per cent in 2013.

Unlike in India, the counting in Pakistan is done at the polling station itself immediately after polling closes. There were several questions raised about the counting. Some parties alleged that the polling agents were not allowed to observe the counting from close up. Some complained that their agents were thrown out of the stations. There were allegations that Form 45 (the result sheet) was neither given to the polling agents nor pasted on the walls of the polling stations. The ECP denied the first allegation, clarifying that only those agents who were in excess of one per party were asked to leave. It, however, admitted to several instances of the second allegation and promised to take action. The ECP also admitted the failure of the 'result transmission system' because it had not been pilot-tested adequately. The foreign minister, whom we met, attributed this, in a lighter vein, to the failure of the British technology on which the app was based.

The conduct of the proscribed militant-dominated religious organizations, a phenomenon of special concern to India, was watched with interest. We noted that the ECP, in accordance with the law, did not allow the registration of such entities and individuals to contest in the election. However, its mechanism for filtering out candidates linked to such organizations was weak, which led to three candidates managing to slip past scrutiny. They were, however, de-listed on the eve of the election after a hue and cry by the media and civil society. It is remarkable that religious parties with extremist connections were totally routed, both in the national and provincial assembly elections. The Tehreek-e-Labbaik managed to get only two seats in Karachi, whereas the Allah-o-Akbar Tehreek drew a blank.

The elections were closely observed by a huge force of civil society volunteers led by the Free and Fair Election Network (FAFEN) and Trust for Democracy Education and Accountability, besides international observers from the European Union, the Commonwealth, and several diplomats. FAFEN deployed 19,683 citizen observers (including 5,846 women) at more than 65,000 polling stations (almost 80 per cent of the total). Most of the observers were satisfied with the arrangements and the conduct of the election. The Commonwealth group commended the ECP for doing a laudable job in the short time it had to implement its mandate for holding transparent elections on schedule. It regarded General Election 2018 as an important milestone in strengthening democracy in Pakistan.

6

In Nepal, With Hope

POLLING FOR THE HISTORIC PARLIAMENTARY AND PROVINCIAL elections in Nepal concluded peacefully on 7 December 2017, despite last-minute attempts by some desperate elements to disturb them. The counting is now going on, 24/7, in three shifts, and is likely to be completed by 15 December. The elections, held in two phases on 26 November in thirty-two pahadi and himali districts and on 7 December in the remaining forty-five districts, are very significant, being the first under the 2015 Constitution of Nepal.

Earlier this year, local government elections were held in three phases—on 14 May, 28 June and 18 September—in six metropolitan cities, eleven sub-metropolitan cities, 276 municipalities and 460 rural municipalities. The holding of two sets of national elections conducted for all three tiers of government, within a span of seven months, is a remarkable achievement of the Election Commission of Nepal (ECN) in fulfilment of its Constitutional mandate.

These elections mark the culmination of the process that started in November 2006 with the signing of the Comprehensive Peace Agreement (CPA) to set up a federal structure in the country. From a Hindu kingdom, Nepal has now formally transformed into a federal democratic republic. The eleven long years of transition have seen important changes. A Constituent Assembly (CA) was elected in 2008 for a term of two years.

It, however, failed to bring out a new Constitution, despite giving itself repeated extensions, till the Supreme Court put its foot down to sack it in 2012. The second Constituent Assembly, elected in 2013, proved much more efficient and productive, coming up with a new Constitution within two years. Credit must be given to the political parties for their spirit of accommodation and their decision to defer, for the post-election period, the most contentious issues, including the delineation and naming of the federal provinces.

A highlight of the elections was the enthusiastic popular participation, as evident from the high voter turnout of 75 per cent in the local elections, and of approximately 68 per cent in the two phases of simultaneous elections to the parliament and the provincial assemblies.

Full credit to the ECN for conducting the elections rather smoothly, despite the time constraints and the fact that it lacked the crucial power to decide the timing of the elections, which was left to the government. Speedy production and distribution of voter identity cards and easy access to voter rolls contributed significantly to the high turnout.

The elections have been widely regarded as free, fair and independent. Arrangements were made for 1.225 crore voters at 15,344 polling booths, in 7,752 polling centres by almost 1,70,000 polling officials. The ECN accredited 45,000 domestic observers and nearly 300 foreign observers. The European Union and the Carter Centre, which sent the biggest teams, have both commented on the fairness of the elections. I also had the privilege of being a member of the observation team consisting of many election commissions from South Asia invited by the ECN.

It was delightful to see the enthusiastic voter participation in what clearly looked like a festival of democracy. Importantly, this was despite very tight enforcement of the stiff code of conduct. There were hardly any noisy processions or defacement of walls with posters and slogans, etc.

A noteworthy feature is that elections were held simultaneously to the provincial assembles and national parliament, something which has been a hot topic of debate in India for the last couple of years. Contrary to apprehensions, the voters, despite a high 35 per cent illiteracy rate in Nepal, had no problem handling as many as three ballot papers—one for the provincial assembly, one for parliament, under the first-past-the-post (FPTP) system, and the third for the proportional representation (PR) system for both tiers. This was made possible by a rather effective voter education programme put together in a short time, the paucity of time being a result of the inevitable debate as to whether voter education is the job of the Election Commission or of the political parties. The training of staff played an important role too. Some reports, however, suggest that many voters were confused with the single ballot for two elections (parliament and provincial) in the proportional representation category and ended up voting only on one part. We will soon know how many blank votes were registered. Lesson for the future: Have separate ballot papers.

It would be interesting to understand the democratic structure of the state, as it is significantly different from India's. The parliament would be bicameral, of which the lower house—the House of Representatives—would consist of 275 members, 165 members directly elected by FPTP (as in India) and 110 indirectly elected by PR. The seven provincial assemblies together have 550 members, of which 330 are directly elected through FPTP and 220 by PR.

The upper house, called the National Assembly, consisting of fifty-nine members, is yet to be constituted. It will have eight members each from the seven provinces, elected by an electoral college consisting of the elected legislators. The remaining three will be nominated by the president.

A bill regarding the formation of the national assembly is still pending, owing to serious disagreements among the political parties on the election process. Constitutional experts now foresee serious post-election challenges, including on matters such as appointment of the province chiefs, determination of provincial capitals and the giving of shape to political structures in the provinces. It is a curious situation, in that the provinces are not even named yet and are identified by numbers. It may be recalled that some amendments to the Constitution which were being demanded by the Madhesis and Janjati groups, leading to massive protests in September of 2015, and in which fifty lives were lost, were postponed in the interest of moving forward. These will come back to haunt the government.

The biggest challenge, of course, is for the government to provide stability and development, the slogan of the winning Left combination. This, in turn, will depend on how the two main parties of the Left alliance, which have long been at loggerheads, even violently, will stick together, sinking their sharp differences.

A potential lesson for India is to learn the working of the PR system to make democracy truly representative—a concern being voiced increasingly, especially since the BSP with 20 per cent of the vote in Uttar Pradesh ended up with zero seats from the state under the questionable FPTP system in the 2014 general election.

7

A UK Election in the Time of Terror

UK's mid-term poll on 8 June 2017 is historic in more ways than one. It will decide the fate of Prime Minister Theresa May's great gamble to seek her own majority, instead of carrying on with what she inherited from predecessor David Cameron, as well as decide the shape of the impending Brexit negotiations. It also marks the death knell of a historic act passed only six years ago, giving the House of Commons a fixed five-year term and a fixed date for its election (5 May, every five years). As per the act, the next election should have been held only on 5 May 2020.

But on 18 April, Theresa May announced her decision to dissolve the house and seek a fresh mandate. Although the Fixed-Term Parliament Act remains on the statute books, it was over-ridden on this occasion by an overwhelming majority; unsurprisingly, neither Opposition party wanted to lose the opportunity to fight an election to unseat the government.

In effect, the PM of the day can now call an early election at will (like before), which makes a mockery of the Act. After the 2015 election, in an article in the *Indian Express,* I had asked what would happen to the fixed term in the event of a snap poll. Even I had not visualized it would happen so soon.

At the time of announcement of the snap poll, I was in London. I asked a number of people their opinion on it. Almost everyone was against Brexit. In that case, May would lose, I ruminated. But many also pointed out that Theresa May could still win because her alternative, Labour leader Jeremy Corbyn, was perceived as untrustworthy. Dislike for a potential leader far outweighed dislike for a more consequential Brexit!

The decision to call a general election must have made sense at the time. May inherited a House of Commons majority of just twelve MPs when David Cameron stood down after the 'Brexit' vote. Even a tiny rebellion among her lawmakers had the potential of ruining policy and putting Brexit negotiations at risk.

Fired by the need for a bigger majority and a personal mandate in mid-April—which would allow her to overcome the opposition to her plans for a 'hard Brexit', whereby the country would not only leave the European Union, but also the bloc's lucrative single market—May seemed buoyed by her comfortable lead of 21 per cent over Labour. By 25 May, according to a YouGov survey, Labour had slashed the Conservatives' lead to 5 points; by 31 May, it had fallen to just 3 points, with Labour polling 39 per cent against Conservatives' 42 per cent.

What led to this dramatic decline? Theresa May's overconfidence in Labour disunity, a manifesto 'full of harsh and draconian policies', especially over social security issues, and an unfortunate underestimation of Corbyn's crowd-pulling ability, are some reasons. Clearly, she had banked on Corbyn's unpopularity among his own lawmakers—on issues such as scrapping the nuclear deterrent, as well as his apparent closeness to certain terrorist organizations, like the Hamas—a wee bit too much.

The contrast became especially acute after the terrorist attack in Manchester on 22 May, when May accused Corbyn of blaming the attack on UK's foreign policy in the Middle East. But, apart from the fact that Corbyn proved unable to put a cost on Labour's plans to offer free childcare to two-year-olds during a radio interview, he ran a smooth election campaign. His far-left electoral promises of re-nationalizing key industries, imposing high taxes on the rich and increasing social spending, are resonating with large parts of the electorate—with young voters in particular.

'Jeremy Corbyn has surpassed people's expectations, which were very low,' says a senior Labour politician. 'Given air time, people have realized he's not so bad.'

So, what has been the impact of the three terror attacks on London and in the rest of the country in the recent weeks? Besides a day's suspension in the campaigning, the impact on parties has been mixed. The Tories, perhaps, stand to gain, because of their hard stand on terrorism. But, as the party in power, their failure to prevent the attacks weighs against them. Many feel the election should be postponed. That is, however, not possible, as only parliament can approve a change of date and it has been dissolved, and unless May declares a full-blown Emergency, which is not the case.

May started this election as a strong favourite. She became prime minister barely a year ago and is still in something of a honeymoon period with the voters. Second, she hasn't made any obvious major public mistakes. Third, Jeremy Corbyn isn't widely popular within his own party. And, as an analyst remarked, it's pretty much 'the iron law' of British elections that divided parties do not win general elections.

In the first couple of weeks after she announced the election, some asked whether the Conservatives were going to win big or very, very big. But during the campaign trail, May has come out weaker than expected, delivering unscripted, unrehearsed interviews with experienced political journalists.

Corbyn, on the other hand, has proven to be rather more adept on the campaign trail. The terror attacks may have actually helped him. His attacks against the Conservatives, accusing them of making Britain more vulnerable by cutting funding for police and security services, have hit home.

So, what's going to be the result?

Truth is, even in the 2015 election, pollsters failed to predict David Cameron's unexpectedly strong victory; as for Brexit, they were completely confused about that referendum. In this election, some foresee a hung parliament, while others have given both Corbyn and May a vote too close to call. No one is willing to predict an outright victory for either.

Much will depend on voter turnout. A member of May's government admitted that Labour 'always turns out its core vote, but the Conservatives may not always'. The younger voter definitely leans toward Jeremy's Labour. If they do turn out to vote, Theresa May may be in big trouble.

All eyes are now focused on 8 May. Will Prime Minister Theresa May win a resounding election victory, scrape home with her authority in tatters, or lose outright? As always, the voter knows best. Twenty-four hours from now, we will know what they think.

8

Their Westminster, And Ours

THE UK IS ALL SET FOR A MID-TERM GENERAL ELECTION ON 8 JUNE 2017, which can only be derailed if there is yet another terror attack. While the poll issues involved and the fluctuating fortunes of the participating political parties are a matter of separate analysis, I will confine myself to the more mundane electoral system and its management issues. When the country had its last general election on 7 May 2015, I was an independent observer along with a sizeable international group—mostly election commissioners, many of whom were my old colleagues and counterparts. I was allotted three constituencies. Interestingly, two of these gave two successive prime ministers—David Cameron and Theresa May (I wonder if a third one is waiting in the wings!).

It is interesting to compare the systems in the UK and India, which hold many similarities as well as significant differences. The first significant difference is that in India, the Election Commission of India (ECI) decides the dates for the elections keeping political parties, including the ruling one, guessing, whereas in the UK, the date has always been decided by the prime minister, giving the ruling party a political advantage. This surely went against the principle of ensuring a level playing field for the competing parties. In 2011, therefore, the old system was changed to a fixed-date election, and Under the Fixed Term Parliamentary Act, the next general election was automatically scheduled for the first Thursday in May of the fifth year after the previous general election.

The 2015 election was the first under this system. But in an article I wrote for a paper ('Britain's electoral plumbing', *Indian Express*, 12 May 2015), I raised a question as to what would happen to the fixed date in case of a mid-term general election. Who imagined that this question would come to haunt the British in less than two years?

The basic common factor is the electoral model itself that we both follow—the Westminster model. Our Lok Sabha and the UK's House of Commons are counterparts to which voters directly elect their representatives. But the size of the house and the parliamentary constituencies differ enormously. The size of the Indian electorate is twenty times that of the UK, which almost corresponds to the state of Rajasthan. Despite the small population of the UK, the House of Commons has a huge strength of 650 MPs, as against the Lok Sabha's 543. The average number of electors for each of these MPs is about 70,000, while in India it is 16 lakh. The campaign styles and logistics in the two countries are thus worlds apart.

In the UK, campaigning is much cheaper, and is confined to door-to-door visits by candidates or agents, and to TV debates. Paid political advertising on TV and radio is not permitted. This is unthinkable in India, where the mass media, despite the exorbitant costs of advertising on them, are the backbone of campaigns. Paid news, which is rampant in India, is unheard of in the UK. There is a cap on election expenditure for both candidates and parties in the UK, whereas in India it extends only to candidates. That's a huge loophole, raising campaign expenditure to obscene levels in India.

Voter participation in both countries was at about the same level—the total turnout in the UK being 66.1 per cent, against 66.4 per cent in India in 2014; however, over the years it has been coming down in the UK and going up in India, thanks to the voter education programme started by the Election Commission of India in 2010. Youth apathy towards elections has been common to both countries, though the Election Commission of India's efforts to increase youth participation have had a dramatic effect, especially since the launch of National Voters Day, focused on young persons, which lead to an addition of nearly 12 crore voters (three UKs!) between the last two general elections.

India is also one-up on the UK, as it has been using EVMs since 1998, while the demand for electronic voting in the UK has never been very audible. The clamour for internet or online voting, however, is gathering slow momentum in both countries. The biggest plus for the UK is that their system is very clean, with no violence, booth capturing, impersonation or rigging. For us in India, these problems make polls a struggle for the nation. The UK system is very trusting; the UK is the only country in the world where no identity proof for voting is required. There is no photo on the electoral rolls, no marking of fingers. There are no party agents in the booths to verify the voter's identity. There are no police at the polling stations, whereas in India, a booth has to be secured like a fort. We are accused of killing the festival of democracy; the British are happy with quiet, civilized polling.

A very significant difference is that poll day is not a holiday in the UK. To enable working-class persons to vote, the voting hours are long—7 a.m. to 10 p.m. People normally vote either early in the morning or late in the evening. Housewives and the elderly vote during the day. So the scene is never chaotic. The UK has about 80 lakh foreigners, nearly 20 lakh of whom are from the Commonwealth countries. The latter are entitled to vote. Of these, there are over 6,15,000 Indian voters, who alone can influence the results in thirty constituencies. Voices are often raised against this anomaly.

Both countries follow the First-Past-The-Post (FPTP) system of election, where the candidate getting the highest number of votes is declared elected. Questions are often raised about the fairness of this system. In the UK, it snowballed to the extent that a referendum was held in 2011, though it failed, with 68 per cent of the votes in favour of the existing system and 32 per cent against. Additionally, the turnout for the referendum was a low 42 per cent.

In India, the demand for replacing FPTP with proportional representation has become louder after the 2014 general election, when a party (the BSP) with the third-largest vote share in the country ended up with zero parliamentary seats. Questions have sometimes been raised about the logistics and management of elections in the UK. In the 2010 and 2015 UK elections, there were complaints about postal ballots and about some polling stations, even in London, falling short of ballot papers before the poll's end—which is unthinkable in India. Our election management, despite its mind-boggling problems—like the Maoist insurgency in certain areas, militancy, the constant shadow of terrorism—is quite fail-safe.

Brexit being at the heart of debate in this election, global interest in this poll is greater than ever. Let us now see how it plays out.

9

Myanmar, Under the World's Eye

FEW ELECTIONS HAVE ATTRACTED AS MUCH WORLD ATTENTION AS the one in Myanmar, scheduled to take place on 8 November 2015. The election is particularly important for India, not just because Myanmar is its immediate neighbour but also because Myanmar borders a very sensitive, militancy-prone region. The fact that the country shares its borders with two giant powers, India and China, makes it geopolitically important. What kind of election Myanmar's is likely to be is the question foremost on the minds of the Myanmarese people and the global community.

Myanmar, like most countries of the region, has a long history of electoral fraud—from contestants and their supporters preventing eligible voters from casting their vote freely to manipulating the results. Fraud can also occur much in advance by altering the composition of the electorate.

The treatment of minorities is an important issue in this election too. For the last fifty years, Myanmar's military rulers have followed a strategic project of Burmanization—aiming for a single religion (Buddhism), language (Burmese) and culture (Burmanj).

In the 2010 election, ethnic Rohingya Muslims constituted three of twenty-nine MPs and two of the thirty-five members of the Rakhine Regional Assembly. The anti-Muslim tide surfaced after reforms started in 2011, erupting in communal violence in which at least 200 Rohingyas were killed and 1,40,000 displaced. Nearly 10 lakh Rohingya Muslims have been debarred from voting by questioning their citizenship itself, under pressure from Buddhist nationalists, and nearly 100 of their candidates have been disqualified from contesting elections. 'I am deeply disappointed by this effective disenfranchisement of the Rohingyas and other minority communities,' said UN Secretary General Ban Ki-moon last month (1 October 2015), adding, 'Barring incumbent Rohingya parliamentarians from standing for re-election is particularly egregious.'

Nine countries had raised concerns that rising religious tensions could spark 'division and conflict'. Aung San Suu Kyi said she 'saw worrying signs of religious intolerance' in an interview to an Indian media outfit on 9 October 2015. Many consider this statement of hers a perfunctory tokenism. Defending her deafening silence on the matter, she said it was the wrong way to achieve reconciliation. Not a single National League for Democracy (NLD) candidate is a Muslim while, ironically, the ultra-nationalist Buddhists accuse Suu Kyi of being pro-Muslim. Many are questioning this attitude of the 'Asian Mandela' and winner of the Nobel peace prize. Perhaps it is a case of 'electoral compulsions' that we in India, too, are familiar with.

A silver lining is an appeal by a civil society organization in Burma, Interfaith for Children, signed by leaders all four religions—Buddhism, Hinduism, Christianity and Islam—for religious tolerance and peace.

The credibility of the election commission in the country itself has come into question. The Union Election Commission (UEC) chairman, Tin Aye, has washed his hands off the matter, with the shocking statement that he could guarantee the accuracy of only 30 per cent of the voters' list. While admitting there was error in the software behind the list, he passed on the blame to voters! It's the people's duty to correct errors in the voters' list and he would bear no responsibility if voters complained without checking the list. President Thein Sein made a radio speech, which, according to the *Daily Eleven*, 'sounded strikingly similar'.

It did not help matters when Tin Aye told a leading media person, 'The president and I are comrades, brothers in arms. We have mutual respect.' Suu Kyi pounced on this statement, calling Tin Aye the bosom pal of Thein Sein and asked the public to be 'vigilant, cautious, careful and very, very brave' in the weeks before the election. The CEC was a high-ranking member of the military junta and the Union Solidarity and Development Party (USDP). The president appoints at least five Election Commission members, and some of the top positions are held by military men. To the UEC's credit, they have invited a large number of independent observers. As many as 11,000 domestic observers from twenty-eight organizations, 905 international observers from at least six international organizations and thirty diplomatic representations are expected.

Despite credibility issues, political enthusiasm is enormous, with 6,074 candidates from ninety-one registered parties in the fray. There are 3.5 crore voters registered to vote at 40,516 polling booths. They will be electing 168 representatives to the Upper House, 330 to the Lower House and 644 to regional and state legislatures. Myanmar has set up polling stations at its forty-four embassies and consulates around the world for advance vote-casting by more than 29,000 overseas Burmese citizens deemed eligible to vote. Domestically, advance voting, from 29 October to 7 November, will be allowed for government officials, political candidates, local observers and media personnel.

Myanmar's refugee problem is another hot issue in the elections. During the five decades of military rule, millions of Myanmarese left—illegally—in search of security to become 'undocumented' migrant workers in neighbouring Thailand, Malaysia and beyond. The UNHCR records 1,30,000 Myanmarese in Thailand, 1,50,000 in Malaysia, and over 10,000 in India. There are 14,000 refugees in Thailand's largest refugee camp, from the eastern Kayah State, which was devastated by the civil war that started in 1957 between the pro-independence groups in the Kayah state and the Myanmar government. They are accused of having connections with armed groups branded as unlawful. Although the Burmese government had invited them to return, seven of the fifteen rebel groups refused to join the ceasefire agreement signed on 24 October 2015.

The main parties in the fray are the USDP, the ruling party floated by the army, and the NLD, led by Suu Kyi. The NLD had won the 1990 election to the constituent assembly, boycotted the 2010 election and participated in the 2012 by-elections for forty-six seats. It won forty-three of the forty-four seats it contested.

The Constitution debars anyone from running for the office of president if s/he has a spouse or children who are foreign nationals. This directly affects Suu Kyi, whose late husband was British, as are her two sons. The Constitution also limits the role of political parties to 75 per cent of the seats, the rest being reserved for the military. The Constitution can be amended only with 75 per cent plus at least one vote. This makes amendments to the Constitution by elected representatives almost impossible, which rules out a Suu Kyi presidency completely. Some feel that she may stand for the post of speaker.

Whatever the outcome, the spotlight will be on Myanmar for the next few months. The election will determine the fate of the country's transition to democracy after five decades of military rule. The US has already announced that its relationship with the state would depend on the quality of the election and its acceptance by all the parties.

10

How Biden Got Elected

A s the United States elected its forty-sixth president after an unusually prolonged counting, election enthusiasts here in India, overwhelmed by result anxiety, began revering the Election Commission of India for its seamless conduct of Indian elections at the national and state levels.

Some went a step further to hold the election process of India in higher esteem than the US's system. It is important to understand how different or similar the US system is, vis-à-vis India's.

The US and India are the world's two largest liberal and secular democracies, whose Constitutions accord universal adult franchise to their citizens, irrespective of their race, caste, creed, sex or religion. Their similarities, however, end here.

Electoral frameworks in India and the US

Even though the election frameworks of both countries have a foundational basis in their respective Constitutions, unlike in India, where national and state elections are guided by two electoral legislations, namely, the Representation of the People Act, 1950 and

1951, in the US, electoral laws and regulations vary across states—even for national legislature and presidential elections.

While the responsibility of conducting and administering elections in India is under an independent constitutional body, the Election Commission of India, the US has no such federal body for management of its elections; there are over 10,000 administrative bodies doing this job in the US with their own rules.

There are two federal bodies with limited roles: the Federal Election Commission (FEC) and the US Election Assistance Commission (EAC). The former monitors campaign funding in presidential elections, and latter assists in administering elections voluntarily.

In terms of electoral methods, India follows the controversial 'winner takes all' first-past-the-post system, whereas the voting system varies across the states and tiers of the government in the US.

For instance, while the majority of the US states have the first-past-the-post system for the presidential elections, Maine uses ranked choice voting (RCV). Similarly, at the tier level, where Alaska and Nevada used RCV for primaries in 2020, Basalt and Berkeley have been using the system for their local elections since the 2000s.

While these are basic yet important intricacies that set the two countries apart, there are two unique features of the American electoral system that invariably either undermine or complicate its electoral democracy.

One of them is the concept of electoral college. The history of the electoral college is, ironically, based on mistrust. The constitutional forefathers were sceptical of the principle of 'direct democracy' as James Madison, the father of the US Constitution, feared a section with majority support could risk 'public good and rights of other people' under the influence of power.

Other objections to presidential elections based on the popular vote included the cropping up of presidential favourites in every state, the possibility of states with large populations having more say in choosing the president of the country and rendering ineffective the 3/5 compromise—a decision that counted three out of five slaves as persons to reward more representation to the southern states. Therefore, the Constitution makers arrived at a bargain called the electoral college. Comprising 538 electors who are distributed amongst the states in the same number as their total strength in the House of Representatives and the senate, the electoral college acts as a joining tunnel between the people's choice and the presidential candidates.

The electors meet in their respective states forty-one days after the election to elect the president of the United States.

US: The electoral college and its limitations

This is where the process gets murkier. Despite the fact that thirty-three states, along with the District of Columbia, legally bind electors to vote as per the popular mandate, seventeen states do not have such requirements, allowing electors to backtrack from their promise.

Even among the thirty-three states, sixteen states and DC have no penalty for such defections. In the last presidential election of 2016, ten electors had retracted from their pledge.

According to FairVote, the election monitoring body, in the fifty-eight presidential elections till now, there were ninety instances of electors (out of 23,507) not voting for the candidates they had pledged to vote for. While numerically backtracking by electors may seem a rare instance, the phenomenon of 'faithless electors' violates the trust bestowed upon them by the central elements of democracy—the voters—hence undermining democracy.

Additionally, the concept of the electoral college tampers with the sacred tenet of 'one person, one vote, one value' in two ways. To understand how this occurs, we must first understand how the electoral votes are allocated to the states. The formula for determining the number of votes for each state is simple: each state gets two votes for its two US Senators, and then one more vote for each member it has in the House of Representatives.

Firstly, regardless of how big or small a state is, they are all accorded two senators. Therefore, one is faced with a situation where a state such as California which has 38 million people has the same number of Senators as the state of Wyoming which has a population of just over half a million. Therefore, this system gives the smaller states an undue advantage by disproportionately increasing their influence in the Senate.

Secondly, unusual in modern democracies, owing to the electoral college, sometimes the winner of the popular vote can lose the election. This is because the President is not chosen by a national popular vote. Instead, the Electoral College vote totals determine the winner, not the statistical majority a candidate may have in the national popular vote totals. Electoral votes are awarded on the basis of the popular vote in each state. 48 out of the 50 states award electoral votes on a winner-takes-all basis. For example, all 55 of California's electoral votes go to the winner of the state election, even if the margin of victory is only 50.1% to 49.9%.

For example, it is for this reason that in 2016, even though the total votes cast for Clinton in the three states combined outnumbered those cast for Trump, Clinton eventually lost. This is because Trump won the electoral votes from Pennsylvania (20) and Texas (38), having won the respective states' popular vote, whereas Clinton only won the electoral votes of California (55).

Even if we set aside these practical problems arising from the electoral college system, that the world's oldest democracy's head of state is not elected by the country's popular vote is an irony worth pondering over.

It becomes a more pressing issue when nearly two-thirds of the American population prefer the popular vote system for presidential elections over the electoral vote system.

If the United States has modified its electoral college thrice in the years 1800, 1933 and 1961 through the twelfth, twentieth and twenty-third constitutional amendments, it follows that there remains no constitutional hindrance for implementation, but only a lack of mutual agreement and the political will of the states to switch to popular vote.

Vote counting process in the US

Another feature that unnecessarily slows down the electoral process in the United States is the counting of votes. The reason for the delay is inextricably linked to the voting equipment used by the states, which is mostly ballot paper, and the mail-in or postal votes.

Although the states begin the counting of votes as soon as voting ends, the final result is not known on the election day. Other than the counting of ballot papers, which is a cumbersome process, the different dates fixed by individual states to open their postal ballots stretches the counting period.

While a slow process is usual in the US elections, vote counting in the 2020 election has been unusually slower as there are large numbers of mail-in votes because of the COVID-19 pandemic.

For instance, while the 2016 presidential election had around 50 lakh early voters/mail ballots, the 2020 presidential election has been projected to have over 10 crore early voters. The problem is exacerbated as the small polling staff of 6,00,000 officials, who include private and public officers, are overworked.

India's vote counting: The EVM

In contrast, though a week or two passes before counting starts, India takes just one day to declare election results, thanks to the use of EVMs. With over ten states resorting to VVPAT, states could once again give EVMs a second thought.

If not, the next feasible option for the US to speed up its counting operation is to scale up its polling staff to India's level. Along this path, the world's largest democracy could become a guiding light to the world's oldest democracy. Considering how different the electoral mechanisms of the United States of America and India are—one being a completely decentralized system and the other fully centralized—it is unfair to compare the two.

Judging them by the same yardstick when the variables are mutually exclusive would be undermining and belittling the efforts electoral management bodies go through to provide for free and fair elections in both countries.

In the end, while India and the US could learn lessons from each other, what matters is that their people's faith in elections must remain intact.

11

Polls Apart

I NDIA AND THE US ARE THE TWO LARGEST DEMOCRACIES IN THE world, but the electoral systems of the two countries are poles apart. While the Indian system is charmingly simple, the US system is extremely complex and confusing.

The basic features of the US system are the following: there is no centralized election management body like the Election Commission in India. All fifty states, and the counties in excess of 3,000 within these states, have different election management bodies. The date of elections has been fixed—the first Tuesday after the first Monday of November—since 1845.

The US polls consist of not just one election but a bunch of simultaneous elections. In many states, a voter will be choosing not just the US president but twenty different contestants on a single ballot, including the members of the US senate and the House of Representatives, the state senate, the governor, the state attorney general and the supreme court judge. Furthermore, there are as many as 162 ballot initiatives (referenda) in thirty-five states. The ballot initiative process allows citizens to propose statutes or constitutional amendments, depending on the state, and collect signatures to place their proposals on the ballot for voters to decide.

The onus to register as a voter lies with the voter, and it is neither compulsory to register as a voter nor to vote. The last date for registration varies from one month prior to the poll to the polling day itself. Online registration is allowed in thirty-one states and also in District of Columbia. Any person turning eighteen even on polling day is eligible to register. Registered voters are a low ratio of the population. While in India over 95 per cent of all persons eligible to vote are already registered as of 2016, in the US it was just above 71 per cent in 2012. The voter identification system varies too—the requirements ranging from different photo identity proofs to self-authentication without a photo.

The polling station can be located in a variety of places, including private precincts, shopping malls, churches, community centres, court houses and fire stations, besides schools. The polling staff are drawn from a variety of sources—private and others.

The voting systems are diverse—voting at polling stations on poll day, early voting in person, absentee voting by mail. The ballot design varies from state to state. The voting technology also varies—from direct-recording electronic voting machines (like Indian EVMs) to paper ballots (marked by pencil or pen). But scanning is invariably used to facilitate counting. Some states have the VVPAT systems.

The turnout in the 2012 presidential election was 61.8 per cent (against India's 66.8 per cent of registered voters in 2014). Given the low voter registration in the US, this effectively means that less than 45 per cent of eligible Americans voted. Voting demographics show that older people—sixty-five-plus—are more likely to vote than eighteen- to twenty-old four-year-olds by as much as 25 percentage points. People with more education and income vote more than the less endowed. Similarly, women vote in larger numbers. Blacks and Hispanics vote less because of lack of interest. The hours of voting are longer—thirteen—than the average of eight hours (usually nine) in India.

The US has two federal bodies pertaining to elections—the Federal Election Commission (FEC) and the US Election Assistance Commission (EAC)—but even together they do not add up to anything as powerful or effective as the Election Commission of India. In fact, they have no control over the election administration. The FEC consists of six members, three each appointed by the two political parties. A decision requires four votes to make it non-partisan. The FEC's role is confined to federal campaign finance regulations. The EAC, also a bipartisan organization, was created only in 2002 to provide funding to states for upgrading their registration and voting systems, besides establishing minimum voter identification standards. Its decisions are, however, not binding.

The complexity of the election process and the multiplicity of authorities in the US is a perfect breeding ground for confusion. It's no surprise that a situation like the infamous Florida fiasco of year 2000 happened, when the results were first challenged in the Supreme Court but not pursued to the hilt by the gentlemanly Al Gore, who lost to Bush by just a few hundred votes. Many Americans called Bush the 'unelected president'. Earlier, too, in 1960, Kennedy defeated Nixon by a very narrow margin (49.7 per cent and 49.5 per cent of the vote, respectively). Many questions were raised about the legality of Kennedy's win, but Nixon chose not to contest the results despite many Republicans, including President Eisenhower, urging him to.

This, however, is perhaps the first time that a candidate—Donald Trump—has cast aspersions on the legitimacy of an election even before the first vote has been cast. Just cancel the election and name me the victor, he seems to suggest. He has also indicated that he may not accept the results if he loses. His supporters have warned of a 'revolution' in case Clinton wins.

It's noteworthy that the validity of results declared by the Election Commission of India has never been doubted—even candidates losing by just one vote have never questioned the results, though election petitions have been filed on grounds of corrupt practices on the part of the opponent. We have at least three cases of one-vote victory and one even of a tie, which was decided by a draw of lots. But the legitimacy of the election itself was never doubted. That's the reason why transition of power in India has always been seamless.

What has worked well for India is a fully empowered but fiercely independent and neutral Election Commission. The biggest reason for the success of the Indian system is its extreme simplicity. All things considered, Indian elections are regarded as a model by a large part of the world. It is always good to be reminded of Hillary Clinton describing the Indian election system as the 'gold standard'.

In the midst of the EVM controversy, we were often asked why we use EVMs when even the US does not. Well, all learnings do not have to come from the US all the time. While India gave equal voting rights to women from day one of it becoming a republic in 1950, the US had taken 144 years to do so. And then, while India elected a woman prime minister within nineteen years of Independence, the US has not had a woman president in 240 years. Hope they finally catch up with India!

12

Nigeria's Difficult Democratic Journey

N IGERIA HAS JUST HAD ITS GENERAL ELECTION IN MARCH 2019, ITS sixth since its return to democracy in 1999. Incumbent President Muhammadu Buhari of the All Progressives Congress (APC) defeated his closest rival, Atiku Abubakar of the People's Democratic Party (PDP), by about 40 lakh votes. Despite his pre-election promise that he would accept the results, Abubakar has rejected them, calling the election a 'sham' and 'militarized', and has decided to question it in court. There were seventy-three registered candidates in the fray. There are ninety-one registered political parties.

Election data

With a population of nearly 20 crore, Nigeria is the most populous country in Africa, accounting for 47 per cent of West Africa's population. It comprises more than 300 ethnic groups. The numbers of Muslims and Christians are almost equal, though the former seem to be politically dominant. Although 8.23 crore voters were registered and issued permanent voter cards (PVCs), 1.12 crore cards were not collected, with over 13 per cent of all registered voters losing an opportunity to vote. Though the observer missions found the register of voters to be generally robust, I feel the figure of 41 per cent, of registered voters among the population, to be low. In India, nearly 62 per cent of the population are registered voters.

Unlike India, counting is done at the polling stations, but the results are collated and declared at collation centres. It took seven days to announce the results of the presidential election, and collation of national assembly election results is still going on.

A federal republic with a presidential form of government, Nigeria has a bicameral national assembly, comprising the 109-member senate and the 360-member House of Representatives, both elected for four years. The country has thirty-six states (besides the Federal Capital Territory), each with an elected governor and a legislative assembly.

Nigeria is Africa's biggest oil exporter and has the largest natural gas reserves in the continent. Yet it ranks near the bottom of UNDP's Human Development Report, 2017, ranking 157 among 189 countries.

The Independent National Electoral Commission (INEC) has enormous power and independence and is considered to be neutral and credible. Each state has a resident electoral commissioner, appointed through a process of parliamentary ratification. When asked what his most important concerns were, INEC Chairman Mahmood Yakubu had mentioned security, fake news and hate speech, followed by 640 pending court cases and expenditure control.

Gaps in the poll

Despite the experience of two good elections in 2011 and 2015 and assurances given by the INEC, the management of the election was fraught with all kinds of flaws. First, there was the last-minute postponement of the poll by a week, just six hours before its commencement, because of a collapse in the logistics. This created extreme anger across the nation, apart from enormous economic loss (estimated at $10–25 billion). Then, despite the week's deferment, there were delays not only in the distribution of materials but also in the arrival of the polling staff, causing a late opening of polling stations. This in turn led to many procedures not being adhered to. Voting booths were often located too close to polling officials, polling agents and voters waiting to vote, potentially compromising the secrecy of the ballot.

The election was also marred by sporadic incidents of violence before and on election day, besides destruction of voting materials, ballot-box snatching and bribing of voters. At least thirty-nine people were killed in election-related violence. However, the death toll this time has been lower than in previous national elections.

Abrupt postponement of the poll, delays and chaos at polling stations and the violence … all contributed to the lowest-ever turnout—35.6 per cent, down from 44 per cent in 2015. In Lagos, there were only 11 lakh valid votes cast, and just above 5 per cent of the people had voted. Further, polling officials, security staff and other essential services personnel were unable to vote and were therefore deprived of their vote. There was also widespread failure of smart card readers as polling officials awaited technical assistance or replacements, compounding the problems.

Despite the complaints of 'militarization', police presence was generally discreet and helpful to the electoral process. A coalition of more than seventy civic organizations monitored the polling, which enhanced the credibility of the election.

Connecting with India

Nigeria is of great interest to India, the country being its biggest trading partner. Over 135 Indian companies have a footprint in Nigeria, including the State Bank of India, New India Assurance and Mecon in the public sector, and Bharti Airtel and the Tata, Bajaj, Birla, Kirloskar and Mahindra groups in the private sector. The number of Indians living in the country is relatively small—about 50,000. Though we have substantial economic interests when it comes to Nigeria, we are no political favourites. But, as the world's largest democracy, India has great interest in the success of the largest democracy in Africa. While the election commissions of the two countries have regular interactions and many officials have visited the flagship institution, the India International Institute of Democracy and Election Management, there is need for enhanced engagement between the two.

13

Kenya Elections, 2013

KENYA JUST FINISHED ITS TENTH BUT MOST HISTORIC NATIONAL election. Uhuru Kenyatta of Jubilee Alliance was sworn in as the president on 9 April after a prolonged counting process and the verdict of the Supreme Court on the election petition of Raila Odinga, the sitting PM.

The elections were extremely significant in the context of the major post-election violence bordering on civil war in 2008, which led to the killing of about 1,300 persons and displacement of over 6 lakh people, besides massive destruction of property. The trauma of the violence has haunted Kenya ever since and has left a deleterious impact on the psyche of the entire nation.

Peace at all costs

The determination of the Kenyans at all levels to maintain peace was writ large everywhere. The Independent Electoral and Boundaries Commission (IEBC), the administration, the judiciary, media and the church, besides the rival political leaders themselves, constantly appealed to the people to maintain peace at all costs. The most reassuring were the promises by the political parties that they would abide by the outcome of the election, whatever it was.

What had happened in 2007–08 was that after the results were announced declaring President Mwai Kibaki re-elected, the rival party claimed that there was a large-scale rigging. There was open incitement to violence. It soon became a full-scale civil war between rival tribes, engulfing most of the country.

The nation was shocked by the developments and started debating the strategy for the future to prevent recurrence of the tragedy that took the country back by a couple of decades. A new Constitution was promulgated (2010) and an Independent Electoral and Boundaries Commission (IEBC) established (2011). The judiciary was revamped. The administration, especially the police, was overhauled. And all entities resolved to put democracy back on the rails with the full support of the media and the citizenry.

The IEBC, from its inception as an Interim Commission in 2008, wanted to establish a transparent and robust system. It organized an 'induction workshop', to which South Africa, Ghana and India were invited. For India, I attended the workshop and shared the Indian experience. Not unsurprisingly, they were all fascinated and overawed by the Indian model. I invited their commission to visit India and see our system first-hand. Six of the nine commissioners, led by the chief, Dr Issack Hassan visited India and had a series of discussions with us besides a field visit. Dr Hassan made two more visits.

Another delegation of five commissioners visited India in June 2010, followed by a visit to Kenya by one of our own officers. IEBC was keen to demonstrate to the world that their elections would be totally fair and transparent. So they invited observers from all over—from the African Union, the European Union, the Commonwealth, the Carter Centre (US) and others, besides hordes of domestic observers. Nearly 32,000 independent observers, including 2,300 foreign observers, witnessed the election. I was invited by the secretary general of the Commonwealth to its seventeen-member observer group.

The ghost of violence

From day one, we came to a positive conclusion about the intention and capacity of IEBC to deliver transparent and free and fair elections. All stakeholders independently vouched for this. The most remarkable feature was the determination and the enthusiasm of the voters. The turnout was 86 per cent.

The mile-long queues from 4 a.m.—a good two hours before the start of the polls—were an amazing sight. We talked to some voters and asked them why they had come out so early. Their said it was because of their keen desire to participate and make the elections a success. Our driver, a local, however, gave us an interesting reason for the massive early turnout. He said that the people were still so haunted by the violence of the previous election that they had decided to come out at the earliest, fearing that violence may happen during the course of the day.

Though this was a lone, stray opinion, I found this to be a great insight into the psyche of the voters. They just did not want to take any chances. This was confirmed by the deserted streets we saw the next five days while the counting was going on. It looked like a curfew, though self-imposed. On the fifth day, I made what would normally be a two-hour journey to the airport in twelve minutes!

The patience of the voters was remarkable. In many places they were in the queue for four to ten hours, but none of them was heard complaining. Even on our probing/provocation, they refused to express any resentment at having to wait seemingly endlessly in the long queues. They told us that this was a small price to pay for a fair election and restoration of democracy.

A complicating feature was that in addition to the presidential election there were five more: national assembly and senate, county governor, county assembly and county woman representative elections. So, each voter had to mark six ballot papers and put them in six different ballot boxes.

Obviously, this was confusing and time consuming, taking the voters between four and ten minutes each to complete the exercise. Then the ballots were to be put into transparent plastic boxes, labelled in English and differentiated by the colour of the lid which matched the colour code on the ballot papers. The pale, faded colours led to a lot of confusion, especially in the dawn hours and late evening when the polling booths were fairly dark. A ballot in the wrong box would be an invalid vote. Despite these drawbacks, the number of invalid votes was surprisingly low (0.88 per cent).

There were problems with the system of identification of voters using the bio-metric reader attached to the laptops of polling officials. The system malfunctioned wholesale after many a delay and was abandoned in favour of the printed voter roll, which was a fortunate standby. I was surprised to see many voters who reached the booth after one and two hours of waiting in the queue only to be told that were in the wrong line leave without a murmur.

It was initially confusing to me that their polling booth corresponded to our polling location, and that what we call a polling booth was called a 'stream'. Thus, the first venue we visited was a school (called a booth) and it had twelve streams. The voter roll was common to all twelve and was divided into twelve sub-parts—not numerically, but alphabetically, by the first name of the voter.

As a result, families were split and joined separate queues, the members completing their voting at different times of the day. This led to funny situations. The families had come well equipped for a long-drawn-out process. But if the umbrella went with the husband, the drinking water went with the wife and the sandwiches with their children. This, of course, was a silly arrangement. I think we need to invite IEBC to India again!

The counting was done at the booth (stream) level just after the end of the polls by the presiding officer who was to convey the results to the returning officer at the tally (counting) centre. The SMS-based encrypted technology to transmit the results, launched with much fanfare, collapsed as soon as it was put to use, and the results could not be transmitted from the booths. The IEBC abandoned the technology and the results were physically carried by the presiding officer (PO) to the ROs. This meant a lot of delay, as the PO could move only after all the six ballots were counted. While the nation waited anxiously for the results of the presidential election, the POs were still counting the ballots of the local councillor elections. Similarly, at the tally centre where I was present, the RO had to announce all six results, one after the other, before moving on to the next booth.

The five days of counting kept the nation on tenterhooks and the people confined to their homes for fear of violence. What added to the suspense was the constitutional provision that the president has to get 50 per cent of the vote plus one vote. Kenyatta was in the lead by over 5–6 lakh votes from day one, a lead which he maintained throughout with minor fluctuations. But it never seemed certain that he would get 50 per cent of the vote, what with six other candidates (besides Odinga) in the fray.

Kenyatta won by the slimmest of margins, earning 50.07 per cent of the vote to clinch a first-round win, in an election that saw a record turnout of 84.9 per cent of registered voters.

If he had failed to cross 50 per cent and lead in twenty-four of forty-seven counties, it would have led to a run–off election within two months. The frightening thought of another election in a tension-ridden country so soon gave anxious moments to everyone.

What almost upset Kenyatta's apple cart was a delayed realization by the IEBC that the 'lead' they had been announcing from the beginning was wrong. They had to take into account the total votes cast, not the total 'valid' votes cast. It was well into the second day when the IEBC realized its mistake and corrected it, leading to protests by Kenyatta followers accusing the IEBC of manipulating the results under foreign pressure.

The Kenyan Constitution provides that any appeal against election results must filed with the Supreme Court within seven days of the results and that the court has to announce its verdict within fourteen days. Expectedly, Odinga filed an appeal alleging several infirmities in the election process. Tension gripped the nation throughout the period. Appeals for peace kept coming from both the leaders, the church, the media and the administration.

The Supreme Court confirmed the results on the last day (of the deadline). Happily, Odinga accepted that he had lost and appealed to his followers for peace. While all the international observers praised the transparency of the elections, some Western media kept attacking Kenyatta as an indictee at the International Criminal Court (ICC) for inciting the 2008 violence in the country.

There were clear suggestions to the Kenyans that the Kenyatta election would be an international embarrassment, as he, as the president of the country, would be appearing in front of the ICC as an accused in April, soon after the elections. Kenyatta converted this threat to his advantage by calling the criticism an infringement on Kenya's sovereignty. The Western diplomats (especially from the US and UK) kept a discreet distance from all this, though the Kenyan media accused them of interfering in the election. After the results, the Western governments, willy-nilly, accepted the verdict and congratulated Kenyatta in calibrated language.

While normalcy was returning, the detailed judgment of the SC came out with a shocker—that though it had found no significant flaw with the verdict, the verdict was far from perfect. It also observed that the failure of the voter identification technology needed detailed investigation, including criminal proceedings against officials of the IEBC. Thus, a well-intentioned reform came under a cloud and showed that all good work could be undone if there were serious glitches in the election management process. One hopes that the IEBC will come out of this inquiry with its reputation intact for a highly commendable effort in conducting credible and transparent elections against heavy odds.

14

Mozambique Elections, 2014

On the day Haryana and Maharashtra went to the polls on 15 October, Mozambique had its elections for their president, parliament and the provincial assemblies. Mozambique has been one of Africa's success stories over the past twenty years, turning from one of the world's poorest countries into one of its fastest-growing economies on the continent with the discovery of windfall natural resources.

I observed the elections as a member of the Commonwealth observers group of fourteen members led by a former prime minister of the Bahamas. The group came from five continents and eighteen time zones. The sun may have set on the British empire, but surely it does not on the Commonwealth.

The group was an interesting mix of politicians, academics, NGOs, media and election managers.

Why should the Mozambique elections be of interest to India? Mozambique has a centuries-old Indian connection through Goa, which—believe it or not—was once the capital of Mozambique, despite 5,500 kms separating the two. Hordes of Goans kept migrating to the country over three centuries, mingling with the locals, blending in totally with the indigenous culture. A sizeable number of Gujaratis followed suit.

The second Indian connection is of very recent origin—our growing business interests. Indian national oil exploration and production major ONGC Limited has lined up investments to the tune of $5 billion to develop the oil and gas reserves in Mozambique.

Coal India Limited too had firmed up undisclosed investments to be pumped into the moatize coal blocks in Tete province in Mozambique. Earlier in September, an Indian consortium, International Coal Ventures Limited (ICVL), completed transactional formalities to pick up Rio Tinto's coal assets in Mozambique for an estimated $50 million. India is, therefore, keeping close tabs on the elections in Mozambique.

Mozambique has presidential form of government and the electoral system is vastly different from ours. There were three simultaneous elections—presidential, parliamentary and provincial assembly (for ten seats)—all held on one day. Voting rights are universal for citizens above eighteen years of age.

As in India, polling booths are put up only in schools or in temporary structures and never in private buildings. The core polling staff consists primarily of teachers. And that's where the comparison ends. The polling party also includes three representatives of political parties. This unique political arrangement was hurriedly arrived at between the ruling Mozambique Liberation Front (FRELIMO, which was responsible for liberating the country from Portugal) and the Opposition Mozambique National Resistance (RENAMO) and Mozambique Democratic Movement (MDM) to increase the transparency of the electoral process.

The main Opposition party, RENAMO, is led by a militant leader, Dhlakama, who has spent more time underground than outside since the country's independence in 1975. He kept the country engaged in civil war till the General Peace Agreement in 1992. He has, however, contested all five elections in the country since 1994 when the single party system gave way to a multi-party system; every time rejecting the victory of the FRELIMO party and going back to the bush. The official results were announced only on 30 October, a full two weeks after the polls. Dhlakama has lost again (36.61 per cent of the vote to FRELIMO's 57 per cent), and has started questioning the legitimacy of the elections yet again.

MDM is the new party of a faction that broke away from RENAMO in 2007. It is increasingly making its presence felt. The most glaring difference between the electoral systems of Mozambique and India is that in the former, the ballots are counted at each polling station immediately after the polls are over, to prevent ballot stuffing. But that's when the complications begin.

Firstly, the tired polling staff who have been working nonstop from 5 a.m. (in fact, since the previous day) have to complete the counting, however long that may take. And that's normally the whole night. Then the result sheets are taken to the district counting centre, where the polling-station-wise figures are collected and consolidated. That's another two days.

Then these are taken to the next level, the provincial tabulation centre. After a similar drill there, the tabulation is taken to Maputo, the national capital. The Constitution provides for fourteen days for this process. Since the numbers of votes polled booth-wise are already known to all political parties from day one, as these were announced at the booth level and pasted on the wall at the booths, the results are not difficult to calculate. This gives scope for speculation and rumour. The obvious losers get the chance to make a noise about the poll process and malpractices as they have nothing more to lose and everything to gain by demanding a re-poll!

Two things were impressive—women and youth participation. Though all three presidential candidates were men, the three contesting parties gave tickets to a very respectable number of women (40 per cent, 27.6 per cent and 20.7 per cent), despite there being no legal requirement to do so. Thirty per cent of the outgoing parliamentary members were women. Even the public's attitude in the matter of gender was very healthy.

Youth Parliament, not an official institution as its rather pretentious name suggests, is a youth NGO that works to promote active youth participation in democracy and development. Its importance lies in the fact that, like India, 70 per cent of the population of Mozambique consists of youths. They use social media extensively, though its penetration is not more than 10 per cent.

The civil society and NGO presence was also sizeable. The institutions that played a proactive role were: Centre for Public Integrity (akin to our Association for Democratic Rights [ADR]), which even takes cases to court; and Women's Law Association, which keeps an eye on gender concerns.

Although there was a lot of talk about voter education and voter registration was 89 per cent, voter turnout was low, at 49 per cent, though up from the last election's 45 per cent five years ago. Most voters were not aware of how to handle the ballot papers. High illiteracy compounded the problem. No wonder that 5.46 per cent of the ballots were found blank! And 3.21 per cent invalid (wrongly marked).

Media

Media is yet to develop as a powerful democratic institution in the country and is remarkably docile. It's known less for its boldness and more for self-censorship, a phrase we often heard. Both fear and bribing were mentioned as the reasons for this attitude. The journalists' union here is weak. The government media is politically influenced and the private media no less behind. There has been a history of punitive action against journalists for publishing unfavourable news. A sizeable number of community and local radio and TV stations cater to local issues but they are equally subject to the controlled environment, besides the influence of religious bodies.

So confident was the Electoral Commission of the transparency of the elections that it invited almost 6,000 observers, of whom 350 were international (European Union, African Union, Carter Centre,

Commonwealth, etc.) besides an equal number of foreign journalists. All the international and domestic observation teams appreciated the transparency of the Electoral Commission and the peaceful and enthusiastic participation of the people. Yet, the losers are questioning the results, as they had on all five previous occasions!

The results have to be validated by the Constitutional Court within forty-five days. Mozambicans are anxiously hoping that the process will be completed without violence so that the country can reap the benefits of its new-found gas reserves.

Although the elections were fairly well conducted, Mozambique could easily learn a thing or two from India, like the forty-odd countries that have sent their election management officials to our own three-year old India International Institute of Democracy and Election Management (IIIDEM).

Constitution and Indian Polity

1

Controversy over Karnataka
RS Polls

THE STING OPERATION BY TWO TV CHANNELS PURPORTEDLY showing Karnataka MLAs negotiating for cash for their votes in a Rajya Sabha election has caused a furore. This is hardly the first instance of horse-trading in the country. Election time has become harvest season for voters electing members to the Vidhan Sabha, Lok Sabha and Rajya Sabha.

We saw MLAs of a party and some independents negotiating for big money—₹5 crore to ₹10 crore—for each vote. Of course, they were not being dishonest; they were just demanding reimbursement of the expenses they incurred on their own election to the Vidhan Sabha! Their party leaders were heard justifying it—'After all, they have to fight an election.'

News anchors and experts were heard advising the Election Commission on what is to be done. Many called the Commission toothless and wanted the elections postponed or even cancelled at once, just on the basis of TV reports. 'What more proof do you need?' they asked the Election Commission. They referred to a similar case in Jharkhand in 2012, when elections to two Rajya Sabha seats were countermanded.

It's important to refer to the Jharkhand case, as it the only precedent we have in this respect. On a complaint brought by three senior political leaders about rampant horse-trading among MLAs, the Election Commission countermanded the poll. It may be recalled that Jharkhand had become notorious for rich people from outside the state queuing up to buy Rajya Sabha membership from the state.

The legal dilemma before the Election Commission in the Jharkhand case was how to prove that the ₹215 crore that was seized was meant for the election. We thought we would face judicial reprimand if the court considered our stand hasty and conjectural. We decided to bite the bullet. Our gamble paid off.

The Jharkhand High Court not only dismissed the writ petition against the order but also hailed it as the most decisive action taken against corruption in the country in sixty years and imposed a fine of ₹1 lakh on one of the petitioners.

In the instant case, no money was seized, but there was a conversation between the MLAs and a decoy journalist, where offers/demands of ₹5–10 crore were made. Does this legally constitute a commission of offence of bribe or at least an attempt to do so? Intention to commit an offence is not a crime, except in the case of dacoity. As expected, the defence being put up by the concerned players is that no money has changed hands.

The rot is deep. Every political party knows it. They also make appropriate noises about it, but have no intention to stem the rot. But their tone changes when they themselves are at the receiving end. So long as we have this volte face and double speak, there can be no solution. I must, however, recall one notable exception when, after the countermanding of elections in Jharkhand, L.K. Advani wrote a blog showering 'kudos to the CEC', despite the fact that his own party was equally hurt by our decision. This is what he wrote. "I hold that today's decision of the Election Commission based on reasonable credible apprehensions is a landmark decision … money bags with no political support would think a thousand times before jumping into the fray.' Sadly, they don't.

What should the Election Commission do? The EC has to ascertain the facts to the fullest extent possible. It has asked for a report from the Karnataka chief electoral officer on the recordings of the sting operation. Going through the recording, transcribing it, and translating the Kannada bits is taking time. While it is clear what the reality is, the law requires evidence. Expecting the Election Commission to act without a detailed report is not fair. We must remember that the Commission's orders are subject to judicial scrutiny. In any case, there is ample time before polling day. The Jharkhand countermand order was given on the night of the election day, after the polling was over, and counting was withheld.

If the Election Commission concludes that there is prima facie evidence that corruption has vitiated a free and fair election, it has to act. What action is possible? One, the immediate ordering of an FIR; two, postponement of the election till the inquiry is sufficiently complete; three, countermanding of the election till a conducive atmosphere for a free and fair election is achieved and a fresh poll notified. An unintended consequence of the countermanding will be that the three other seats where the numbers are clear (and the candidates are stalwarts) will also be put on hold. Can this be turned into an opportunity? It may force the two biggest national parties to debate the evil of money power and consider the electoral reforms they have been avoiding.

What are the desirable reforms? Foremost is amendment of Section 58 of the Representation of the People Act to make abuse of money a ground for the countermanding of polls, as the Election Commission has demanded. In the Jharkhand case, we had resorted to the plenary power granted by Article 324 of the Constitution. This is a weapon the Election Commission uses sparingly. It's important that an enabling legal provision is made.

Two, political parties must discuss the overall problem of money power vitiating the election process and carry out the necessary electoral reforms. Three, there must be a ceiling on the expenditure allowed by political parties to their candidates. Political parties spend crores of rupees, and when they do they will need to collect crores of rupees too.

Four, state funding of political parties, not elections, must be considered, and private funding totally banned. Based on the number of votes obtained, ₹100 per vote can be given to a party. Five, the domicile condition for candidates, which was done away with in 2003, must be restored to stop wealthy candidates from outside a state from jumping into the election fray in another state. Six, to prevent cross-voting by horse-trading, the anti-defection law should be amended to declare violation of the party whip as defection.

The Karnataka situation is a defining moment in India's democracy. Let's seize the opportunity. When people lose faith in democracy, the consequences are disastrous. We have enough examples of this in our neighbourhood.

2

Karnataka Horse-Trading

THE KARNATAKA ELECTIONS AND THE SUBSEQUENT EVENTS OF JUNE 2018 have raised important questions about horse-trading in politics, the anti-defection law, the pros and cons of post-poll alliances, as well as the discretionary powers of the governor.

The dirty dance of politics in Karnataka has brought to light the various challenges facing Indian democracy. With regional parties gaining importance across states, we have moved towards a truly multi-party system, with fractured mandates becoming the norm. In such a scenario, it is essential to have a set of rules that will prevent a repeat of the natak that played out in Karnataka.

Horse-trading, which has become a catch-phrase in Indian politics, referring to political defections and the buying and selling of MLAs or MPs, has been around for a long time. It started in Haryana in 1967, when a Congress MLA named Gaya Lal defected thrice in a span of fifteen days—and twice in nine hours! Congress leader Rao Birender Singh presented him before the Chandigarh press with the historic words phrase 'Gaya Ram is now Aya Ram'—an expression that has come to describe political defections in India.

In order to curb the menace, an anti-defection Act was passed by parliament in 1985. The fifty-second amendment to the Constitution added the Tenth Schedule, which laid down the process by which legislators may be disqualified on grounds of their defection to another political party. According to the Act, an elected member is disqualified if he/she voluntarily gives up his/her membership of a political party, or votes against the party whip or abstains from voting.

However, a 'defection' by one-third of the elected members of a political party to another party was considered a 'merger' and would not lead to their disqualification. While this Act failed to curb the menace, the ninety-first Constitutional Amendment Act, 2003, changed the proportion of 'defectors' to two-thirds of elected members of a party having to be in favour of a 'merger' for it to have validity in the eyes of the law. The Act further states that the speaker's decision on questions of disqualification on the grounds of defection shall be final, as all such proceedings shall be deemed to be legislative and thus out of judicial review. The Supreme Court, however, declared this provision to be unconstitutional (*Kihoto Hollohan vs. Zachillhu and Others*, 1991), making the speaker's decision subject to judicial review, as the speaker would be acting as a tribunal while deciding cases under the anti-defection law.

The law, however, does not seem to be doing much to stop MLAs from defecting. This is primarily because MLAs are offered back-door entry to assemblies by rival parties. There is not much that an MLAs loses if he/she defects or abstains from voting. In fact, if figures are to be believed, the MLAs in Karnataka stood to gain ₹100 crore each! I believe a defecting MLA must be disqualified from contesting or from becoming a minister for at least six years. A distinction, though, needs to be drawn between a member leaving a party over ideological differences and one simply leaving for greener pastures.

Another question that cropped up related to the ethicality of post-poll alliances. Unlike pre-poll alliances, where the voters are aware of whom they are voting for, post-poll alliances present a new set of challenges. With the Congress and JD(S) having aggressively campaigned against each other before the elections in Karnataka, the post-poll alliance between the two rival parties is being seen by many as a betrayal of the trust of the voters, who call it an 'unholy' or opportunistic alliance. But how is the Congress-JD(S) alliance 'unholy' when the BJP post-poll alliances in Goa, Manipur and Meghalaya along similar lines were 'holy' just a few months ago? Public memory is short, but not so short. We can't have double standards.

Is there a way out? When multiple parties contest elections and the results show fractured mandates, there are only two options—re-election or a post-poll alliance. Re-elections will lead to enormous wastage of money and intensified polarizing of the hate discourse, and still not guarantee a single party coming to power. Post-poll alliances, therefore, present a trade-off that a lesser evil.

The third issue that has been highlighted in recent months is that of the discretionary powers of the governor. Government formation now seems to be a race to determine who can run to the governor the fastest to stake claim to form the government. 'Athletic' qualities rather than the number of seats have become the deciding factor! The questionable conduct of the governors in the exercise of their discretionary powers has raised serious questions about whether these powers are safe in their hands. Many voices have been raised demanding abolishment of the post itself.

As far back as in 1983, the Sarkaria Commission set up to examine the relationship and balance of power between the state and central governments dealt with this issue in depth and recommended the following order of priority to the governor as options to be considered when elections returned a hung assembly: One, an alliance of parties formed prior to elections; two, the single-largest party staking claim to form the government with the support of others, including independents; three, a post-electoral coalition of parties, with all the partners in the coalition joining the government; four, a post-electoral alliance of parties, with some joining the government and some extending support from outside.

The commission rightly makes the post-poll alliance, with all parties joining or offering outside support, the last option.

The Punchhi Commission set up in 2007 to take a fresh look at the relative roles and responsibilities of various levels of the government and their inter-relations, reiterated the need for adoption of the recommendations of the Sarkaria Commission. Whether the single-largest party is called first (ideal), or a post-poll alliance, the process must be uniform across the country. That these recommendations have been brushed under the carpet shows the ruling dispensation of the times in poor light. Since ruling parties always think they are going to be at the helm forever, they sacrifice long-term national interests for their immediate political interests.

The time has come now to put a stop to all this. What is required is a set of rules that will curb the menace of defection as well as the misuse and abuse of the powers of the governor's office. The following steps seem imperative: One, the anti-defection law must be made tighter, disqualifying a 'traded horse' for six years, if not more. Two, the governors' discretionary powers must be abolished and replaced with clear guidelines based on the Sarkaria Commission. Democracy is precious and must be protected from politicians and their rubber stamps at all costs.

3

When Defection Is a Mere Detour for an MLA

THEY DEFECTED, RE-CONTESTED, AND BECAME MEMBERS AGAIN, ALL in six months. Some are even likely to become ministers soon.

The Karnataka 2018 by-election results have widely put to display the ineffectiveness of the anti-defection law. Of the seventeen defecting Congress-Janata Dal (Secular) MLAs, eleven were re-elected on BJP tickets. Not only did this set of events lay down a well-structured framework for elected representatives to side-step the law, it even set a dangerous precedent for neutralizing the consequences of the law altogether.

The phenomenon of defections is not new in Indian politics. It has been plaguing the political landscape for over five decades. The most prominent case was that of Haryana's Gaya Lal, originally an independent MLA who, in 1967, shifted his loyalties between the Congress and Janata Party thrice over two weeks. The recurrence of this evil phenomenon led to the 1985 anti-defection law, which defined three grounds for disqualification of legislators—relinquishing of party membership; going against the party whip; and abstaining from voting.

Resignation not a condition

An individual's resignation as an MLA was not one of the conditions. Exploiting this loophole, the seventeen rebel MLAs in Karnataka resigned from their posts. This was aimed at ending the majority of the ruling coalition and at the same time avoiding disqualification. However, the speaker refused to accept the resignations and declared the legislators disqualified. This was possible as the legislation empowers the presiding officer of the house (i.e., the speaker) to decide on complaints of defection, and the speaker is under no time constraint.

The law originally protected the speaker's decision from judicial review. However, this safeguard was struck down in *Kihoto Hollohan vs. Zachillhu and Others* (1992). While the SC upheld the speaker's discretionary power, it underscored that the speaker functioned as a tribunal under the anti-defection law, thereby making her/his decisions subject to judicial review. This judgment enabled the judiciary to become the watchdog of the anti-defection law instead of the speaker, who had increasingly become a political character, contrary to the neutral constitutional role he or she was expected to fulfil. It was much the same in the case of *Shrimanth Balasaheb Patel & Ors vs. Speaker Karnataka Legislative Assembly & Ors* (2019), where a three-judge SC bench upheld the then Karnataka speaker's decision to disqualify the seventeen rebel MLAs in question. However, it struck down his ban on the MLAs from contesting elections till 2023, negating the only possible permanent solution to the problem. The Supreme Court played the role of a neutral umpire in this political slugfest. But the spectacle of MLAs being hoarded into a bus and being sent to a resort openly exposed not just the absence of ideological ties between a leader and his party, but also the moral character of each of these persons. It was also upsetting to see public acceptance of such malpractices as part of politics, with some even calling it *Chanakya niti*!

Exit, and swift return

The anti-defection law provided a safeguard for defections arising from genuine ideological differences. It accepted a 'split' in a party if at least one-third of the party members in the legislature defected, and allowed the formation of a new party by them; it also allowed the defectors' 'merger' with other political party if not less than two-thirds of the party's legislative members committed to it. The ninety-first Constitutional amendment introduced in 2003 deleted the provision allowing a split.

The ninety-first amendment also barred the appointment of defectors as ministers until their disqualification period is over or they are re-elected, whichever is earlier. But, obviously, such laws have not put to rest the trend of defection.

The main issue, as witnessed in Karnataka, is that the defectors treat their disqualification as a mere detour before they return to the house or to the government by re-contesting. This can only be stopped by extending the disqualification period for re-contesting and appointment to chairmanships/ministries to at least six years. The minimum time limit of six years is needed to ensure that the defectors are not allowed to enter the election fray for least one election cycle, which is five years.

Of course, MLAs can still be bought for hefty sums from the ruling dispensation to reduce it to a minority, simply to stay at home for six years.

Almost every political outfit has been party to such devious games, and has hardly any political will to find a solution to put a stop to it.

THE BAR, THE BENCH AND THE ELECTION COMMISSION: THE CUSTODIANS OF INDIAN DEMOCRACY

THERE IS GROWING REALIZATION, NAY, RECOGNITION, ALL OVER THE world that democracy—where 'a little man, walking into a little booth, with a little pencil, making a little cross on a little bit of paper', in the words of Sir Winston Churchill—is the ultimate ruler and the best system of governance in the modern era.

Even centuries-old monarchies are now making way for democracy; the latest examples can be seen in our immediate neighbourhood, in Bhutan and Nepal. So are dictatorships turning a new leaf, like in Pakistan and Iraq.

India is a Democratic Republic, as enshrined in the Preamble to its Constitution, and is now regarded in the comity of nations as one of the most stable democracies in the world. It is the largest democracy, but that is accidental because of its sheer numbers. But being regarded as a stable democracy speaks volumes about its qualitative strength.

Democracy survives and thrives on free and fair elections. 'Elections supply vis viva to a democracy' (*Mohinder Singh Gill and another vs. Chief Election Commissioner and others*—AIR 1978 SC 851). Free and fair elections constitute the bedrock of all democratic institutions.

For deepening democracy and firming and strengthening its roots in the country, the Election Commission can, without any reservation but with humility, claim due credit, because of the manner in which it has been able to deliver free and fair elections during the last six decades after Independence.

As senior Supreme Court advocate, K.K. Venugopal has said, 'While the three pillars of State unite to ensure good governance, it is the independent functioning of the Election Commission that has ensured that a democratically elected Government is put in place.'

It cannot, however, be gainsaid that but for the wholehearted support of the judiciary, the Election Commission would not have been able to discharge its constitutional obligations and perform its onerous task.

The liberal construction which the Hon'ble Supreme Court has always been pleased to place on the various provisions in the Constitution and the laws enacted by parliament, particularly relating to the powers of the Commission in its allotted domain of elections, has greatly strengthened the hands of the Commission in conducting free and fair, peaceful, smooth and periodic elections—paving way for smooth transfer of power, based on exercise of the ballot by the multitudes of ultimate rulers, and not by a few by dint of the bullet.

The path for holding uninterrupted elections as per the schedule laid down by the Election Commission was in fact laid in 1952 itself by the Hon'ble Supreme Court, when it held in N.P. Ponnuswami vs. Returning Officer, Namakkal–AIR 1952 SC 64 that,

> Having regard to the important functions which the legislatures have to perform in democratic countries, it has always been recognized to be a matter first importance that elections should be concluded as early as possible according to time schedule and all controversial matters and all disputes arising out of elections should be postponed till after the elections are over, so that the proceedings may not be unduly retarded or protracted.

But the path-breaking and illuminating pronouncements of the courts on the various provisions of electoral laws could not have come without the constructive role played by the bar.

The Election Commission has also been vested with some quasi-judicial functions and powers, like the tendering of opinion to the president and governors under Articles 103 and 192 in the matter of disqualification of sitting MPs, MLAs and MLCs, determination of disputes between rival sections or groups of recognized political parties under the Election Symbols (Reservation and Allotment) Order, 1968, etc. In dealing with those matters, the Commission sits like a court, where the distinguished members of the bar assist it in its deliberations, enabling it to reach well-considered decisions. Its decisions are open to judicial scrutiny before the high courts under Article 226 and before the Supreme Court under Article 136, and the courts' illuminating judgments have crystallized and settled the law in several grey areas, e.g., the Supreme Court's decision in the Sadiq Ali case (AIR 1972 SC 187) relating to the first split in Indian National Congress in 1969–70, upholding the test of majority applied by the Commission, and a much later judgment of the Supreme Court in Jaya Bachchan's case (AIR 2006 SC 2119) upholding the Commission's opinion about the office of profit held by her.

The most potent weapon given by the Supreme Court to the Commission for ensuring free and fair elections and providing a level playing field to political parties is the power given to it to enforce the Model Code of Conduct from the date of its announcing the election schedule. Though the MCC has no statutory sanction, yet, with the sanction of the Supreme Court in the case of Union of India vs. Harbans Singh Jalali (SLP No. 22724 of 1997) decided on 26 April 2001, the Commission has been able to enforce it with great efficacy and most expeditiously, and with the desired effect.

Another great power enjoyed by the Commission to keep the election machinery under tight control and to ensure its impartiality is the power to discipline the staff and transfer those who are found wanting in the performance of their functions. This, again, the Commission owes to the decision of September 2001 of the Supreme

Court in Writ Petition No. 606 of 1993 filed by the Commission against the Union of India.

In the judicial system of our country, which is wedded to the rule of law, the bench and the bar are complementary to each other. Members of the bar are regarded as officers of the court. The independence of the judiciary would collapse if there is no fearless bar, not afraid of placing its considered views with honesty of purpose so that the Bench comes to the right conclusions to render justice, which is the ultimate object of any judicial system. The historic decisions that the Hon'ble Supreme Court rendered in the long catena of cases on electoral matters, like the cases of Ponnuswami (AIR 1952 SC 64), M.S. Gill (AIR 1978 SC 851), Rameshwar Prasad (Bihar dissolution of Legislative Assembly case, [AIR 2006 SC 980]), B.R. Kapur (relating to appointment of Ms Jayalalithaa as CM of Tamil Nadu, 2001 (7) SCC 231), Kuldip Nayar (secrecy of voting at elections to the Rajya Sabha [AIR 2006 SC 3127]), Special Reference No. 1 of 2002 (relating to Gujarat elections [AIR 2003 SC 87]) manifest the collective knowledge and wisdom both of the bench and the bar, which made significant contributions in their lucid submissions.

The bar's singular contribution to making the right of electors really effective needs special mention. It was only because of the constructive role of the bar that the apex court gave those landmark directions requiring candidates to disclose their criminal antecedents, assets, liabilities and educational qualifications (*Peoples Union for Civil Liberties vs. Union of India and others* – 2003 (4) SC 399).

Some Grievances and Recommendations

But I have one grievance, and a serious grievance, against the bar. Our experience has shown that even where the law is unambiguously and unequivocally settled by the Hon'ble Supreme Court, not once but repeatedly, as in the cases of Ponnuswami and Gill, cases are often filed on frivolous grounds seeking courts' intervention when elections are in progress. This results in sheer wastage of the invaluable time of the courts. At the same time, this unnecessarily diverts the attention of the Commission, and its energies and administrative effects are distracted from its primary task of conduct of its operations and spent in running from court to court in various corners of the country.

Another example of unnecessary litigation into which the Commission is often dragged relates to election petitions. The Hon'ble Supreme Court has repeatedly held in Jyoti Basu's case (AIR 1982 SC 983) and the Michael Fernandes case (AIR 2002 SC 1041) that the Election Commission cannot be made a party respondent in an election petition. Yet, quite often, the Commission gets notices from several high courts where the election petitioners have named the Commission as a respondent. The Commission is then under obligation to make its appearance before the court, engage a counsel for the purpose, put in an application for deletion of its name from the array of respondents, and so on. How much administrative effort and expense from the public exchequer is involved in this unnecessary and avoidable exercise can be anybody's guess.

One of the great blessings of our electoral system has been the supportive and protective role of the higher judiciary. Many reforms in the electoral system have come from it. The order that candidates must declare their criminal and financial antecedents at the time of filing their nomination papers has been the biggest single contribution of the Supreme Court in making elections more transparent. Now, at least the voters can make an informed choice. Politicians should realize that when they fail in their duty to enact electoral reforms, the judiciary has been stepping into their political space. They cannot blame judicial activism when they have themselves become so passive and unresponsive to the signs of the time.

While the judiciary has been a great protector of democracy, it has been disappointing in at least one area, namely, disposal of election petitions. The Representation of the People Act, 1951, requires the high courts to decide on election petitions within six months, but all high courts, except that of Kerala, have been taking four to five years or more to dispose of such petitions, making the exercise worthless, since by then the impugned MP or MLA has finished his full term.

And when these election petitions are dismissed as infructuous after the term of the house, the MPs and MLAs, accused of corrupt practices in the petitions also escape punishment of disqualification from contesting for six years. As the upholder of all the laws of the land, this is one law that the judiciary itself has failed to uphold. I wonder if there has been any introspection on its part on this failure to discharge its legal obligation, which does cast a shadow on the judiciary's own moral authority. The government and judiciary together must address this issue, either by setting up fast-track election tribunals or by ensuring time-bound disposal of cases. If the Kerala High Court can do it, so can the others, if they choose to.

Another extremely crucial area where more prompt judicial action is desired concerns the plea against the electoral bonds scheme. The issue has been hanging fire since February 2017 when, in his budget speech, Finance Minister Arun Jaitley made two profound statements: One, without transparency of political funding, free and fair elections are not possible, and two, that despite seventy years of concern we have failed to achieve the transparency required. After these momentous statements, one expected that these issues would be resolved. However, what he announced was the opposite of the desires expressed.

Electoral bonds were born. And transparency died. Till then, every transaction of more than ₹20,000 was reported to the Election Commission. Now, even ₹20 crore or ₹200 crore could be donated anonymously. The reason given for the change was that the donors want secrecy.

The current electoral bonds scheme was introduced through the Finance Acts of 2016 & 2017, which amended four legislations—the Foreign Contribution Regulation Act, 2010, Representation of the People Act, 1951, Income Tax Act, 1961 and the Companies Act, 2013.

The petitioners (Association for Democratic Reforms [ADR], CPI [M]) argue that the scheme should not have been introduced through the Finance Acts, as this bypasses scrutiny by the Rajya Sabha.

They argue that the four amendments should have been examined by the Rajya Sabha. Additionally, ADR has filed a stay application on the scheme on two grounds:

1. Almost all electoral bond donations have been in favour of the political party leading the Union government.
2. Most bonds use the ₹10 lakh and ₹1 crore denominations. This suggests that the scheme is primarily used by corporations (who benefit from anonymity under the scheme) rather than by individuals.

The tenures of five chief justices of India—Chief Justices Dipak Misra, Ranjan Gogoi, S.A. Bobde, N.V. Ramana, and U.U. Lalit—have passed, and the current Chief Justice D.Y. Chandrachud has only deferred hearings so far, and finally the issue remains undecided. This is a matter of great national importance with serious implications for the electoral process, which is the foundation of our democracy. The Supreme Court therefore must act more promptly and honour its historical role as the custodian of India's democracy.

In the economy and polity of the globalized world, if India has one USP, it is our democracy. Though the little man, the voter, is the principal player, the bar, the bench and the Election Commission—jointly—are its custodians.

While the bench and the bar deserve three cheers, at least one cheer could be reserved for the Election Commission, which has not betrayed the nation's trust even once in seven decades.

ON THE OFFICE OF PROFIT ISSUE

THE OFFICE-OF-PROFIT ISSUE KEEPS COMING UP EVERY NOW AND then, leaving behind several questions. The most recent case pertains to appointments made by Delhi's AAP government on 13 March 2015. As many as twenty-one MLAs were appointed as parliamentary secretaries and attached to various ministers. One Prashant Patel petitioned the president on 22 June 2015, questioning the appointments on the ground that it violates Article 191A. The very next day, the Delhi assembly passed the Removal of Disqualification Bill 2015 with retrospective effect and forwarded it to the president for post-facto approval. After nearly a year, the president declined assent on 7 June 2016. He forwarded the petition to the Election Commission (EC) for its 'opinion', as mandated by the Constitution.

While this petition was pending with the President, the Rashtriya Mukti Morcha petitioned the Delhi High Court saying the appointments were illegal, since the lieutenant governor's prior approval—which is mandatory—was not taken for them. The court upheld this contention and held the appointments void ab initio.

On 19 January, a day before Chief Election Commissioner A.K. Joti was to retire, the Election Commission forwarded its 'opinion' to the president, declaring AAP MLAs disqualified , who accepted it within a day—despite the fact that it was a Sunday and the president was travelling. These developments raised a question: Did all this happen in undue haste? The bona fides of the matter are being examined. Interestingly, there is also a counter allegation—that the Election Commission took too long to decide the matter.

The origin of the concept of office of profit for ministers dates to eighteenth-century Britain. From 1701 to 1919, legislators who were appointed ministers lost the right to be members of the House of Commons as they were entitled to salaries and perks. India adopted this concept through Articles 102 and 191 to ensure the independence of MPs and MLAs from the government. To bypass these Articles, the Parliament (Prevention of Disqualification) Act was enacted in 1959. It exempted several posts from the purview of Articles 102 and 191, and has been amended five times—in 1993, 1994, 2000, 2006 and 2013. The long list of exemptions has made the office-of-profit safeguard a big farce. It is clear that exemptions were granted according to the whims and fancies of the government of the day. If we were to examine the list, case-by-case, most of the exemptions would be impossible to justify.

A.P.J. Abdul Kalam was probably the first president who saw through the absurdity in this practice, when in 2006 as many as fifty-five new categories were proposed to be exempted by an amendment bill—with retrospective effect from 1959. He refused to sign the bill and returned it to parliament. The Lok Sabha passed the bill again without change and returned it to the president. Defying constitutional requirement, President Kalam chose to sit on the file for over two weeks instead of refusing to sign it, making the government panic.

After a great deal of personal persuasion by then Prime Minister Manmohan Singh, the president signed the bill, on the assurance that on the first working day of parliament, the government would constitute a Joint Parliamentary Committee (JPC) to address his concerns over the justification for such a long list.

Not many know that the Election Commission was all set to issue notices to twenty-two MPs (including the then Lok Sabha Speaker Somnath Chatterjee) against whom there were complaints about holding offices of profit. If the notices had been sent, there would have been a demand for the resignation of all twenty-two. In fact, Chatterjee, who got wind of the impending notice, was all set to resign. If that had happened, parliament could have ended in commotion and the JPC would not have been constituted that day. The president would not have signed the bill, making the confrontation between him and the government uglier.

President Pranab Mukherjee's refusal to give assent to the Delhi assembly bill in 2016 without assigning any reason for it can be seen in this light. The Delhi bill aimed to protect 21 party legislators who were appointed as parliamentary secretaries from the prospect of disqualification. But the same president had approved another amendment along the same lines as the Delhi bill in 2013. Is this selectivity a case of the famous bureaucratic aphorism: Show me the face and I would show you the rule?

The indiscriminate use of exemptions has created a situation where the same posts are exempt from the purview of some Acts in some states, while they are deemed as offices of profit in others. What is good for the goose must be good for the gander. Another anomaly was that while there were many posts of parliamentary secretary in several states, such posts were denied to Delhi—and indeed to some other states. The selective operation of the process does raise questions as to its legitimacy. Many jurists are wondering if the office-of-profit concept is relevant or should be done away with.

The Delhi assembly case has left a number of questions unanswered, which the AAP has challenged. Did the Election Commission give sufficient opportunity to the defendants to be heard, as per the law of natural justice? Is the Commission's stand, that the petitioner is like a whistle-blower who cannot be cross-examined, justified? Was there undue haste in the way the CEC issued the order disqualifying

AAP MLAs on his last working day? Was the action of Election Commissioner O.P. Rawat, who had first recused himself but rejoined the proceedings without informing the parties, legally correct? Was the newly appointed commissioner, who had not heard the case at any stage, right in joining in the verdict? Another relevant question is whether the president was obliged to accept the Delhi assembly bill. The matter is sub-judice.

The AAP seems to be depending solely on its argument of 'no pecuniary benefit', whereas the Election Commission has based its decision on the third of the three criteria laid down by the Joint Parliamentary Committee—that is: 'Whether the body in which an office is held enables the holder to wield influence or power by way of patronage.' It will be interesting to see how the court adjudicates on these questions.

The bigger concern, however, is that there seems to be no other reason for creating posts of parliamentary secretary except to bypass the ninety-first constitutional amendment of 2004, which restricted the number of ministers in a cabinet to 15 per cent of the Lok Sabha or the state legislatures. It is a shame that to keep a flock of MPs and MLAs happy, various governments created the post of parliamentary secretary, with full salary and perks, and with powers almost identical to those of ministers. It's also a pity that the legislators have no attachment to ideology and the only force that keeps them tied to their parties are the loaves of office. I am pained to say that the long list of exemptions is a joke on the Constitution. The wholesale creation of posts of parliamentary secretary is a fraud on the Constitution.

ON RAHUL GANDHI'S DISQUALIFICATION

WITH RAHUL GANDHI'S DISQUALIFICATION FROM PARLIAMENT, many questions pertaining both to the legal and political ramifications of the disqualification have been doing the rounds. I intend here to both clarify many questions being raised and also to raise new and significant questions which are consequential, not only to the present case but also more broadly to the fate of our parliamentary democracy.

On 23 March 2023, the chief judicial magistrate, Surat, sentenced Congress MP Rahul Gandhi to two years' imprisonment and also imposed a fine of ₹15,000 on him after convicting him for the offence of criminal defamation under Sections 499 and 500 of the Indian Penal Code. The court suspended his sentence for thirty days and granted him bail to enable him to file an appeal in a higher court against its verdict. Following this, the very next day, the Lok Sabha secretariat issued Rahul Gandhi's disqualification notification.

Congress workers rushed to the streets in many parts of the country, instead of Rahul Gandhi's lawyers rushing to the court in appeal. The solution only lies with the courts. The disqualification can only be reversed if a higher court grants a stay on the conviction or reverses the conviction. After the Lily Thomas judgment of the Supreme Court in 2013, disqualification comes into immediate effect.

On 1 October 2013, Rasheed Masood became the first MP to lose his membership of parliament upon his conviction in a criminal case. After that, over twenty other legislators, including Lalu Prasad Yadav, have been disqualified under the same provision.

Did the Lok Sabha secretariat act in undue haste, as alleged by some? A former attorney general pointed out that the secretariat has no option. He clarified that as soon as the judge signs the conviction order, disqualification kicks in. He, however, did not mention a violation of this principle which happened in a similar case from Lakshadweep.

The Lakshadweep MP, Mohammed Faizal was convicted in an attempt-to-murder case and was awarded a ten-year sentence. Two days later, the Lok Sabha secretariat issued a notification disqualifying him. On 18 January 2023, the Election Commission declared a by-poll for the Lakshadweep seat. However, on 25 January, the Kerala High Court stayed Faizal's conviction. The Supreme Court thereafter stayed the by-poll which the Election Commission had ordered with equal promptness.

But to this day Faizal has not yet been reinstated to parliament. What the legal luminary has not mentioned is whether removal of disqualification also comes into effect the moment the court signs the order suspending a conviction. Does this not lend credence to the allegation of selective haste? Besides, isn't this wilful disobedience of the orders of the high court contempt of court? In Lok Prahari v Election Commission of India (2018), the Supreme Court held that once a conviction has been stayed during the pendency of an appeal, the disqualification which operates as a consequence of the conviction cannot remain in effect.

Some puzzling questions remain, which need to be answered. How come the petitioner who filed the suit against Rahul Gandhi sought a stay from the high court on Gandhi's trial last year and was successful in delaying the proceedings for nearly twelve months? And what specific circumstances prompted him to seek a vacation of the stay when no additional evidence was produced for it? Why was the magistrate changed in February? No reason has surfaced.

Thirdly, did Rahul Gandhi's remarks constitute criminal defamation, as opposed to civil defamation? This is what he had said at a rally in Kolar, Karnataka, on 13 April 2019: 'Nirav Modi, Lalit Modi, Narendra Modi … how come they all have Modi as common surname? How come all the thieves have Modi as the common surname?'

Did it call for a sentence of the maximum possible prison term of two years? Incidentally, this is the minimum period of punishment which attracts disqualification under the Representation of the People Act, 1951.

Fourthly, and perhaps most importantly of all: In a political atmosphere such as ours, which is being increasingly charged with high levels of hate speech and vitriolic politics, how many of our politicians can truly survive the tests of Section 153 (a) and Section 505, both of which, if someone is convicted, can lead to disqualification under Section 8 of the Representation of People Act, 1951 for that person? Both the aforementioned sections deal with offences that promoting enmity based on religious and linguistic grounds, among others. Therefore, why this selective efficiency in disqualifying members of the Opposition while turning a blind eye towards members of the ruling dispensation? Surely, as the ruling party themselves are stating repeatedly, equality before the law is a cardinal principle, and no one is above the law.

I believe it is high time that we review and rethink the use and legitimacy of defamation cases in general. Many democratic countries around the world, including the UK, USA and Sri Lanka, have decriminalized defamation and it is no longer a criminal offence. It may do us well to follow suit.

Finally, in conclusion, it must be remembered that the best and correct way to proceed from hereon will be through the due process of the courts. The judgment determining the legality of such a disqualification as Rahul Gandhi's cannot be deliberated in the streets. The political fallout of this issue is slowly unfolding as we await the final outcome of this, especially in the light of the 2024 general elections.

But whatever may be the electoral results and legal verdicts, it is an indisputable fact that a healthy Opposition is an imperative for a healthy democracy. We must not allow it to be killed.

THE GOVERNOR'S ROLE: MEDDLER OR STABILIZER?

In the 2023 disqualification proceedings against Maharashtra MLAs in the Supreme Court, Chief Justice of India D.Y. Chandrachud, heading the five-judge Constitution bench, dropped a bombshell with his hard-hitting remarks about the role and powers of the governor of a state.

In the course of the arguments, the chief justice severely criticized the Maharashtra governor's actions and raised questions about the legitimacy and limits of the governor's role in this case, though, as obiter dicta. The CJI observed that the 'Governor should not enter political arena', adding that a governor 'cannot enter into any area by which his action would precipitate the fall of a government', and that unless this principle is maintained it would be 'very, very serious for our democracy'.

The crucial issue at hand is regarding the procedural and constitutional powers conferred on the governor. A governor who is expected be non-partisan cannot function in a way that precipitates a crisis and leads to the toppling of a duly elected government. Furthermore, being an executive appointee, the governor has no role to play in legislative issues, and if at all he does the circumstantial constraints and exceptions that will legitimately allow his interference need to be delineated.

While the argumentative and circumstantial nuances specific to the particular case concerning the Maharashtra crisis are sub judice, we cannot lose sight of the highly significant underlying issue—the role and scope of the governor.

In India, in recent years, there has been a spate of controversies about the conduct of governors across the country, from Jharkhand and West Bengal to Tamil Nadu and Kerala. This issue has gotten to such a worrying level that many governors are being called 'agent provocateurs of the Centre'. We only have to take the very recent case of R.N. Ravi, the Tamil Nadu governor. Exceeding his powers, he skipped certain parts of his speech, omitting words such as 'secularism' and names such as 'Periyar' and 'B.R. Ambedkar'. Further, he made denigrating remarks, stating that the Dravidian model of politics is regressive, and at a gathering of civil aspirants advised them that in matters of dispute between Centre and the state, they should always undoubtedly take the side of the Centre. He went on to show the impertinence to suggest changing the name of the state of Tamil Nadu itself!

Likewise, we may look at what happened in the case of Jharkhand in August 2022. On 26 August, the Election Commission of India sent a report to Jharkhand governor Ramesh Bais ostensibly recommending the disqualification of chief minister Hemant Soren as a member of the assembly for allegedly holding a mining licence, and thus violating electoral law regarding "office of profit". Former Jharkhand governor (now Maharashtra governor) Ramesh Bais withheld the opinion of the Election Commission on Hemant Soren's office-of-profit case and did not act on it, thereby causing chaos and destabilizing the house. In fact, by keeping the ECI's verdict a secret, despite repeated requests by both CM Soren and the ruling UPA, he violated Article 192(2) of the Constitution, which says that he 'shall act' according to such opinion. Thereafter, in a move that casts serious aspersions on his bonafides, Bais claimed that his delay in revealing the ECI's report was due to his taking a 'second opinion'. Second opinion? Even by a charitable interpretation, this explanation was not only facetious but betrayed his utter ignorance of the Constitution. The 'opinion' in this case is a quasi-judicial order of the Election Commission which a governor (or even the president, in the case of MPs) cannot change even a comma of and has to implement in toto. The Constitution has mandated the word of ECI to be final in the matter of disqualification in an office-of-profit case.

The act of the governor keeping to himself the 'opinion' of the ECI is a mystery. If the ECI found Soren guilty of holding an 'office of profit', the governor would have lost no time in sacking him. If the ECI's verdict was 'not guilty', he should have made that public to remove the uncertainty hanging over the government. The suspense was enough for an exodus to start from the government. Which is presumably what the governor intended. Soren's act of seeking a vote of confidence pre-empted that, but even he probably didn't know the law. If the ECI had found him guilty, no vote of confidence could have saved him. The vote was irrelevant. All this political drama could have been avoided if the governor had not kept the ECI's opinion close to his chest. It was not his personal property to sit over. Article 192(2) clearly says that the governor 'shall act' according to the ECI's opinion. By not acting, he was clearly in violation of the Constitution.

As an unelected appointee of the Centre, the governor is expected to not get involved in political controversies or ideological rifts. He must display non-partisan statesmanship, and not become confrontational and meddlesome in legislative matters. It is also necessary to restrict the discretionary powers of the governor, because a politically active and partisan governor would be usurping the power of elected representatives.

The question mark on the role of governors is not a new phenomenon, but has been in evidence for decades. Demands have been raised, ranging from calls to restrict their discretionary powers to even abolishing the post of governor. Their questionable role in the wake of elections, in choosing which leader to invite to form the government, has often been observed. A hung mandate becomes a fertile ground for some governors who are happy to play puppet in the hands of an overbearing Centre.

Laying down a clear procedure in cases of a hung mandate would do great good to Indian democracy. The Justice Sarkaria commission, established in 1983 to examine the relationship and balance of power between state and Central governments, had recommended the following order of choice to be followed by a governor in the case of a hung assembly:

1. An alliance of parties that was formed prior to the elections
2. The single-largest party staking a claim to form the government with the support of others, including independents
3. A post-electoral coalition of parties, with all the partners in the coalition joining the government
4. A post-electoral alliance of parties, with some of the parties in the alliance forming a government and the remaining parties, including independents, supporting the government from outside.

Two decades later, the Justice Punchhi Committee (2007) reiterated the recommendations, but successive governments have not bothered to take them seriously. History has shown that constitutional morality and values are too serious to be left to the discretion of governors. We must design institutional safeguards to ensure that governors do not cross the Lakshman rekha. The Sarkaria and Punchhi Commissions have dealt with the subject at length. For strengthening our democracy and its federal structure, we need to act. And urgently too.

ON THE SUPREME COURT VERDICT ON THE APPOINTMENT OF ELECTION COMMISSIONERS

In a decision on 3 March 2023, the Supreme Court of India directed that appointment of election commissioner must be made on the advice of a committee comprising the Prime Minister, the leader of the Opposition and the chief justice of India. This decision is a significant step towards ensuring the impartiality and independence of the Election Commission, which is an essential pillar of India's democracy.

As a former chief election commissioner of India, I believe this is a landmark decision that will strengthen the Election Commission's functioning and enhance public trust in the electoral process. The Election Commission of India is responsible for conducting free and fair elections in the country and for ensuring that they are conducted in an impartial and transparent manner.

The Supreme Court's decision comes in response to four writ petitions challenging the system of appointment of Election Commissioners unilaterally by the executive. The petitioners argued that this practice compromised the independence of the Election Commission and made it susceptible to political interference. The court agreed with this argument and directed the government to pass a law to provide for the appointment of election commissioners on the advice of a committee comprising the prime minister, the leader of the Opposition, and the chief justice of India.

The inclusion of the leader of Opposition in the committee is a crucial element to ensure that the appointment of election commissioners is not subject to the whims and fancies of the ruling party alone. This move is in line with the principles of checks and balances, which are fundamental to a robust democracy. It is important to note that the Election Commission of India is widely regarded as one of the most credible and impartial electoral bodies in the world. This is largely due to the independence and integrity of its members, who have played a crucial role in ensuring the conduct of fair elections in the country. However, on many occasions, questions have been raised about the fairness of its actions. With the Supreme Court's decision, the Election Commission will be able to continue its work with renewed confidence, knowing that it has universal acceptance across party lines.

The unanimous verdict of the five-judge Constitution bench of the court is a significant step towards enhancing the credibility and integrity of the electoral process in India. This decision reinforces the independence of the Election Commission and safeguards it from government interference.

A question is being asked is—what will be the response of the government? Well, their top lawyers had strongly opposed the petitions and had argued that the system has been working well all these years and has acquired international prestige, so where is the need to tinker with it. The counter argument is that hoping that the system will work well in the future is not a pragmatic solution. 'Hope' is not a strategy. There have to be systemic checks in place.

Many people are asking whether the government will implement this decision by bringing up a bill in parliament. I am optimistic that the government will accept the verdict gracefully and implement it fully. Till an Act is passed, the norms laid down by the court have to be applied. Hopefully, the Act will consider electoral reforms in all its dimensions, including protection to commissioners from removal, as has been provided for the chief election commissioner.

The kind of collegium suggested is not new to the country. Appointments to the National Human Rights Commission, Central Vigilance Commission and Central Information Commission are, after all, done on the recommendation of a collegium. And these institutions have been free from any controversy.

The court examined the practice in several countries, each of which had a bipartisan system of selection of the election commissioners. The collegium was the least of the options. In some countries, a select committee of parliament oversees the appointments. In some, the entire parliament debates on the names. In some countries, this debate or interviews of the candidates are nationally televised. India is the only country in the entire democratic world where the election Commissioners are appointed unilaterally by the incumbent government.

Article 324(2) of the Constitution stipulates that the president will make these appointments according to a law which parliament may pass. After seven decades, the law is still nowhere to be seen.

Is there a guarantee that those appointed through the collegium system will be totally free from pressure or the influence by the government? Surely, there can be no guarantee of this. But appointments by consensus would certainly enhance the credibility of the institution in the eyes of the public. Opposition leaders will not be able to criticize the decisions of the Commission since the LOP would be involved in the selection process. However, it will be appropriate to admit that the verdict is not a magic wand. After all, many judgments of even the apex court have been viewed with suspicion and questioned by legal experts.

LINKING VOTER ID TO AADHAR

T HE ELECTION LAWS (AMENDMENT) BILL WAS PASSED ON 21 December 2021, amid protests by the Opposition in both houses of parliament. The crux of this new Bill is that the Aadhaar, a unique identification system, is to be linked to the electoral rolls as a way to authenticate voters. The opponents of the Bill have several suspicions about it, which need to be addressed.

The government has said that the Bill sought to address the Election Commission's concern of identifying duplicate voters so as to clean up the rolls, and that the linking is designed to do exactly that. There are two principal reasons for the proposal to link the two systems. One is improved accessibility to voting: with over 30 crore migrant workers across the country, the Voter ID-Aadhaar linking will allow the Election Commission to track them and allow them to participate in elections in their home states. The second is prevention of voter fraud: since Aadhaar information is linked to biometrics, which cannot be replicated, the Election Commission had contended that voter fraud on the basis of this information would be very difficult. Voter cards linked with biometrics would be difficult to falsify.

The Election Commission had sent its proposal for voter card and Aadhaar linking in August 2019, suggesting that the electoral law be amended to allow it to gain access to the Aadhaar records of both registered voters and first-time voters getting registered. Earlier, in 2015, the Election Commission had launched a pilot programme—the National Electoral Roll Purification and Authentication Programme—to use Aadhaar information to remove duplicate voters from the electoral rolls.

The Supreme Court had stayed this action until such time as it would adjudicate on whether this would violate citizens' privacy. In August 2017, a nine-judge bench of the Supreme Court delivered a unanimous verdict in *K.S. Puttaswamy vs. Union of India*, affirming that the Constitution guarantees to each individual the fundamental right to privacy. Before the Supreme Court stay on the linking, the Election Commission had already collected and verified the Aadhaar data volunteered by 32 crore voters. The Bill was met with a storm of opposition even at the time of its introduction in the Lok Sabha. The opposition is based on primarily three grounds:

1) Linking the electoral roll with Aadhaar information could lead to personal information getting leaked. This could lead to targeted electoral campaigns and even disenfranchisement of groups of voters. What was mentioned as proof of this having already happened was the tracking of lakhs of voters in Andhra Pradesh and Telangana in 2019, and even the actual deletion of 55 lakh voters from the electoral rolls.

2) Scope for voter fraud remains, even with the use of Aadhaar. In 2020, the Unique Identification Authority of India (UIDAI) had admitted that it had had to cancel 40,000 fake Aadhaar cards. There are multiple examples of Aadhaar identities having been faked, such as the incident in 2018 in which a Bangladeshi national was arrested at Bengaluru airport with a fake Aadhaar card and other documents that he had procured from an agent in the city. Voter ID-Aadhaar linking could thus potentially give

non-citizens the right to vote, as Shashi Tharoor pointed out during the debate on the bill.

3)   Justice B.N. Srikrishna, who was the chairman of the committee which drafted the original Personal Data Protection bill, has said that voter ID-Aadhaar linking could allow the government to profile voters. Precedent for this exists in Latin America, where authoritarian governments had brought in legislation to use a single form of identification (a national ID), which had actually led to disenfranchisement of citizens and a reduction in the number of voters as marginalized communities failed to procure the ID and thus the vote. India, with its hundreds of marginalized communities, could very easily face a similar problem.

A number of electoral reform proposals sent by the Election Commission to the government from time to time have been languishing. If the reason the bill was rushed through parliament was truly to purify the electoral rolls and system, then why have the other reforms been left out? Why has the government brushed the fears and apprehensions of the Opposition under the carpet instead of addressing them and taking the Opposition along?

In my view, the fear of leakage of voter information is perhaps unfounded, as the information contained in the electoral rolls is already in the public domain, in pdf format. The other information concerns the voting pattern, which in any case is secret and not linkable to any database or network. The government has said, in view of the Supreme Court judgment on Aadhaar, that the linking will be voluntary.

How exactly can the voluntary assent of 90 crore voters be taken? Will a door-to-door campaign be conducted? What is the motivation for a voter to give consent to his or her data to be linked with Aadhaar? What if a majority—or even a small number—refuse to consent? That will not ensure a clean roll, defeating the purpose of the whole exercise. The Bill answers none of these questions.

The electoral roll is the foundation of the integrity of the entire election process. Doubts about it should not be allowed to cloud its credibility. Every political party wants clean rolls. They should have been taken into confidence on how the linking is being attempted. If the government has no malafide intention or a secret plan behind the linking, why could it not attempt to take all parties along? By pushing it down the throat of the Opposition, it has itself created suspicion in minds of the people, as it did in the case of the three farm laws. Why burn your fingers again?

THE J&K DELIMITATION REPORT

O N 5 MAY 2022, THE JAMMU AND KASHMIR DELIMITATION Commission headed by the (Retired) Supreme Court Justice Ranjana Prakash Desai submitted its final report, two years after it was appointed to redraw the electoral cartography of J&K, as per the mandate set by the Jammu and Kashmir Reorganisation Act, 2019. A day before its term ended, the commission, also consisting of Chief Election Commissioner Sushil Chandra and the J&K State Election Commissioner K.K. Sharma as ex-officio members, notified the new boundaries, names and number of assembly constituencies in J&K, paving the way for its first-ever assembly elections since it was deemed a Union Territory after the abrogation of Article 370.

Delimitation is carried out in accordance with the Delimitation Act, 2002, and is currently based on the 2011 census data. Before the repeal of Article 370, which accorded special status to J&K, delimitation of the state assembly seats was carried out by the Jammu and Kashmir Constitution and the Jammu and Kashmir Representation of the People Act, 1957. Delimitation for the Lok Sabha seats was governed by the Constitution of India itself. Now, after the abrogation of J&K's special status in 2019, delimitation of both assembly and parliamentary seats is governed by the Constitution of India.

The last delimitation exercise in J&K was done in 1995. In 2002, the then J&K government led by Farooq Abdullah amended the J&K Representation of the People Act to freeze the delimitation exercise until 2026, when it could coincide with the exercise for the rest of the country. This was challenged, in both the J&K High Court and the Supreme Court, both of which upheld the freeze. Owing to this, political parties in Kashmir have been pointing out that the Delimitation Commission is mandated by the Reorganisation Act. Delimitation is carried out primarily on the basis of the population as shown in the Census, and the commission has said it is considering other factors, such as geographical features, means of communication, public convenience and contiguity of areas. The final report, published in the Gazette of India, has announced changes which have been intensely debate over the last week. However, regardless of the merits of the grievances, the orders made by this independent commission are not subject to judicial arbitration.

There are several important takeaways from the final report. Firstly, seven additional constituencies have been added to the J&K assembly, with Jammu getting six of those. This takes Jammu, the bastion of the BJP party in the region, from thirty-seven seats to forty-three, whereas Kashmir goes up only by one constituency, taking its count from forty-six seats to forty-seven seats. According to the 2011 Census data, the Kashmir region accounts for 56 per cent of the total population of J&K, and therefore deserves a greater number of additional seats and a greater number of seats in total.

Additionally, they also point out the discrepancies with regard to the division of voter demography. The average number of voters per constituency in Kashmir is 1.45 lakh, and in Jammu 1.25 lakh. This effectively means that 44 per cent of the population (Jammu) will vote in 48 per cent of the legislators, whereas the 56 per cent living in Kashmir will vote in 52 per cent of the seats. In the earlier set-up, Kashmir's 56 per cent had 55.4 per cent of the seats and Jammu's 43.8 per cent had 44.5 per cent of the seats.

The Kashmir-based parties are alleging a pro-ruling party bias. They have unanimously rejected the report, claiming that it is politically motivated and certain to disempower the Kashmiris. They have also questioned the reservation of two seats for Kashmiri Pandits, since there can be no reservation for religious groups.

This has been taken care of by calling them 'Kashmiri migrants'.

The commission has also made important changes to the structural set-up of the Lok Sabha seats here. The commission has redrawn the boundaries of Jammu and Anantnag seats. Jammu's Pir Panjal region, comprising the districts of Rajouri and Poonch, which were previously part of the Jammu parliamentary seat, has now been added to the Anantnag seat in Kashmir. This restructuring will practically change the influence of various demographic groups in these seats.

For instance, the commission has reserved for the first time nine assembly seats for scheduled tribes, six of which are allocated in the redrawn Anantnag parliamentary seat, including Poonch and Rajouri, which have the highest STpopulations in Kashmir. The erstwhile Anantnag seat had a small ST population, but in the current restructured set-up, the electoral outcomes would be strongly determined by Rajouri and Poonch. Kashmir-based parties emphasize that this move effectively reduces the influence of the ethnic Kashmiri-speaking Muslim voters.

Interestingly, twenty-four seats have been traditionally reserved for Pakistan-Occupied Kashmir, or PoK, in the assembly. I don't know why the same logic is not extended to reserve a few seats for PoK in the Lok Sabha too.

Finally, what remains is for the Centre to fix a date from which the delimitation order will come into effect. Chief Election Commissioner Sushil Chandra has said the polling stations and electoral rolls will subsequently be revised. This, therefore, will prepare the way for the much-awaited assembly polls in Jammu and Kashmir post-abrogation of Article 370. We will then need to wait and see how the various implications of the changes will substantially manifest in the electoral outcomes.

Model Code Violations in Multi-Phase Elections

E VER SINCE PRIME MINISTER NARENDRA MODI'S INTERVIEW TO THE news agency ANI, which was broadcast on several TV channels a day before the first phase of the Uttar Pradesh elections in 2022 when the 'silence period' was in operation, my phone has not stopped ringing. Media persons have been asking for clarification as to whether this was a violation of the electoral laws and the Model Code of Conduct. To compound the problem, the very next day of this interview, the prime minister gave a public speech at Saharanpur when polling was going on in the neighbourhood. And subsequently, before the second phase, Chief Minister Yogi Adityanath also gave an interview.

Many people reminded us of a similar violation in 2017 by Rahul Gandhi, for which he was indicted by the Election Commission. FIRs were filed against him citing his violation as a criminal offence.

Several years before that, NDTV had broadcast an opinion poll during the period when there was a ban on such polls, and several

FIRs were filed against Prannoy Roy and the news channel at different places in the country.

Given this background, the common question is about the violation of the provisions of the laws and the Model Code of Conduct in the 'silent period' by Modi and Adityanath.

Let us first see what the law says: Section 126, the Representation of People Act, 1951 lays down the following:

> Prohibition of public meetings during period of 48 hours ending with hour fixed for conclusion of poll –
> (1) No person shall –
> (a) convene, hold, attend, join, or address any public meeting or procession in connection with an election; or
> (b) display to the public any election matter by means of cinematograph, television or other similar apparatus –
> (2) Any person who contravenes the provisions of this section shall be punishable with imprisonment for a term which may extend to 2 years or with fine or with both.
> (3) In this section the expression 'election matter' means any matter intended or calculated to influence or affect the result of an election.

The problem is not new. For years, complaints have been pouring in about violation of this section of the RP Act. This has been aggravated by multi-phase elections, which seem to be the root cause of these violations.

Prime Minister Modi's speech cannot be legally questioned, though ethical questions are raised because the law has to be followed not only in letter but also in spirit. Modi was 'campaigning' in an area where no silence zone was in operation and where campaigning was allowed. But people questioned this since his speech was carried by all the TV channels and could be viewed in those areas which were going through the phase of polling and where a ban on political speeches was in operation. The question is, how can an electronic signal be barred from being seen in a silence zone? In view of this technical impossibility, I feel the time has come to reconsider Section 126 altogether.

Section 126 of the Representation of the People Act, 1951 prohibits public meetings, processions and electronic media campaigns during the silent period. It, however, allows door-to-door campaigns and print media campaigns during the silent period. My suggestion is that electronic campaigns, which are technically impossible to stop, must be permitted. Since all parties will have this facility, a level playing field will be ensured. On the other hand, door-to-door campaigns should be banned because the spirit of this silent period is that after a blitzkrieg of many different campaigns, the voters should have a quiet time to reflect on the choices before them and decide who they are going to vote for. Door-to-door campaigns can be troublesome, often resulting in arguments and quarrels. It is also during this period that voters are bribed with liquor, money or other goodies. It is not possible for the Election Commission to check this fully, especially as these transactions take place in the dark of the night.

Complaints against a leader making a speech or giving an interview outside the silence zone put undue pressure on the Election Commission. It is a Hobson's choice for the Commission: should it go by the letter of the law, or by the spirit of the law?

In my opinion, there is only one solution: amendment of Section 126 of the RP Act. All electronic campaigns (alongside the already permitted print media campaigns) must be allowed, but physical contact, namely, door-to-door campaigns, must be stopped. This is all the more important in the COVID era, when the physical proximity of even one person can be dangerous for an individual.

There is another dimension to the problem—the tenability of multi-phase elections. At the time when multi-phase elections were introduced, the situation was radically different. Muscle power was rampant and murders on the day of polling or during the campaign period were a common occurrence. In the middle of the 1990s, T.N. Seshan introduced the deployment of Central armed police forces, commonly called paramilitary forces. Since the number of security personnel made available to the Election Commission was limited, not enough to cover all the identified sensitive and hypersensitive polling booths, elections had to be held in multiple phases so that the forces could be rotated from one geography to another.

While this measure definitely made elections peaceful, in the electronic age and, more recently, the social media age, it has created more problems than it has solved. While the forces take three to five days to move from one polling area to another other as one phase of voting gives way to the next, the criminals move much faster, landing up in the next election phase zone within a few hours. Rumours and fake news spread in seconds which, during a prolonged period of multi-phase election, has disastrous consequences.

Now the question would be whether going back to single-phase polling would ensure peaceful elections. My feeling is that it is certainly possible, given the range of steps introduced by the Election Commission in the last two decades. The EC has introduced vulnerability mapping of polling stations, which clearly identifies potential troublemakers, who are brought to book under the Criminal Procedure Code with a bond for good conduct. Campaigns to seize illegal arms have been effective. Even licensed arms are ordered to be surrendered. Most importantly, the non-bailable warrants (NBW) issued against criminals, which used to stay unexecuted under political pressure for months and even years, with the absconders reported as 'untraceable' (while they could be seen moving freely and even appearing regularly on page three in the newspapers), are now a thing of the past. Every single NBW is executed under the watch of the Election Commission. The criminals are kept under video watch 24x7, with nearly 1 lakh video cameras doing the rounds.

A single-phase election would require availability of a sufficient number of Central armed police personnel, which every political party now demands. Currently, the ministry of home affairs (MHA) makes available, say, 1000–1200 companies for nearly three months for a seven-phase election. If the number of companies could be increased to 3,000 and their deployment period reduced to two weeks, this can easily reduce the duration of the campaign period without jeopardizing security deployment in sensitive areas.

Even a national election can easily be completed in thirty to thirty-five days, instead of in two to three months as at present. A prolonged election creates its own problems—of an extended campaign full of communal and caste tensions and abuse of money power. This will also take care of the constant irritant of opinion and exit poll instructions getting violated regularly.

Pragmatism demands that we move with the times and adjust our regulations to the changing and evolving situation. And the sooner we do it, the better. It will do away with a lot of the vitiation of the purity of the poll process that currently goes on.

Gender and the State of Democracy

1

The Lawmakers We Need

INCLUSION OF ALL SECTIONS OF THE SOCIETY IN THE PUBLIC SPHERE IS critically important for any democracy. For all its successes in giving representation to different social groups, India has a mixed track record when it comes to women's participation and representation in politics. Women were given the right to vote the day India became independent, something that took the UK and the United States 100 and 144 years, respectively, to achieve. India has also produced a number of powerful and consequential women politicians—more than most democracies—who have held, and still hold, power at the highest levels in state and national politics. The seventy-third Constitutional amendment ensures, by reserving seats for women in the panchayat system, that at least a third of India's 32 lakh elected representatives are women (the 33 per cent quota was raised to 50 per cent in 2009. Several states have since introduced gender parity in representation in municipal bodies).

But the presence of strong women politicians, and 10 lakh elected women representatives at the grassroots level, has not ensured gender parity in the state assemblies or parliament. The right to vote in itself is insufficient to guarantee gender parity in voting. During the first two decades after Independence, women's participation in elections lagged behind men's by nearly 20 points. In recent years, women's participation has caught up with the average, to the point that in the last round of elections to state assemblies, women outvoted men in seventeen states.

The Election Commission (EC) has to be party credited for that success, since it has improved the conduct of elections in ways that encourage women's participation. Improvement of the electoral rolls, provision of separate queues for women voters, the securing of the process after 1996, have gone a long way in making voting easier and safer for women. Since 2006, the EC has been closely studying the gender composition of the electoral rolls. It prohibits the publication of voters' photographs in the electoral rolls, barring a small stamp-size photograph in the hard copy distributed to political parties.

In Uttar Pradesh, during the 2012 election, the EC decided to let in two women into the polling booths after every male voter cast his vote. This was done to quicken the voting process for women. This practice was a success and has since been adopted throughout the country. Voting conditions for women have also improved, notably on account of the compulsory presence of female polling staff, who are responsible for identifying women voters and marking their fingers with indelible ink. This addresses the reluctance of many women—including those wearing purdah or other headscarves—to be screened by men. Women police forces are also deployed with a view to encourage women to turn up to vote.

That there is gender parity in voter turnout in most states is remarkable—particularly so in a country that suffers one of the world's worst sex ratios. The fact that women out-vote men in many states where their literacy rate is significantly lower than the average literacy rate (65.46 per cent against 82.14 per cent in 2011, for all of India) must also be noted. In 2010, the Election Commission started conducting surveys on the gaps within social categories with respect to voter turnout, and highlighted areas where interventions were required. The surveys revealed that concern for personal security, dependence on approval of family elders and lack of adequate toilet facilities were some of the reasons that kept many women away from voting. The Commission rolled out a comprehensive voter education drive that targeted women in particular. It sought to directly encourage women to vote. The results in Bihar and UP were immediate. In the 2010 and 2012 assembly elections in the state, women out-voted men for the first time, by a small margin. In the 2014 general election, women turnout rose from 55.82 per cent to 65.63 per cent, a jump of nearly 10 percentage points. The overall gender voting gap shrank to an all-time low of 1.46 percentage points. The trend has continued in the subsequent state elections.

Information suggests that women out-voted men in the recent elections to the state assemblies. Punjab witnessed a female turnout of 78.14 per cent, against 76.9 per cent for men. In Uttarakhand, 69.76 per cent of the women electors voted, against 63.23 per cent of the men. In Goa, the ratio was 83.98 to 78.48 in favour of women. Uttar Pradesh is expected to follow that trend, based on the turnout figures for the first five phases.

In spite of this progress, women's representation in the elected assemblies remains abysmally low. In 1952, women comprised 6 per cent of India's first Lok Sabha. Sixty-two years later, representation of women in the Lok Sabha in 2014 reached an all-time high of 12.15 per cent. The situation is worse at the state level, where the average representation ratio of women is only 7.3 per cent. Some states, Nagaland or Mizoram, for example, have no women MLAs. Among the other worst performers are Jammu and Kashmir (2.27 per cent) Goa (2.5 per cent), Karnataka (2.65 per cent) and Arunachal Pradesh (3.28 per cent). India's best-performing state is Haryana (14.44 per cent), followed by West Bengal (13.95 per cent), Rajasthan (13.48 per cent) and Bihar (11.67 per cent).

Women face many obstacles when it comes to contesting and getting elected, including traditional and cultural barriers. But the greatest obstacle that women face are the political parties, who refuse to field a fair number of women candidates. Their reservations—

that women make weaker, less 'winnable' candidates—could be easily addressed by passing the Women's Reservation Bill, which was introduced for the third time in 2008 and lapsed for the third time in 2014. Changing the prejudices and stereotypes in India will remain a herculean task for generations to come. The only way to address it in the short run is through bold legislation, the kind of spectacular gestures the prime minister seems inclined to make.

2

On the Status of Women in India

International Women's Day is a good occasion to reflect on the status of women in India. The best measure of a civilized nation is the degree to which its women are treated with respect, dignity and equality. We seem to fall short in this area. Even though they make up nearly half the population of India, women here have endured discrimination for centuries. It's a national shame that India ranks 132 on the Gender Development Index and 127 on the Gender Equality Index. It doesn't befit a country whose ancient scriptures placed women on a high pedestal.

The most effective tool is perhaps women's political empowerment. As American social reformer Susan Anthony remarked, 'There will never be complete equality until women themselves help to make laws and elect lawmakers.' It's not that our track record has always been bleak. When India chose democracy in 1950, it surprised the world by giving equal voting rights to men and women at one go, whereas the US took 144 years and the UK 100 years. As early as in 1917, Sarojini Naidu had joined a delegation of women to meet the viceroy of India to demand suffrage for women. In 1919, Madras became the first province to take the revolutionary step of extending franchise to women. Britain was shocked. In 1917, Britain had decided to extend suffrage to women over thirty years of age and that too, with conditions attached as to their education level and ownership of property. It was only in 1928 that Britain extended unconditional universal adult suffrage. By that time, a forty-one-year-old medical practitioner, Dr Muthulakshmi Reddy, had become the first Indian woman to become a member of the legislative council in Madras in 1927.

Britain, in its 300 years of democratic history, had the first and only woman leader of a major party in 1977, when Margaret Thatcher took over the Conservative Party, a good fifty-two years after Sarojini Naidu had become president of the Congress. In 1979, when Thatcher became the first woman prime minister of the UK, Indira Gandhi had already been the Indian PM for a decade and a half.

Today, the Lok Sabha speaker and the chief ministers of four states are women. Just a few years ago we had a woman president. But women's empowerment at the top has not trickled down. The obstacles to political empowerment of women are mainly in three areas—their registration as voters, their actual participation in voting, and their contesting in elections. The Election Commission of India (EC) has sought to deal with this through some innovative methods.

India suffers from one of the lowest sex ratios (940/1000 in 2011) in south Asia. The gender ratio on the electoral rolls is even lower, at around 800 women for every 1,000 men. Since 2006, gender analysis has been made a critical element in the updation of electoral rolls.

Gender sensitivity is also taken into account when it comes to carrying photos of the voters in the electoral rolls. It is mandatory to provide a hard copy of the rolls to recognized parties. The EC stopped handing out soft copies of rolls, as women's photos could be subjected to abuse, such as morphing. Separate queues for women and deployment of women police and polling staff are some of the standard measures for facilitating voting for women.

Studies by the Election Commission have revealed several reasons why female voter turnout is generally lower than male voter turnout.

Concern for personal security, dependence on the approval of family elders, especially the men, and lack of adequate toilet facilities were some of them. These were all addressed. To motivate women to come out and vote, local women icons—Sharda Sinha in Bihar and Malini Awasthi in UP—became the face and voice of a voter education campaign. This proved a game changer. Areas with relatively large gender gaps were identified for increased intervention. As a result, female voters, at 54.85 per cent, outnumbered male voters, at 50.77 per cent, in Bihar (2010). In UP, the corresponding figures were 60.28 per cent and 58.68 per cent (2012). Similar results followed subsequently in all the other states. In the general election of 2014, female turnout shot up from 55.82 to 65.63 per cent—a jump of nearly 20 per cent. Moreover, in sixteen states, women voters outnumbered their male counterparts. The gender gap, which used to be higher than 10 per cent, came down to an all-time low of 1.46 per cent.

In terms of participation of women as candidates in elections, India is way behind more backward countries in south Asia. It's ironic that even conservative Muslim countries like Afghanistan, Pakistan and Bangladesh have higher female representation. However, a breakthrough came with the enactment of the seventy-third and seventy-fourth amendments to the Constitution in 1992. In 2009, the Union cabinet approved an increase in reservation for women from 33 to 50 per cent in panchayati raj institutions. However, the bill for women's reservation in the legislatures has been pending in parliament.

Reservation apart, parties give far fewer tickets to women. The reason given is it is difficult for women to win elections. This isn't borne out by the facts. In 2014, women constituted 7.9 per cent of the total number of candidates, but 11.6 per cent of the elected MPs. In all elections since 1957, women's 'strike rate' has been 50 per cent to 350 per cent higher. It clearly demonstrates that women's ability to win is greater than men's. Till women's reservation becomes a reality, parties must give women more tickets. Voters should vote only for those parties that give a fair share of tickets to women.

Meanwhile, there's a great success story brewing at the local level, where political participation by women is increasing not only numerically but qualitatively too. Their increased participation in local government will gradually reflect in the assemblies and parliament. All we need is stronger and more supportive political will and a sense of urgency.

3

A Democracy for Her

DESPITE THE MANY HORRORS WE HAVE WITNESSED SINCE THE COVID-19 pandemic began, there have been some positive developments, the most pertinent being the growing role of women in strengthening the political and civic life of democracy in South Asia. At the global level, much has already been written about the superior performance of women leaders such as Jacinda Ardern (New Zealand), Tsai-Ing Wen (Taiwan), Sanna Marin (Finland) and K.K. Shailaja (Kerala, India), in handling the pandemic. Likewise, the highly effective contributions of local-level panchayat sarpanches and health officials such as Roorkee's Daljit Kaur, Singhwahini's Ritu Jaiswal and the mayor of the Chandannath municipality in Nepal, Kantika Sejuwal, have been justly exalted. One must not, however, turn a blind eye to the more systemic and ground-level realities of women, which are fraught with various contradictions, contestations and quiet calamities. Therefore, for a proper appraisal of the relations between gender and democracy, we ought to examine the links between violence, representation and political participation by women.

Historically, one of the peculiar paradoxes of South Asian democracy has been the continued presence of strong women leaders at the executive Centre and the generally appalling condition of women in the society at large. South Asia has had the largest number of women heads of state—including Sirimavo Bandaranaike, Chandrika Kumaratunga, Indira Gandhi, Khaleda Zia, Sheikh Hasina and Benazir Bhutto—of any region in the world till recently. However, this seemingly empowering image is disproved when we take a broader view of the electoral representation and social condition of women in the region. While women have played very visible and important roles at the higher echelons of power and at the grassroots level in social movements, they have been under-represented in political parties as officials and as members of key decision-making bodies.

In electoral representation, India, for instance, has fallen several places in the Inter-Parliamentary Union's global ranking of women's parliamentary presence, from 117 after the 2014 election to 143 as of January 2020. India is currently behind Pakistan (106), Bangladesh (98) and Nepal (43), and ahead of Sri Lanka (182). Prior to the 2019 election, scholars such as Carole Spary and S.M. Rai estimated that it would take another forty years to have a 33 per cent female membership of the Lok Sabha, based on historical election trends and assuming that no gender quota is introduced, such as the heavily undermined and ignored the Women's Reservation Bill.

However, there are two main points to be noted here. In India, women currently make up 14.6 per cent of MPs (seventy-eight MPs) in the Lok Sabha, which is a historic high. Although the percentage is modest, it is remarkable because women barely made up 9 per cent of the candidates in 2019. BJP women candidates won at a strike rate of 73 per cent, as opposed to their male counterparts, at 66 per cent. Additionally, twenty-seven of forty-one women MPs were able to retain their seats too. Similarly, of the fifty women candidates fielded by the Trinamool Congress in last year's West Bengal assembly elections, forty won. This proves that the winnability (the basis on which political parties claim to give tickets) of women is much higher than the winnability of men.

In terms of electoral quotas, there were two outstanding exceptions in the 2019 general election. West Bengal, under Mamata Banerjee, and Odisha, under Naveen Patnaik, opted for voluntary parliamentary quotas, fielding 40 per cent and 33 per cent women candidates, respectively.

Interestingly, in countries such as India and Bangladesh, the presence of women may be more powerfully felt as voters than as candidates. In 1962, the male voter turnout in India was 16 percentage points higher than for women. Six decades later, in the 2019 Lok Sabha election, women's participation exceeded that of men for the first time. This suggests an increasing assertion of citizenship rights among women. The growing turnout of women voters could influence political parties' programmatic priorities and improve their responsiveness to women voters' interests, preferences and concerns, including issues related to sexual harassment and gender-based violence.

The TMC ran and highlighted many women-centric schemes, which played a central role in their victory. Schemes such as Swasthya Sathi, under which health cards were issued in the name of female heads of families, and Kanyashree Prakalpa and Rupashree Prakalpa, which provided financial support for girls' education and marriage, respectively, proved immensely popular.

Likewise, the Central government must be commended for its achievements in two areas in particular: Its DBT schemes, such as the Pradhan Mantri Vaya Vandana Yojana and the Pradhan Mantri Surakshit Matritva Abhiyan, due to which maternal mortality rate has reduced from 167 (2011–13) to 113 (2016–18). The Maternity Benefit (Amendment) Bill, 2017 is another landmark achievement, extending paid maternity leave to twenty-six weeks from the existing twelve.

The extent to which parties represent women and take up their interests is closely tied to the health and vitality of democratic processes. However, the strength of civil society initiatives is not entirely dependent on the strength of political institutions—a case in point would be the Aurat marches in Pakistan. Another is the Shaheen Bagh protest that proved remarkably active in mobilizing women.

The BJP must use its parliamentary majority to finally pass the Women's Reservation Bill, as was promised in their 2014 election manifesto. Until that happens, the initiative taken by the governments of Banerjee and Patnaik to increase women's parliamentary presence must serve as an inspiration to other Indian states. At this crucial juncture, to cherish our democratic values, we will need to sympathize with the voice of the fifteenth century Bengali poet, Ramoni, a low-caste washerwoman, who sang, 'I'll not stay any longer in this land of injustice/ I'll go to a place where there are no hellhounds.'

4

Faith and Her Freedom

Ever since the Taliban captured power in Afghanistan in June 2021, the media has been speculating on how they will conduct themselves, particularly towards women. Images of women wrapped in blue burqas from the Taliban's earlier rule in 1996–2001 are being flashed. Atrocities against women—especially girls being prohibited from going to school—are being recapitulated.

Mercifully, the Taliban's first statement gives cause for optimism. 'We are going to allow women to work and study. We have got frameworks, of course. Women are going to be very active in the society but within the framework of Islam,' Zabihullah Mujahid, the group's spokesman, said at a press conference in Kabul on Tuesday, 17 August 2021. '… there will be no discrimination against women,' he declared, adding, 'they are going to work shoulder to shoulder with us'.

This incited another flood of questions: What is the 'framework of Islam'? What's the Taliban's version of it? Since the Taliban claims to act according to Shariah, let's understand the meaning of Shariah. In Arabic, it means the path to be followed by Muslims. It can be described as Islamic law. The original sources of Shariah are the

Quran, the Sunnah or the 'habitual practices' of the Prophet (PBUH) and Ahadees (recorded sayings of the Prophet). Based on these, and subservient to them, are two other sources—the Ijma (the consensus of jurists) and Qiyas (analogy/interpretation).

The international media often projects Islam as a religion that cages women. These perceptions ignore, or are unaware of, the Islamic tenets with respect to women, as specified in the holy Quran and the traditions of Prophet Muhammad.

Fourteen centuries ago, Islam recognized women as equal partners to men: They participated in business, war and several other activities. Islam was also the first religion to recognize property and inheritance rights for women—which many other religions granted only in the twentieth century.

The Holy Quran and the Hadith are replete with injunctions on gender equality. Here are some samples from the Holy Quran:

> 'And one of His signs is this: He created for you mates from yourself that you might find tranquility in them, and He ordained between you love and mercy … ' (Surah Ar Rum—The Romans 30:21).
>
> 'And for women are rights over men similar to those of men over women.' (Surah Al Baqarah—The Cow 2:228)
>
> 'They (your wives) are your garment, and you are a garment for them.' (Surah Baqarah 2:187)
>
> 'I never fail to reward any worker among you for any work you do, be you male or female—you are equal to one another.' (Surah Al e Imran—The Family of Imran 3:195)
>
> 'The believers, men and women, are helpers, supporters, friends and protectors of one another.' (Surah At Tawbah—The Repentance, Quran, 9: 71)
>
> The Ahadees supplement the verses of the Quran with explanations and elaboration. Here are some samples:
>
> 'Verily, women are the twin halves of men.' (Abu Dawud, Tirmidhi).

'Men and women are equal halves.' (Abu Dawud).

'The most complete believer in faith is the best in morals, and the best among you is the best to their wives.' (Tirmidhi).

'Observe your duty to Allah in respect to the women, and treat them well.' (Prophet Muhammad's Last Sermon).

Please note: Respecting women is seen as a duty to Allah.

The following anecdote is also educative:

A man asked the Prophet, 'Who deserves my companionship most?' The Prophet said, 'Your mother.' The man asked, 'Who next'? The Prophet said, 'Your mother.' The man asked, 'Who next?' Prophet said, 'Your mother.' He asked, 'Who next?' The Prophet said, 'Then your father'. (Narrated by Abu Hurairah-Bukhari and Muslim)

It is well known that many Indians, driven by the traditional preference for sons, continue to have children until they get a male child and end up with a large family. Lately, with the invention of sex determination tests, female foeticide has become rampant, despite stringent laws against it. The Quran forbade female infanticide fourteen centuries ago:

'When one of them gets a baby girl, his face becomes darkened with overwhelming grief. Ashamed, he hides from the people, because of the bad news given to him. He even ponders: Should he keep the baby grudgingly or bury her in dust? Miserable indeed is their judgement.' (Surah An Nahl— The Bee 16:58-59)

'Do not hate having daughters, for they are the comforting dears.' (Al-Tabarani)

'Whoever has three daughters, and cares for them, is merciful to them, and clothes them, then paradise is certain for him.' (Jabir ibn Abdullah)

Abdel Rahim Omran, professor of Islamic Law at the University of Al-Azhar, Cairo, has summed up the position of women in Islam, as enunciated in Surah An Nisa 4:11,12:

> Islam championed equality for women in all matters—religious, social, economic and familial. A woman cannot be forced into marriage by her family or guardian—she has to give her consent. Islam endorses a woman's consent to such an extent that a marriage could be annulled when it has been forced on a woman by her guardian.

One of the most significant facets of Islam's recognition of a woman's individuality pertains to her retaining her maiden name. She can do with her money as she pleases, while her husband—or father or brother—is responsible for providing for her and her children. She has total control of her possessions. As a mother, she is placed ahead of her husband in regard to the children's loyalty and affection. She has a right to demand, at the time of the marriage contract, the power of divorce and also the power to disallow polygyny by her husband.

Islam gives women equal legal status. This means she has the right to enter into all kinds of contractual arrangements and to conduct business on her own without the need of her husband's consent. As regards girls' right to education, Prophet Muhammad told his followers: 'Acquisition of knowledge is binding on all Muslims, male and female … The person who goes forth in search of knowledge is striving hard in the way of Allah, until his/her return.'

It is unfortunate that not only the Taliban but also Muslims in many other parts of the world do not understand and follow the tenets of Islam. It is clearly a case of Islam versus the Muslims.

5

This Women's Day, Enable Them to Get Fair Share of Electoral Power

IN AN EXTREMELY DIVERSE COUNTRY LIKE INDIA, INCLUSIVITY OF ALL sections of the society, big or small, is critically important. The foremost act of inclusivity in our democracy certainly would be to give equality to women—our largest minority.

When India chose to become a democratic republic, we started off by giving equal voting rights to women from day one—a fact which looks hugely significant, given that the US had taken 144 years and UK exactly 100 to do so! But Indian women are way behind their counterparts in these two countries when it comes to active participation in the electoral process.

Today, 8 March 2018, the speaker of the Lok Sabha and the chief ministers of two states in India are women. Just a few years ago, we had a female president and five women chief ministers, who all were very efficient. But the empowerment of women at the top has not trickled down. There are obstacles that hinder the engagement of women in the election process.

The hindrances include traditional and cultural barriers, and social norms, which are compounded by gender stereotypes, illiteracy, lack of awareness, lack of motivation, safety and security issues, including intimidation by males and inability of women to step out of their roles as mothers, wives and homemakers.

Registration of women voters

India suffers from one of the lowest sex ratios among South Asian countries. Provisional figures in the 2011 Census of India put the sex ratio in the country at 940 to 1,000. Among the ten most populous countries of the world, only China is behind us, with a sex ratio of 926 to 1,000.

Similarly, female literacy rate in India is also low. It was 65.46 percent in 2011, and the male literacy rate 82.14 per cent. Keeping this socio-economic-political milieu in mind, several steps were taken by the Election Commission to ensure that women are not prevented from exercising their right to vote.

To ensure equality for women in the democratic process, an analysis of the gender ratio of the electoral rolls has been done meticulously since 2006. A major concern related to the publishing of photos of voters on the electoral rolls, which is problematic due to our socio-cultural sensitivities. It is mandatory to give hard copies of these rolls to the recognized political parties.

However, the Election Commission decided to share the soft copy of the rolls without the photographs of the voters. It was felt that a soft copy of women's photos could be subjected to abuse, like morphing. The printed copies carrying only a small postage-stamp-size photo of the voter were considered good enough for identification purposes.

Female participation in voting

The next logical step after their registration in the voter lists is for women to out to vote on the day of polls. Here too women were lagging behind, because of socio-cultural prejudices. The Election Commission has been taking several steps to encourage and facilitate women's participation on polling day. For one, there are separate queues for men and women.

To make it convenient for women to vote in the Uttar Pradesh elections in 2012, for a single man allowed to cast his vote, it was decided to allow two women in the queue to proceed to vote. This worked wonders, as their queues moved faster and the women were able to return from the booths quickly, which motivated other women to go and vote. This has been made a nationwide practice.

There is invariably one female polling staff member to take care of the sensibilities of female voters, especially those veiled in burqa or ghunghat, who may have reservations about a male polling staff member applying indelible ink on their fingers or identifying their faces. Women police forces are also deployed with a view to encouraging female voters to turn up at the booths.

This issue recently hit the headlines when a BJP leader demanded deployment of women police to identify the burqa-clad women in the last two phases of the UP election. It created an unpleasant controversy, with a communal twist. The fact is, identification of every voter, including those wearing burqa, is mandatory. The Election Commission has a standard provision that there must be at least one woman staff member in the polling team to ensure that the rule is followed without violating cultural sensitivities.

Pre-election surveys

An analysis of gender-disaggregated data from the electoral rolls indicated a considerable gender gap, much below the national population ratio. The survey highlighted areas where interventions were required. Concern for personal security, dependence on the approval of family elders, especially men, and lack of adequate toilet facilities were some of the factors that kept many women away from voting.

The Election Commission's voter education programme sought to address these concerns. Its brand ambassadors, celebrity folk singers like Sharda Sinha in Bihar and Malini Awasthi in UP, led lakhs of women to the polling booth, recording a phenomenal jump in female voter turnout. In fact, female voters, at 54.85 per cent of registered voters, outnumbered male voters, at 50.77 per cent of registered voters—which was a clear lead of eight per hundred.

Women voter turnout

The persistent efforts of the Election Commission have yielded remarkable achievements. In the 2014 Lok Sabha election, women voter turnout went up from 55.82 per cent to 65.63 percent—a jump of nearly 10 percentage points, as against 8 percentage points for men. Moreover, in sixteen out of thirty-five states, women voters outnumbered their male counterparts, despite their adverse gender ratio in those states. This also meant the shrinking of the gender voting gap nationally to an all-time low of 1.46 percent. The trend has continued unabated. In the 2017 assembly elections, in every state, women outvoted men. Punjab, with a very poor sex ratio of 895 females per 1,000 males, witnessed a female turnout of 78.14 per cent, against 76.9 per cent among males. In Uttarakhand, it was 69.76 (F) against 63.23 (M), in Goa 83.98 (F) against 78.48 (M); and in UP (first five phases) 60.28 (F) against 58.68 (M).

Participation of women as candidates

While the registration of women as voters has increased phenomenally, their representation in the legislature is abysmally low.

Representation of women in the Lok Sabha is a mere 12.15 per cent, there being only sixty-six women representatives. It is embarrassingly low when compared with the numbers in conservative Muslim countries in south Asia, like Afghanistan, Pakistan and Bangladesh, which have very high female representation.

The saving grace for India is the enactment of the seventy-third and seventy-fourth amendments to its Constitution, which provided 33 per cent reservation for women in panchayati raj Institutions (PRIs). On 27 August 2009, the Union cabinet approved an increase in reservation for women from 33 per cent to 50 per cent in PRIs.

A number of states have also introduced 50 per cent reservation for women in municipalities and corporations. Regarding state assemblies and parliament, a Bill for women's reservation is pending with the parliament; it has been debated ad nauseum for the past several years, but is yet to be passed.

The reluctance of the male-dominated Indian political leadership to provide fair representation to women in the legislature is a matter of concern. Reservations apart, political parties are not willing to give more tickets to women. Hardly 10 per cent of electoral candidates are women. The excuse offered is their poor 'winnability'.

Even this is not borne out by facts. Throughout Indian electoral history, the winnability of women has always been higher than the winnability of men.

Prime Minister Narendra Modi is a man of bold initiative. Let's see if he would like to break this glass ceiling.

6

Beyond Binaries

TRANSGENDER PEOPLE HAVE A GENDER IDENTITY OR EXPRESSION that differs from their assigned sex at birth. They are sometimes also referred to as transsexuals, if they desire medical assistance in order to make the transition from one biological sex to another.

Numbering approximately 4,90,000, as per the last count (2011), transgender people in India are perhaps among the most visibly invisible populations in the country. Historically, Indian society has been tolerant of diverse sexual identities and sexual behaviours. The 'hijra' community evolved to form a unique sub-culture within the Indian society, existing alongside the ubiquitous heterosexual unit of the family. They had cultural and social significance across the country in various avatars. The same is evident in Indian mythology and ancient literature, such as the Kamasutra, or the epics such as the Mahabharata, in which the transgender community has been portrayed with dignity and respect.

However, transgender people have been increasingly recognized as one of the most socio-economically marginalized communities in the country. Since the late nineteenth century, they have been pushed to the margins of society and have lost the social-cultural position they once enjoyed. Often shunned as a menace to society, they are now only visible in streets and localities where they are found begging, and never as a part of the mainstream.

They are subject to extreme forms of social ostracization and exclusion from basic dignity and human rights. They remain highly vulnerable to gender-based violence. As a direct result of their acute mistreatment, vilification, ostracization and dehumanization, they also remain highly vulnerable to fatal communicable diseases like HIV-AIDS.

The typical life cycle of a transgender person in India is, perhaps, is one of great misery. Most often, boys who do not conform to the gender construct binary in our society leave, or are forced to leave, their families and live in vulnerable conditions. More often than not, these children or young individuals begin their journey alone and in search of individuals of their kind, a journey that is marred by unspeakable hardships and abuse.

Despite laws, policies and their implementation, the community continues to remain quite marginalized and highly vulnerable. We have numerous examples of higher education institutions providing quotas and giving special consideration to transgender people, but the takers remain few and far between. This is mostly because school education among most transgender people is either incomplete or non-existent. Their lack of basic schooling is a direct result of the bullying they are victims of, because of which they are forced to leave school. And schools remain unequipped to handle children with alternative sexual identities.

However, an increasing number of activists work at the grassroots level for the welfare of the community and have managed to bring society's attention to their socio-economic deprivation.

In 2009, it was brought to the notice of the Election Commission that some voters weren't getting registered as they refused to declare themselves as male or female—the traditional gender binary, earlier found on voter registration forms to be filled in order to get registered as a voter. This is especially significant when it comes to local body elections in constituencies which are reserved for women. As a result, in November 2009, appropriate directions were issued by the Election Commission to all districts to amend the format of the registration form to include an option of 'others'. This enabled transsexual people to tick the column if they didn't want to be identified as either male or female.

This decision of the Election Commission also went a long way in opening the nation's eyes to the realities of a deprived community that still continues to be at the margins. One member of the community, in conversation with the BBC before the 2014 general election, said, 'The Election Commission has given us the most important aspect of our life—freedom.'

The Supreme Court, in *National Legal Services Authority vs. Union of India* (2014), recognized transgender people as the 'third gender'. In the landmark ruling, Justice K.S. Radhakrishnan, who headed the two-judge bench, observed that 'recognition of transgenders as a third gender is not a social or medical issue, but a human rights issue'.

Only a year after the verdict, it was encouraging to see India's first transgender mayor, Madhu Kinnar of Raigarh city in Chhattisgarh, who was elected to office in 2015. The Transgender Persons (Protection of Rights) Bill, 2016, has been passed in the Rajya Sabha. It is now pending in the Lok Sabha.

According to a report in April 2018, the number of registered transgender voters nearly doubled in the Karnataka polls from 2013. Over 5,000 transgender people cast their ballots in the Karnataka assembly polls, which is historic.

Transgender people are forced to beg, dance at events and religious functions, or even provide sex services. Their vulnerability to fatal diseases can be extreme in the conditions they work in, and thus they have a higher prevalence of HIV, tuberculosis as well as a whole host of other sexually transmitted infections.

According to a recent UNAIDS report, HIV prevalence among transgenders is 3.1 per cent (2017), which is the second highest amongst all communities in the country. But only about 68 per cent of the people in general are even aware that they are infected, which is worrying. High instances of substance abuse and low levels of literacy only complicate matters.

World AIDS Day, celebrated on 1 December every year, serves as a stark reminder to us as a nation that communities such as the transgender people warrant special attention, not only from the state machinery but also from the society at large.

There are encouraging trends. HIV services for the community are rapidly improving in a targeted manner after the Supreme Court verdict. For example, the National Aids Control Organisation (NACO) reported that 2,40,000 hijras were provided with HIV prevention and treatment services in 2015, against 1,80,000 the previous year.

A multi-pronged approach is needed on a war footing in the form of mass awareness campaigns, generation of avenues for dignified employment of transgender people, gender sensitization of society and affirmative action. Only then can the trailblazing efforts of the Election Commission and the judiciary to ensure inclusive elections in the world's largest democracy also result in a meaningful and inclusive democracy.

1

Sixty-Seven Years Young

Soon after India got freedom, we made a new beginning. We chose democracy as the way forward. New institutions were created and nurtured—parliament, the Election Commission, the Supreme Court, the Planning Commission, and others. The country has indeed made phenomenal progress. It has become a major military, industrial and economic power, an IT superpower and a space giant eyeing the moon and Mars. As I write this article on the eve of Independence Day in 2014, I have great expectations that the prime minister's address will touch upon some of the following issues.

India is now the tenth-largest economy by GDP and the third-largest by purchasing power parity. We have the sixth-largest number of billionaires. But we also have the largest disparities between the haves and have-nots. After all, we take pride in being a country of diversity!

We are ranked 135th in UNDP's human development index (out of 187 countries). One in every three Indians is below the poverty line.

One in every four is still illiterate. We still have high infant and maternal mortality rates—far worse than even Sri Lanka's. More than half the population is malnourished. The rate of unemployment is so high that it contributes to disgruntlement, frustration and even criminal tendencies among the youth. This could make for a breeding ground for disruptive forces of various hues. Drug abuse in some states has reached alarming proportions. The education system has let the country down, producing lakhs of unemployables. Ironically, there is no dearth of policies, programmes and funds to deal with these issues. Massive corruption is preventing their percolation to the intended beneficiaries.

While many old problems persist, we also have new challenges and opportunities. We are a country of young people. More than 70 per cent of Indians are below thirty-five years of age. They have new aspirations. Are we equipping them to meet these aspirations? Let there be an employment mission to coordinate all the relevant programmes. Nearly 25 crore of our young people are adolescents, who have their peculiar problems. They are no longer children but not yet adults. They worry about what is happening to them, physically and emotionally. Their curiosity and sense of experimentation make them vulnerable to exploitation and abuse. This is the time to educate them in life skills.

Population issues have gone off the political radar altogether. As a result, India's population will overtake China's by 2028. The Department of Family Welfare was quietly abolished a decade ago. One factor contributing to the population explosion is child marriage. One in every three marriages in India is illegal, involving parties below the legal age for marriage. Yet not a whimper is heard. Early marriage leads to early pregnancy, which creates health complications for adolescent girls not physically or mentally equipped to deal with it. We should adopt an integrated adolescent development programme (and not just for health) and implement it in mission mode.

Crime and violence against women are a major issue, one that is getting uglier every day. A large number of assault cases takes place when rural and slum women go to answer the call of nature, usually at dusk or at dawn. That is when they are most vulnerable to predators on the prowl. Where is freedom for women?

India has the dubious distinction of being a country with the highest number of open defecators—60 per cent of the population. In his election campaign, Narendra Modi rightly flagged toilets for women as a high-priority issue. It is hoped that his vision will be translated into action soon. But why leave it to the government alone? The corporate sector should assign it top priority while meeting its CSR obligations. If the entire country takes it up on a war footing and resolves to end this national shame within the time frame of a year or two, it can be done. Synergy has great strength.

The 16 December 2012 gangrape in Delhi shocked the conscience of the nation. In a knee-jerk reaction, we came up with a law that may not necessarily strike at the root of the problem. Nobody uttered a word about society's gender attitudes. No solutions were offered to educate the youth and inculcate in them the right values. The result is that we still see the crime being repeated with sickening regularity. An attitude change is more important than any law. It cannot be left to the government alone to bring about. Society as a whole must take up the responsibility. Do we look critically at the gender attitudes of our sons? A national gender education drive must be considered.

Incidentally, we rank 132 on the gender development index and 127 on the gender inequality index, both of which are conducted by UNDP.

Another threat to freedom and development percolating down to all sections of society is social disharmony and unrest. It's an irony that elections have become the root cause of corruption as well as of communal and caste polarization, the three curses of our society that constantly pull the country back. Rooting out these problems is imperative. All institutions of freedom and democracy must unite to ensure that these problems are buried forever.

The social polarization that is rearing its ugly head can do unfathomable damage. Absence of intermixing among communities creates ignorance about the 'other', which breeds a vicious circle of fear, hate and aggression. Growing up in an atmosphere of hate and fear is destructive for children's psyche. Mental pollution is the worst kind of pollution.

Infighting weakens the nation. Peace and harmony are the prerequisites for development. Nothing should be done to hamper realization of the PM's slogan, '*Sab ka saath, sab ka vikaas*', a very inclusive vision, which has received global acclaim. Pluralism is one of India's core strengths, its great USP. It should be strengthened and not weakened.

A government with a strong majority should be an opportunity to strengthen all institutions of democracy. The sanctity of the Constitutional wisdom of separation of powers between the government—judiciary, the executive and the legislature must be respected. At the same time, all constitutional institutions themselves have a duty not to allow erosion of their moral authority, which seems to be under stress.

This is India's defining moment. I hope we choose the right course. That would be the best tribute to those who died for our freedom.

2

India Remains a Flawed Democracy Despite Being an Electoral Wonder

THE PRESIDENT OF TAIWAN, TSAI ING WEN, ONCE SAID, 'DEMOCRACY is not just an election, it is our daily life.' In this context, World Democracy Day, celebrated on 15 September, is an opportune day to ponder over the state of democracy in the world.

The South Asian Region requires special attention because a quarter of the world's population and half of the world's democracy lives here.

The Global State of Democracy Index, 2018

The International Institute for Democracy and Electoral Assistance (International IDEA), an inter-country organization of thirty-two countries, of which India is a founding member, has recently evolved the Global State of Democracy Index (GSoD).

It scores 158 countries on five major attributes—fundamental rights, checks on government, impartial administration, participatory engagement and representative government.

These are measured in terms of sixteen attributes and ninety-seven sub-indicators. The main aim of the exercise is to reflect on trends in democratization in the world since 1975 and present a picture of democracy involving not only the process, but also the substance of it. The latest report, expected to be released in November 2019, classifies countries into three categories: democracies, hybrid regimes, and non-democracies, based on their GSoD scores.

The Asia Pacific Region (APR)

Overall, the picture appears to be moderately positive for this region (see Annexure). There has been an increase in the conduct of elections throughout the world, with less manipulation, irregularities and fraud. In APR, there has been significant democratic expansion in the last four decades. The number of democracies has gone up (from seven to fifteen) and the number of non-democracies has come down (from fourteen to ten) between 1975 and 2018. Six countries, however, have had democratic disruptions too.

Under the measures of representative government, fundamental rights and impartial administration, the region as a whole has consistently scored below the world average since 1990. The local democracy gap has widened since 1989, and electoral participation since 2007. The gap in civil society participation has remained stagnant since 1990. Nearly 40 per cent of the region's democracies are mid-range in their performance across all attributes.

A closer look at countries within the region gives us more insight into deepening autocratization and democratic backsliding. For instance, Thailand became a non-democracy from a democracy in 2013–14. In 2019, a civilian government has taken charge again. Pakistan became a hybrid regime in 2017 from being a democracy. There have been significant declines in scores across three or more sub-attributes in some countries.

The most populous democracy in the world, India, declined on four sub-attributes. The Philippines and even New Zealand have declined on three each. Vietnam, already a non-democracy, slid further in scores.

The South Asian Region (SAR)

SAR is a sub-region within APR in the GSoD, and comprises eight countries of SAARC.

The Maldives and Bhutan have not been evaluated. While the region fares better than both APR and the world average in representative government, checks on government and civil society participation, it fares below both averages in fundamental rights, impartial administration and electoral participation.

Afghanistan, Bangladesh, Nepal and Pakistan have had periods of non-elected regimes. The entire South Asian region has, most notably, declined on checks on government and representative government since 2015. In fundamental rights, Afghanistan and Nepal have seen the most relative overall improvement. Several fragile democracies such as Bangladesh (since 2014) and Pakistan (since 2018) have regressed in their scores.

India, the cause for concern

While talking of democracy, India merits special attention. After all, it is home to a fifth of humanity and 70 per cent of the SAARC population.

India has heralded the conduct of free and fair elections since Independence, and the Election Commission has won accolades from across the world for making the process more inclusive and transparent since 1951–52.

Additionally, our judicial structure has preserved the balance of power, barring a few hiccups, which explains our good scores in the checks-on-government category. As a result, India has held the highest rating among South Asian democracies.

It is ironical that even with all the great elections it has had, India is consistently characterized as a flawed democracy across various democracy indices. Although there was a drastic increase in civil society participation between 1978 and 2012, its decline has also been drastic since 2015. The same is the state of civil liberties in the country.

There has been a significant dip in the country's record under the measures of personal security, freedom of association, gender equality and basic welfare. Media integrity has taken a special beating.

Similarly, on media integrity, India fared better than both the global and South Asian averages till 2012. But the country's score has since plummeted.

Not a one-off case

I would like to mention here that the trends above are not exclusive to the GSoD. The latest Economist Intelligence Unit's (EIU) World Democracy Index, published in February 2019, shows India along, with its South Asian neighbours, slipping on democracy.

India (41) and Sri Lanka (71) were classified as flawed democracies, followed by Bangladesh (88), Bhutan (94) and Nepal (97) as hybrid regimes, and Pakistan (112) and Afghanistan (143) as authoritarian. After having reached the highest-ever position of twenty-seven in 2014, just two points short of being considered a 'full democracy', India slipped to forty-two in 2017, its worst-ever ranking.

Even though we improved one rank to forty-one in 2018, our score is the same (7.23/10). This is because it hardly crossed 7.5 in any of the measures, even though it ranked a high 9.17 in the electoral process and pluralism categories of the EIU. Hence, GSoD trends only serve to corroborate the EIU index.

India's plummeting media integrity has also been confirmed by the 'Freedom in the World' Report, 2019 and the World Press Freedom Index, 2019, which ranked India at an abysmal 140 out of

160 countries, below South Sudan! Unfortunately, the evidence of declining democracy in India is incontrovertible.

It is an embarrassing paradox that India is a flawed democracy despite being an electoral wonder. On this World Democracy Day, let all stakeholders pledge to engage constructively to arrest these trends.

3

A Moderate Performance

TODAY, THE 15 SEPTEMBER 2018, THE WORLD CELEBRATES THE eleventh International Day of Democracy in pursuance of a UN resolution. This is an appropriate occasion to have a look at the state of democracy in south Asia, especially India.

The world saw a huge wave of democratization after World War II. The newly liberated states in Latin America, Africa and Asia adopted democratic forms of government after centuries of colonial subjugation. Today, more people than ever before live under various forms of democracy. More than 120 of the 192 countries in the world have some form of democracy, whereas only eleven parliamentary democracies existed in 1941. This indicates the appeal of democratic ideas and systems.

South Asia is home to 3 per cent of the world's area and 21 per cent of the world's population. It is significant that 50 per cent of the world's population living under some form of democratic rule resides in this region. Despite the democratic upsurge, there are significant challenges in the region, like poverty, inequality, gender injustice, nepotism and corruption. Elected despots and authoritarian leaders are weakening democracies across the world. Political experts have argued that democratic values are on the decline, especially in the West.

The International Institute for Democracy and Electoral Assistance (IDEA), an inter-country organization, tried to evaluate the state of democracy in the world in the light of such worrying claims. At the time of writing this, the Global State of Democracy Index (GSoD) had looked at the trends in democratization from 1975 to 2017. With the help of a set of ninety-eight indicators, IDEA has aimed to study the factors that threaten democracy throughout the world and those that make it strong and resilient. The study covers a variety of important indicators, such as representative government, fundamental rights, checks on the government, impartial administration and participatory engagement. These have many sub-indicators to make for an in-depth indices-based analysis.

When it comes to representative government, India and Sri Lanka have maintained relatively high scores. Afghanistan, Bangladesh, Nepal and Pakistan have had periods of non-elected regimes. The general trend in south Asia in this respect has, however, been positive.

With respect to ensuring fundamental rights, the region's score matches that of Asia Pacific, but it is slightly below the global average. At the country level, Afghanistan and Nepal have seen the most improvement. Sri Lanka and Pakistan saw a slight decline in the 1970s and 1980s. India's score has been stable since the late 1970s. However, a decline has been observed since 2015.

South Asia shows steady improvement on the yardstick that measures gender equality, with Nepal standing out. India's score was better than the world average till 2003, but there has been a dip in the country's performance on the gender equality yardstick since.

When it comes to checks on government, south Asia has shown a steady increase from 1975 to 1994. Afghanistan, Nepal and Pakistan have shown the most improvement. Bangladesh, India and Sri Lanka have remained relatively stable, their scores in line with the global average.

On the yardstick of impartial administration, south Asia follows both the regional and global trends, showing no significant difference, except Nepal, which has seen a significant improvement. However, the 'absence of corruption' sub-index within the 'impartial administration' category shows a worrying tendency in south Asia. The region has the lowest scores in the world, despite showing slight improvement between 2012 and 2015.

A robust civil society is essential for deliberative decision making. Civil society participation increased in India by leaps and bounds between 1978 and 2012, after which it declined drastically to fall below the Asia Pacific and world averages. In 2017, it was the lowest since 1975.

In 2017, the gap between the Indian score and the world average on the yardstick that measures 'personal integrity and security' was the widest since 1977. This is worrying. In the past ten years, south Asia's scores for electoral participation are in line with the global average but slightly below the Asia Pacific average. Recently, there has been a decrease in voter participation in Bangladesh, but a slight increase in India and Sri Lanka.

One of the major challenges to democracy is people losing faith in it. There are many reasons for such disillusionment, including corruption, nepotism and unemployment. This often leads to people disengaging with key public policy issues which, in turn, makes those in power less accountable. Other factors, in contrast, contribute to the popularity of democracies. These include transparency in political processes, accountability of elected representatives, basic freedoms for all citizens, equal rights for women and minorities, and high rates of voter participation.

The GSoD report analyses India's performance on all the above-mentioned indicators and shows that the country has done moderately well. On yardsticks such as elected government, effective parliament and impartial administration, the country scores hover around the world average, but in the last decade there has been a significant dip in the country's record on civil liberties, personal integrity and security, freedom of association, media integrity, gender equality and basic welfare.

In fact, India's performance on the measure of media integrity was better than the global and South Asian averages between 1994 and 2012. However, the country's score has fallen below those averages in 2017. Given that a free and fair media is crucial to a meaningful democracy, this is a worrying tendency.

The Election Commission has played an important role in conducting free and fair elections in the country. The Commission's Systematic Voters Education for Electoral Participation Programme's role has been crucial in this respect.

An independent judiciary is another reason for the resilience of democracy in India. The apex court has given judgments that keep the government in check and ensure a transparent and accountable democratic system.

Democracy does not merely mean voting rights for people; it also means empowering people by granting them equality. It also means creation of mechanisms to resolve differences among the people through dialogue and with mutual respect and understanding.

India does have the highest rating among South Asian democracies. But its performance on several yardsticks makes it a flawed democracy. If we want the largest democracy to count among the world's greatest too, there must be serious introspection among all stakeholders in the country.

4

Ease of Democracy

THE PAST FEW YEARS HAVE APPARENTLY NOT BEEN GOOD FOR INDIAN democracy, hailed globally as the largest democracy in the world. It has performed poorly in every major global democracy report during this period. This is troubling news, for several reasons.

The Freedom House Index for 2021 pushed India down four points from last year, bringing its score from 71 to 67. This demoted the country from being a 'free' to a 'partially free' country. V-Dem, the world-renowned think tank from Sweden, has, similarly, downgraded India. It has labelled India an 'electoral autocracy', an even more devastating blow to the pride of a country that boasts of a completely independent and impartial electoral management body. The Economist Intelligence Unit (EIU) has also been scathing in its report of 2021. A comparative study by the organization has shown India's score dropping from an all-time high of 7.92 in 2014 to 6.61 in 2020, and its ranking taking a nosedive from 27 to 53 out of 167 countries.

The reports and findings of these reputed agencies point to several factors contributing to India's declining performance. The country has seen increased pressuring of human rights organizations and civil rights groups. Journalists and activists have been intimidated and incarcerated, and minorities have been specifically targeted. Hate and polarization are rampant. It has even led to Amnesty International halting all activities in India. The most worrying trend has been the government's crackdown on freedom of speech, with statistics showing a 165 per cent increase in sedition cases between 2016 and 2019.

The latest controversy surrounding India's waning status as a democracy has been its engagement with the EIU after it released its 2021 report *Democracy Index* earlier this year. The report sparked outrage in the Indian government, which sought to challenge the rating. A national daily wrote:

The assessment of the EIU has been called false, biased, and misinformed (amongst other names) and Indian officials reached out to the EIU head office in London for clarification regarding the report… . Elucidation was reportedly asked regarding the sample size used and the details of organisations and authors providing data, amongst other methodology minutiae. An offer made by the Indian government to supply 'accurate' data pertaining to the democratic index was firmly refused by the EIU as mentioned in the Hindustan Times report.

The democracy index has, in fact, itself spelt out that it is a weighted average of answers to sixty questions based on five parameters: electoral process and pluralism, functioning of government, political participation, political culture, and civil liberties. Most answers are 'expert assessments'. The report, however, does not give any details of who the experts are. Some answers are provided by public opinion surveys from the respective countries. It is noteworthy that these questions are not specific to India but are common to all 167 countries surveyed. It is puerile on our part to feel that we are being singled out.

As the Indian government's offer to supply data was rejected, a parallel global democracy index formulated by Indian think tanks is reportedly being considered by government officials, with 'accurate' reports on Indian and global democratic progress. India's rejection of the global democratic indices is a pathetic move to hide the country's downslide on most parameters.

The EIU is not alone in its assessment of India. The Reporters without Borders' Press Freedom Report has placed India at 167 out of 183 countries. Freedom House has also given India a score of 2 out of 4 in terms of press freedom, stating that the Indian press is 'partially free'. EIU has reportedly asserted that incidents like the shutdown of Kashmir in 2019 and the Citizenship Amendment Act have brought about this demotion for India. India has become so used to a sycophantic media that it cannot tolerate any assessment which is not flattering to it. Sadly, no Enforcement Directorate raids or income tax 'surveys' are possible against these organizations.

Commenting on this episode, Kaushik Basu, formerly chief economist at World Bank, referred to the 'burgeoning tendency of fabricating data to present an alternative image that has beset the Indian administration'. For several years now, there have been active efforts to suppress data pertaining to, inter alia, the nosediving economy, record unemployment and even COVID cases. This, according to Basu, 'is detrimental to the reputation of a country which has pioneered data collection under greats like P.C. Mahalanobis. On the other hand, not showcasing actual data is making it difficult for policymakers to attempt to remedy the situation'.

The Indian indignation at global reports citing a decline in the country's democratic values seems to be a clear case of shooting the messenger. Facts point irrevocably to the aforementioned incidents actually having taken place. The Indian refusal to acknowledge and remedy them is irreparably harming its democracy.

The government, instead of facing the reality and taking corrective action, continues to be in denial mode. Recently, a question asked by a Member of Parliament on India's declining performance in democratic indices was disallowed as it was 'very sensitive in nature'. Paradoxically, the law ministry took shelter behind a rule which allows refusal of a reply if it constitutes 'information on trivial matters'. Trivial or sensitive?

It appears from the media reports that the concern about the unflattering EIU data has been engaging the attention of the government for two years. The government's move to monitor the indices and work on improving its rankings goes back that long. A committee of secretaries' met on 30 January 2020 to discuss how India fared on various important parameters based on thirty-two internationally recognized indices in order to improve its performance on these indices.

The desire to introspect and analyse what needs to be done to improve the country's performance on this front is correct and laudable. But trying to bully or to influence the rating agencies to doctor data to suit us is reprehensible. The NITI Aayog and all concerned organizations should focus on improving our performance in all the declining indicators. In this regard, our focus on 'ease of doing business', which led to a phenomenal improvement in our ranking on that front within a year, is a success story to emulate.

5

Issues and Solutions for Indian Democracy

DEMOCRACY DOES NOT COME EASY. IT TAKES A LONG TIME TO TAKE root but can be dislodged in a jiffy if the public gets disillusioned with the quality of governance and by the corruption. India is fortunate to have achieved a level of maturity in that sustains its democratic character, unlike most of our neighbours, and indeed many countries in Africa that won independence at around the same time as India did but are still struggling to establish a working, let alone credible, democracy.

In its six-decade existence, India's democracy has gone from strength to strength and has achieved a credibility—albeit with some aberrations—which is the envy of the democratic world. The mind-boggling magnitude of our electoral processes fascinates election watchers worldwide. The general election earlier in 2014 was the biggest the world has ever seen. As many as 55.4 crore of the 83.4 crore eligible voters exercised their franchise at 9,30,000 polling booths, nearly 1.18 crore more than were registered to vote in 2009.

The voter turnout was 66.4 per cent, the highest in India, though it needs to increase further.

One of the most interesting features of the 2014 election was the decisive role played by the new media, including mobile telephony and social media. There are an estimated 90 crore mobile devices in India, 16.5 crore of which are connected to the internet. Of this online population, 75 per cent are under thirty-five years of age. There were 14.9 crore first-time voters between eighteen and twenty-three years of age, and they were the primary target of the social media campaign. And not without reason. The Internet and Mobile Association of India estimates that a well-executed social media campaign can swing 3–4 per cent of the vote, which can be decisive in a multi-cornered contest. The BJP was smart enough to realize this and reaped a rich harvest from its social media strategy. Other parties are now waking up to this potential of social media.

The increasingly peaceful, free and fair conduct of elections has made our electoral system a respected global 'brand'. One of the secrets of its success lies in its dynamism and constant evolution, based on its vast experience and the response called for by changing needs. From candidate-specific ballot boxes to ballot paper to EVM, the system has evolved continuously. A good part of the success is owed to a powerful Election Commission. Several factors have helped make the Commission the powerful institution that it is. First and foremost, the Constitution gave it an autonomous and independent character to go with the sweeping powers it has. Laws passed by parliament and the overwhelming support of the Supreme Court further strengthened it and made it, as is commonly believed, the most powerful Election Commission in the world. But an institution is often only as strong as its head. Fortunately, no chief election commissioner, though appointed unilaterally by the government of the day, has betrayed his constitutional trust. Appointment of the CEC through a collegium will institutionalize this expectation, so such a system must be put in place as soon as possible.

Regular credible elections are the life blood of a democracy, and the Election Commission of India has ensured this without fail. Electoral violence is largely history, as are rigging and booth capturing. Deployment of the EVM, which even developed countries are wary of adopting, has made voting and counting less cumbersome and more credible. The recent introduction of VVPAT has further enhanced the transparency and credibility of the system.

That said, grave problems persist. The role of money in elections seems to have grown out of control, as political finance is opaque, with 75 per cent of the funds coming from undeclared sources. Then there is little, if any, evidence of inner-party democracy. This year's election sent a record number of MPs with criminal cases filed against them to the Lok Sabha—187 out of the total of 543 MPs, up from 162 in 2009 and 128 in 2004. This adversely affects the image of not only the political class but also of the legislature and governance. Candidates facing cases of heinous offences shame and disgrace the system. And public contempt for politicians is not healthy for democracy. It is a reason why democracies collapse. It must be remembered that democracy is a fragile system that needs continuous nurturing. Loss of credibility can be disastrous, as we have seen in struggling democracies across the world.

It is, therefore, imperative to effect urgent electoral reforms. First, criminals must be taken out of politics. A start has been made with the Supreme Court directing courts to dispose of cases against MPs and MLAs within a year, or report reasons for failing to do so to the chief justices of their respective high courts. Then, many electoral reform proposals pending for more than two decades with the Centre must be passed and effectively implemented. So far, governments have cited lack of consensus among the political parties and coalition compulsions as excuses for inaction on this front. But the present government, which won an overwhelming mandate on a promise of clean and effective governance, has a historic opportunity, and sacred duty, to bring about reform. It must not flinch from doing so.

6

Elections in the Time of Cambridge Analytica

CAMBRIDGE ANALYTICA HAS BEEN IN THE LIMELIGHT EVER SINCE whistle-blower Christopher Wylie revealed that the UK-based company used illegally obtained data from 5 crore Facebook users to influence the result of the US presidential election and the voting on Brexit. The controversy has raised new concerns regarding misuse of data on social media sites, the privacy of users and the power of social media to influence important political outcomes.

While the controversy unfolded, allegations were made about Cambridge Analytica's connection with Indian politics. Irrespective of whether these allegations are correct or not, the truth is that the details of Indian social media users have been out in the open, unprotected, for quite some time now, and can be plumbed for data.

Statistica, an online data portal, estimates that India will have about 49.27 crore mobile phone internet users by 2022. The data portal also reckons that in 2019 there would be around 25.83 crore social network users in India—up from 16.81 crore in 2016. Facebook is projected to have close to 31.9 crore users in India by 2021.

Digital networking on such a massive scale has given people the opportunity to communicate with one another and exchange ideas from across the world. But the flip side of such exchanges is that they can be exploited to extract personal information about social media users. Information about them, including their browsing history, is used for targeted cross-platform advertising. The problem, however, as senior journalist Mandira Moddie points out, this information, analysed in bulk, can aid intimate psychological profiling, including the users' ideological preferences, which can help campaign managers to influence crucial political outcomes in democracies.

All of this has naturally raised concerns about the country's data protection laws. India follows the Information Technology Act, 2000. Under the Act, only passwords, financial information such as bank details, information pertaining to a person's physical, physiological and mental health conditions and sexual orientation, medical records and biometrics are identified as 'sensitive personal data'. Entities handling such data are required to follow 'reasonable security practices and procedures'. This means that different entities can choose their own reasonable security procedures to protect sensitive data. Such a law points to how vulnerable social media users are to their data being accessed, and to the need for more stringent data protection laws.

After the recent data breach in the case of Cambridge Analytica, questions were raised about the security of data held by the Election Commission of India. I believe that the worry regarding Election Commission data is unnecessary. The Commission holds two kinds of data—electoral rolls and election results. The electoral rolls do not consist of sensitive information that might reveal people's personal history or their ideological preferences. All they have are the voter's name, age, name of father/spouse, and address. All this is already in the public domain. This data has already been used to target specific audience segments. The BJP's famous panna pramukhs—in charge of one page each of the electoral rolls—conduct such analyses on a regular basis to reach out to voters. This, to my mind, is a perfectly legitimate democratic activity. In this context, technology is a labour-saving and not intrusive instrument.

The other set of data pertains to voting information, including election results. Such data is, of course, very sensitive, sacrosanct and secret. It is, however, contained in the EVMs and is not linked to any external sources. The results data is, therefore, absolutely secure.

Questions have been raised as to whether linking ECI data with Aadhaar will compromise privacy and security for citizens. There, too, my answer is no. The only objective of linking ECI data with Aadhaar is to detect duplicate voters—a major concern. Biometrics will involve checking impersonation only.

Where does Facebook come into this? The ECI has, time and again, collaborated with Facebook for its voter outreach and education programmes. Facebook has helped the ECI reach out a large number of voters, especially the youth. The collaboration has been a productive one for Indian democracy. The ECI, in fact, recommended a special award to Facebook for this work, to be given by the president of India on National Voters Day on 25 January 2018. After the recent events, Chief Election Commissioner O.P. Rawat did say that there was a need to review the ECI-Facebook collaboration. Subsequently, though, the ECI has affirmed that its partnership with Facebook will continue.

There is no doubt, however, about the need for a stricter data regulation framework in India to avoid data abuse and prevent undue influencing of voters. Any element that can influence election results is a concern and must be kept under close scrutiny. It is relevant here to refer to Section 171C of the IPC, which deals with 'Undue Influence at Elections'. 'Whoever voluntarily interferes or attempts to interfere with the free exercise of any electoral right commits the offence of undue influence at an election,' the section notes. This includes threatening a candidate or voter 'with injury of any kind' or 'inducing or attempting to induce a candidate or voter to believe that he or any person in whom he is interested will become or will be rendered an object of divine displeasure'. Violation carries punishment of a year's imprisonment and/or fine.

Winning elections and defeating rivals in an electoral contest is a normal democratic activity. Segmentation of targeted audiences and selective targeting are old marketing practices, which are also followed by election campaigners. But the content of their messaging must be ethical and legal. It should not violate laws, regulations or codes such as the Representation of the People Act, the Indian Penal Code and the Model Code of Conduct. The messages should not carry hate speech, amount to disrupting election campaigns or contain personal attacks or appeals on the basis of religion or caste.

The rules that apply to the traditional media must apply to social media too. Application of these rules cannot be ignored just because they might be 'tougher' to implement in the latter's case.

Profiling of citizens on the basis of their political orientation for intimidating them or subjecting them to undue influencing by governments, political parties and individuals has serious implications and points to the need for adequate legal/technical safeguards. Stricter data protection laws, more security and safeguards for individual privacy are, therefore, essential if we are to survive this age of technology and emerge as a stronger and more efficient democracy.

1

The Age of Social Media

THE SCALE AND THE VARIOUS WAYS IN WHICH DIGITAL infrastructures intrude into our social and personal lives demand closer study. The media, functioning as a system of communications, public information and networking, by its very origins was always definitively social. However, with the new social media platforms, we are encountering something unprecedented and understudied. We ought to pay critical attention to the new forms of civic imagination, mediatized citizenship and political economy that are slowly but powerfully emerging.

The rise of data to become a key component of encounter and interaction has profoundly changed both the way we live our daily lives and how the world operates globally. The big question for us is to delineate the ways in which these digital infrastructures are reconstituting our public life. To understand their social and electoral impact and, consequently, their larger impact on the fate and functioning of our democracy, is of utmost significance.

Firstly, however, we must begin by understanding the reach and intrusion of social media nationally. Taking on from there, in this essay, I pay particular attention to the way social media impacts our electoral democracy, by analysing the role of political advertising and the extant media regulations that govern these developments.

I show that contemporary statecraft has become data dependent, fundamentally altering established norms in the public sphere and in political mobilization. It is precisely for these reasons that the party which can utilize these digital technologies most effectively can also shape its public image, ideology, electoral influence and voter mobilization most powerfully.

General trends in India

In 2021, out of 466 crore active internet users, 420 crore utilized social media. In India, Facebook has 27 crore members, making it the most popular social networking site. Center for the Study of Developing Societies' (CSDS) data shows that nearly four times more people use Facebook today than they did during the time of the previous general election.

Internet users in India went up by eight times between May 2014 (6.53 crore) and May 2019 (58.15 crore). Estimates vary as to how many of these users were active, but most accounts agree that by 2019, about half of India's voting population had access to information in ways that were simply not possible earlier.

Particularly, platforms like Twitter are perfect for political organizations to broadcast information on a worldwide stream for debate and discussion. With an estimated 5.31 crore active users, (as per the figures available of 2015), India is the third-largest user of Twitter in the world.

In early 2019, Google estimated that there were 40 crore active internet users in India, with an average of 4 crore users being added each year. More significantly, Google also reported that more than half of its searches were now coming from 'Bharat', or non-metro Indian cities. Crucially, this rise in the number of users was being driven by the fact that India's average mobile data consumption per user (over 8 GB per month in 2018) was on par with the consumption in developed markets. By May 2019, roughly one third of Indians had access to Facebook (up from 9 per cent in 2014), WhatsApp and YouTube. This cheap data revolution, triggered by the launch of the Jio phone network in September 2016, profoundly transformed Indian politics.

In contrast to traditional media, these new forms of social media provide many features, which are useful from the point of view of statecraft and electoral mobilization. The rapidity of information transmission, the heightened interactivity possible with targeted users, the easier and larger scope for data manipulation, the relatively cheaper costs necessary to set up a powerful IT cell, and moreover, the social image of public modernity ascribed to digital savviness, provide political parties with an amazing range of options. Given these features, alongside the increasingly mediatized form of citizenship, we have citizens who are also becoming 'prosumers', in that they are at once both active producers and consumers of public information.

Political advertising and social media

The aforementioned transformations have made social media a ripe platform for political advertisement and electoral mobilization. Between February and May 2019, Google and Facebook declared cumulative political online advertising of ₹58.67 crore in India. The money spent on each platform was more or less equal, though Facebook's ad library received a far higher volume of individual advertisements. Google declared 12,276 political advertisements worth ₹29.3 crore. Facebook, in its India Ad Library, declared a total of 1,32,419 advertisements worth ₹29.28 crore.

The takeaway from these numbers is significant. The BJP dominated digital political spending on both platforms. On Google, it accounted for 41.4 per cent (₹12.19 crore) of the political advertising, with Tamil Nadu's Dravida Munnetra Kazhagam (DMK) a distant second, accounting for 13.6 per cent (₹4 crore) of the spending, and the Congress third, with 10 per cent (₹3 crore) of the spending. The

BJP also dominated Facebook, accounting for 14.7 per cent (₹4.3 crore) of the political advertising, with the Congress a distant second, with 6.1 per cent (₹. 1.8 crore) of the political advertising. The declared political advertising on digital platforms is extremely low. The Congress's declared digital spend, for example, was minuscule when compared with the ₹820 crore it declared to the ECI as campaign expenditure in 2019. At the time of writing this book, the BJP was yet to submit its 2019 accounts to the ECI. But, for the sake of comparison, its declared spending in 2014 was ₹714 crore.

The data clearly indicates that the BJP dominated the digital domain, at the very least in terms of declared spending. The online trend in electoral spending is not an outlier. It mirrors offline trends in party earnings. In 2017–18, the BJP declared a total income of ₹1,027.34 crore, while the Congress declared an income of ₹199.15 crore.

In March 2021, Facebook revealed that the BJP had been leading in political ad spend on Facebook. According to official Facebook data, the BJP and its affiliates accounted for over 50 per cent of the total ad spend as of February 2022 while the Opposition party, the Congress, and its affiliates were in third position, behind the regional parties.

CSDS data shows that while 47 per cent of people with high social media exposure feel close to the BJP, that figure is only 18 per cent for the Congress. Moreover, for voters with no exposure to social media, the Congress figure actually increases slightly, to 21 per cent, while the BJP's drops to 38 per cent.

Given these realities, it is often assumed that, somehow, digital platforms are tailored for the right wing and are easier to dominate with polarizing messaging. However, the truth is slightly more complicated. On Twitter and Facebook, while Modi swept the field in 2014, then Congress president Rahul Gandhi started getting his online strategy together from 2017 onwards, after the Uttar Pradesh (UP) assembly elections, and made significant strides. While Modi remained significantly ahead in terms of both followers and total posts (see Annexure), in absolute terms the level of engagement for Rahul Gandhi increased significantly in the last two years.

Media regulation for the new age

It may come as a surprise to the reader that despite the enormous impact of social media and the increasing flows of investment and finances into it, there is simply no established framework of regulations and legal governance on the scale and of the coherence necessary to effectively tackle the many problems it is fraught with.

So far, in measures that can only be termed pseudo-regulatory, the Election Commission has developed, prior to the Lok Sabha 2019 election, a set of 'Voluntary Code of Ethics' for general elections. This Code has been developed to ensure free, fair and ethical use of social media platforms and to maintain the integrity of the electoral process.

In addition to this, there is also what is called a 'Media Certification and Monitoring Committee' (MCMC). This committee clears political advertisements before they are telecast on television and cable networks by any registered political party or by any group or organization/association or by any contesting candidate during elections. MCMC's three major functions are (i) pre-certification of political advertisements on electronic media, and as well as social media, (ii) monitoring of and acting against paid-news cases, and finally (iii) monitoring of cases of violations by the media during the election process. For the purpose of examination, a social media specialist was also designated under the district and state-level Media Certification and Monitoring Committees.

Apart from these external bodies, there are many laws and provisions that regulate the offensive language on social media, such as the Information Technology Act 2000 (Amendment 2015), the Indian Penal Code, 1860, etc. Section 66A of the IT Act had been the provision for online abuse or defamation. However, in 2015, the Supreme Court, upholding the provisions of Article 19(1)(a), had struck down Section 66A of the IT Act, 2000 in the landmark case *Shreya Singhal and Ors vs. Union of India*. But there are many provisions in the IPC for offences relating to cyber-crime and abuse by the trolls, which are: Section 295A (intentionally insulting religion or belief), Section 153A (promoting enmity between people), Section 499 (defamation), Section 505 (statements conducing to public mischief), 506 (criminal intimidation), and Section 124A (sedition), among others.

Globally, we see similar measures. For instance, as a result of the 2016 US presidential elections, the European Union created a proposal called the Digital Services and Digital Markets Act in 2020, which spelled out requirements for digital platforms to follow.

Against the enormous presence of social media, these regulatory measures described above prove to be evidently weak and ineffective. Instead of these dispersed scatterings of legal provisions which are forever being amended and the contingent external bodies with pseudo-powers, we need a coherent, well-established, all-encompassing body of regulations for legal governance and administration of these newly emerging digital infrastructures. We need laws that can effectively cover issues ranging from user privacy and digital data proprietorship to penalizing of digital disinformation and hate speech.

Our democracy is going through something profoundly new with the rise of social media. The time has come for us to re-evaluate, reform and regulate these digital infrastructures so that the nation may realize the utopian promises made to its citizens.

2

Social Media in a Violent Democracy

WHAT HAPPENS TO OUR NOTIONS OF PUBLIC GOVERNANCE AND civic morality when the reign of social media severely exacerbates the politics of hatred and division? What happens when the virtual world of digital technology assimilates into the real world of practical politics to such an extent that each world becomes indiscernible? Given these newly emerging forms of digital polity, what kinds of new dangers or dynamics will disrupt the functioning of democracy? While there may be legal provisions, however unsatisfactory, to deal with the spread of intense polarization and disinformation on social media, it increasingly appears that they are beyond our firm control. We need now to revise and reappraise our ideals of democracy in light of these emerging realities. For that, we must first stop and consider what is at stake and what, in fact, is happening.

I have always believed that the state of the national media is a robust indicator of the overall health of a nation's democracy. The independence, integrity and collective morality of the citizenry is intricately tied to the proper functioning of its media. We seem to have forgotten, all too tragically, that our great national leaders in the freedom struggle, from Ram Mohan Roy to Aruna Asaf Ali, and from Gandhi to Tilak, were also in fact pioneering journalists who ran multiple and multi-lingual newspapers and publications. They knew very well that a fearless and democratic media is an imperative for achieving a fair and democratic republic.

In our contemporary world, we are witness to a new chapter in this history of media technology, with the extraordinary onset of social media and digital infrastructures. In order to gauge the situation in India today, we ought to study the affiliations and intersections between the traditional and the new social media, or in other words, what may be called the media ecosystem. It is worth reiterating that the fate of the media ecosystem is closely intertwined with the fate of our national democracy.

Assessing the media ecosystem

In India today, we are witnessing increasing degeneration of the media ecosystem, which is working in nexus with partisan corporatism, and an absolutely unaccountable proliferation of 'cyber-armies' of party-sponsored IT cells. What is particularly worrying is that this is happening within an overall context of punitive anti-dissident government policing, heavily compromised digital rights (such as privacy and cyber security laws), access to unprecedented levels of electoral funding and, in the case of BJP, access to a superbly entrenched, hierarchized, grassroots-level manpower of party workers and volunteers, owing mainly to the century-long work of the Rashtriya Swayamsevak Sangh, which is now the biggest volunteer group in the world.

Traditional media continue to be the dominant source of information for Indians. Among those aged fifteen to thirty-four, 57 percent watch TV news a few days a week, 53 per cent read the newspapers at the same frequency, and about 18 per cent consume their news on the internet, according to a 2016 study by the Centre for the Study of Developing Societies, a think tank based in New

Delhi. But social media is playing a growing role. As many as 23 crore Indians use WhatsApp, making the country the messaging platform's biggest market. One-sixth of them are members of chat groups started by political parties, according to another CSDS study. These groups, ostensibly used to organize rallies, recruit volunteers, or disseminate campaign news, are capped at 256 members. In 2018, 'horrified by terrible acts of violence', WhatsApp limited the number of chat groups and individuals that messages could be forwarded to in India from 256 to five, making it harder to forward images, audio clips and videos to a very large number of people.

The disruptions to democracy being caused by social media are not simply on some abstract, vaguely discernible, macroscopic level that is somehow only a matter of concern to ivory-tower scholars of media theory and political science. In fact, we have in India certain appalling incidents that can reveal to us the directly and viscerally-felt nature of social media–induced violence—namely the 'WhatsApp lynchings'.

They are a uniquely Indian phenomenon, and there have been more than a dozen innocent civilians who have been murdered or lynched in broad daylight, influenced by WhatsApp-fuelled hate-spewing, paranoia-inducing fake news. Across the country (with cases in places such as Bengaluru, Assam, Tamil Nadu, Telangana and Uttar Pradesh), members belonging to minority or marginalized groups such as Muslims, nomadic tribes, LGBTQI+ and Dalits have been killed. It is to be noted that most of these cases were concentrated in urban centres, where members from these marginalized groups come in as rural migrants looking for jobs and livelihoods. These cases were so severe and recurrent that WhatsApp even made (arguably insufficient) changes to the app to restrict the number of people messages could be forwarded to, exclusively for Indian users, although some of these restrictions have since been rolled out worldwide.

Who, then, are to be blamed for these killings? The murderers themselves may end up in courts and prisons, but it is all too important that we understand the roots of the problem, which in turn requires us to contend with the larger digital culture of fake news, hate speech, disinformation and polarization. Merely on technical terms, it is hard to trace down and cut fake-news sources on platforms such as WhatsApp, Helo and ShareChat. WhatsApp has end-to-end encryption. What that means is, every message sent between two parties has a unique set of keys, regardless of whether it is the same message being passed on. This means that when fake news happens, there is no trail. It becomes tough for even WhatsApp to track.

Facebook and WhatsApp are not the only social networks where this phenomenon of polarizing disinformation is violently raging. Smaller platforms such as ShareChat, which has 4 crore monthly active users, and Helo, which has about 2.5 crore, operating in fourteen Indian languages and target first-time internet users, are both rife with litanies of false claims and misinformation.

BJP in the age of social media

Regardless of the BJP's image as being 'medieval', 'antiquated' and 'reactionary', they are actually front-runners in and have mastered the use of digital technology to target, collectivize, mobilize and manipulate social media expertly. In fact, they currently have the largest social-media ecosystem of any party in India. Although all the major parties now have IT cells, the BJP is unique in having apps centred exclusively on Modi, such as 'NaMo'.

The NaMo app—which came preloaded on free Android phones distributed by at least two BJP-led state governments and in low-cost phones sold by Reliance Jio—has been installed by more than 1 crore people. It is used to promote the prime minister and has a built-in social network with Twitter-like features. Apart from being vulnerable to use as a vehicle for spread of misinformation, it reveals the party's attempts to manufacture personality cults as an ostensibly ideal alternative to dynastic politics.

The national convenor of BJP's IT cell, Amit Malaviya, has said that about 12 lakh volunteers will help run the party's social media campaign for the national election. In India's most populous state, Uttar Pradesh, for example, the BJP's IT department has a six-tier hierarchical structure covering the state from the capital city of Lucknow down to the most remote village. At what is known as 'booth level', which is the last point of contact with voters, each party worker has been directed to create a WhatsApp group consisting of at least fifty users.

Apart from utilizing these popular social media platforms, BJP has designed its own applications, such as the surprisingly under-known 'Tek Fog' app. This is a highly sophisticated app, used and accessible to online operatives of BJP IT cells, *only* to hijack private social media accounts and encrypted messaging platforms to amplify right-wing propaganda to a domestic audience. This is extremely scary use of technology. Using this, the operatives can hijack and literally control Twitter and Facebook trends, and they have a cloud base with access to information about private citizens, like their phone numbers, online history, and so on. They use these information points to hijack inactive WhatsApp numbers for targeted messaging and so on.

Moreover, the government's use of the Information Technology (Intermediary Guidelines and Digital Media Ethics Code) Rules, 2021 as a threat and inducement to get major platforms to play ball has been extensively documented. Meta's (earlier Facebook) hesitation to take action against Hindutva handles spreading hate and disinformation has already been pointed out by two important whistle-blowers. Take, for instance, the case of former Facebook data scientist and whistle-blower Sophie Zhang. She uncovered how networks of inauthentic accounts were using fake engagements to flood the information pipelines and revealed that the social media giant did nothing about it once it found that a BJP MP, Vinod Sonkar, was involved.

There is another disturbing, hugely emerging and uniquely BJP phenomenon: the rise of 'Hindutva Pop'. Across north India, pop singers such as Laxmi Dubey (whose songs have over 5 crore YouTube views), Sandeep Acharya, Sanjay Faizabadi, Prem Krishnavanshi and

Kanhiya Mittal are propagating Hindutva ideology, Islamophobia, anti-Kashmiri and anti-Pakistan sentiments, even calling for genocide and massacres in their song lyrics. One of these singers, Prem Krishnavanshi, was even given a Uttar Pradesh state award during Adityanath's oath-taking ceremony.

What is the way forward

Therefore, this is entrenched, heavily sophisticated digital machinery working in nexus with big-tech corporates, traditional media houses and surveillance companies, such as Pegasus and Tek Fog, for establishing a surveillance state.

This is clearly highly formidable machinery, often working insidiously and invisibly, and to contend with this will surely be a challenge, which must involve digital activism for internet rights, awareness campaigns, alternative journalism and systematic efforts at dismantling the dominant ideologies.

Truth and non-violence were the great virtues around which were organized our national struggles for freedom. In independent India, as disinformation and violence are becoming inescapable and integral to our national life, we must battle to reassert and reinforce those same great ideals upon which our republic was founded. Perhaps, then, the struggle for independence is still ongoing, and it must continue to do so until freedom is truly manifested.

3

Accountability of Social Media Platforms

O N 29 OCTOBER 2019, SOCIAL MEDIA FIRM WHATSAPP BLASTED THE world—India, in particular—with news that its platform was infiltrated by the use of a spyware, Pegasus, sold by Israeli surveillance firm NSO Group, to snoop on over 1,400 people across four continents, including 100 academics, human rights activists, journalists and lawyers. It claimed that Pegasus was secretly installed in the mobile phone of the targeted persons by means of a missed WhatsApp call, adding that the spyware was capable of accessing their call logs, photos and emails, among other private data. This revelation was followed by WhatsApp suing the Israeli firm in a US federal court. Without any doubt, the outcome of this lawsuit would be path-breaking. The incident has once again brought to fore the fragility of privacy rights in the age of the information technology revolution.

It is not the first time that social media has been in the eye of a cyber storm. It is popularly known that social media platforms—in particular, Facebook and Twitter, with 2.12 billion and 250.8 million users, respectively—have become convenient media for political campaigning for their function of sheer accessibility. In 2018, a scam involving Cambridge Analytica (CA) opened a Pandora's box of illegal data breaches made for political influence. Whistleblower Christopher Wylie revealed that to influence the US presidential elections and the voting on Brexit, UK-based political strategizing company Cambridge Analytica used illegally obtained data of 50 million Facebook users by means of floating several quizzes on Facebook for viewers' entertainment. It helped create 30 million profiles of users and sold them to politicians without the users' consent. Journalist Mandira Moddie has pointed out that the combination of data they obtained can reveal users' ideological preferences and other personal psychological factors.

While the Cambridge Analytica scam allowed one-time analysis of users' social media activities, the Pegasus scam enabled surveillance of the users' cell phones. In simpler analogy, the CA scam is a single photograph and the Pegasus scam is live video-streaming of the targeted audience's social media activities. The consequences of both are grave.

With cyber-attacks of such a massive scale, there have been concerns over the security of the voter data that lies with the Election Commission of India (ECI) and the privacy rights of the voters. The electoral rolls consist of publicly available information, like the voter's name, name of father/spouse, age and address. Political campaigning based on this data has been a regular practice by parties, which selectively target households based on their composition, which is a legitimate practice.

However, it needs to be noted that the content shared to influence voters must be legal and ethical and must not disturb communal harmony. The other dataset with the ECI includes voting information that is secret, and this data not connected to any network or device. However, with the addition of VVPAT, concerns have been raised over its vulnerability to manipulation. The ECI must initiate measures to allay fears regarding this.

Even though our electoral data is secure with the ECI, there remains an immediate need for the Indian government to frame a foolproof legislation against data breach. The current legislation—the Information Technology Act (2000)—fails to match up to the technological advancements that are happening. The Act only considers passwords, banking details and information on the person's sexual orientation and bodily conditions, along with his or her biometrics, as sensitive information. Instead of an objective data protection framework, it instructs the entities owning data to formulate their own security practices to prevent misuse of their data. Passing the buck won't do. It is imperative for the country to have a stringent framework to avoid and punish any future illegal transaction in data without user consent.

In terms of surveillance, the legislation dates back to the colonial times: the Indian Telegraph Act (1885). The Act allowed the government and some law enforcement agencies to conduct surveillance in case of threat to public safety or public emergency. Its provisions regarding surveillance were suitably adopted into the Information Technology Act (2000), and the grounds of surveillance under the Act were broadened with amendments in 2008. However, neither of the laws closely covers private agency-led wiretapping.

It would be unfair not to mention the brazen misuse of social media in spreading fake news and propagating hate speeches. With no effective regulation, these two phenomena on social media have also played a role in influencing elections. Ahead of the general election, as per a survey conducted by Social Media Matters and Institute for Governance, Policies and Politics, over 53 per cent of the respondents claimed that they had received fake news in the run-up to the election on various social media platforms in the past thirty days. The survey report went on to state that approximately one in two persons received fake news via Facebook and WhatsApp.

To cope with the hazard of fake news and hate speech on social media, the ECI, along with the Internet and Mobile Association of India (IAMAI), adopted the Voluntary Code of Ethics, which required social media sites to take down posts violating Section 126 of the Representation of the People Act, 1951 within three hours of a complaint by the EC. However, in these times of single-tap forwards, three hours' action period is an eternity. Underlining the Internet's tendency to 'cause unimaginable disruption to the democratic polity', the government has stated that it plans to release revised IT Rules (2011) in January 2020. Though this move offers a ray of hope, it would be a tightrope walk to balance individual right to expression and privacy with national security.

With data being the 'new oil', and given the rapidly growing technological advancements, where a 27.5 per cent increase in social media users is anticipated between 2019 and 2023, the debate over balancing citizens' rights to privacy and free speech and the demands of national security needs to be clinched on a war footing. Social media platforms cannot be allowed to go on without being accountable. We are sitting on a ticking time bomb. Urgency is imperative.

4

Fake News: A Big Threat to Democracy

THE TERM 'FAKE NEWS' WAS NAMED COLLINS DICTIONARY'S Official Word of the Year for 2017. Even though rumour-mongering is as old as history, fake news has influenced events internationally, ever since the explosion of digital technology. Back home, according to the Quint tracker, ninety-two people have been lynched since 2015 as a result of fake news, and the count is rising.

A November 2018 BBC study titled 'Duty, Identity, Credibility: Fake News and Ordinary Citizen in India' goes into the genesis of fake news. It interviewed eighty people in three countries—India, Nigeria and Kenya—over a one-week period, analysing their media consumption habits and how they used Facebook and WhatsApp on their phones for sharing information.

They found that respondents made little effort to figure out the original source of what they shared. Confirmation biases, coupled with trustworthiness of the source (relatives, friends etc.), have served to exacerbate such a disastrous phenomenon. As a respondent said,

'My friend has sent this to me, why would he send anything fake to me?'

Analysing Twitter in India, it found that 'right-leaning fake news spreads faster and wider than left-leaning fake news'. Equally dangerous are the WhatsApp groups. This is for obvious reason that the right wing has highly organized social media groups in the thousands, with a cumulative reach of millions. Fact-checking is almost impossible. After all, when one is being bombarded with a thousand stories every day, will one care to fact-check them to see how much of it is true? The attractive narrative of fake messages discourages fact checking.

The report goes on to recommend some measures. It calls for the involvement of all actors—platforms, media organizations, the government and civil society—to work together towards curbing false news. Fake news has always existed, it's the pace at which it spreads which has increased manifold because of the communication channels of the twenty-first century.

Most importantly, it suggests that 'journalists investigate further whether or not there is an organised ecosystem of fake news production and dissemination'. This is crucial, as there is sufficient proof that a majority of fake news is systematically targeted at voters and sympathizers by the IT wings of political parties.

During the biggest electoral show in history, no wonder fake news on social media, coupled with paid news, is having a field day—with disastrous consequences. Money power is in full play, to bombard voters with fake and paid news. In the aftermath of the Balakot airstrikes, Trushar Barot, who heads Facebook India's efforts to counter fake news, said on Twitter that he had 'never seen anything like this before'. It is reported that Facebook is removing as many as 1 million fake Indian accounts per day!

To stem the tide of fake news, the Election Commission announced a slew of measures at a press conference on 11 March. All candidates have to reveal their social media information in their nominations. The 'silence' period of forty-eight hours before the polls shall come into force on social media too. The rules of political advertising shall apply to social media the same way as they apply to other news media. Only pre-certified advertisements will be accepted by Google, WhatsApp, Twitter, Facebook and WeChat. The district and state-level Media Certification and Monitoring Committees will have a social media expert to monitor content.

The Internet and Mobile Association of India (IMAI) has formulated a 'Voluntary Code of Ethics' for social media, and this came into force on 20 March. The code highlights the commitment of social media companies towards ensuring that they are not misused during elections. In accordance with Section 126 of the Representation of the People Act, 1951, social media companies will implement the forty-eight-hour silence period and 'valid legal orders' of the EC by taking down objectionable content within three hours of being notified of it. A 'high priority dedicated notification' mechanism is being created for the purpose.

WhatsApp has already taken various measures in the past, such as tagging of forwarded messages to track trouble-makers. A new service called 'WhatsApp Tipline' has provided a number to which users can send information for verification. Facebook and Twitter have assured that they will be putting in place an online library of election advertisements for public access. Google announced its plans to launch an 'Advertising Transparency Report'.

While these are welcome developments, the Code itself seems to be vague. There is no definition of the term 'fake news' in the Code. It highlights the commitment of the social media companies 'to provide an update on the measures taken by them to prevent abuse of their platforms', but the magnitude of the problem far exceeds the measures they have committed themselves to.

Fake news is not only an election-related problem, but also a serious social and security issue in the twenty-first century. It's a source of extremism and a boon for anti-social elements and militants. It is most important for social media companies to ensure that they take steps to counter this burgeoning social menace. Profit must come after people.

The Code of Ethics cannot be ignored or taken lightly on the pretext of free speech and must be stringently applied, as 'reasonable restrictions' must protect citizens against hate and bigotry spread through misinformation. We can't simply ignore this phenomenon just because rules might be 'tougher' to implement for social media.

With the great power of technology comes great responsibility. The content of messaging must be ethical, factual and legal. It should not violate laws, regulations or codes such as the RPA and the Model Code of Conduct. The messages should not carry hate speech, personal attacks, or appeal on the basis of religion or caste; all these terms need to be properly defined within the Code too.

Citizens, too, must take individual responsibility to fact-check before forwarding material to their kin. All information must be taken with a pinch of salt, keeping in mind the business model of social media. Citizens must remember that if a service is free, you are the product.

1

The Unsung Organizer of India's First Election

DEMOCRACY IN INDIA IS A SOURCE OF IMMENSE NATIONAL PRIDE and a cornerstone of the identity of this country. It did not, however, have a smooth start. Immeasurable struggle and the indomitable will of India's nation builders and its people combined to make the second most populous country the largest democracy in the world.

The foundation of all democracies is free and fair elections. The first Indian election was held from 25 October 1951 to 21 February 1952, with an astronomical (for the times) 17,32,12,343 registered voters, of whom 10,59,50,083 exercised their newly acquired voting right. Most observers and experts held that the geographical vastness of India, which even today poses a formidable challenge, was insurmountable for a countrywide election to be organized in the 1950s.

Interestingly, the backdrop for the 1952 elections was as much a strategic consideration as it was a political one. While India became independent in 1947, it remained a dominion. A British governor general remained at the head of the Indian political system, greater in stature than the country's prime minister. As the Constitution, promulgated on 26 November 1949, came into effect on 26 January 1950, Prime Minister Jawaharlal Nehru was anxious to get elections underway as soon as possible. Democracy and establishment of the will of the people were the main premises on which the struggle for independence was waged, and without elections that premise would remain unfulfilled. The man this mammoth task was entrusted to was Sukumar Sen, an unsung hero of Indian democracy.

Sen, an Indian Civil Service officer, was the chief secretary of West Bengal when he was called to be the first chief election commissioner of India. A month after he was appointed in March 1950, the Representation of the People Act was passed in parliament, which provided the framework for elections, mainly the electoral rolls. A year later, the Representation of the People Act, 1951 was passed, dealing with all the remaining matters pertaining to the conduct of elections. It is not clear why the two Acts were given the same name.

It was decided that the electoral process would be started as early as in 1951. It was mandated that any Indian citizen twenty-one years of age or more, residing in a particular constituency for more than 180 days, would be eligible to vote from that constituency.

It is significant that poor and backward as India was, it still gave its people, men and women, an equal vote, while it took the so-called greatest democracy, the US, 144 years (from the Deceleration of Independence in 1776) and the UK almost 100 years from the (Reform Act of 1832) to give equal voting rights to women.

In a country with massive illiteracy (84 per cent) and where lakhs of residents did not possess key identification documents owing to the turmoil of Partition, this was perhaps a significant challenge. But at the same time, the step was a befitting homage to the ideals of democracy and representation that had fuelled an independence struggle spanning over half a century. In the heralded democracies of the West, such as the US or the UK, elections are held with two or at best three competing political parties. In India, however, the first election saw fifty-three registered political parties (including fourteen national parties) competing for 489 seats for the lower house of parliament.

At the time of Independence, there were seventeen provinces in British India, which were reorganized into states. And then there were princely states, 565 of them, dotting the country. These had to be reconfigured into the existing provinces, which ultimately led to fourteen new states and six Union Territories, which formed independent India. This reorganization was the first challenge the Constituent Assembly Secretariat (CAS), the body in charge of preparing the electoral rolls, faced. This was before the Election Commission of India was created and took over the task.

The second challenge India faced was the aftermath of the Partition riots, including the rehabilitation of refugees. The Bengal and Punjab borders were porous, with refugees coming in almost every day throughout the later months of 1947 and even after. There was widespread confusion amongst both administrators and the masses regarding where exactly the international borders between India and Pakistan were. It was in the midst of this confusion that the CAS undertook the task of preparing the first electoral rolls for registering 17.3 crore first-time voters, two years before the Election Commission came into existence. This made the formidable task easier for Sukumar Sen.

Not to be missed in this exercise is the foresight of the bureaucracy of the Constituent Assembly Secretariat led by B.N. Rau, constitutional adviser (CA), to start advance action. The other staff members who were directly and continuously involved in the work of preparation of the electoral rolls, in what came to be known as the Franchise Section, were the joint secretary, S.N. Mukherjee and under-secretaries K.V. Padmanabhan and P.S. Subramaniam, the latter of whom joined in late 1948 and then took over from Rau. Interestingly, as Ornit Shani, the author of *How India Became Democratic,* observes, the CAS made Indians voters before they even became citizens.

The Election Commission of India (ECI) was created as an independent autonomous constitutional body. While introducing draft

Article 289 (which later became Article 324 in the final Constitution) on 15 June 1949 in the Constituent Assembly, B.R. Ambedkar, chairman of the Drafting Committee, explained the rationale for an independent central and federal Election Commission. Thus, an independent Election Commission was constituted, and vested with the superintendence, direction and control of preparing electoral rolls and conducting elections to parliament as well as the state legislatures and to the offices of the president and vice-president of India.

The first elections of 1952 under Sukumar Sen were pivotal, because they set the standard for all subsequent elections. Sen started from scratch. There was no staff, permanent or temporary, no infrastructure, no training facilities and no institutional memory, as a large number of the staff who had conducted the 1944 assembly elections had either migrated or were killed in the riots. Sen started with a blank slate.

Of the 489 parliamentary constituencies, 314 were single-seat constituencies, 172 double seat (including one general category candidate and one SC or ST candidate) and three were triple-seat constituencies (containing one candidate from each category). A total of 1,874 candidates, including 533 independents, contested.

Ballot papers were printed at the Government Security Press in Nasik. A whopping 1,96,084 polling stations were set up, of which 27,527 were exclusively for women voters. Each candidate was allotted a coloured box with his or her name and a symbol painted on it. The turnout was 45.7 per cent, which was considered quite decent under the prevailing circumstances. However, a voter turnout as high as 80.5 per cent was recorded in Kottayam district of Kerala, a testament to the potential enthusiasm of the Indian people to exercise their franchise.

These elections proved to be a benchmark for future endeavours; every minute detail was taken care of to make the elections a success.

Transport to the remotest parts of the country was arranged by any means available, including camels and elephants. Ballot sheets, ballot boxes and indelible ink were prepared, political party symbols were designed and allotted to make things easier for the mostly illiterate voters. There was attention in the matter of every possible factor, including the weather. In certain tehsils like Chini in what is now Himachal Pradesh, locals went to the polls earlier than the rest of the country as the winter snow would make the routes leading to the tehsil impassable. In village Kalpa in Kinnaur valley, a young man called Shyam Saran Negi became the first known voter to cast his vote. He hasn't missed a single election since, and is now the oldest living voter, a media celebrity.

Interestingly, the polls were held in sixty-eight phases between 25 October 1951 to 21 February 1952.

What makes the first Indian elections even more extraordinary in context was the international situation at the time. When India was going to polls in late 1951, Prime Minister Liaquat Ali Khan in neighbouring Pakistan had just been assassinated, pushing the country towards the first of its many military dictatorships. The government of South Africa had just disenfranchised the Cape Coloureds, the last non-white people who had voting rights in the country. Vietnam had plunged into war against the French, and the prime minister of Iran was assassinated. It was amidst this chaos of war and violence on the global stage that a fledgling nation fought to establish and uphold its democratic values and its promise to a colonized people who had fought for decades to gain their independence.

Today, after over seven decades, the great Indian election has become a global benchmark for free, fair and credible elections. There have been several electoral reforms during this period, the most prominent of which has been the journey from the individual, coloured ballot boxes to ballot papers and eventually EVMs. But perhaps 80 per cent of the system remains what its founder, Sen, had created from scratch. In the absence of mass media exposure, he did his job discreetly. He remains an unsung hero of Indian democracy.

2

Goodbye, Mr Seshan

THE PASSING ON OF MR T.N. SESHAN MARKS THE END OF A GLORIOUS era of resurgence of democracy about three decades ago. In the first half of the nineties, the very mention of his name was enough to put the fear of God in the hearts of recalcitrant politicians and respect in the heart of every Indian ever since. I have no hesitation in saying that all his successor CECs basked in his glory, though we also always carried the burden of being compared with him all the time.

I worked under him as an election observer several times. He once sent me to Danapur in Bihar, which was Lalu Prasad Yadav's constituency. On another occasion, I was deputed to Mylapore, where Jayalalithaa lived (and where Mr Seshan too had his house). Mr Seshan had a battle running with both, which made my tough job doubly difficult.

I recall the Bihar election in 1996, when I was posted as an observer. Mr Seshan concluded his briefing with these reassuring words: 'Don't worry. Nothing will happen—except a bomb on your face and a bullet through your stomach!' Sure enough, I saw witnessed two bomb explosions a few yards away from me. Fortunately, I returned with my stomach unpunctured!

The awe and fear he evoked in us bordered on terror. Nobody had the guts to argue with him, not to speak of falling foul of him. Yet, behind a tough exterior he had a soft heart. Once I was posted as an observer in the Maoist area of Jharkhand. I had just got up from a slipped disc and could not have stood the bad roads in the tribal belt. In the briefing he had called, I gathered the courage to request a change of my posting to an urban constituency because of my medical condition. Very sweetly, he ordered that I be exempted altogether from observer work.

When I became the CEC myself, I went to his house in Chennai to seek his blessings. He was extremely affectionate and asked his extremely gentle wife to give me a present. She brought a few things, from which I picked a sandalwood Ganesh, a souveneir I have cherished.

A few months ago, I published a book titled *The Great March of Democracy: Seven Decades of India's Elections*. It carries a chapter written by Mr Seshan about the problems he faced in turning things around in the electoral system. Interestingly, it also carries a chapter on Mr Seshan by a French professor, Christophe Jaffrelot. I am happy I dedicated the book to two legends—Sukumar Sen, the first CEC, and Mr T.N. Seshan, who took the Commission to new heights of authority, credibility and visibility.

I pray I get to see another Seshan in my lifetime.

Religion and the Future of India

1

On Politics of Hatred in India

WHAT IS TO BE DONE WHEN THE INDIAN REPUBLIC, COMMITTED to working within the framework of constitutional democracy and the rule of law, starts to accommodate elements that are stridently anti-constitutional and anti-secular? What once belonged to the fringes of Indian society has now become increasingly mainstream, and the fringe elements' disruptive actions are being registered in the public sphere more frequently and viciously. Hate speech is at the root of many forms of violence being perpetrated, and has become one of the biggest challenges to the rule of law and to our democratic conscience.

One of the most visible consequences of hate speech is increased electoral mobilization along communal lines, which is also paying electoral dividends for some.

Hate speech must be unambiguously condemned and the law must take its course when there are instances of it, although not merely because it can lead to events of violence in the future. Hate speech, in itself, must be understood and treated as a violent act, and urgently so, for it has become an indispensable resource for the ruling powers. No wonder it becomes louder during elections.

Several instances of hate speech and religious polarization have been reported in Yogi Adityanath's poll campaign in the recently concluded UP elections, for instance. In 2019, the Supreme Court reprimanded the Election Commission, calling it 'toothless' for not taking action against candidates engaging in hate speech during the election campaigns in UP. The Commission responded by saying it had limited powers to take action in this matter. So far, the Supreme Court does not appear to have acted decisively in response to allegations of hate speech in electoral campaigns, indicating that the Election Commission must assume more responsibility for it; and the Commission has argued that in matters of hate speech it is largely 'powerless'. In any case, the Commission's role is confined to events that happen during the election period. So, who is responsible for dealing with hate speech taking place in non-election times?

Is the state powerless? Not at all. There is a whole bunch of laws meant to curb hate speech. The Indian Penal Code, as per Sections 153A, 295A and 298, criminalizes the promotion of enmity between different groups of people on grounds of religion and language, alongside acts that are prejudicial to the maintenance of communal harmony. Section 125 of the Representation of the People Act deems that any person, in connection with elections, promoting feelings of enmity and hatred on the grounds of religion and caste is punishable with imprisonment up to three years and fine, or both. Section 505 criminalizes many kinds of speech, including statements made with the intention of inducing, or which are likely to induce, fear or alarm among the public, instigating them towards public disorder; statements made with the intention of inciting, or which are likely to incite, class or community violence; and discriminatory statements that have the effect or the intention of promoting inter-community hatred. The Act covers incitement of violence against the state or another community, as well as promotion of class hatred.

While examining the scope of hate speech laws in India, the Law Commission in its 267th report published in March 2017, recommended introduction of new provisions within the Penal

Code—in addition to the existing ones—that specifically punish incitement to violence. In my view, any recommendation for more laws is a red herring and provides an excuse for inaction. It's the lack of political will, blatant inefficiency and bias of the administration, and the shocking apathy of the judiciary that is killing the secular spirit of the Constitution.

Another watchdog should have been the media. In recent years, hate speech in all its varieties has acquired a systemic presence in the media and the internet, whether in electoral campaigns or in everyday life. Abusive speech directed against minority communities, particularly Muslims, and disinformation campaigns on media networks have made trolling and fake news significant aspects of public discourse. By desensitizing the citizenry with a constant barrage of anti-minority sentiments, the ethical and moral bonds of our democracy are taking a hit.

This epidemic of 'mediatized' hate speech is, in fact, a global phenomenon. According to the *Washington Post*, 2018 can be considered as 'the year of online hate'. Facebook, in its Transparency Report, disclosed that it ended up taking down 30 lakh hateful posts from its platform, while YouTube removed 25,000 in one month alone.

On 2 April 2022 amidst unconcerned police officials and cheering crowds, Mahant Bajrang Muni Udasin, chief priest of the Badi Sangat Ashram in Uttar Pradesh's Sitapur district, publicly threatened sexual violence against Muslim women and violence against Muslims in general—'you and your pigsty will cease to exist,' he said. Although this particular video went viral recently and Udasin has now been arrested by the Sitapur police, he has a long history of spewing hate and stoking communal polarization with apparent impunity. In the past, Udasin celebrated Dara Singh, a Bajrang Dal member who is currently serving a life sentence for leading a mob on 23 January 1999 in Orissa and setting fire to a wagon in which the Christian missionary Graham Staines and his two sons were sleeping. All three were burnt to death. Likening Dara Singh to a godman, Udasin appealed to Hindu monks to declare him a Shankaracharya. With this, Udasin joins the ranks of a multitude of 'holy' men and women, most prominent among them being Yati Narsinghanand, Pooja Shakun Pandey and Jitendra Tyagi, who have been at the forefront of the politics of fear and hatred.

With elected members currently sitting in the legislative assemblies and Parliament giving political sanction to these self-styled mahants, with ordinary citizens mobilized into mob violence and complicit public officials, hate speech is becoming the dominant mode of public political participation. Two people died in the Ram Navami violence in April 2022, while many more were arrested across states for perpetrating violence. Shocking images also surfaced from Jawaharlal Nehru University—of students injured during a face-off between two groups on Ram Navami day on campus.

This should prick the conscience of the nation. Enough damage has been done. We cannot wait another day to address this growing challenge.

2

The Secular Constitution

THE PUBLIC DISCOURSE IN INDIA RESOUNDS WITH TRIUMPHALISM ON the one hand and nihilistic lament on the other over the defeat or death of secularism. The former group, mostly in affiliation with the ruling regime, denigrates the virtues of secularism by calling it a pernicious product of the latter group, who are termed 'pseudo-seculars', 'sickularists', 'urban naxals' and 'anti-nationals'. This attack on secularism and democracy can be said to have increased, especially over the last decade.

The political dominance of the BJP's brand of Hindutva nationalism since the 2014 election has put into question the future viability of the nation's secularist tradition and its commitment to diversity. Not only does this crisis disfigure the moral and socio-cultural fabric of the nation but it also undermines Constitutional governance. In fact, the state's engagement with religion can be said to have been one of the abiding themes of conflict in India's democratic experiment.

Therefore, in order to gauge the damage being done and to fix the problem at its root, we must begin by understanding the nature and evolution of Indian secularism. We must remember that secularism is not an isolated and separate category within the larger realm of democratic governance and social equality. Instead, it is *a definitive and fundamental feature* of any equal democracy, or in other words, we cannot have one without having the other. It is for this reason that this essay claims that a crisis in democracy and constitutional governance is directly a product of degenerating secularism.

Moreover, in this essay I also argue that constitutional secularism is of immense import to our notions of citizenship, nationality and civic freedom. Apart from the obvious effects that a crisis in secularism is registering in the electoral realm, we must also pay attention to how that crisis is creeping into other sectors of our nation's life, ranging from our national media to education to the everyday life of the citizen.

Towards the end of the colonial regime, in December 1946, the Constituent Assembly of India was convened and tasked with drafting the Constitution of India. On 17 October 1949, the Constituent Assembly devoted a significant part of its discussions to incorporating the principle of secularism in the Preamble of the Constitution. An amendment proposed by H.V. Kamath, which sought to begin the Preamble of the Constitution with the words 'In the name of God' was defeated. Noteworthy amongst the voices opposing the amendment was Pandit Kunzru, who stated that invoking the name of God was inconsistent with the freedom of faith guaranteed in the Constitution and amounted to showing a 'narrow, sectarian spirit'. This debate signals the core issue, namely, the unique challenge for the Constituent Assembly to create a secular Constitution for a deeply religious population.

The Constituent Assembly, and subsequently independent India, sought to resolve this challenge in three main ways, (i) by establishing the framework of fundamental rights that synthesizes religious issues, namely the rights-based approach, (ii) by highlighting the role of the judiciary as a manager and arbiter of religious concerns, that is, judicialization of religion, and finally, (iii) by way of innovative conceptualization and reworking of the model of secularism itself, especially as opposed to its European counterparts.

The rights-based approach

Articles 25 to 28 of the Constitution of India, all of which are facets of the freedom of religion, or more broadly what is constitutionally referred to as 'freedom of conscience', were incorporated in Part III of the Constitution of India as, fundamental rights. Likewise, Articles 29 and 30, which provided certain cultural and educational rights to minorities, were also incorporated in Part III of the Constitution. Such are the cruel ironies and contradictions at play in our nation today that by the logic of the current ruling regime, these constitutional provisions themselves may be charged with being 'anti-national'!

Apart from these fundamental rights, there are other related rights that also broaden and further strengthen the doctrine of secularism. Articles 14 and 15, which grant equality before the law and equal protection for all without discrimination, and Article 16(1), which grants equal opportunity for all citizens in matters of public employment, regardless of their religion, etc., also reinforce the secularist impulse of our Constitution. Moreover, in order to constitutionally extend the cultural and social import of religious equality, Article 51(A) obliges all citizens to promote harmony and the spirit of common brotherhood and to value and preserve the rich heritage of our composite culture.

Importantly, the freedom of religion guaranteed in the Constitution is not confined to its citizenry alone but extends to all persons, including 'aliens'—that is, non-citizens, refugees etc. This point was underlined by the Supreme Court in *Ratilal Panchand vs. State of Bombay*, 1954, and is significant because a substantial number of foreign Christian missionaries were engaged at the time in propagating their faith among adherents of other religions.

Therefore, we see very clearly that in all the major realms of a republican democracy—namely, economics, law, education, private and civic life of the citizenry—the Constitution has mandated equality of all religions, and secularism.

The judicialization approach

The courts play a significant role in implementing this secular vision for two main reasons. Firstly, the Supreme Court India is engaged not only in interpreting the law but also in actively promulgating values; as such, it has played a dominant role in shaping Indian secularism. Secondly, since courts act as arbiters of the legality and constitutionality of legislative and executive action, their decisions provide a more holistic overview of the conflicts and contentions in a democracy.

In *Kesavananda Bharati v. State of Kerala* , 1973, which has since been said to have become 'the bedrock of constitutional interpretation in India', a majority of seven out of a record thirteen-judge-bench of the Supreme Court held that a constitutional amendment could not alter the basic structure of the Constitution. Justice Sikri, one of the thirteen judges, in his judgment, stated that the 'secular character of the Constitution' was one of the features that formed part of the basic structure of the Constitution. Likewise, the other panelists, Justice Shelat and Justice Grover, in their judgments not only stated that the 'secular and federal character of the Constitution' formed part of the basic structure of the Constitution, but also reiterated the following position:

> India is a secular State in which there is no State religion. Special provisions have been made in the Constitution guaranteeing the freedom of conscience and free profession, practice and propagation of religion and the freedom to manage religious affairs as also the protection of interests of minorities ...

Likewise, a 1994 case that solidified the position of secularism in India's Constitutional framework was that of *S.R. Bommai v. Union of India*. The most significant contribution of the judgment was to hold in no uncertain terms that secularism is part of the basic structure of the Constitution (*S.R. Bommai* in paras. 29, 153, 186). The judgment goes on to hold that not only is encroachment of religion into the secular activities of the State prohibited but also said:

> We have accepted the said goal (of secularism) not only because it is our historical legacy and a need of our national unity and integrity but also as a creed of universal brotherhood and humanism. It is our cardinal faith. Any profession and action which go counter to the aforesaid creed are a prima facie proof of the conduct in defiance of the provisions of our Constitution …

These landmark judgments are important not only because they instituted what is called the basic structure doctrine in constitutional legality, but also because they claim that secularism is inherent to this basic structure. These judgments, along with the rights-based approach, show how anti-constitutional and in fact anti-national the Hindutva ideology is, given its main purported aim of establishing a 'Hindu rashtra'.

The conceptualization of 'Indian secularism'

Given the above-discussed constitutional background, we can easily understand how our founding figures re-conceptualized a uniquely Indian form of secularism.

This Indian model of secularism consists of two main features. Firstly, unlike the European model, ours is not blindly anti-religious but respects and maintains a critical distance from all religions. However, given that religion affects the social as well, as Ambedkar famously observed, every aspect of religious doctrine or practice cannot be respected.

Therefore, the second feature is that reverence for religion must be accompanied by a critiquing approach. It follows that although the state must respectfully leave religion alone, it must however intervene if any aspect of religion causes communal disharmony and discrimination. Therefore, untouchability, religion-based gender discrimination and other negative practices must be abolished constitutionally.

The recent decade has witnessed an unprecedented rise in the politics of hatred and division. From social media and corporate news channels infused with hate speech and polarizing disinformation, to the alleged targeted demolition of Muslim houses and shops in the name of anti-encroachment drives, the tinkering with school curricula to favour the ruling ideology, the constant controversies raked up by calls for banning azaan, namaz and hijabs, and the frequent calls for genocide by self-styled mahants, often in the presence of elected leaders … democracy and the nation's future itself is put on trial.

The worrying depths to which our secular republic has sunk under right-wing rule is unprecedented. The right rages a controversy over the hijab while one of their chief ministers is seen at all times smugly draped in Hindu liturgical robes of saffron. Official state and parliamentary ceremonies begin with coconut-cracking and aarti puja, making a mockery of the secular tenets. During the peak of a deadly pandemic, when people were literally dying on pavements, the Union health minister sits down with a self-proclaimed corporate baron of a baba to promote an ostensibly Ayurvedic company. Children are being taught ideological mythologies in place of academically astute histories. Mahatma Bapu appears as demon Mahishasur under Ma Durga's feet in Hindu Mahasabha mandals. Statues are built while statutes are being broken, and the republic is roiled to ruin as riots rage and dissenters are caged.

In this worrying context, in order to protect the moral fabric of our republic and to exorcise the demons against democracy, we must redeem ourselves of these elements of hate and fear, both in speech and action, by powerfully reasserting the great values of non-violence, equality and communal solidarity of our founding fathers. Moreover, we must remember that the book by which we rule our nation should not be any religious epic or revelation, but our extraordinary Constitution, which is secular and indispensable.

1

Consequences of Divisive Politics on Children

THE CASTE AND COMMUNAL CONFLICT DIVIDING INDIAN SOCIETY today is doing a great harm to the country. Unfortunately, it's the younger generation that gets affected the most. Systematic efforts to pollute young minds are visible. Children are mercilessly getting indoctrinated into hatred. The seeds of poison are planted without much notice. The consequences are unimaginably dangerous.

The child's mind is most impressionable, like wet clay waiting to be moulded into shapes—good, bad or ugly. The child is the prime, and softest, target. In my professional upper-middle-class setting, my seven-year-old son returns from a plush Delhi school and asks me, 'Papa, are we Musalmaans?' Bewildered at first, I questioned him, 'Why do you ask?' He replied, 'A boy in my class was telling other children.' This was thirty years ago. It has become worse now.

This 'we and they' instilled in young minds not only fills them with anger and hatred for the 'other', it also fills them with 'fear' of the other, which is disastrous for a child's mental development. As Edmund Burke observed, 'No passion so effectually robs the mind of all its powers of acting and reasoning as fear.' Making our children live in fear is a punishment inflicted on our children.

> No child is born a bigot. Hate is learned, and there is no doubt it can be unlearned. Leading experts on child development argue that the problem begins as early as preschool, where children have already learned stereotypes or acquired negative attitudes towards 'others'. The process of countering those negatives with positives should also begin at an early age'. (Educationist Caryl M. Stern-LaRosa).

A word of clarification here: Children are born into religions, and there is nothing negative about religion. Religious teaching that anchors children in ethics actually does them a world of good. What is wrong is when children grow up in religious bigotry, hatred and fear. A simple analogy is: water is life, but polluted water is poison.

Mind-pollution or brainwashing is not confined to any community. Among the Muslims, some lunatic fringe talks of 'jihad against the infidel' as a religious duty and as a passport to jannat (paradise). But en route the jannat, hell is created. They conveniently forget the fact that the concept of jihad in Islam meant struggle to overcome illiteracy, ignorance and immoral desires. The condemnation of the acts of the fringe elements by Muslim scholars and institutions like the Darul Uloom, Deoband, unfortunately, does not attract much attention.

It is time to conduct serious research to quantify the damage caused by mind pollution, as by environmental pollution. For healthy mental development, the child's mind must be exposed to positive symbolism and imagery around him: of human kindness, of moderate nationalism, of moral values, of brotherhood, of the beauty of pluralism.

The laws to deal with hate activities are adequate, but the enforcement machinery is not only lackadaisical but often complicit. This is disastrous. We must remember that Phoolan Devi became Phoolan Devi when the system failed to give her justice. When a terrorist act is used as an opportunity for community profiling and the launching of false cases with fanfare (which years later are dropped by the courts very quietly), the whole community feels demonized and besieged.

Children require a happy and congenial environment during their growing-up years and not fear and hatred. 'Hate hurts the hater more than the hated,' says famous American writer Madeleine L'Engle.

2

The Pollution of Young Minds

THE DAMAGE TO OUR PLANET FROM ENVIRONMENTAL POLLUTION HAS been a hot topic of discussion for decades. There are, however, equally serious if not greater dangers which no one talks about—the consequences of the pollution of minds, especially those of the young.

A child's mind is most impressionable, like wet clay waiting to be moulded into shapes—good, bad or ugly. According to Benjamin Spock, an American paediatrician whose book *Baby and Child Care* is amongst the best-selling books in history, 85 per cent of the child's mind is developed by the age of five. This is spelt out lucidly by Robert Fulghum in his magnum opus *All I Really Need to Know, I Learned in Kindergarten*: 'Share everything, play fair, don't hit people, put things back where you found them, clear up your mess, don't take things that are not yours, when you go out into the world, watch out for traffic, hold hands, and stick together!'

If the formative years are so crucial, it is vital that what a child is exposed to is healthy and positive. In the global village, there are streams of messages floating around, generated by mutual hatred. Children are mercilessly left to infer what they can from these. The consequences are unimaginably disastrous. The seed of poison is planted without much notice. This cancer affects the soul, curbs the development of the individual and constrains his or her personality. Fear and aggression get ingrained in the psyche.

With the phenomenal expansion of TV, children's exposure to the outside world is enormous. Hate and violence predominate TV content. According to an American study, by the time a child is eighteen, (s)he has been exposed to 2,00,000 acts of violence, including 25,000 killings. (American Psychiatric Association, 1998). So much exposure to violence brutalizes children more than adults. They tend to take murder as a way of life.

Experts believe that violence shown in the media is the single-largest source of pathogenic and criminogenic imagery. Aggressive characters become children's role models, and many of them grow up to be angry young men and women. Their belief in the established legal system is subverted. The cases of mob lynching and people taking the law into their own hands prove the point.

Pollution of the minds of adolescents is as severe, if not more. Crisis of identity at this stage makes this age segment vulnerable to physical and psychological behavioural problems. Adolescents are overtaken by several emotional problems like anger, aggression, depression, loneliness, insecurity and guilt. The physiological changes lead to adolescents getting involved in high-risk behaviours, like sexual experimentation and drugs. Crimes by and against adolescents surface in many forms, like harassment of young women, abduction, rape, incest, prostitution and sexual harassment. How can we forget that in the horrendous December 2012 Delhi rape and murder case, the most brutal offender was a teenager? In many cases of mob lynching and communal and caste violence, teenagers have been in the forefront.

Mind pollution typically expresses itself in the creation of stereotypes. This could be about gender, communities, religion, ethnic groups, or any other distinction. Targeting a group with hate and violence is often the next step. One particularly severe pollutant is communalism, which calls for some elaboration as an example. The child's mind is the worst victim of this pollution.

In my professional upper-middle-class setting, my seven-year-old son returns from a posh Delhi school and asks me, 'Papa, are we Musalmaans?' Bewildered at first, I said, 'Why do you ask?' 'A boy in my class was telling the other children this,' he replied. This was thirty years ago. It is a hundred times worse now. Nazia Erum, in her book *Mothering a Muslim,* has amply documented this phenomenon, where Muslim children as young as three have been called terrorists by their classmates. Communal content in textbooks, demonizing some communities in the process, is aggravating the situation.

The idea of 'we and they' being instilled in young minds is a terrible form of mental pollution. This not only fills them with anger and hatred for the 'other', but also instils in them fear of the other. As Edmund Burke has observed, 'No passion so effectually robs the mind of all its powers of acting and reasoning as fear.' It will not be wrong to say that living in fear is self-inflicted punishment.

All pollution spreads through agents or carriers. Propaganda is a major carrier. In the wake of a few unfortunate terrorist acts, a well-orchestrated campaign dubs the entire Muslim community as terrorists. Some obscurantists trumpet derisive slogans about Muslims like, '*Hum paanch, hamare pachees*' (we are five–husband and four wives–and have twenty-five children), and an image is deliberately or mischievously created projecting Muslims as polygamists.

This is designed to cause a rift between communities. The perpetrators of communal hatred have achieved tremendous success in this, with their travesty of facts.

The only study on marriage customs ('Towards Equality—The Report of the Committee on the Status of Women in India, 1975') found that there was incidence of polygamy in all communities in India, including Hindus. Muslims, in fact, had the least! The 227th report of the Law Commission of India (2009) on prevention of bigamy via conversion to Islam stated that as many as 1 crore Hindu men had more than one wife, against 12 lakh Muslim men who did, as per the 1971 census.

The media, unfortunately, has played a key role in the propagation of distorted images. With the proliferation of social media, fear and hatred have become visceral. Individuals can easily find others who share those feelings, and this soon leads to a mob mentality.

Now, let us turn to the Muslims. Some on the lunatic fringe talk of 'jihad against the infidel' as a religious duty and as a passport to *jannat* (paradise). But en route to *jannat*, hell is created. They conveniently forget the fact that the concept of jihad in Islam meant a struggle within to overcome illiteracy, ignorance and immoral desires.

Resistance to mind pollution has to start with the realization that it has disastrous consequences—direct and imminent. We need serious research to quantify the possible damage created by mind pollution, as has been done for environmental pollution. We cannot wait a day longer. Mind pollution has to be stopped. Moreover, the pollution that has already taken place has to be addressed.

While parents have to rise to play their role, the responsibility of the state, the education system, the judiciary and the media needs to be especially recognized. Children require a happy and congenial environment when they are growing up, not one of fear and hatred. The coronavirus will, hopefully, disappear soon. But the communal virus will continue to haunt us for a long time. Let's not build a nation at war with itself.

3

The Duty of the Young

12 January is National Youth Day, celebrated on the occasion of the birthday of the great youth icon Swami Vivekananda. Around this day, the nation must take stock of the status of the youth of the country, on whom depends the future of our democracy. 1 January 2018 marked a very important day for Indian democracy. On this day, people born in the twenty-first century became eligible to vote. The prime minister had this very thought in mind when, in the last session of 'Mann ki Baat' for 2017, he focused on and encouraged the youth to participate in huge numbers in the voting process.

He urged all youths turning eighteen by 1 January to enrol as voters so that they can be active participants in Indian democracy in the following year and the years to come, telling them that their votes would be the bedrock of a New India. He also suggested the holding of a mock parliament, comprising youths selected from every district, to deliberate on the various issues the country faces today. Specifically addressing youths aged eighteen to twenty-five, the prime minister called them the 'New India Youth' and urged them to participate in Indian democracy and make it corruption- and casteism-free.

Over the years, the PM has time and again reiterated the role that the youth have to play in shaping a new and better India. That makes PM Modi one of the few politicians who has understood the importance of youth power. The role of the youth in shaping the course of any democracy is undeniable. More than 50 per cent of India's population is below the age of twenty-five, and more than 65 per cent below thirty-five. Given that democracy is the will of the majority, and the majority of India's population—nearly 40 crore voters—consists of the youth, it is essential to look at the way this majority can be harnessed to participate in democracy and contribute towards the development of the country. One of the most important ways they can do this is by exercising their right to vote.

The right to vote is not just a right enjoyed by every individual over the age of eighteen; it is also a responsibility to make an informed and responsible choice and to bring to power the most well-suited candidate to govern the country. For a long time now, there has been a trend of voting for candidates who give the maximum amount of freebies to their voters in return. Instead of following this path, the youth must make a conscious decision to vote on the basis of the agenda of the candidates and their past work.

It is only when the youth become aware of the problems the country is facing and choose candidates who are most likely to bring about change that the right representatives will come to power and India's future will be in safe hands. The task is not a long and tedious one. All it requires is a bit of effort to examine all the contesting candidates, their histories and their agendas, and vote for the one deemed most fit to govern the country. Several websites are making this task easier by simplifying analysis of the comparative performance of competing candidates.

In my book, *An Undocumented Wonder: The Making of the Great Indian Election* (2014), I had pointed out that the youth, who should be the most important participants in the Indian democracy, are mostly absent from the daily discourse on democracy. While they are visible at protest marches, on cricket grounds, at music concerts and cultural events, and can be seen blocking roads, stopping trains, throwing stones, burning tyres and raving and ranting against corruption and bad governance, when the time comes to actually participate in the decision-making process and change the system and its culture by electing the right leaders, most of them disappear.

When I started my tenure as chief election commissioner, I was distressed to find out that the voter enrolment ratio amongst eighteen- to twenty-year-olds was as low as 12 per cent. We in the Election Commission decided to make this issue our top priority. Through a programme called Youth Unite for Voter Awareness (YUVA), we argued that the best way to convert a country's demographic dividend into democratic dividend is through the mass participation of the youth in elections. National Voters Day (NVD), celebrated on 25 January 2011, was launched as an annual event dedicated to the youth.

This seeks to create an enlightened movement of voters who see voting as an opportunity to bring about change, who are aware of their role and are neutral with respect to caste, religion, community and other identity differences, those who have their own views about a party and its performance and change their preference from election to election if needed. The NVD not only encourages the youth to enrol in huge numbers and vote without fail but also seeks to involve them in increasing awareness amongst other voters.

Democracy cannot survive without both citizens' participation and accountability on the part of politicians. Since the politicians will do nothing to inform the youth about the socioeconomic problems facing the nation today and only exploit them, it is the responsibility of civil society organizations and the media to educate young people about the issues involved and their high stakes in the fruits of development.

It is important to remember that instead of always pontificating to the youth about their role and responsibilities, political leaders should remind themselves of their own role in fulfilling the needs and aspirations of the youth, particularly with respect to jobs. If their expectations are not met, a backlash is unavoidable. Once the youth become restive, chaos cannot be far behind.

Conclusion

S INCE THE FOUNDING OF THE REPUBLIC, INDIA HAS BEEN THE LARGEST democracy in the world. In many respects it was considered a model democracy, largely owing to the ideals that India strove to attain. Its abiding features have been non-discriminatory management of religious, caste, and linguistic diversity, concern for an equitable and equal society that is alert to the issues of gender and sustainable development, and ultimately, a profound reverence towards the promise of our founding document, the Constitution. This is not to mention maintenance of the integrity and non-partisanship of the Election Commission, and of an active public sphere where dialogue and debate are energetically and freely undertaken.

However, over the years, the inevitable tussle between historical reality and theoretical idealism ensured that at times the social contract was disrupted, with multitudinous conflicts and conundrums obstructing complete and total achievement of democracy. In recent times, for instance, the Economist's Intelligence Unit reports have classified India as a 'flawed democracy'. Since the inception of the report in 2006, it has shown India as registering regular ups and downs, mostly downs. More recently, a 2021 report by the Sweden-based V-Dem Institute ranked India as an 'electoral autocracy'; with deteriorating federalism, degeneration of secular bonds, increasing inequality and an unraveling economy contributing to the downfall of democracy.

India today is a republic of contradictions. It boasts of producing world-domineering billionaires while its poor die of hunger and curable diseases in greater numbers. More women vote now in numbers hitherto unseen in the history of elections while it elects merely one female chief minister. It ranks high globally in ease of doing business while its youth are left unemployed in the millions. The Preamble to its Constitution preaches secularism and tolerance while the country riots in the name of religion and caste. Media houses driven by the motives of agenda and profit are celebrated and popularized, while other journalists and activist–investigators are arrested and subject to unending detentions. Rapists are garlanded while the high rhetoric of women's rights echoes forth from national podiums.

To arrive therefore at a sustainable and egalitarian resolution, to fix our historical and contemporary crises, to redeem and reshape our political landscape and social priorities, to uphold the virtues and vitality of our Constitution, and to manifest the glorious visions of our founding figures, our first and foremost step is to achieve a proper self-understanding. We must first pause to evaluate our contemporary condition. In this book I have endeavoured to do precisely that. Understanding India is, however, a truly daunting task, for it is always evolving and takes on new shapes and colours ever so often.

As the chief election commissioner, I have been fortunate to have had a ringside view of elections, which I believe to be the foundation of our democracy. Elections themselves are such a significant and fascinating field of study because they serve as a useful microcosm of our country. Through studying our elections, we can access the core issues and realities of the Indian republic. Within the drama of elections, therefore, our nation's anxieties and aspirations, ideologies and insecurities, perils and promises, triumphs and tribulations, are all revealed and engaged with. Not only do elections serve as a shining symbol of a working democracy, but they also, time and again, disclose to us the darker, criminal elements that form part of democracy's subterranean reaches. Effectively, and at the very least, symbolically, it is in elections that our leaders are both birthed and judged, our public empowered and honoured, and the tenets of representative democracy celebrated and attested to. It is for these reasons that I believe electoral politics to be the litmus test of a democracy.

Strong institutions are the bedrock for democratic and open societies like ours. Not only do institutions have to be strong and objective, but the overall social and cultural contexts within which they operate must also be free of conflict and insecurity. This is necessary to instil confidence among the public. Our judiciary is in dire need of reform. Justice delayed is justice denied. Similarly, the Election Commission must fearlessly uphold the integrity of our elections, as it has done consistently since the first general election in 1951. A strong and credible political Opposition is essential for the health of any democracy.

While institutions are crucial to a democracy, we must not forget that institutions are not some abstract machinery; that indeed it is the people of a country that make, sustain and serve in the institutions. Therefore, a harmonious citizenry is indispensable for the proper functioning of national institutions. In order to protect the moral fabric of our Republic, we must redeem ourselves of elements of hate and fear by powerfully reasserting, like our founding figures, the great values of non-violence, equality and communal solidarity.

It has now been seventy-five years since we achieved independence from the British Raj, and we have come a long way from where we started. India has succeeded in sustaining a consistent and rapid economic growth for decades now. Especially since the early 1980s, the country has enjoyed an average gross domestic product (GDP) per capita growth rate of 4.6 per cent. In nearly forty years (ending 2018), no decadal average fell below 3 per cent. To put these numbers in context, the economists note that since 1950, India is the only continuous democracy, other than possibly Botswana, to maintain an average GDP growth rate of between 3 per cent and 4.5 per cent for nearly four decades. Needless to say, this has had positive impacts on poverty rates.

Owing to this, more Indians have had greater access to basic private goods, from fuel and electricity to toilets and bank accounts. Currently, India is enjoying a digital payments revolution. Since 2014, over 460 million bank accounts have been opened across the country. According to the International Monetary Fund (IMF), India's digital payment volume has grown at an average annual rate of 50 per cent over the past five years. A study conducted by Boston Consulting Group and PhonePe estimates that 40 per cent of payments (in value terms) in India are now conducted digitally. If the current trends persist, this $3 trillion market could more than triple by the year 2026.

Alongside the digital revolution, India is also currently witness to what is being called a 'participatory revolution'. For the first time, more women came out to vote in 2019 than at any other time in our nation's history, even slightly overtaking their male counterparts. In many respects, 2019 was a banner year for female representation, yet women accounted for just 8.9 per cent of all Lok Sabha candidates and 14.6 per cent of winning members of parliament, according to data collected by the Trivedi Centre for Political Data. While we have been tremendously successful in achieving excellent women voter turnouts, owing to voter education programmes, we need to balance it out with having more women leaders. Therefore, it is high time we finally pass the Women's Reservation Bill, which will ensure 33 per cent of Lok Sabha seats for women.

Fertility and family planning have been a vexed issue in India since Independence. The latest National Family Health Survey (NFHS) data significantly allays concerns about the potential of a 'population bomb'. According to the most recent figures, as of 2019–20, India's total fertility rate (TFR) stood at 2.0, a slight reduction from the TFR of 2.2 clocked in the previous NFHS round (2015-16), A TFR of 2.1 is considered replacement level, which means the population replenishes itself without growing or shrinking. Currently, India's population is 5 million more than China's.

Contrary to popular perception, however, India's population growth rate has also actually slowed down in the last few decades—from 24.7 per cent between 1971 and 1981 to 17.7 per cent between 2001 and 2011. This has been due to the rising levels of education and healthcare, as well as the alleviation of poverty. Currently, 650 million Indians—nearly half the country's population—are below the age of twenty-five. In 2021, the working-age population of India stood at a whopping 900 million, according to Organisation of Economic Co-operation and Development (OECD) data. This group isn't just young, it's also dynamic: it grew up in a market economy with access to the Internet and a hunger to compete on the global stage. Two thirds of the Indian population has access to smartphones, thanks to the cheap data plans that have been offered in the last decade. India must find not only democratic measures to control its population but must also use its vast human resources to grow economically and socially.

We must encourage small and medium enterprises and increase opportunities for the rural economy. In order to capitalize on our unmatched human resources, we must encourage labour-intensive manufacturing exports, just as Japan did in the early nineteenth century, which catapulted it into becoming an economic superpower. To absorb the young working population, India will need to create at least 90 million new non-farming jobs by 2030. We will need to design and implement urban employment guarantee schemes, much like MGNREGA, which addresses rural employment, to tackle the rising youth unemployment and decreasing labour-force participation. We must provide greater quality of education to the young of the nation. Quality of education directly benefits the quality and quantity of employment, which itself is further related to the quality of life. Therefore, to improve the life of the nation, we must holistically improve the lives of our young populace.

Seventy-five years ago, when the bloody horrors of Partition were still raging, princely states were warring with the Union and the greater majority of the country were illiterate and poor, many experts and observers prophesied India's ultimate disintegration, deeming the very idea of India an impossibility. The country's people themselves, however, were full of hope and ambition. The midnight hour of freedom handed to us, in equal parts, respite and responsibility. I myself aged alongside India. And, ever since, the theatre of history has relayed to us a bewildering tale of pain and progress, wealth and dearth, triumph and despair, success and sorrow. So much has been achieved and yet there is much that remains to be achieved. As has always been the case, at this juncture too, much is at stake. We need to collectively work towards making India a greater country, one that was the dream of our founding figures. We must proudly and persistently strive to enshrine and achieve the values and virtues for which many a million sacrifices were made.

At all times, we all must, with hope, harmony, and righteousness, strive for an India that is just and equal. Our greatest priority must always be to protect from danger and decay the life of our democracy.

ANNEXURE

1

Constitution of India: The following Articles of the Constitution provided the framework for the electoral system of India

Article 324

324. Superintendence, direction and control of elections to be vested in an Election Commission

(1) The superintendence, direction and control of the preparation of the electoral rolls for, and the conduct of, all elections to Parliament and to the Legislature of every State and of elections to the offices of President and Vice President held under this Constitution shall be vested in a Commission (referred to in this Constitution as the Election Commission)

(2) The Election Commission shall consist of the Chief Election Commissioner and such number of other Election

Commissioners, if any, as the President may from time to time fix and the appointment of the Chief Election Commissioner and other Election Commissioners shall, subject to the provisions of any law made in that behalf by Parliament, be made by the President.

(3)   When any other Election Commissioner is so appointed the Chief Election Commissioner shall act as the Chairman of the Election Commission

(4)   Before each general election to the House of the People and to the Legislative Assembly of each State, and before the first general election and thereafter before each biennial election to the Legislative Council of each State having such Council, the President may also appoint after consultation with the Election Commission such Regional Commissioners as he may consider necessary to assist the Election Commission in the performance of the functions conferred on the Commission by clause (1).

(5)   Subject to the provisions of any law made by Parliament, the conditions of service and tenure of office of the Election Commissioners and the Regional Commissioners shall be such as the President may by rule determine; Provided that the Chief Election Commissioner shall not be removed from his office except in like manner and on the like grounds as a Judge of the Supreme Court and the conditions of service of the Chief Election Commissioner shall not be varied to his disadvantage after his appointment: Provided further that any other Election Commissioner or a Regional Commissioner shall not be removed from office except on the recommendation of the Chief Election Commissioner.

(6)   The President, or the Governor of a State, shall, when so requested by the Election Commission, make available to the Election Commission or to a Regional Commissioner such staff as may be necessary for the discharge of the functions conferred on the Election Commission by clause (1)

Article 325

No person to be ineligible for inclusion in, or to claim to be included in a special, electoral roll on grounds of religion, race, caste or sex. There shall be one general electoral roll for every territorial constituency for election to either House of Parliament or to the House or either House of the Legislature of a State and no person shall be ineligible for inclusion in any such roll or claim to be included in any special electoral roll for any such constituency on grounds only of religion, race, caste, sex or any of them.

Article326

Elections to the House of the People and to the Legislative Assemblies of States to be on the basis of adult suffrage. The elections to the House of the People and to the Legislative Assembly of every State shall be on the basis of adult suffrage; but is to say, every person who is a citizen of India and who is not less than twenty one years of age on such date as may be fixed in that behalf by or under any law made by the appropriate legislature and is not otherwise disqualified under this Constitution or any law made by the appropriate Legislature on the ground of non residence, unsoundness of mind, crime or corrupt or illegal practice, shall be entitled to be registered as a voter at any such election.

Article 327

Power of Parliament to make provision with respect to elections to Legislatures.

Subject to the provisions of this Constitution, Parliament may from time to time by law make provision with respect to all matters relating to, or in connection with, elections to either House of Parliament or to the House or either House of the Legislature of a State including the preparation of electoral rolls, the delimitation of constituencies and all other matters necessary for securing the due constitution of such House or Houses.

Article 328

Power of Legislature of a State to make provision with respect to elections to such Legislature. Subject to the provisions of this Constitution and in so far as provision in that behalf is not made by Parliament, the Legislature of a State may from time to time by law make provision with respect to all matters relating to, or in connection with, the elections to the House or either House of the Legislature of the State including the preparation of electoral rolls and all other matters necessary for securing the due constitution of such House or Houses.

Article 329

Bar to interference by courts in electoral matters Notwithstanding anything in this Constitution

(a)   the validity of any law relating to the delimitation of constituencies or the allotment of seats to such constituencies, made or purporting to be made under Article 327 or Article 328, shall not be called in question in any court;

(b)   No election to either House of Parliament or to the House or either House of the Legislature of a State shall be called in question except by an election petition presented to such authority and in such manner as may be provided for by or under any law made by the appropriate Legislature.

Article 101

Focuses on vacation of seats:

(1)   No person shall be a member of both Houses of Parliament and provision shall be made by Parliament by law for the vacation

by a person who is chosen a member of both Houses of his seat in one House or the other.

(2)   No person shall be a member both of Parliament and of a House of the Legislature of a State and if a person is chosen a member both of Parliament and of a House of the Legislature of a State, then, at the expiration of such period as may be specified in rules made by the President, that person's seat in Parliament shall become vacant, unless he has previously resigned his seat in the Legislature of the State.

(3)   If a member of either House of Parliament

(a) becomes subject to any of the disqualifications mentioned in clause (1) or clause (2) of Article 102, or

(b) resigns his seat by writing under his hand addressed to the Chairman or the Speaker, as the case may be, and his resignation is accepted by the chairman or the Speaker, as the case may be, his seat shall thereupon become vacant: Provided that in the case of any resignation referred to in sub-clause (b), if from information received or otherwise and after making such inquiry as he thinks fit, the chairman or the Speaker, as the case may be, is satisfied that such resignation is not voluntary or genuine, he shall not accept such resignation.

(4)   If for a period of sixty days a member of either House of Parliament is without permission of the House absent from all meetings thereof, the House may declare his seat vacant: Provided that in computing the said period of sixty days no account shall be taken of any period during which the House is prorogued or is adjourned for more than four consecutive days.

Article 191

Focuses on the grounds for disqualification of membership:

(1)   A person shall be disqualified for being chosen as, and for being, a member of the Legislative Assembly or Legislative Council of a State

(a) if he holds any office of profit under the Government of India or the Government of any State specified in the First Schedule, other than an office declared by the Legislature of the State by law not to disqualify its holder;

(b) if he is of unsound mind and stands so declared by a competent court;

(c) if he is an undischarged insolvent;

(d) if he is not a citizen of India, or has voluntarily acquired the citizenship of a foreign State, or is under any acknowledgement of allegiance or adherence to a foreign State;

(e) if he is so disqualified by or under any law made by Parliament. Explanation: For the purposes of this clause, a person shall not be deemed to hold an office of profit under the Government of India or the Government of any State specified in the First Schedule by reason only that he is a Minister either for the Union or for such State.

(2)   A person shall be disqualified for being a member of the Legislative Assembly or Legislative Council of a State if he is so disqualified under the Tenth Schedule.

2

Representation of the People Act

Representation of the People Act, 1950

The Preamble of this Act states that it is an Act to provide the allocation of seats in, and the delimitation of constituencies for the purpose of election to the House of the People and the Legislatures of States, the qualifications of voters at such elections, the preparation of electoral rolls, and matters connected.

This Act makes provisions for:

1. Seat allocation in the Lok Sabha and the Legislative Assemblies through direct elections.
2. Voter qualifications for the elections.
3. Delimitation of constituencies for both Lok Sabha and Assembly elections. The extent of the constituencies would be determined by the Delimitation Commission.
4. The Indian president can alter the constituencies after due consultation with the Election Commission.

5. Preparation of the electoral roll. A person cannot be enrolled in more than one constituency. He or she can be disqualified and barred from voting if found to be of unsound mind or is not an Indian citizen.

Representation of the People Act, 1951

This Act makes provisions for the conduct of elections in India.

The Preamble of this Act states that it is an Act to provide for the conduct of elections to the Houses of Parliament and to the House or Houses of the Legislature of each State, the qualifications and disqualifications for membership of those Houses, the corrupt practices and other offences at or in connection with such elections, and the decision on doubts and disputes arising out of or in connection with such elections.

The following constitute its prime focus:

1. It highlights corruption and other illegal activities related to elections.
2. It makes provisions for dispute redressal in matters connected to elections.
3. It focuses on the qualifications of as well as grounds for the disqualification of MPs and MLAs.

Election Commissioners (Conditions of Service) Amendment Act, 1991

An Act to determine the conditions of service of the Chief Election Commissioner and other Election Commissioners and to provide for the procedure for transaction of business by the Election Commission and for matters connected therewith or incidental thereto.

The Commission consists of a chief election commissioner and two election commissioners. Until October 1989, there was just one chief election commissioner. In 1989, two election commissioners were appointed, but were removed in January 1990. In 1991, however, parliament passed a law providing for the appointment of two election commissioners. This law was amended and renamed in 1993 as the Chief Election Commissioner and other Election Commissioners (Conditions of Service) Amendment Act 1993.

Landmark Judgments of the Supreme Court

The Supreme Court of India has played a crucial role in forcing electoral reforms. Some of the landmark judgments in this regard are summarized below:

(i) N.P. Ponnuswami vs. Returning Officer, Namakkal Constituency, 1952

Whether the high court has the power to decide on election matters under Article 226, and to review the orders of returning officers

Facts: The appellant, N.P. Ponnuswami, was one of the applicants who filed his nomination papers in the Madras legislative assembly elections from Namakkal constituency located in Salem district. The returning officer for the same constituency, while scrutinizing the nomination papers of various candidates on 28 November 1951, rejected the appellant's nomination paper on certain grounds. Aggrieved by the order of returning officer, the appellant moved the Madras High Court under Article 226 claiming the writ of certiorari and prayed for quashing of the order of the returning officer and his inclusion in the valid candidates' list. The high court dismissed the appellant's petition, on the ground that it had no jurisdiction, under the constraint of Article 329(b) of the Constitution, to interfere with the order of the returning officer.

Judgment: The Supreme Court dismissed the appeal, confirming the view of the high court. The Supreme Court held that the word 'election' in Article 329(b) connotes the entire electoral process, commencing with issue of the notification calling the election and culminating in declaration of the result, and that the electoral process, once started, could not be interfered with at any intermediary stage by the courts.

(ii) Sadiq and Anr. vs. Election Commission, 1972

Regarding the Election Symbols Order 1968 and party splits

Facts: The Indian National Congress is a recognized national party under the provisions of the Election Symbols (Reservation and Allotment) Order, 1968. There was a split in the party in 1969 which resulted in the formation of two groups, one led by Shri Jagjivan Ram and the other by Nijalingappa. After the recording of evidence and hearings of detailed submissions by both groups, the Commission came to the conclusion that the group led by Jagjivan Ram enjoyed majority support, both in the organizational and legislature wings of the party, and recognized that group as the Indian National Congress in its order. Each group contended that it was the original party; the Election Commission adjudicated the dispute between the two rival groups of the party under para. 15 of the 1968 Order. The rival group led by Nijalingappa felt aggrieved by the Election Commission order and filed an appeal before the Supreme Court by way of petition for special leave to appeal under Article 136 of the Indian Constitution.

Judgment: The Supreme Court held that the test of majority or numerical strength applied by the Commission for resolving the dispute was a relevant and valuable test, and rightly applied by the Commission. The Supreme Court held that para. 15 of the Symbols Act was not ultra vires the powers of the Election Commission under Article 324 of the Indian Constitution. The court held that an election symbol is not the property of the party concerned.

(iii) Mohinder Singh Gill vs. Chief Election Commissioner, 1978

Regarding Article 329(b), which bars the interference of courts in electoral matters

Facts: At the 1977 general election to the house of the people, the poll in the Firozepur Parliamentary constituency was conducted on 16 March 1977. The constituency consists of nine assembly segments. Counting in five of these segments was completed on 20 March 1977, and in the remaining four on 21 March 1977. Until then, according to the result sheets, Mohinder Singh Gill, the petitioner, was leading over his nearest rival by 1,921 votes. Only 769 postal ballot papers then remained to be counted by the returning officer, who took up the counting of these postal ballot papers at his headquarters at Firozepur on 21 March 1977, at 3 p.m. He rejected 248 out of the 769 postal ballot papers. At that stage, there was some mob violence in the counting hall and the postal ballot papers remaining to be sorted out and counted candidate-wise were burnt in various assembly segments. The Election Commission, on 22 March 1977, on receipt of reports about these disturbances and destruction of election records, declared the poll taken on 16 March 1977 in the entire Firozepur parliamentary constituency as void and directed a fresh poll, to be taken on a date it would notify later. This order of the EC was challenged by the petitioner, Mohinder Singh Gill, in a writ petition before the Delhi High Court.

Judgment: The Supreme Court dismissed the appeal, holding that the order of the EC directing a re-poll was a step in the process of an election and, as the election process was not yet complete, the writ petition under Article 226 challenging the Commission's order was not maintainable in view of Article 329(b) of the Constitution. The Supreme Court also held that Article 329(b) was a blanket ban on litigative challenges to electoral steps taken by the EC and its officers to complete an election. Election, in this context, has a very wide connotation, commencing from the notification calling for the election and culminating in the final declaration of the returned candidate.

(iv) A.C. Jose v. Sivan Pillai and Others, 1984

Whether the casting of ballot by EVMs is valid and legal, and concerns Articles 324, 327 and 329 of the Constitution

Facts: At the election to the Kerala legislative assembly held in May 1982 in the assembly constituency of Parur, the EC used for the first-time EVMs at fifty out of the eighty-four polling stations in the constituency for recording and counting of votes. A.C. Jose, who lost the election, questioned before the Kerala High Court the use of EVMs at the fifty polling stations in the Parur constituency, on the ground that the Representation of the People Act, 1951 and the Conduct of Elections Rules, 1961 did not provide for use of EVMs in the conducting of polls and the counting of votes in elections in India.

Judgment: The Supreme Court (reversing the order of the high court, which held that under Article 324, the EC was empowered to use EVMs) held that the EVMs could not be used in elections without an express provision in the law. The Supreme Court also held that the Election Commission has to conduct elections according to law enacted by Parliament and it could, in exercise of its powers under Article 324 of the Constitution, supplement the law but not supplant it. The Supreme Court, therefore, declared the election in the Parur assembly constituency as void and directed a re-poll to be held in the fifty polling stations where EVMs were used.

(V) R.C. Poudyal vs. Union of India, 1993

Regarding reservation of seats in the legislative assembly

Facts: The case focuses on the constitutional validity of the reservations made by parliament in the then newly constituted legislative assembly of Sikkim and determines the concerns related to such representations. In order to fathom the context for an argument the court largely relies on, it is imperative to know the historical circumstances because of which these reservations were put into question.

Judgment: The Supreme Court constituted a five-judge bench to adjudge the matter and the majority opinion was 'negative' on both the issues. The court, observing that the Sangha community is Buddhist, examined whether Buddhism is a religion that observes discrimination under Article 15 of the Constitution. The court held that even though the Sangha community received privileges under its Buddhist ruler until 1973, after the merger of the state with India, however, such reservation is discriminatory because it is made solely on the basis of religion.

(vi) Gadakh Yashwantrao Kankarrao vs. EV Alias Balasaheb Vikhe Patil, 1994

Concerning Section 123 (4) of the Representation of the People Act which defines 'corrupt practices' and 'electoral Offences' in Chapter 4A of the IPC

Facts: In this case, Vikhe Patil filed an election petition at the Aurangabad bench of the Bombay High Court praying that the election of Gadakh be declared as void and that he (Patil) be declared to have been duly elected from that constituency. The challenge to the validity of Gadakh's election was made by Vikhe Patil on the ground that Gadakh was guilty of corrupt practices under Sub-section (4) of Section 123 of the Representation of the People Act. This was based on the allegation that Gadakh had made certain false statements in his speeches relating to the personal character and conduct of Vikhe Patil, accusing him of having used corrupt methods, with a view to prejudice the prospects of Vikhe Patil's election, in meetings held by him at Sonai on April 30, 1991, Ahmednagar on May 2, 1991, Newasia on May 3, 1991 and in an interview given to a journalist on May 10, 1991 which was published in the daily newspaper Maharashtra Times on May 13, 1991..

Judgment: The Supreme Court in this case held that when a corrupt practice is committed by a candidate, or by someone else with his consent, it has the effect of vitiating the whole election and will result in the election of the candidate being declared void; the commission of an electoral offence does not have such fatal bearing on the election result. In the former, the whole constituency suffers, inasmuch as the candidate loses his seat and the constituency goes without representation in the legislature till another election is held to replace the unseated member; in the latter, only the persons committing the electoral offences suffer their criminal liability. The other noteworthy point here is that any grievance relating to commission of corrupt practices can be agitated only after the election is over, but commission of an electoral offence can be taken cognizance of as soon as it is committed and the process of law set in motion immediately thereafter.

(vii) Election Commission of India through Secretary vs. Ashok Kumar, 2000

Regarding Section 59(A) of the Conduct of Election Rules, 1961, concerning counting of votes and Article 329(B), about the interference of courts in electoral matters

Facts: In this case, while exercising the powers conferred by rule 59A of the Conduct of Election Rules, 1961, the Election Commission of India published a notification according to which in areas where voting was to be done by ballot paper, the counting of such votes were to be done by mixing the ballot papers and not station-wise. Writ petitions were filed before the Kerala High Court against this particular notification, claiming that the counting must be done station- wise. The High Court ordered in favour of the petitioner. Aggrieved by this order, the ECI filed an SLP in the Supreme Court.

Judgment: The Supreme Court overturned the order of the high court, claiming that according to Article 329(b) of Indian Constitution, the elections couldn't be called in question until the process is not finished.

(viii) Union of India vs. Association of Democratic Reforms, 2002

Regarding the citizen's right to know the educational background, assets and criminal records of electoral candidates

Facts: In this case, the petitioner—the Association for Democratic Reforms—filed a writ petition before the High Court of Delhi for direction to implement the recommendations made by the Law Commission in its 170th Report and to make the necessary changes under Rule 4 of the Conduct of Election Rules, 1961. The Law Commission had recommended debarring of candidates from contesting elections if charges have been framed against them by a court in respect of certain offences, and the necessity for a candidate seeking to contest election to furnish details regarding criminal cases, if any, pending against him/her. It has also suggested that a true and correct statement of assets owned by the candidate, his/her spouse and dependant relations should also be made.

Judgment: In this case, the Supreme Court held that a voter has the right to know his or her public functionaries and candidates running for office, and this would include their educational background, assets and criminal background. This right is said to be derived from Article 19(1) (a) of the Indian Constitution. The court ruled that a candidate's records should not be kept hidden from the citizens because it helps the citizens to make an informed choice and use their freedom of speech and expression, as voting in a democratic country is an act that comes under the freedom of expression.

(ix) Indian National Congress vs. Institute of Social Welfare & Ors. 2002

Whether the Election Commission of India under Section 29A of the Representation of the People Act, 1951, has power to de-register or cancel the registration of a political party

Facts: In the writ petitions filed before the Kerala High Court it was alleged that despite Supreme Court having declared that calling for a bandh is unconstitutional, political parties in Kerala state continue to call for bandhs under the name and cover of hartal, and so sought to de-register the CPM party for having violated the law. The petitioners prayed for enforcement of decision in the case of CPI (M) v. Bharat Kumar & Others, 1998. The Court held that there is no express provision in the law which empowers the Election

Commission to de-register any party on the ground of violation of the Constitution of India except in certain exceptional cases where a party is found to have obtained registration by fraud, when a case arises out of sub-section (9) of Section 29A of Representation of the People Act, 1951, or when a party is declared unlawful.

Judgment: The Supreme Court observed the plea that Section 21 of General Clauses Act, 1897 does not apply to the Commission as its functions are quasi-judiciary and not legislative or executive and the Commission has no power to de-register a party through it has the power to register it.

(x) People's Union for Civil Liberties (PUCL) vs. Union of India & Ors, 2003

Whether Section 33B of the Representation of People Act, 1951, was unconstitutional or not

Facts: The petitioners in this case filed a writ petition under Article 32 challenging the constitutionality of the Representation of the People Act (Amendment) Ordinance, 2002. The petitioners challenged it as being arbitrary and violative of the fundamental right of the citizens to know their electoral candidate, and as deviating from a previous judgment of the Supreme Court. The Election Commission had issued directives to effect the judgment made in the previous case of *Union of India vs. Association for Democratic Reforms, 2003*, which clearly declared that the voter/citizen has the right to seek information about an electoral candidate; this judgment is derived from the fundamental right of freedom to speech and expression, but the Act of 1951 made it ineffective. The right to speech and expression comes under Article 19(1) and is a fundamental right, which cannot be taken away by an amendment. PUCL contended that parliament cannot nullify a judgement by a Court by passing an ordinance or order, which is an arbitrary action.

Judgment: Section 33B of the Representation of the People Act, 1951, was held invalid and unconstitutional. However, disclosure of educational qualifications was not be part of this, and refusal to make a disclosure in this respect would not violate Article 19(1) since it was not absolutely necessary information. The court directed the Election Commission to issue revised directions in accordance with the judgment. The public's right to know their electoral candidates was dealt with using a liberal approach in the judgment instead of a restricted one.

(xi) Lily Thomas vs. Union of India & Ors., 2013

Whether MLAs or MPs should be disqualified after they are convicted in a criminal case

Facts: The petitioner, Lily Thomas, filed a writ petition in the Supreme Court of India under Article 32 as a public interest litigation contending that sub-section (4) of Section 8 of the Representation of the People Act, 1951, be declared as inconsistent with the Constitution. This sub-section allowed convicted MPs, MLAs and MLCs to continue in their posts provided they appealed against their conviction/sentence in the higher courts within three months of the date of judgment by the trial court. The defendant here was Union of India itself, supporting the fact that the parliament enacted the provision under the shadow of the Constitution, and that the Constitution itself, under Articles 102 and 191, has given them the right to set certain more provisions relating to disqualification of members of parliament and member of the legislative assembly or council.

Judgment: The apex court in its judgement held that Section 8(4) is indeed ultra vires the constitutional provisions. It also accepted the contention of the petitioners that the grounds for disqualification of a candidate and a member are the same. Thus, parliament has exceeded its powers by bringing in Section 8(4). The Court further observed that the sitting members who have already benefitted from Section 8(4) would not be affected by this judgment. However, if any sitting member of parliament or state legislature is convicted by virtue of subsections 1, 2 and 3 of Section 8, he/she shall stand disqualified by virtue of this judgment.

(xii) People's Union for Civil Liberties vs. Union of India & Anr., 2013

Regarding NOTA and secrecy of ballot

Facts: The People's Union of Civil Liberties (PUCL), a civil rights NGO, brought a case before the Supreme Court arguing that the Representation of the People Act of 1951 violated the right to freedom of expression, because while it recognized the right to not vote, it did not adequately protect voter secrecy. Under the Act, whenever someone exercises the right not to vote, a note is taken of this by the presiding officer. The government objected, arguing that the right to vote is not a fundamental constitutional right, but rather, a right granted and regulated by statute. The government argued that the Act was meant to protect those who had voted for one of the candidates and could not be extended to those who did not exercise their right to vote.

Judgment: The Supreme Court concluded that the rules, as they stood, violated the fundamental rights and ruled that a 'none of the above' option should be provided through the EVMs. The Court emphasized that secrecy of ballot was essential; fear of disclosure of one's vote would act as a constraint on the voter's expression and decision not to vote. Finally, the court held that an arbitrary distinction had been drawn between voters who decide to vote and those who do not. This violated the right to equality under Article 14 of the Indian Constitution.

(xiii) Dr Subramanian Swamy vs. Election Commission of India, 2013

Regarding implementation of VVPATs

Facts: In this case, with the introduction of EVMs, the ECI contemplated introduction of a paper trail of the vote, which was pilot-tested. The Supreme Court studied the results of this test in of the voter-verified paper audit trail (VVPAT) system in the Noksen assembly constituency in Nagaland; the ECI had reported that it had been successfully used in twenty-one polling stations. The paper slips produced by the VVPAT system would not be counted by Returning Officer unless applied for by a candidate. But to ascertain that there was no discrepancy in the pilot case, the ECI had counted the paper slips in Noksen and found them to be accurate. The appellant contended before this court that the present system of EVMs, as utilized in the last few general elections in India, does not meet all the requirements of international standards, and though the ECI maintained that the EVMs cannot be tampered with, the fact is that EVMs, like all electronic equipment, are open to hacking.

Judgment: The Supreme Court noted that the paper trail provided verification to the voter of his or her vote and was indispensable for free and fair elections. The Court also observed voter confidence in EVMs would be 'achieved only with the introduction of the "paper trail"'. It felt VVPAT could restore voter confidence and make the system more transparent.

(xiv) Krishnamoorthy v. Shiv Kumar & Ors., 2015

Regarding non-disclosure of criminal cases by candidate at the time of filing for nomination

Facts: The appellant was elected as the president of Thekampatti panchayat, Mettupalayam taluk, Coimbatore district, in the State of Tamil Nadu in the elections held for the said purpose on 13 October 2006. The validity of the election was called into question on the sole ground that he had filed a false declaration suppressing the details of the criminal cases, pending trial, against him; therefore, his nomination deserved to be rejected by the returning officer before the Coimbatore District Court in election O.P. no. 296 of 2006.

Judgment: The Supreme Court had argued that disclosure of criminal antecedents by a candidate was a 'categorical imperative', as mandated by law. Non-disclosure hindered the 'free exercise of electoral right" as voters were prevented from making an informed choice and is therefore, interference in their right to vote. As the candidate himself would have the knowledge of the pending cases against him where cognisance had been taken or charges framed, non-disclosure of the same during filing for nomination as an electoral candidate 'would amount to undue influence and, therefore, the election is to be declared null and void by the Election Tribunal under Section 100(1)(b) of the 1951 Act'.

(xv) Abhiram Singh vs. C.D. Commachen, 2017

Electoral appeals case

Facts: The election in 1990 of Abhiram Singh to the no. 40 Santa Cruz legislative assembly constituency of Maharashtra was successfully challenged by Commachen in the Bombay High Court. While hearing the appeal against the decision of the Bombay High Court, a bench of three learned Supreme Court judges expressed the view that the content, scope and what constitutes corrupt practice under sub-sections (3) or (3A) of Section 123 of the Representation of the People Act, 1951 needs to be clearly and authoritatively laid down to avoid miscarriage of justice in interpreting 'corrupt practice'. The bench was of opinion that the appeal requires to be heard and decided by a larger bench of five judges of the same court on three specific questions of law.

Judgment: The Court, by a 4:3 majority, held that appealing to the ascriptive identities of any candidate as well as to **the voters'** constitutes a 'corrupt practice' under Section 123(3).

(xvi) Anoop Baranwal vs. Union of India, 2023

Regarding ECI appointments to be made under the collegium system

Facts: In January 2015, Anoop Baranwal filed a PIL on the ground that the current system for appointing members of the Election Commission of India (ECI) is unconstitutional. Currently, the executive enjoys the power to make appointments, which the

PIL contended had degraded the ECI's independence over time. The PIL pleaded for the court to issue directions to set up an independent, collegium-like system for ECI appointments. It claimed that the current system of appointments violated Article 324(2) of the Constitution.

Judgment: After hearing four days of substantial arguments in November 2022, the Constitution bench decided to change the process for Election Commission appointments in order to secure their independence. The bench created a committee comprising the prime minister, the leader of the Opposition in parliament, and the chief justice of India. This committee will make recommendations and advise the president on Election Commission appointments until parliament enacts a separate law on the subject.

3

Tables

List of Chief Election Commissioners

S. No.	Name of Chief Election Commissioners and their Tenure	Tenure Dates
1	Sukumar Sen	21 March 1950 to 19 December 1958
2	Kalyan Sundaram	20 December 1958 to 30 September 1967
3	S. P. Sen Verma	1 October 1967 to 30 September 1972
4	Nagendra Singh	1 October 1972 to 6 February 1973
5	T. Swaminathan	7 February 1973 to 17 June 1977
6	S. L. Shakdhar	18 June 1977 to 17 June 1982

S. No.	Name of Chief Election Commissioners and their Tenure	Tenure Dates
7	R. K. Trivedi	18 June 1982 to 31 December 1985
8	R.K. Peri Sastri	1 January 1986 to 25 November 1990
9	V.S. Ramadevi	26 November 1990 to 11 December 1990
10	T.N. Seshan	12 December 1990 to 11 December 1996
11	M.S. Gill	12 December 1996 to 13 June 2001
12	James Michael Lyngdoh	14 June 2001 to 7 February 2004
13	TS Krishnamurthy	Feb 2004– May 2005
14	B.B. Tandon	16 May 2005 to 29 June 2006
15	N. Gopalaswami	30 June 2006 to 20 April 2009
16	Navin Chawla	21 April 2009 to 29 July 2010
17	S.Y. Quraishi	30 July 2010 to 10 June 2012
18	V. S. Sampath	11 June 2012 to 15 January 2015
19	Harishankar Brahma	16 January 2015 to 18 April 2015
20	Nasim Zaidi	18 April 2015 to 5 July 2017
21	Achal Prakash Jyoti	6 July to 22 January 2018
22	Om Prakash Rawat	23 January 2018 to 1 December 2018
23	Sunil Arora	2 December 2018 to 12 April 2021
24	Sushil Chandra	13 April 2021 to 14 May 2022
25	Rajiv Kumar	15 May 2022– Incumbent

4

Indian Elections at a Glance

(Courtesy: Election Atlas of India, 2022 edition)

India Population

(2011 census)

DEMOGRAPHICS	
Household	24,66,92,667
Population	121,08,54,977★
Percentage of Total Population	
Rural	69
Urban	31
SC	16.63
ST	8.61
Hindu	79.8
Muslim	14.23
Christian	2.3
Buddhist	0.7

DEMOGRAPHICS	
Sikh	1.72
Jain	0.37
Others	0.9
Literacy Rate	72.99

*   As per 2011 census. The current population of India is 1,418,533,462 as of Monday, May 8, 2023, based on Worldometer elaboration of the latest United Nations data.

Electors, Voters and Polling (2019-1952)

Year	Total PCs	Electors			Total Voters	Poll %age
		Total	Male	Female		
2019	543	91,19,50,734	47,33,73,748	43,85,37,911	61,46,85,268	67.4
2014	543	83,40,82,814	43,70,35,372	39,70,18,915	55,41,75,255	66.44
2009	543	71,69,85,101	37,47,58,801	34,22,26,300	41,72,36,311	58.19
2004	543	67,14,87,930	34,94,90,864	32,19,97,066	38,99,48,330	58.07
1999	543	61,95,36,847	32,38,13,667	29,57,23,180	37,16,69,104	59.99
1998	543	60,58,80,192	31,66,92,789	28,91,87,403	37,54,41,739	61.97
1996	543	59,25,72,288	30,98,15,776	28,27,56,512	34,33,08,090	57.94
1991–92	543	51,15,33,598	26,89,62,610	24,25,70,988	28,58,56,465	55.88
1989	543	49,89,06,529	26,20,45,142	23,68,61,387	30,90,50,451	61.95
1984–85	542	40,01,19,657	20,79,12,918	19,22,06,739	25,62,94,963	64.05
1980	542	35,62,05,329	18,55,39,439	17,06,65,890	20,27,52,893	56.92
1977	542	32,11,74,327	16,70,19,151	15,41,55,176	19,42,63,915	60.49
1971	518	27,41,89,132	14,35,64,829	13,06,24,303	15,15,36,802	55.27
1967	520	25,02,07,401	–	–	15,27,24,611	61.04
1962	494	21,63,61,569	–	–	11,99,04,284	55.42
1957	403	19,36,52,179	–	–	12,05,13,915	45.44
1952	401	17,32,12,343	–	–	10,59,50,083	44.87

Polling Stations and Reserved Constituencies

Polling Stations (PS)			Month and Year of Poll	Reserved PCs
No. of PS	Electors per PS	Voters per PS		
10,37,848	879	592	April–May, 2019	SC – 84, ST – 47
9,27,553	899	597	April–May, 2014	SC – 84, ST – 47
8,34,919	859	500	April–May, 2009	SC – 84, ST – 47
6,87,473	977	567	April–May, 2004	SC – 79, ST – 41
7,74,651	800	480	Sept.–Oct., 1999	SC – 79, ST – 41
7,72,681	784	486	Feb.–March & June, 1998	SC – 79, ST – 41
7,67,462	772	447	April–May, 1996	SC – 79, ST – 41
5,91,020	866	484	Feb., May, 1991–92	SC – 79, ST – 41
5,80,798	859	532	November, 1989	SC – 78, ST – 39
5,05,288	792	507	Sept. & Dec., 1984–85	SC – 79, ST – 40
4,36,813	815	464	January, 1980	SC – 79, ST – 41
3,73,910	859	520	March, 1977	SC – 78, ST – 38
3,42,918	800	442	Jan-Feb., April-July & Oct. 1971	SC – 76, ST – 36
–	–	–	February, 1967	SC – 77, ST – 37
2,38,031	909	504	February, 1962	SC – 79, ST – 30
–	–	–	Feb-March & May, 1957	SC – 0, ST – 16
–	–	–	March, 1952	SC – 0, ST – 8

Electoral Results (Top 5 Parties 2019-1952)

Top 2 Parties

Year	1st Position			2nd Position			Margin Votes (%)
	Party	Won (Contested)	Votes (%)	Party	Won (Contested)	Votes (%)	
2019	BJP	303 (436)	22,90,76,879 (37.3)	INC	52 (421)	11,94,95,214 (19.46)	10,95,81,665 (17.84)
2014	BJP	282 (428)	17,16,60,230 (31)	INC	44 (464)	10,69,35,942 (19.31)	64,7,24,242 (11.69)
2009	INC	206 (440)	11,91,11,019 (28.55)	BJP	116 (433)	78435381 (18.8)	4,06,75,638 (9.75)
2004	INC	145 (417)	10,34,08,949 (26.53)	BJP	138 (364)	8,63,71,561 (22.16)	1,70,37,388 (4.37)
1999	BJP	182(339)	8,65,62,209 (28.3)	INC	114(453)	10,31,20,330 (23.75)	1,65,58,121 (4.54)
1998	INC	141 (477)	9,51,11,131 (25.82)	BJP	182 (388)	9,42,66,188 (25.59)	8,44,943 (0.23)
1996	INC	140 (529)	9,64,55,493 (28.8)	BJP	161 (471)	6,79,50,851 (20.29)	2,85,04,642 (8.51)
1991-92	INC	244 (500)	10,12,85,692 (36.4)	BJP	120 (477)	5,58,43,074 (20.07)	4,54,42,618 (16.33)
1989	INC	197 (510)	11,88,94,702 (39.53)	JD	143 (244)	5,35,18,521 (17.79)	6,53,76,181 (21.74)
1984-85	INC	414 (517)	12,01,07,044 (48.12)	BJP	2 (229)	1,84,66,137 (7.4)	10,16,40,907 (40.72)
1980	INC(I)	353 (492)	8,44,55,313 (42.69)	JNP	31 (432)	3,74,93,334 (18.95)	4,69,61,979 (23.74)
1977	BLD	295 (405)	7,80,62,828 (41.32)	INC	154 (492)	6,52,11,589 (34.52)	1,28,51,239 (6.8)
1971	INC	352 (441)	6,40,33,274 (43.68)	NCO	16 (238)	1,52,85,851 (10.43)	4,87,47,423 (33.25)

| Year | Party | 1st Position | | Party | 2nd Position | | Margin Votes (%) |
		Won (Contested)	Votes (%)		Won (Contested)	Votes (%)	
1967	INC	283 (516)	5,94,90,701 (40.78)	BJS	35 (249)	1,35,80,935 (9.31)	4,59,09,766 (31.47)
1962	INC	361 (488)	5,15,09,084 (44.72)	CPI	29 (137)	1,14,50,037 (9.94)	4,00,59,047 (34.78)
1957	INC	371 (490)	5,75,79,589 (47.78)	PSP	19 (189)	1,25,42,666 (10.41)	4,50,36,923 (37.37)
1952	INC	364 (479)	4,76,65,951 (44.99)	SP	12 (254)	1,12,16,719 (10.59)	3,64,49,232 (34.4)

Top 3 and 4

| | 3rd Position | | | 4th Position | |
Party	Won (Contested)	Votes (%)	Party	Won (Contested)	Votes (%)
AITC	22 (62)	2,49,29,330 (4.06)	BSP	10 (383)	2,22,46,501 (3.62)
BSP	0 (503)	2,29,46,106 (4.14)	AITC	34 (131)	2,12,62,665 (3.84)
BSP	21 (500)	2,57,28,920 (6.17)	CPM	16 (82)	2,22,19,111 (5.33)
CPM	43 (69)	2,20,70,614 (5.66)	BSP	19 (435)	2,07,65,229 (5.33)
CPM	33 (72)	1,96,95,767 (5.4)	BSP	14 (225)	1,51,75,845 (4.16)
CPM	32 (71)	1,89,91,867 (5.16)	SP	20 (166)	1,81,67,640 (4.93)
JD	46 (196)	2,70,70,340 (8.08)	CPM	32 (75)	2,04,96,810 (6.12)

3rd Position			4th Position		
Party	Won (Contested)	Votes (%)	Party	Won (Contested)	Votes (%)
JD	59 (312)	3,26,28,400 (11.73)	CPM	35 (63)	1,70,74,699 (6.14)
BJP	85 (225)	3,41,71,477 (11.36)	CPM	33 (64)	1,96,91,309 (6.55)
JNP	10 (219)	1,66,30,596 (6.66)	CPM	22 (64)	1,42,72,526 (5.72)
JNP(S)	41 (294)	1,86,11,590 (9.41)	CPM	37 (64)	1,23,52,331 (6.24)
CPM	22 (53)	81,13,659 (4.29)	ADK	18 (21)	54,80,378 (2.9)
BJS	22 (157)	1,07,77,119 (7.35)	CPM	25 (85)	75,10,089 (5.12)
SWA	44 (178)	1,26,46,847 (8.67)	CPI	23 (109)	74,58,396 (5.11)
SWA	18 (173)	90,85,252 (7.89)	PSP	12 (168)	78,48,345 (6.81)
CPI	27 (110)	1,07,54,075 (8.92)	BJS	4 (130)	71,93,267 (5.97)
KMPP	9 (145)	61,35,978 (5.79)	CPI	16 (49)	34,87,401 (3.29)

Fifth Position

5th Position			Others Votes (%)	Polarity (Party)
Party	Won (Contested)	Votes (%)		
SP	5 (49)	1,56,47,206 (2.55)	19,62,54,921 (31.95)	Other
SP	5 (197)	1,86,73,089 (3.37)	20,63,21,972 (37.26)	Other
SP	23 (193)	1,42,84,638 (3.42)	15,73,80,212 (37.73)	Other
SP	36 (237)	1,68,24,072 (4.32)	14,03,39,359 (36)	Other
SP	26 (151)	1,37,17,021 (3.76)	12,61,66,122 (34.62)	Other
BSP	5 (251)	1,71,86,779 (4.67)	12,46,53,095 (33.84)	Other
BSP	11 (210)	1,34,53,235 (4.02)	10,94,46,557 (32.68)	Other
JP	5 (350)	92,95,062 (3.34)	6,20,96,460 (22.32)	Other
TDP	2 (33)	99,09,728 (3.29)	6,45,90,686 (21.47)	Other
LKD	3 (173)	1,40,86,691 (5.64)	6,60,22,340 (26.45)	Other
INC(U)	13 (212)	1,04,49,859 (5.28)	3,44,61,847 (17.42)	Other
CPI	7 (91)	53,22,088 (2.82)	2,67,26,962 (14.15)	Bipolar (BLD-INC)
CPI	23 (87)	69,33,627 (4.73)	4,20,62,316 (28.69)	Other
SSP	23 (122)	71,71,627 (4.92)	4,55,18,003 (31.21)	Other
JS	14 (196)	74,15,170 (6.44)	2,78,61,002 (24.19)	Other
SCF	6 (21)	20,38,890 (1.69)	3,04,05,428 (25.23)	Other
BJS	3 (94)	32,46,361 (3.06)	3,41,97,673 (32.28)	Other

Electors

Growth of Electors by Gender

Growth of Electors by Gender			
Year	**Electors (In Crore)**		
	Total	**Male**	**Female**
2022	95.25	49.19	46.06
2019	91.20	47.34	43.85
2014	83.41	43.70	39.70
2009	71.70	37.48	34.22
2004	67.15	34.95	32.20
1999	61.95	32.38	29.57
1998	60.59	31.67	28.92
1996	59.26	30.98	28.28
1991–92	51.15	26.90	24.26
1989	49.89	26.20	23.69
1984–85	40.04	20.80	19.23
1980	35.62	18.55	17.07
1977	32.12	16.70	15.42
1971	27.42	14.36	13.06
1967	25.02	–	–
1962	21.64	–	–
1957	19.37	–	–
1952	17.32	–	–

Note: Total include "28.5; 39.08; & 45.90 thousand other/third gender" electors in 2014, 2019 and 2022 respectively.

1. Candidates

C1. Growth of Candidates by Gender & Average No. of Contestants Per Seat

Year	Total No. of Contestants	Total Male candidates	Total Female candidates	Average No. of Contestants Per Seat
2019	8054	7328	726	14.83
2014	8251	7583	668	15.20
2009	8070	7514	556	14.86
2004	5435	5080	355	10.01
1999	4648	4364	284	8.56
1998	4750	4476	274	8.75
1996	13952	13353	599	25.69
1991	8749	8419	330	16.11
1989	6160	5962	198	11.34
1984	5492	5321	171	10.13
1980	4629	4486	143	8.54
1977	2439	2369	70	4.50
1971	2784	2698	86	5.37
1967	2369	2302	67	4.56
1962	1985	1919	66	4.02
1957	1519	1474	45	3.77
1952	1874			4.67

C2. Percentage of Winners (Strike rate) among Male and Female Contestants

Year	Male	Female
2019	6.35	10.74
2014	6.36	9.13
2009	6.44	10.61
2004	9.80	12.68
1999	11.32	17.25
1998	11.17	15.69
1996	3.77	6.68
1991	5.89	11.52
1989	8.62	14.65
1984	9.40	25.15
1980	11.46	19.58
1977	22.08	27.14
1971	18.42	24.42
1967	21.33	43.28
1962	24.13	46.97
1957	32.02	48.89

C3. Parliamentary Constituencies with Highest and Lowest No. of Candidates

Year	PC with Maximum No. of Candidates	PC with Minimum Number of Candidates
2019	Nizamabad (Telangana) – 185	Tura (Meghalaya) – 3
2014	Chennai South (Tamil Nadu) & Varanasi (Uttar Pradesh) – 42	Tura (Meghalaya) – 2
2009	Chennai South (Tamil Nadu) – 43	Kokrajhar (Assam) & Nagaland – 3

Year	PC with Maximum No. of Candidates	PC with Minimum Number of Candidates
2004	Madras South (Tamil Nadu) – 35	Godhra (Gujarat), Tura (Meghalaya) & Cuttack (Odisha) – 2
1999	Gonda (Uttar Pradesh) – 32	Banswara (Rajasthan) – 2
1998	Ongole (Andhra Pradesh) – 34	Anand (Gujarat), Lakshadweep, Satara (Maharashtra) & Nagaland – 2
1996	Nalgonda (Andhra Pradesh) – 480	Lakshadweep – 2
1991–92	East Delhi (Delhi) – 105	Lakshadweep – 2
1989	Bhiwani (Haryana) – 122	Srinagar (Jammu and Kashmir) – 1
1984–85	East Delhi (Delhi) – 42	Tirupati (Andhra Pradesh), Lakshadweep, Sangli (Maharashtra), Nabarangpur (Odisha), Chidambaram, Pollachi, Rasipuram, Tenkasi, Wandiwash (Tamil Nadu), Dum Dum, Durgapur & Katwa (West Bengal) – 2
1980	Chandigarh – 39	Srinagar (Jammu and Kashmir) – 1
1977	Bombay South (Maharashtra) & Moradabad (Uttar Pradesh) – 14	Arunachal West (Arunachal Pradesh) & Sikkim – 1
1971	Secundrabad (Andhra Pradesh) & Bombay South (Maharashtra) – 16	Laccadive, Minicoy Amindivi Islands – 1

Year	PC with Maximum No. of Candidates	PC with Minimum Number of Candidates
1967	Kairana (Uttar Pradesh) – 14	Vijayawada (Andhra Pradesh), Kokrajhar (Assam), Anantnag, Ladakh (Jammu and Kashmir) & Nagaland – 1
1962	Jaipur (Rajasthan) – 11	Tiruchendur (Madras), Angul (Odisha) & Tehri Garhwal (Uttar Pradesh) – 1
1957	Outer Delhi (Delhi) – 13	Rajahmundry, Vicarabad (Andhra Pradesh), Darrang (Assam), Mandla (Madhya Pradesh) & Hassan (Mysore) – 1
1952	Karnal (Punjab) – 14	Bilaspur (Bilaspur), Yadgir (Hyderabad), Coimbatore (Madras), Rayagada Phulbani (Odisha) & Halar (Saurashtra) – 1

C4. Number of Independent Candidates and Elected Members

Number of Independent Candidates and Elected Members		
Year	Total No. of Independent Candidates	No. of Independent Candidates Elected
2019	3460	4
2014	3234	3
2009	3831	9
2004	2385	5
1999	1945	6
1998	1915	6

Number of Independent Candidates and Elected Members		
Year	Total No. of Independent Candidates	No. of Independent Candidates Elected
1996	10635	9
1991	5546	1
1989	3712	12
1984	3894	13
1980	2826	9
1977	1224	9
1971	1134	14
1967	866	35
1962	479	20
1957	481	42
1952	533	37

C5. Muslim Representation in Lok Sabha

Muslim Representation		
Year	Muslim in Lok Sabha	Percentage of Representation
2019	27	5.0
2014	23	4.2
2009	30	5.5
2004	36	6.6
1999	32	5.9
1998	29	5.3
1996	28	5.2
1991	28	5.2
1989	33	6.2
1984	46	8.5
1980	49	9.3
1977	34	6.3

Muslim Representation		
Year	Muslim in Lok Sabha	Percentage of Representation
1971	30	5.8
1967	29	5.6
1962	23	4.7
1957	24	4.9
1952	21	4.3

C6. Women Representation

Year	Number of Women contestants	Number of Women Members elected	Percentage out of total strength of Lok Sabha
2019	726	78	14.36
2014	668	62	11.42
2009	556	59	10.86
2004	355	45	8.29
1999	284	49	9.02
1998	274	43	7.91
1996	599	40	7.36
1991	330	39	7.11
1989	198	29	5.48
1984	171	43	7.94
1980	143	28	5.29
1977	70	19	3.50
1971	86	21	4.05
1967	67	29	5.57
1962	66	31	6.27
1957	45	22	4.45
1952		24	4.91

Poll Percentage

D1. Voter Turnout by Gender

Growth of Poll Percentage by Gender			
Year	Total	Male	Female
2019	67.40	67.01	67.18
2014	66.44	67.00	65.54
2009	58.19	60.24	55.82
2004	58.07	61.66	53.30
1999	59.99	63.97	55.64
1998	61.97	65.72	57.88
1996	57.94	62.06	53.41
1991	55.88	61.58	51.35
1989	61.95	66.13	57.32
1984	64.01	61.20	58.60
1980	56.92	62.16	51.22
1977	60.49	65.63	54.91
1971	55.27	60.09	49.11
1967	61.04	66.73	55.48
1962	55.42	–	–
1957	45.44	–	–
1952	44.87	–	–

Note: Male/Female breakup is not available for 1952–1962 elections.

D2. Top Ten Parliamentary Constituency with Highest Poll Percentage

Rank	Year	Constituency	State	Poll %
1	2004	Nagaland	Nagaland	91.77
2	2019	Dhubri	Assam	90.66
3	2009	Tamluk	West Bengal	90.32
4	2009	Nagaland	Nagaland	89.99
5	2009	Kanthi	West Bengal	89.97
6	1996	Panskura	West Bengal	89.88
7	1996	Tamluk	West Bengal	89.80
8	1996	Cooch Behar	West Bengal	89.56
9	1996	Basirhat	West Bengal	89.20
10	1984–85	Barpeta	Assam	89.04

(Excluding bye-elections)

D3. Top Ten Parliamentary Constituency with Lowest Poll Percentage

Rank	Year	Constituency	State	Poll %
1	1989	Anantnag	Jammu and Kashmir	5.07
2	1989	Baramulla	Jammu and Kashmir	5.48
3	2019	Anantnag	Jammu and Kashmir	8.98
4	1991–92	Tarn Taran	Punjab	9.50
5	1991–92	Sangrur	Punjab	10.90
6	1999	Srinagar	Jammu and Kashmir	11.93
7	1962	Bhanjanagar	Odisha	12.04
8	1962	Koraput	Odisha	12.17
9	1962	Phulbani	Odisha	13.92
10	1991–92	Bathinda	Punjab	13.92

(Excluding bye-elections)

D4. Growth of Polling Stations and Average Number of Electors & Voters in a Polling Station

Growth of Polling Stations and Average Number of Electors & Voters in a Polling Station					
Year	Electors	Voters	Number of Polling Stations	Average Number of Electors	Average Number of Voters
2019	91,19,50,734	61,46,85,268	10,37,848	879	592
2014	83,40,82,814	55,41,75,255	9,27,553	899	597
2009	71,69,85,101	41,72,36,311	8,34,919	859	500
2004	67,14,87,930	38,99,48,330	6,87,473	977	567
1999	61,95,36,847	37,16,69,104	7,74,651	800	480
1998	60,58,80,192	37,54,41,739	7,72,681	784	486
1996	59,25,72,288	34,33,08,090	7,67,462	772	447
1991	51,15,33,598	28,58,56,465	5,91,020	866	484
1989	49,89,06,129	30,90,50,451	5,80,798	859	532
1984	40,03,75,333	25,62,94,963	5,06,058	791	506
1980	35,62,05,329	20,27,52,893	4,36,813	815	464
1977	32,11,74,327	19,42,63,915	3,73,910	859	520
1971	27,41,89,132	15,15,36,802	3,42,918	800	442
1967	25,02,07,401	15,27,24,611	2,43,693	1027	627
1962	21,63,61,569	11,99,04,284	2,38,031	909	504
1957	19,36,52,179	12,05,13,915	2,20,478	878	547
1952	17,32,12,343	10,59,50,083	1,96,084	883	540

D5. Top Ten Parliamentary Constituencies with Largest Geographical Area in India

Rank	Constituency	State	Area (Sq KM)	Electors	Density of Electors (Per square KM)
1	Ladakh	Jammu & Kashmir	172374	179232	1.04
2	Barmer	Rajasthan	55074	1941231	35.25
3	Kachchh	Gujarat	41414	1744321	42.12
4	Arunachal East	Arunachal Pradesh	39704	339788	8.56
5	Arunachal West	Arunachal Pradesh	39613	463775	11.71
6	Mandi	Himachal Pradesh	32017	1281462	40.02
7	Bikaner	Rajasthan	31401	1851628	58.97
8	Bastar	Chhattishgarh	28614	1379122	48.20
9	Jodhpur	Rajasthan	24258	1956755	80.67
10	Mizoram	Mizoram	20268	792464	39.10

D6. Top Ten Parliamentary Constituencies with Smallest Geographical Area in India

Rank	Constituency	State	Area (Sq KM)	Electors	Density of Electors (Per square KM)
1	Lakshadweep	Lakshadweep	30	55189	1821.84
2	Mumbai South	Maharashtra	39	1554176	39458.17

Rank	Constituency	State	Area (Sq KM)	Electors	Density of Electors (Per square KM)
3	Kolkata Uttar	West Bengal	44	1444082	32588.63
4	Mumbai North Central	Maharashtra	45	1679891	36987.10
5	Mumbai South Central	Maharashtra	49	1440380	29362.92
6	Chennai Central	Tamil Nadu	63	1332300	21287.90
7	Hyderabad	Andhra Pradesh	66	1957931	29647.33
8	Mumbai North East	Maharashtra	69	1588693	23173.76
9	Mumbai North West	Maharashtra	73	1732263	23820.35
10	Chandni Chowk	Delhi	78	1562283	20157.22

Parties' Performance

E1. Largest Single Party in Lok Sabha with Vote Share Percentage

Election Year	Party Securing Majority	Total Seats	Seats won	% of Votes
2019	BJP	543	303	37.30
2014	BJP	543	282	31.00
1984	INC	542	414	48.12
1980	INC	542	353	42.69
1977	BLD (Janata Party)	542	295	41.32

Election Year	Party Securing Majority	Total Seats	Seats won	% of Votes
1971	INC	518	352	43.68
1967	INC	520	283	40.78
1962	INC	494	361	44.72
1957	INC	494	371	47.78
1951	INC	489	364	44.99

E2. Seats Won & Vote Share by Major Parties

Year	Seats Won & Vote Share by Major Parties					
	INC		BJP		CPI+CPM	
	Seat	Vote Share	Seat	Vote Share	Seat	Vote Share
2019	52	19.46	303	37.30	5	2.33
2014	44	19.30	282	31.00	10	3.80
2009	206	28.55	116	18.80	20	6.76
2004	145	26.70	138	22.16	53	7.07
1999	114	28.30	182	23.75	37	6.52
1998	141	25.82	182	25.59	41	4.99
1996	140	28.80	161	20.29	44	8.09
1991	244	36.26	120	20.11	49	8.65
1989	197	39.53	85	11.36	45	9.12
1984	414	48.12	2	7.74	28	8.58
1980	353	42.69	-	-	47	8.73
1977	154	34.52	-	-	29	7.11
1971	352	43.68	-	-	48	9.85
1967	283	40.78	-	-	42	9.39
1962	361	44.72	-	-	29	9.94
1957	371	47.78	-	-	27	8.92
1952	364	44.99	-	-	16	3.29

E3. Top Five parties with number of seats won and vote share

Top 3 Parties

Year	1st Position			2nd Position			3rd Position		
	Party	Seat	Vote Share	Party	Seat	Vote Share	Party	Seat	Vote Share
2019	BJP	436	37.3	INC	421	19.46	AITC	62	4.06
2014	BJP	428	31	INC	464	19.31	BSP	503	4.14
2009	INC	440	28.55	BJP	433	18.8	BSP	500	6.17
2004	INC	417	26.53	BJP	364	22.16	CPM	69	5.66
1999	INC	453	28.3	BJP	339	23.75	CPM	72	5.4
1998	INC	477	25.82	BJP	388	25.59	CPM	71	5.16
1996	INC	529	28.8	BJP	471	20.29	JD	196	8.08
1991–92	INC	500	36.4	BJP	477	20.07	JD	312	11.73
1989	INC	510	39.53	JD	244	17.79	BJP	225	11.36
1984–85	INC	517	48.12	BJP	229	7.4	JNP	219	6.66
1980	INC(I)	492	42.69	JNP	432	18.95	JNP(S)	294	9.41
1977	BLD	405	41.32	INC	492	34.52	CPM	53	4.29
1971	INC	441	43.68	NCO	238	10.43	BJS	157	7.35
1967	INC	516	40.78	BJS	249	9.31	SWA	178	8.67
1962	INC	488	44.72	CPI	137	9.94	SWA	173	7.89
1957	INC	490	47.78	PSP	189	10.41	CPI	110	8.92
1952	INC	479	44.99	SP	254	10.59	KMPP	145	5.79

4th and 5th Ranks

4th Position			5th Position		
Party	Seat	Vote Share	Party	Seat	Vote Share
BSP	383	3.62	SP	49	2.55
AITC	131	3.84	SP	197	3.37
CPM	82	5.33	SP	193	3.42
BSP	435	5.33	SP	237	4.32
BSP	225	4.16	SP	151	3.76
SP	166	4.93	BSP	251	4.67
CPM	75	6.12	BSP	210	4.02
CPM	63	6.14	JP	350	3.34
CPM	64	6.55	TDP	33	3.29
CPM	64	5.72	LKD	173	5.64
CPM	64	6.24	INC(U)	212	5.28
ADK	21	2.9	CPI	91	2.82
CPM	85	5.12	CPI	87	4.73
CPI	109	5.11	SSP	122	4.92
PSP	168	6.81	JS	196	6.44
BJS	130	5.97	SCF	21	1.69
CPI	49	3.29	BJS	94	3.06

E4. Top Ten Winner Candidates Securing Highest Number of Votes

Rank	Year	Candidate	Constituency	State	Party	Votes	Votes %
1	2019	Shankar Lalwani	Indore	Madhya Pradesh	BJP	1068569	65.59
2	2019	Queen Oja	Gauhati	Assam	BJP	1008936	57.20
3	2019	Chandra Prakash Joshi	Chittorgarh	Rajasthan	BJP	982942	67.38
4	2019	C. R. Patil	Navsari	Gujarat	BJP	972739	74.37
5	2019	Vijay Kumar Singh	Ghaziabad	Uttar Pradesh	BJP	944503	61.96
6	2019	Subhash Chandra Baheria	Bhilwara	Rajasthan	BJP	938160	71.59
7	2019	Ramcharan Bohra	Jaipur	Rajasthan	BJP	924065	63.45
8	2014★	Munde Pritam	Beed	Maharashtra	BJP	922416	71.05
9	2019	Krishan Pal	Faridabad	Haryana	BJP	913222	68.80
10	2019	Sanjay Bhatia	Karnal	Haryana	BJP	911594	70.08

E5. Top Ten Winner Candidates Securing Lowest Number of Votes

Rank	Year	Candidate	Constituency	State
1	1967	P.M. Sayeed (INC)	Laccadive, Minicoy Amindivi Islands	Laccadive, Minicoy Amindivi Islands
2	1971	Ramubhai Ravjibhai Patel (INC)	Dadar and Nagar Haveli	Dadra and Nagar Haveli
3	1977	Muhammed Sayeed Padannatha (INC)	Lakshadweep	Lakshadweep
4	1980	Muhammad Sayeed Padannatha (INC)	Lakshadweep	Lakshadweep
5	1984–85	Mohammad Sayeed Padannatha (INC)	Lakshadweep	Lakshadweep
6	1967	S. R. Delkar (INC)	Dadar and Nagar Haveli	Dadra and Nagar Haveli
7	1977	Patel Ramubhai Ravjibhai (INC)	Dadar and Nagar Haveli	Dadra and Nagar Haveli
8	1991–92	Tandel Dev Ji Jogi Bhai (BJP)	Daman and Diu	Daman and Diu
9	1991–92	P.M. Sayeed (INC)	Lakshadweep	Lakshadweep
10	1989	P. M. Sayeed (INC)	Lakshadweep	Lakshadweep

E6. Top Ten Women Winner Candidates Securing Highest Number of Votes

Rank	Year	Candidate	Constituency	State	Party	Votes	Votes %
1	2019	Queen Oja	Gauhati	Assam	BJP	10,08,936	57.20
2	2014★	Munde Pritam	Beed	Maharashtra	BJP	9,22,416	71.05
3	2019	Ranjanben Bhatt	Vadodara	Gujarat	BJP	8,83,719	72.30
4	2019	Sadhvi Pragya Singh Thakur	Bhopal	Madhya Pradesh	BJP	8,66,482	61.54
5	2019	Diya Kumari	Rajsamand	Rajasthan	BJP	8,63,039	69.61
6	2014	Sumitra Mahajan (Tai)	Indore	Madhya Pradesh	BJP	8,54,972	64.93
7	2019	Darshana Vikram Jardosh	Surat	Gujarat	BJP	7,95,651	74.47
8	2019	Nusrat Jahan Ruhi	Basirhat	West Bengal	AITC	7,82,078	54.56
9	2014	Bijoya Chakravarty	Gauhati	Assam	BJP	7,64,985	50.60
10	2019	Rathva Gitaben Vajesingbhai	Chhota Udaipur	Gujarat	BJP	7,64,445	62.03

E7. Top Ten Women Winner Candidates Securing Lowest Number of Votes

Rank	Year	Candidate	Constituency	State	Party	Votes	Votes %
1	1998*	Smt. Nirmala Devi	Pragpur	Himachal Pradesh	BJP	22651	65.59
2	1977	Parvati Devi	Ladakh	Jammu and Kashmir	INC	23130	53.32
3	1962	Savitri Nigam	Banda	Uttar Pradesh	INC	45919	36.62
4	1952	Amrit Kaur	Mandi Mahasu	Himachal Pradesh	INC	47152	26.89
5	1952	Suchetia Kripalani	New Delhi	Delhi	KMPP	47735	46.72
6	1952	Bonily Khongmen	Autonomous District	Assam	INC	59326	54.10
7	1952	Tarkeshwari Devi	Patna East	Bihar	INC	62238	46.90
8	1962	Lalita Rajya Laxmi	Aurangabad	Bihar	SWA	64552	39.19
9	1967	V. Raje	Chatra	Bihar	IND	66329	34.57
10	1952	Nayar Shakuntala	Gonda District (West)	Uttar Pradesh	HMS	66330	50.54

E8. Top Ten Winner Candidates with Highest Number of Winning Margin

Rank	Year	Candidate	Constituency	State	Party	Votes
1	2014★	Munde Pritam	Beed	Maharashtra	BJP	696321
2	2019	C. R. Patil	Navsari	Gujarat	BJP	689668
3	2019	Sanjay Bhatia	Karnal	Haryana	BJP	656142
4	2019	Krishan Pal	Faridabad	Haryana	BJP	638239
5	2019	Subhash Chandra Baheria	Bhilwara	Rajasthan	BJP	612000
6	2004	Anil Basu	Arambagh	West Bengal	CPM	592502
7	2019	Ranjanben Bhatt	Vadodara	Gujarat	BJP	589177
8	1991★	P.V.N. Rao	Nandyal	Andhra Pradesh	INC	580297
9	2019	Parvesh Sahib Singh Verma	West Delhi	Delhi	BJP	578486
10	2019	Chandra Prakash Joshi	Chittorgarh	Rajasthan	BJP	576247

E9. Top Ten Winner Candidates with Lowest Number of Winning Margin

Rank	Year	Candidate	Constituency	State	Party	Votes
1	1989	Konathala Ramakrishna	Anakapalli	Andhra Pradesh	INC	9
1	1998	Som Marandi	Rajmahal	Bihar	BJP	9
2	1996	Gaekwad Satyajitsinh Dilipsinh	Baroda	Gujarat	INC	17
3	1971	M. S. Sivasamy	Tiruchendur	Tamil Nadu	DMK	26
4	2014	Thupstan Chhewang	Ladakh	Jammu and Kashmir	BJP	36
5	1998	Dr. H. Lallungmuana	Mizoram	Mizoram	IND	41
6	1957	Missula Suryanarayana Murthy	Golugonda	Andhra Pradesh	INC	42
6	1962	Rishang	Outer Manipur	Manipur	SOC	42
7	1957	T. D. Muthukumarasamy Naidu	Cuddalore	Madras	IND	59
8	1962	Surendranath Dwivedy	Kendrapara	Odisha	PSP	66
9	2004	Dr. P. Pookunhikoya	Lakshadweep	Lakshadweep	JD(U)	71
10	1980	Ramayan Rai	Deoria	Uttar Pradesh	INC(I)	77

E10. Top Ten Candidates with Highest Percentage of Winning Vote Margin

Rank	Year	Candidate	Constituency	State	Party	Votes %
1	1989	P. L. Handoo	Anantnag	Jammu and Kashmir	JKN	97.19
2	1967★	Dr. K. Singh	Udhampur	Jammu and Kashmir	INC	93.92
3	1989	Saif Ud Din Soze	Baramulla	Jammu and Kashmir	JKN	91.87
4	1972★	M. Ray	Raiganj	West Bengal	INC	89.71
5	1991–92	Dil Kumari Bhandari (W)	Sikkim	Sikkim	SSP	86.86
6	2002★	Ganti Vijayakumari	Amalapuram	Andhra Pradesh	TDP	83.32
7	1991★	P.V.N. Rao	Nandyal	Andhra Pradesh	INC	82.92
8	1971	M. S. Sanjeevi Rao	Kakinada	Andhra Pradesh	INC	81.84
9	1971★	C. Subramaniam	Krishnagiri	TAMIL NADU	INC	81.58
10	1971	Partap Singh	Shimla	Himachal Pradesh	INC	81.53

E11. Top Ten Candidates with Lowest Percentage of Winning Vote Margin

Rank	Year	Candidate	Constituency	State	Party	Votes %
1	1989	Konathala Ramakrishna	Anakapalli	Andhra Pradesh	INC	0.001
2	1998	Som Marandi	Rajmahal	Bihar	BJP	0.002
3	1996	Gaekwad Satyajitsinh Dilipsinh	Baroda	Gujarat	INC	0.004
4	1971	M. S. Sivasamy	Tiruchendur	Tamil Nadu	DMK	0.006
5	1957	Missula Suryanarayana Murthy	Golugonda	Andhra Pradesh	INC	0.009
6	1998	Dr. H. Lallungmuana	Mizoram	Mizoram	IND	0.013
7	2019	Bholanath (B.P. Saroj)	Machhlishahr (SC)	Uttar Pradesh	BJP	0.017
8	1999	Pyare Lal Sankhwar	Ghatampur	Uttar Pradesh	BSP	0.019
9	2006*	Jhansi Lakshmi Botcha	Bobbili	Andhra Pradesh	INC	0.022
10	1980	Ramayan Rai	Deoria	Uttar Pradesh	INC(I)	0.023

Election Exercise

F1. Schedule for Parliamentary Elections

Year	Dates of Poll	Days of Poll	Date of Counting[1]	Date of Constitution of Lok Sabha
2019	11-04-2019 to 19-05-2019	7	23-05-2019	31-05-2019
2014	07-04-2014 to 12-05-2014	10	16-05-2014	04-06-2014
2009	16-04-2009 to 13-05-2009	5	16-05-2009	18-05-2009
2004	20-04-2004 to 10-05-2004	4	13-05-2004	17-05-2004
1999	05-09-1999 to 03-10-1999	8	06-10-1999	10-10-1999
1998	16-02-1998 to 28-02-1998[2]	4	08-03-1998[3]	10-03-1998
1996	27-04-1996 to 07-05-1996[4]	3	08-05-1996 to 11-05-1996[5]	15-05-1996[6]
1991	20-05-1991 to 05-06-1991	4		20-06-1991
1989	22-11-1989 to 26-11-1989	3		02-12-1989
1984	24-12-1984 to 28-12-1984	3		31-12-1984
1980	03-01-1980 and 06-01-1980	2		10-01-1980
1977	16-03-1977 to 20-03-1977	4		23-03-1977
1971	01-03-1971 to 10-03-1971[7]	9		15-03-1971

Year	Dates of Poll	Days of Poll	Date of Counting[1]	Date of Constitution of Lok Sabha
1967	15–02–1967 to 28–02–1967[8]	13		04–03–1967
1962	19–02–1962 to 25–02–1962	7		02–04–1962
1957	24–02–1957 to 15–03–1957[9]	20		05–04–1957
1951	02–01–1952 to 25–01–1952[10]	17		02–04–1952

Note:

1. Except in Travancore, Cochin, Punjab, and Bilaspur (October 1951 and in Himachal Pradesh 10th September 1951)
2. One of the date of poll in Jammu and Kashmir was 07-03-1998 also
3. Dates of Counting in Meghalaya was 23-02-1998 and date of counting for Jammu and Kashmir were on 08-03-1998 & 09-03-1998
4. Dates of poll have gone up to 23rd and 30th May 1996 in Jammu and Kashmir
5. Dates of counting for Jammu and Kashmir were 01-06-1996 and 10-02-1998 also
6. One of the date of notification in Jammu and Kashmir was 10-02-1998 also
7. Dates of poll have gone upto 6th June 1971 in Jammu and Kashmir
8. Dates of poll have gone upto 31st May 1967 in hilly areas of Himachal Pradesh
9. Dates of poll have gone upto 15th July 1957 in hilly areas of Punjab and Himachal Pradesh
10. UP polled in February, 1952 also, Trancore Cochin and Hyderabad polled in December 1951. Also Himachal Pradesh polled from 25-10-1951 to 30-11-1951.

Also note: Until the year 1996, date of announcement of Election by Commission and date of counting was not part of the published election programme.

F2. Duration of Parliamentary Elections

Lok Sabha	Span	No. of Days
First Lok Sabha (1951–52)	25 October – 21 February, 1952	119
Second Lok Sabha (1957)	24 February – 14 March, 1957	18
Third Lok Sabha (1962)	19 February – 25 February, 1962	6
Fourth Lok Sabha (1967)	17 February – 21 February, 1967	4
Fifth Lok Sabha (1971)	1 March – 10 March, 1971	9
Sixth Lok Sabha (1977)	16 March – 20 March, 1977	4
Seventh Lok Sabha (1980)	3 January – 6 January, 1980	3
Eighth Lok Sabha (1984)	24 December – 28 December, 1984	4
Ninth Lok Sabha (1989)	22 November – 26 November, 1989	4
Tenth Lok Sabha (1991)	20 May – 15 June, 1991	26
Eleventh Lok Sabha (1996)	27 April – 30 May, 1996	33
Twelfth Lok Sabha (1998)	16 February – 23 February, 1998	7
Thirteenth Lok Sabha (1999)	5 September – 6 October, 1999	31
Fourteenth Lok Sabha (2004)	20 April – 10 May, 2004	20

Lok Sabha	Span	No. of Days
Fifteenth Lok Sabha (2009)	16 April – 13 May, 2009	27
Sixteenth Lok Sabha (2014)	7 April – 12 May, 2014	35
Seventeenth Lok Sabha (2019)	11 April – 19 May, 2019	39

F3. Election Commission's Expenditure on Lok Sabha Elections

Year	Expenditure (In Crore ₹)	No. of Electors	Expenditure per elector (In ₹)
2014	3468.73 (₹. 350 Cr released on provisional basis to all States/UTs)	83,41,01,479	41.6
2009	846.67 (₹. 840.15 Cr released on provisional basis to 35 States/UTs)	71,69,85,101	12
2004	1113.89 (₹. 679.12 Cr released on provisional basis to 30 States)	67,14,87,930	17
1999	947.68	61,95,36,847	15
1998	666.22	60,58,80,192	11
1996	597.34	59,25,72,288	10
1991	359.1	51,15,33,598	7
1989	154.22	49,89,06,129	3.1
1984	81.51	40,03,75,333	2
1980	54.77	35,62,05,329	1.5
1977	23.04	32,11,74,327	0.7

Year	Expenditure (In Crore ₹)	No. of Electors	Expenditure per elector (In ₹)
1971	11.61	27,41,89,132	0.4
1967	10.8	25,02,07,401	0.4
1962	7.32	21,63,61,569	0.3
1957	5.9	19,36,52,179	0.3
1952	10.45	17,32,12,343	0.6

Note:

$: Elections were held separately for States of Assam & Punjab in 1985.

\# : Elections were held separately for State of Punjab in 1992.

^ : Duly audited expenditure from 23 States.

@ : Duly audited expenditure from 17 States.

!!! : A proposal for additional allocation of the amount for further release to states/ UTs is under consideration of the Ministry of Finance.

G. President and Vice President Elections

G1. Schedule for Presidential Elections

Year	Notified on	Last Date for Making the Nominations	Date of Poll & Hours	Counting on
1952	04–04–1952	12–04–1952	02–05–1952	06–05–1952
1957	06–04–1957	16–04–1957	06–05–1957	10–05–1957
1962	06–04–1962	16–04–1962	07–05–1962 10 A.M.–4 P.M.	11–05–1962
1967	03–04–1967	13–04–1967	06–05–1967	09–05–1967

Year	Notified on	Last Date for Making the Nominations	Date of Poll & Hours	Counting on
1969	14-07-1969	24-07-1969	16-08-1969	20-08-1969
1974	16-07-1974	30-07-1974	17-08-1974	20-08-1974
1977	04-07-1977	18-07-1977	06-08-1977	Elected Unopposed
1982	09-06-1982	23-06-1982	12-07-1982	15-07-1982
1987	10-06-1987	24-06-1987	13-07-1987	16-07-1987
1992	10-06-1992	24-06-1992	13-07-1992	16-07-1992
1997	09-06-1997	23-06-1997	14-07-1997	17-07-1997
2002	11-06-2002	25-06-2002	15-07-2002	18-07-2002
2007	16-06-2007	30-06-2007	19-07-2007	21-07-2007
2012	16-06-2012	30-06-2012	19-07-2012	22-07-2012
2017	14-06-2017	28-06-2017	17-07-2017	20-07-2017

G2. Results of Indian President Election

Year	Votes Polled	Winner Candidate	Votes (%)	Runner-up Candidate	Votes (%)	Others Vote (%)	Total Candidates
1952	605386	Dr. Rajendra Prasad	507400 (83.81)	Shri K.T. Shah	92827 (15.33)	5159 (0.85)	5
1957	464370	Dr. Rajendra Prasad	459698 (98.99)	Shri Nagendra Narayan Das	2000 (0.43)	2672 (0.58)	3
1962	562945	Dr. Sarvapalli Radhakrishnan	553067 (98.25)	Chowdhry Hari Ram	6341 (1.13)	3537 (0.63)	3
1967	838048	Dr. Zakir Hussain	471244 (56.23)	Shri Kota Subbarao	363971 (43.43)	2833 (0.34)	17
1969	836337	Shri V.V. Giri	401515 (48.01)	Shri Neelam Sanjeeva Reddy	313548 (37.49)	121274 (14.5)	15
1974	954783	Shri Fakhruddin Ali Ahmed	765587 (80.18)	Shri Tridib Chaudhuri	189196 (19.82)	0 (0.00)	2
1977		Shri Neelam Sanjeeva Reddy	Unopposed				1
1982	1036798	Gyani Zail Singh	754113 (72.73)	Shri H.R. Khanna	282685 (27.27)	0 (0.00)	2

Year	Votes Polled	Winner Candidate	Votes (%)	Runner-up Candidate	Votes (%)	Others Vote (%)	Total Candidates
1987	1023921	Shri R. Venkataraman	740148 (72.29)	Shri V. Krishna Iyer	281550 (27.50)	2223 (0.22)	3
1992	1026188	Dr. Shanker Dayal Sharma	675804 (65.86)	Shri G.G. Swell	346485 (33.76)	3839 (0.37)	4
1997	1006921	Shri K.R. Narayanan	956290 (94.97)	Shri T.N. Seshan	50631 (5.03)	0 (0.00)	2
2002	1030250	Dr. A. P. J. Abdul Kalam	922884 (89.58)	Smt. Lakshmi Sahgal	107366 (10.42)	0 (0.00)	2
2007	969422	Smt. Pratibha Devisingh Patil	638116 (65.82)	Sh. Bhairon Singh Shekhawat	331306 (34.18)	0 (0.00)	2
2012	1029750	Sh. Pranab Mukherjee	713763 (69.31)	Sh. Purno Agitok Sangma	315987 (30.69)	0 (0.00)	2
2017	1069358	Shri Ramnath Kovind	702044 (65.65)	Smt. Meira Kumar	367314 (34.35)	0 (0.00)	2

G3. Schedule for Vice-Presidential Elections

Year	Notified on	Last Date for Making the Nominations	Scrutiny on	Last Date for the Withdrawal of Candidature	Date of Poll & Hours	Counting on
1952	12-04-1952	21-04-1952	22-04-1952	25-04-1952	12/05/1952	Uncontested
1957	09-04-1957	18-04-1957	20-04-1957	23-04-1957	11/05/1957	Uncontested
1962	06-04-1962	16-04-1962	18-04-1962	21-04-1962	07/05/1962	07/05/1962
1967	03-04-1967	13-04-1967	15-04-1967	18-04-1967	06/05/1967	06/05/1967
1969	31-07-1969	09-08-1969	11-08-1969	14-08-1969	30/08/1969	30/08/1969
1974	26-07-1974	09-08-1974	10-08-1974	12-08-1974	27/08/1974	27/08/1974
1979	23-07-1979	06-08-1979	07-08-1979	09-08-1979	27/08/1979	Uncontested
1984	20-07-1984	03-08-1984	04-08-1984	06-08-1984	22/08/1984	22-08-1984
1987	04-08-1987	18-08-1987	19-08-1987	21-08-1987	07/09/1987	07/09/1987
1992	17-07-1992	31-07-1992	01-08-1992	03-08-1992	19/08/1992	19/08/1992
1997	15-07-1997	29-07-1997	30-07-1997	01-08-1997	16/08/1997	16/08/1997
2002	10-07-2002	24-07-2002	25-07-2002	27-07-2002	12/08/2002	12/08/2002
2007	09-07-2007	23-07-2007	24-07-2007	26-07-2007	10/08/2007	10/08/2007
2012	06-07-2012	20-07-2012	21-07-2012	23-07-2012	07/08/2012	07/08/2012
2017	04-07-2017	18-07-2017	19-07-2017	21-07-2017	05/08/2017	05-08-2017

G4. Results of Indian Vice-President Election

Year	Votes Polled	Winner Candidate	Votes (%)	Runner-up Candidate	Votes (%)	Others Vote (%)	Total Candidates
1952		Dr. S. Radhakrishnan	Unopposed				
1957		Dr. S. Radhakrishnan	Unopposed				
1962	582	Dr. Zakir Hussain	568 (97.59)	N.C. Samantsinhar	14 (2.41)		2
1967	676	Varahagiri Venkata Giri	483 (71.45)	Prof. Habib	193 (28.55)		2
1969		Gopal Swarup Pathak					6
1974	662	B.D. Jatti	521 (78.7)	N.E. Horo	141 (21.3)		2
1979		Mohammad Hidyatullah	Unopposed				
1984	715	Ramaswami Venkataraman	508 (71.05)	Bapu Chandrasen Kamble	207 (28.95)		2

Year	Votes Polled	Winner Candidate	Votes (%)	Runner-up Candidate	Votes (%)	Others Vote (%)	Total Candidates
1987		Dr. Shankar Dayal Sharma	Unopposed				
1992	701	K.R. Narayanan	700 (99.86)	Kaka Joginder Singh	1 (0.14)		2
1997	714	Krishan Kant	441 (61.76)	Surjit Singh	273 (38.24)		2
2002	759	Bhairon Singh Shekhawat	454 (59.82)	Sushil Kumar Shinde	305 (40.18)		2
2007	752	Mohd. Hamid Ansari	455 (60.51)	Dr. Najma A. Heptulla	222 (29.52)	75 (9.97)	3
2012	728	M. Hamid Ansari	490 (67.31)	Jaswant Singh	238 (32.69)		2
2017	760	Venkaiah Naidu	516 (67.89)	Gopalkrishna Gandhi	244 (32.11)		2

Note:

★ : Gopal Swarup Pathak secured 400 votes and get the required quota of votes in the first round of counting and were declared elected.

Bibliography

Aajeevika Bureau, 'Political Inclusion of Seasonal Migrant Workers in India: Perceptions, Realities, Challenges', (Udaipur: Aajeevika Bureau, 2012), https://www.aajeevika.org/assets/pdfs/Political%20Inclusion%20of%20Migrant%20Workers%20in%20India.pdf.

BBC, 'Duty, Identity, Credibility: Fake News and Ordinary Citizen in India', November 2018, https://downloads.bbc.co.uk/mediacentre/duty-identity-credibility.pdf.

BJP manifesto, 2014, https://www.bjp.org/bjp-manifesto-2014.

BJP manifesto, 2019, https://www.bjp.org/files/2019-10/BJP-Election-english-2019.pdf.

Creating the United States, https://www.loc.gov/exhibits/creating-the-united-states/formation-of-political-parties.html.

CSDS, https://www.csds.in/.

Damini Nath, 'Total Recall: From Ambedkar to Advani, concerns over how ECI appointments are made', *The Indian Express*, https://indianexpress.com/article/explained/explained-politics/ambedkar-advani-election-commissioners-appointment-debate-8475143/.

Dieter Nohlen and Florian Grotz, 'External Voting', https://www.researchgate.net/profile/Florian-Grotz/publication/277266613_External_Voting_Legal_Framework_and_Overview_of_Electoral_Legis-lation/links/585d3acd08aebf17d38a30e5/External-Voting-Legal-Framework-and-Overview-of-Electoral-Legis-lation.pdf

Donald Horowitz, 'Electoral Systems: A Primer for Decision Makers', *Journal of Democracy* 14, no. 4 (October 2003): 115-27.

Indian Penal Code, 1860, https://www.indiacode.nic.in/handle/123456789/2263?sam_handle=123456789/1362.

Information Technology Act, 2000, https://www.indiacode.nic.in/bitstream/123456789/13116/1/it_act_2000_updated.pdf.

International Institute for Democracy and Electoral Assistance, 'Political Finance Regulations Around the World', 2012, https://www.idea.int/sites/default/files/publications/political-finance-regulations-around-the-world.pdf.

Jagdeep Chhokar, 'The declining aura of the Election Commission', Civil Society, 2015, https://www.civilsocietyonline.com/column/election-tracker/the-declining-aura-of-the-election-commission/.

Jatin Verma, 'A Welcome Debate On Electoral Reforms', 12 July 2019, https://www.jatinverma.org/a-welcome-debate-on-electoral-reforms.

Landmark Judgements on Election Law, http://ceojk.nic.in/pdf/LandmarkJudgementsVOLIII.pdf.

Law Commission of India, Seventeenth Commission, https://lawcommissionofindia.nic.in/report_seventeenth/.

Mann ki Baat, https://www.pmindia.gov.in/hi/%E0%A4%AE%E0%A4%A8-%E0%A4%95%E0%A5%80-%E0%A4%AC%E0%A4%BE%E0%A4%A4/.

Model Code of Conduct, https://eci.gov.in/mcc/.

National Legal Services Authority vs. Union of India (2014),https://indiankanoon.org/doc/193543132/

Ornit Shani, How India Became Democratic: Citizenship and the Making of the Universal Franchise (Cambridge: Cambridge University Press, 2017).

Oxfam India, 2021-2022, https://www.oxfamindia.org/oxfam-annualreports.

Press Council of India, 'Norms of Journalistic Conduct', 2022, https://presscouncil.nic.in/WriteReadData/Pdf/Norms2022.pdf.

Proposal to amend the Representation of the People Act, 1951, https://loksabhadocs.nic.in/Refinput/New_Reference_Notes/English/The%20Representation%20of%20People%20(Amendment)%20Bill%202017.pdf

PTI, 'India falls to 53rd rank in EIU's Democracy Index, dubbed as flawed democracy', 4 February 2021, https://economictimes.indiatimes.com/news/politics-and-nation/india-falls-to-53rd-position-in-eius-democracy-index-dubbed-as-flawed-democracy/articleshow/80665859.cms?from=mdr

Rajiv Khandelwal, Amrita Sharma and Divya Varma, 'Creative Practices and Policies for Better Inclusion of Migrant Workers: The Experience of Aajeevika Bureau', https://www.aajeevika.org/assets/pdfs/Creative%20Practices%20and%20Policies%20Paper_Final.pdf.

Social Media Matters and Institute for Governance, Policies and Politics, https://www.socialmediamatters.in/impact-of-fake-news.

Susan B. Anthony, Universal Declaration of Human Rights at 70: 30 Articles on 30 Articles - Article 7, United Nations, https://www.ohchr.org/en/press-releases/2018/11/universal-declaration-human-rights-70-30-articles-30-articles-article-7.

Tanushree Basuroy, 'Internet usage in India - statistics & facts', Statista, 22 September 2022, https://www.statista.com/topics/2157/internet-usage-in-india/#topicOverview.

Thomas Carothers, 'Democracy without Illusions', Foreign Affairs 76, no. 1 (1997): 85–99. https://doi.org/10.2307/20047911.

Index

Aam Aadmi Party (AAP), 44, 71,
  325–328
Abubakar, Abdulsalami, 261
Abubakar, Atiku, 290
Acharya, Sandeep, 415
Adityanath, Yogi, 36, 83, 86, 348,
  416, 436
Advani, L.K., 34, 36, 84, 121, 130,
  242, 308
agenda setting, 179–180
AIADMK, 5, 61, 65, 182, 219
Ali, Aruna Asaf, 412
alliances: post-poll, 106–107,
  312–315; pre-poll, 106
All India Radio, 15
All Progressives Congress (APC),
  290
Ambedkar, B.R., 8, 213, 428
Amnesty International, 395
Anthony, Susan, 359

anti-defection law, 17, 48–49,
  103–105, 315, 317; Gujarat
  Vidhan Sabha elections in 2017,
  241; a piece of paper, 105
appointment in ECI: broad-based
  collegium, 30; chief election
  commissioner (CEC), 31–33;
  election commissioners (eCs),
  31–33
Ardern, Jacinda, 363
Arora, Sunil, 486
assembly polls, 96, 188, 260, 346,
  378
Association for Democratic
  Reforms (ADR), 16, 18, 140,
  145
Association of Asian Election
  Authorities (AAEA), 245
Awasthi, Malini, 361, 374
Aye, Tin, 279

Bahujan Samaj Party (BSP), 32–33, 71, 198, 214–215, 276
Bais, Ramesh, 334
Bajrang Dal, 437
ballot box and papers, 32–33, 48, 51, 68, 71, 75, 92, 96, 98, 104, 203, 215, 230, 234, 237, 267, 276, 284–285, 287, 292, 296, 378, 399, 428–429; debate on secrecy of, 50; e-postal ballot, 236, 239–240; printed at Government Security Press (Nasik) during first general elections, 428; stuffing, 302; use post introduction of EVMS, 76
Bandaranaike, Sirimavo, 364
Banerjee, Mamata, 365
Barot, Trushar, 422
Basu, Kaushik, 396
Bhutto, Benazir, 364
Biju Janata Dal (BJD), 32–33, 214–215
BJP, xix, xx, 32–34, 44, 50, 76, 87–88, 96–97, 205, 216, 241; on EVMs, 215; expenditure in 2019 elections for advertisement, 93; manifesto of: (2014, 129; 2019, 130); NDA government, 53, 186, 195; panna pramukhs, 402; political advertising, 408; political dominance on brand of Hindutva nationalism, 439; rise of Hindutva Pop, 415–416; Tek Fog app, 415; use of social media, 399, 412, 414–416; winning rate of women candidates, 364

black money use in elections, 19, 146, 152, 155, 158–159, 161–164, 191, 400
Bobde, S.A., 324
Brahma, Harishankar, 486
Brexit, 269–270, 276, 401, 418
British Polling Council, 176
Broadcast Audience Research Council (BARC), 168
Buhari, Muhammadu, 290
Burke, Edmund, 445–446

CAG, 147
Cambridge Analytica (CA): and elections in India, 405–408; scam on illegal data breaches for political influence, 418
Cameron, David, 269–270, 273
Campaign for Free and Fair Elections (CaFFE), 246
Carothers, Thomas, 12
cash-for-votes, 188
cashless economy, 159
caste-based hierarchy, 4
Central Bureau of Investigation (CBI), 46, 111, 113, 138
Central government schemes: Maternity Benefit (Amendment) Bill, 2017, 365; Pradhan Mantri Surakshit Matritva Abhiyan, 365; Pradhan Mantri Vaya Vandana Yojana, 365
Central Information Commission, 46, 339
Central Vigilance Commission, 46, 339

Centre for the Study of Developing Societies, New Delhi, 412–415

Chandrachud, D.Y., 63, 324, 333

Chandra, Sushil, 344, 346, 486

Chatterjee, Somnath, 327

Chatterji, Pulok, 39

Chawla, Navin, 486

Chhattisgarh by-election scam in 2014, 109–118

Chhokar, Jagdeep, 16

Chief Election Commissioner (CEC), 6, 22–23, 26, 27, 32, 36–37, 39, 46, 84, 188, 456

Chief Election Commissioner and other Election Commissioners (Conditions of Service) Amendment Act 1993, 471

children and youth of India: divisive politics on children, impact of, 445–447; duty to participate in voting process, 452–454; need to create non-farming jobs by 2030, 459; pollution of adolescents young minds, 448–451

Churchill, Sir Winston, 318

Citizenship Amendment Act, 396

Clinton, Hillary, xxii, 110, 284

Code of Criminal Procedure, 1973, 88

Code of Election Rules, 1961, 50, 241

common pool of funding, 19

communal hostilities, xvii

Communist Party of India (CPI), 32–33, 214–215

Communist Party of India- Marxist (CPI-M) (CPI (Marxist)), 32–33, 55–56, 140, 214–215

Companies Act: Section 182, 150

comptroller and auditor general (CAG) of India, 150, 195

Conduct of Election Rules, 1961, 55, 61, 230

Conduct of Elections Act, 15

Congress (I), 54, 61, 65

Congress (Indira), 54

Congress (O), 54, 61, 65

Congress (Tiwari), 54

Constituent Assembly of India, xvii, 4, 10, 13, 123, 213–214, 440

Constitutional governance, 439

Constitutional morality, 5

Constitution of India: Article 14, 441; Article 15, 441; Article 19, 174; Article 19(1)(a), 228, 232; Article 25 to 28, 441; Article 51(A), 441; Article 101, 466–467; Article 191, 467–468; Article 192(2), 334–335; Article 243K, 211; Article 243ZA, 211; Article 324, 4–5, 99, 309, 463–464; Article 324(2), 339; Article 325, 465; Article 326, 465; Article 327, 465–466; Article 328, 466; Article 329, 32, 49, 466; Article 370, 344, 346; ninety-first Constitutional amendment (2003), 317; promulgated on 26 January 1950, 4, 7, 12; seventy-third and seventy-fourth amendments, 5

Constitution of India Bill (1895),
  3–4
Corbyn, Jeremy, 270–271
corporate tax rates, 225
COVID-19 pandemic, 225,
  257–258, 285, 349, 363, 396;
  and Bihar elections, 91–94,
  98; challenge for conducting
  elections during, 95–98; (to
  avert political crisis, 99–101;
  lessons to be learnt from South
  Korea, 91–92, 95, 100–102);
  positive voters, 102; virtual
  rallies during, 97
criminalization in elections:
  criminal charges against Lok
  Sabha MPs, 140; ECI safeguards,
  134–135; Supreme Court
  directives and judgement on,
  133–134, 136–139, 142–143
cyber-attacks, 418

Dasmunshi, Priya Ranjan, 167
Dattatreya, Bandaru, 76
Debroy, Bibek, 125
defamation, 329, 331, 409
Delhi gangrape (16 December
  2012), 383, 449
Delimitation Commission Report
  2022, 344–346
democracy: expansion in Asia
  Pacific Region (APR), 386–387;
  in South Asian Region (SAR),
  387, 390–392
democracy (India), 6, 455; cause of
  concern and issues, 398–400;
  creation and importance of

new institutions, 381, 457;
  crime and violence against
  women, 382–383; custodians
  of, 318–324; drug abuse, 382;
  greatest democracy, 8; and
  independent judiciary, 393;
  and social media, 405–410;
  solutions, 398–400; source
  of national pride, 7; tenth
  largest economy by GDP, 381;
  unemployment rate, 382
democratic elections, 92, 96;
  platform for civil and political
  rights, 3
democratic pluralism, 12
demonetization of currency notes
  (8 November 2016), 191; bank
  transactions to disclose by BJP
  party legislators, 162; experts
  opinion on, 187; logistical
  challenges post, 162; objective
  of, 158–159, 161
Desai, Kishore Arun, 125
Deshapriya, Mahinda, 246
Devi, Rabri, 100
digital: infrastructure, 405;
  networking, 402
Digital Services and Digital Markets
  Act in 2020, European Union,
  410
Dinesh Goswami Committee, 19
direct-to-home (DTH) television,
  168–169
disinformation, 175, 181, 183,
  410–411, 414–416, 437, 444
Doordarshan (DD), 15, 165, 169
door-to-door campaigns, 349

Dravida Munnetra Kazhagam
(DMK), 32, 214, 407
drug abuse, xviii, 382
Dubey, Laxmi, 415

Easter terror attack in Sri Lanka (21
April 2019), 254
Election Commissioners
(Conditions of Service)
Amendment Act, 1991, 470–471
Election Commission of India
(ECI), 4–6, 8–9, 17, 20, 22–24,
26, 30, 83, 178, 216, 260, 273,
282, 288, 319–320, 381, 418,
427–428, 455; advocating for
common electoral roll for all
elections, 209; appointments
and removals of ECs, 33–34;
cancellation of Tamil Nadu
assembly seats in 2009, 188;
conference on scourge of money
power in elections (2015), 164;
data, kinds of, 402; expenditure-
control mechanisms (2010),
161; -Facebook collaboration,
403; flaws in appointment
system, 36–37; grievances and
recommendations, 321–324;
issues and debates on, 48–51;
to make fully independent,
45–46; measures on fake
news, 422; motto of no voter
left behind, 227; neutrality,
39–42; points of concern,
35–36; power to contempt of
Constitution, 43–45; proposal
for expansion of postal ballots,
227; to provide protection to
two commissioners, 46–47; role
of, 14–16; seeking power to
de-register political parties for
violations, 37–38; systematic
voter education for electoral
participation (SVEEP)
programme, 92, 96, 184, 393;
trust deficit, 31–33; Voluntary
Code of Ethics, 94; voter ID-
Aadhar linking, 340–343, 403;
Youth Unite for Voter Awareness
(YUVA), 454
Election Laws (Amendment) Bill
2021, 340
election management bodies:
Election Commission of India
(ECI), 210; State Election
Commissions (SECs), 209–210
elections at a glance (2019-1952):
candidates growth, 491–496;
election exercise, 517–521;
electors, 488–494; performance
of parties, 505–516; polling,
488–494; poll percentage,
501–505; Presidential elections,
521–524; Vice-Presidential
elections, 525–528; voters,
488–494
Election Symbols (Reservation and
Allotment) Order, 1968, 15, 56,
137, 316; Section 15, 53–54,
63–64
election-time corruption, 115–116
electoral autocracy, 394, 456
electoral bonds, 28, 145–148, 150–
151, 214, 323; advantages of,

152; Electoral Bonds Scheme, 151; heavy bias in favour of ruling party, 153–154; hidden alphanumeric number, 151; increase in funding in Union Budget 2017, 149; issue with, 152–153; life of, 152; period of purchase, 152

electoral democracy, 6, 9, 85, 187, 248, 282, 406

electoral frameworks comparison between India and US, 281–283

electoral mobilization, 407, 435

electoral process, 4, 6, 8, 36; and role of judiciary, 111, 113

electoral reforms, 6, 198; advocacy over years for, 30; consideration of three reforms, 209; Goswami Committee report on electoral reforms (1990), 28, 214; Indrajit Gupta Committee report on state funding of elections (1998), 28; issues and debates on: (advocacy over years, 216; appointment process of election commissioner, 213–215; simultaneous elections, 215–216); need for, 16–21; short-duration discussion in Rajya Sabha, 213

electoral representation in India vs other countries, 364–365

electoral results between 2019-1952, 490–493

electoral rolls, 20; common, 33–34; fidelity of, 33; process of making, 210; proposal to link with Aadhaar, 212; Registration of Electors Rules, 1960, 210

electoral voting system, consequences of: corruption in elections by using money power, 191–192; election trust fund, 194–195; independent auditor, 195; political parties ignore ECI demands, 193–194; state funding of polls, 192; transparency in donations, 192–193

electronically transmitted postal ballot system (ETPB system), 233–235

electronic voting machines (EVMs), xvi, 31, 33, 35, 44–45, 97–98, 275, 289, 399–400; ballot papers use to conduct elections in Andhra Pradesh, 76; declared illegal in Germany, 68; ECI on excessive heat for malfunctioning of, 67; ended invalid votes problem, 69; issue of hackability, 73; judicial scrutiny, 74; makes election process transparent, 69; security, four tiers of, 73–74; stringent trials, 77; tamperability issue of, 68; three generations of, 72; voter-verified paper audit trail (VVPAT), 31, 36, 67–70, 75, 77, 232, 285, 400, 418; (audit, 78; procurement of machines before 2019, 74)

Erum, Nazia: *Mothering a Muslim*, 446

European Society for Opinion and Market Research (ESOMAR), 185–186

Faizal, Mohammed, 330
Faizabadi, Sanjay, 415
Federation of Indian Chambers of Commerce and Industry (FICCI), 168
Finance Bill, 150
financial fraud, 169
first general elections of India (1951 to 1952), 457; ECI expenditure on per elector, xx; electoral process, 8; held from 1951 to 1952, 7, 9; to make first electoral roll, 9–11; organizers and challenges in conducting, 425–429; registered voters, 7
first-past-the-post (FPTP) system, 201–202, 204, 267–268, 275–276; advantages of, 198; defined, 197; in India, 198–199; winner-takes-all nature of, 199
Foreign Contribution (Regulation) Act (FCRA), 214
Forum of the Management Bodies of South Asia (FEMBoSA), 245
freebies (revdi culture) promises during election: and ECI guidelines, 218–219; true interventionist, 222–223; types of, 217–218; vs welfarism, 223–226
frequent elections: benefits of, 122–127, 130–132

Fulghum, Robert: *All I Really Need to Know, I Learned in Kindergarten,* 448

Gandhi, Indira, xvi, 61, 199, 360, 364
Gandhi, Mahatma, xv, 248; International Day of Non-violence to commemorate, xvi
Gandhi, Rahul, 347, 409; disqualification from parliament on Modi surname remark, 329–332
Gandhi, Rajiv, 104
gender sensitization, xxi, 360
general elections: 2014, 26, 125, 131; (voter turnout, 398–399); 2019, xxi, 22–24, 86; (course correction, 208; expensive election, xx; MCC violations and counting, 206–208; role of three Ms (money, media and mafia), 206; seven phases, controversy over, 205–206; Voluntary Code of Ethics, 409)
Gill, M. S., 486
Gogoi, Ranjan, 324
Gopalaswami, N., 34, 36, 240, 486
Government of India (Transaction of Business) Rules, 1961, 107
Governments Acts of 1919 and 1935, 4
Governor: role of, 106–107; role in Maharashtra MLAs disqualification, 333–336
Gowda, Rajeev, 214

Grover, A.N., 55, 64–65
Gupta, Indrajit, 192

Habermas, Jürgen, 179
Harishankar Brahma, 486
Hasina, Sheikh, 364
Hassan, Issack, 295
hate speech, 24, 32, 79–81, 170, 207,
    259, 291, 331, 404, 410, 414,
    419, 424, 435–438, 444
Hazare, Anna, 46
Hegde, K.S., 55, 64–65
Hindustan Times, xxiii
Horowitz, Donald, 197

Independent Electoral and
    Boundaries Commission
    (IEBC), 294–299
Inderjeet Gupta Committee on
    State Funding of Elections, 19
India International Institute of
    Democracy and Election
    Management (IIIDEM), 293,
    304
Indian National Congress (INC),
    xvi, 13, 109, 185, 313; political
    advertising, 408; split in 1969
    and 1978, 54–56, 65
Indian Penal Code (IPC), 1860, 79,
    81, 88, 117–118, 174, 180–181,
    329, 403–404, 409, 436
Indian Polling Council, 177, 186
Indian Telegraph Act (1885), 419
Information Technology (IT) Act,
    2000, 402, 409–410, 419
Information Technology
    (Intermediary Guidelines and
Digital Media Ethics Code)
    Rules, 2021, 415
inner-party democracy, 215
intermixing among communities,
    impact of, 383–384
International Coal Ventures Limited
    (ICVL), 301
International Criminal Court
    (ICC), 299
international general elections:
    Kenya, 294–299; Mozambique,
    300–304; Myanmar, 277–280;
    Nepal, 265–268; Nigeria:
    (connecting with India,
    292–293; election data,
    290–291; gaps during poll,
    291–292); Pakistan, 261–262;
    Sri Lanka elections in 2015,
    2019 and 2020, 245–260;
    (People's Action for Free and
    Fair Elections (PAFFREL),
    246, 250); UK, 269–276;
    United States; (bunch of
    simultaneous elections, 286–
    287; election system, features
    of, 286; electoral college
    and its limitations, 282–284;
    electoral framework, 281–283;
    federal bodies to elections, 292;
    polling station, 291; turnout
    in presidential election (2012),
    287; voting process, 284–285;
    voting systems, 287)
International Institute for
    Democracy and Electoral
    Assistance (International IDEA),
    Stockholm (2012), 385, 391;

study on Political Finance Regulations Around the World, 156–157, 195

International Monetary Fund (IMF) on India's digital payments revolution, 458

International Republican Institute (IRI), 253, 256

Internet and Mobile Association of India (IAMAI): on social media campaign, 399; Voluntary Code of Ethics, 419–420, 423

internet users in India, 406

Islamophobia, 416

Jaffrelot, Christophe, 431

Jaitley, Arun, 145, 323

James Michael Lyngdoh, 486

Jammu and Kashmir: abrogation of special status in 2019, 344–345; Constitution, 344; Kashmiri migrants, 346; Kashmiri Pandits, 346; last delimitation exercise in 1995, 345; pro-ruling party bias, 346; Reorganisation Act, 2019, 344; Representation of the People Act, 1957, 344–345; seats reserved for Pakistan-Occupied Kashmir (PoK), 346

Janaki, 54

Janata Dal, 54, 65

Janata Dal (United) (JD(U)), 53–54, 140, 215

Janata Dal (S), 54, 313

Jawaharlal Nehru University, 438

Jayalalithaa, J., 54, 61, 65, 430

Jogi, Ajit, 115

Joint Parliamentary Committee (JPC), 326–327

Joshi, C.P., 98

Joti, A.K., 44, 325–326

judicial activism, 139

Justice B.N. Srikrishna Committee, 342

Justice Punchhi Commission (2007), 107, 336

Justice Sarkaria Commission (1983), 106–108, 313–315, 336

Justice V.R. Krishna Iyer Committee (1994), 17

Jyoti, Achal Kumar, 51, 486

Kalam, A.P.J. Abdul, 26, 326

Kamath, H.V., 440

Kejriwal, Arvind, 44, 224–225

Kerala Vidhan Sabha, 123

Khan, Liaquat Ali, 429

Khanna, H.R., 55, 64–65

Khan, Saumitra, xix

Khurshid, Salman, 41, 87–88

Ki-moon, Ban, 278

Kovind, Ramnath, 5

Krishnamurthy, T. S., 240, 486

Krishnavanshi, Prem, 415–416

Kumaratunga, Chandrika, 364

Kumar, Rajiv, 486

Kunzru, Pandit, 440

Lal, Chaudhary Bansi, xxiv

Lal, Gaya, 104, 315

Lalit, U.U., 324

Law Commission, 84, 128; 227th report (2009), 450–451; 255th report (March 2015), 192; 267th report (March 2017), 436–437; seventeenth report on Reform of the Electoral Laws, 17

L'Engle, Madeleine, 447

Locke, John, 179

Lok Janshakti Party (LJP): split of, 53–56

Lok Sabha, 5–6, 121, 123, 202–204, 208–209, 360, 371

LTTE, 250

Lyngdoh, James Michael, 486

Madison, James, 12, 282

Mahalanobis, P.C., 396

Maharastra politics: BJP-Shiv Sena alliance, 106; involvement of president and prime minister offices, 107–108; Shiv Sena-Congress-Nationalist Congress Party (Maha Vikas Aghadi), 106

Malaviya, Amit, 414–415

Marin, Sanna, 363

May, Theresa, 269–270, 272–273

Media Certification and Monitoring Committee (MCMC), 409

media ecosystem, 412–414

MGNREGA, 459

migrants right to vote: cause of issue, 232–235; ECI decision for pilot remote voting for domestic migrants, 231, 234; electronically transmitted postal ballot system (ETPB system), 233–234; Multi-Constituency Remote Electronic Voting Machine (RVM), 231–232, 234

ministry of home affairs (MHA), 350

ministry of information and broadcasting (MIB), 167; Policy Guidelines for Television Rating Agencies in India (2014), 168

Mishra, Kapil, 93

Misra, Dipak, 20, 136, 324

Mitra, Amit, 168

Mittal, Kanhiya, 416

mixed-member proportional (MMP) voting system: in Germany, 201–202; in Nepal, 203

Moddie, Mandira, 402, 418

Model Code of Conduct (MCC) during elections, 16, 35, 47, 83, 121, 131, 161, 173, 189, 205, 217–218, 404, 424; code of self-discipline evolved by political parties, 86; laws, 79–82; legalization of, 83–87; political leaders views on, 87; violations, 79–82; (in multi-phase elections, 347–351)

modern democracy, xvi

Modi: A Common Man's Journey web series, 36

Modi, Narendra, xvi, 34, 36, 51, 124–125, 128–129, 160–161, 199, 204, 215, 220, 229, 241–242, 375, 408–409; advocacy of compulsory voting, 27; ANI interview before first phase of Uttar Pradesh elections in 2022, 347–348; anti-satellite (ASAT) test, 35; *Mann Ki Baat,* 27, 452;

NaMo app, 414; NaMo TV, 35;
on role of youth and New India
Youth, 452–453; *Sab ka saath, sab
ka vikaas* slogan, 384; suggestions
for simultaneous elections, 121;
toilets for women priority, 383;
vision for new India, 47
Modi, Sushil Kumar, 211
Moily, Veerappa, 41
money-laundering industry, 189
money power role during elections,
xx–xxi, 116–118, 188–191
Mukherjee, Pranab, 202, 327
Mukherjee, S.N., 11, 427
multiple single-vote victory
margins, 183
Muslim representation in India, xix

Naidu, N. Chandrababu, 61, 76
Naidu, Sarojini, 359–360
Narsinghanand, Yati, 438
Nasim Zaidi, 486
National Aids Control Organisation
(NACO), 379
National Committee to Review
the Working of the Constitution
(NCRWC), 17, 20
National Crimes Record Bureau,
138
National Democratic Institute
(NDI), 253–254, 256
National Disaster Management
Authority, 96
National Human Rights
Commission, 339
Nationalist Congress Party, 140
national media, 411

National Youth Day (12 January),
452
Negi, Shyam Saran, 429
Nehru, Jawaharlal, 7, 426
Nehru Report of 1928, 4
New Delhi Declaration of Guiding
Principles for Regulating
Political Finance in South Asia,
2015, 118, 189
New Education Policy, xxi
news: fake, 20, 419, 421–424; paid,
20, 160, 274
NFHS on total fertility rate (TFR)
of India, 458–459
NITI Aayog, 33, 125–126, 215,
397
non-bailable warrants (NBW), 350
None of the Above (NOTA),
48–50, 75, 184; option in Rajya
Sabha polls, 241–242
non-resident Indians (NRIs)
voting, 235–236; proxy voting,
236–238; (arguments against,
238–239); right to free and fair
elections, 239–240

O'Brien, Derek, 213; cheat India
platforms, 213; initiated electoral
reforms in Rajya Sabha,
213–214
office of profit, 335; appointments
of AAP government case,
325–328
open-list variant of the system, 200
Opposition parties, 31, 78, 92–94,
96, 161, 207, 213, 219, 222, 224,
246, 257, 269, 408

Organisation of Economic Co-operation and Development (OECD), 459

Padmanabhan, K.V., 11, 423
panchayat elections, 123, 127, 209, 220
Pandey, Pooja Shakun, 438
Parrikar, Manohar, 84, 87
participatory democracy, 44
participatory revolution, 458
Partition of India, xvii, 4, 8–10, 426–427, 460
party systems in other countries, 13–14
Pascal, Blaise, 179
Paswan, Chirag, 53
Patnaik, Naveen, 24, 130, 365
Pawar, Ajit, 100
Pawar, Manturam, 117
Pegasus spyware, 416–417
People's Democratic Party (PDP), 290
Phoolan Devi, 446
Planning Commission, 381
PMO, 39–42, 211
political leaders, 5, 31, 34, 80, 86–87, 92–93, 100, 113, 118
political parties in India: capping of election expenditure for, 32; exhibit collective political, 21; horse-trading in, 48, 50, 105, 159, 241–242; post-election funding of, 155–157; public funding of, 150; state funding of, 18
politician-bureaucracy nexus, 191

politics of hatred in India, 435–438
polls: exit, 174–177, 180–181, 186; online, 186; opinion, 174–183, 185
population growth rate of India, 458–459; as per 2011 census, 487–488
Prasad, Lalu, 100
Press Council of India, 183–184
PRI Act, 1993, 210
Prime Minister, 5, 7, 27, 34, 35–36, 39, 46–47, 83, 100, 107, 128, 158–159, 207–208, 222
prisoners right to vote: guilty or marginalized, 228–229; international trends, 229–230; solution for, 230
proportional representation (PR) system of voting, 201, 267–268, 276; defined, 200; features of, 200; International Institute for Democracy and Electoral Assistance report (2017), 203; issues in, 200–201
proxy voting, 237
public contempt for politicians, 400
public governance, 411
public interest litigation (PIL), 227
public opinion, 179–180
Pudo, Rupdhar, 116–117
Punchhi Commission (2007), 314

Quraishi, S.Y., xxiii–xxv, 242, 486; *An Undocumented Wonder - the Making of the Great Indian Election,* 110, 115, 189, 248, 453; *The Great March of Democracy:*

Seven Decades of India's Elections, 431

Quraishi, Zubair, xxii–xxiii

Radhakrishnan, K.S., 378

Rai, S.M., 364

Raja, D., 215

Rajapaksa, Gotabaya, 259–260

Rajapaksa, Mahinda, 247–248, 250–251, 254–256, 259

Rajya Sabha, 48–50, 91, 213, 378; Election Laws (Amendment) Bill (2017), 209; Jharkhand elections, 308; Karnataka elections, horse trading in, 307–317; votes buying in Jharkhand in 2012, 111, 114

Ramadevi, V.S., 486

Ramana, N.V., 224, 324

Ramoni, 366

ranking of India: Borders' Press Freedom Report, 396; Economist Intelligence Unit (EIU) report of 2021, 394–397, 455; Freedom House Index for 2021, 394; Gender Development Index, 359, 383; Gender Equality Index, 359; Global Democracy Index, xxii; Global State of Democracy Index (GSoD), 381–388, 391–393; UNDP's human development index, xviii, 381

Rao, D. Subba, 190

Rashtriya Mukti Morcha, 325

Rashtriya Swayamsevak Sangh, 412

Rau, B.N., 11, 427

Ravi, R.N., 334

Rawat, Om Prakash, 44, 51, 328, 403, 486

Reddy, Muthulakshmi, 360

referendum in UK on voting system, 197–198

Reliance Jio, 414

Representation of People Act (RPA), 1951, 68, 79–80, 88, 117, 160, 174, 176–177, 180, 280–281, 322–323, 331, 404, 423–424, 426; provisions for: conduct of elections in India, 470; preparation of electoral rolls and connected matters, 489–470; Section 8, 20, 137; Section 14(b), 211; Section 20 (8), 230; Section 29(A), 15, 37, 85; Section 54, 309; Section 60, 230; Section 60(c), 233; Section 62(5), 227–228; Section 123, 181; Section 125, 436; Section 126, 348–349, 420; Section 153, 100; Section 169A, 43

returning officer (RO), 50

Right to Information Act (RTI), 18

Roy, Prannoy, 348

Roy, Ram Mohan, 412

RTI Act, 163

SAARC countries: Conference on Regulating Campaign Finance: Ensuring Free and Fair Elections (2014), 189

Sahasrabuddhe, Vinay, 215

Samajwadi Party (SP), 30, 214, 216; war on symbol, 57–58

Sampath, V. S., 486

Sarma, K.S., 167

Sastri, R.K. Peri, 486

secrecy of ballot, 48

secularism in India: constitutional
secularism, 440; features of, 443–
444; judicialization approach,
442–443; rights-based approach,
441; and rise of BJP, 439

Sen, Amartya, 6, 9

Sen, Sukumar, 426, 428, 431, 485

Sen, Verma, S. P., 485

Seshan, T.N., 349–350, 430–431, 486

sex education, xxii

Shah, Amit, 33

Shaheen Bagh anti-CAA NRC
protest, 82

Shailaja, K.K., 363

Shakdhar, S. L., 485

Shakespeare, William: on public
opinion, 179

Shani, Ornit, 11; *How India Became
Democratic,* 431; *How India
became Democratic,* 9–10

Sharma, Anand, 198

Sharma, K.K., 344

Shinde, Eknath, 63

Shiva Sena: split in 2022 and claim
for party symbol, 63–66

Sibal, Kapil, 214

simultaneous elections, 121–124,
215–216, 224; concerns over,
130–131; hurdles in, 131–132;
need for healthy debate,
132; obstacles in conducting,
125–128

Singh, Dara, 437–438

Singh, Kalyan, 36

Singh, Manmohan, 39, 46, 326

Singh, Nagendra, 485

Singh, Raman, 115

Sinha, Sharada, 361, 374

Sirisena, Maithripala, 247, 251–252

social media in India: media
regulation for new age, 409–410;
political advertising, 407–408;
rise of data, 405; trends, 406–407

social media platforms, 451;
accountability of, 417–420;
Google, 93, 406–407, 423;
Helo, 414; Meta (earlier
Facebook), 93–94, 97, 401, 403,
406–408, 414–415, 417, 423,
437; ShareChat, 414; Twitter,
93, 224, 406, 408, 414–415,
417, 422–423; WeChat, 423;
WhatsApp, 417, 423; use among
Indians, 413–414; YouTube, 72,
407, 415, 437

social polarization, 383

Sonkar, Vinod, 415

Soren, Hemant, 334–335

South Asian democracy, 363–366

Spary, Carole, 362

Spock, Benjamin: *Baby and Child
Care,* 448

Sri Lanka Freedom Party (SLFP),
251

Stern-LaRosa, M., 446

Subramanian, P.S., 11, 427

Sundaram, Kalyan, 485

Supreme Court of India, 34, 37, 40,
55–56, 113, 147–148, 324, 381,
399; on Aadhaar, 212; *Abhiram
Singh vs. C.D. Commachen* (2017),
482; *A.C. Jose vs. Sivan Pillai*

and Others (1984), 473–474; *Anoop Baranwal vs. Union of India* (2023), 482–483; appointment of election commissioners, 337–339; *Bhim Singh vs. the Election Commission* (1996), 14; *Dr Subramanian Swamy vs. Election Commission of India* (2013), 480–481; *Election Commission of India through Secretary vs. Ashok Kumar* (2000), 476; *Gadakh Yashwantrao Kankarrao vs. EV Alias Balasaheb Vikhe Patil* (1994), 475–476; on hate speeches, 36–37; *Indian National Congress (I) vs. the Institute of Social Welfare & Ors.* (2002), 15–16, 477–478; *Kesavananda Bharati vs. State of Kerala* (1973), 442; *Kihoto Hollohan vs. Zachillhu and Others* (1992), 104, 312, 316; *Krishnamoorthy vs. Shiv Kumar & Ors.* (2015), 481–482; *K.S. Puttaswamy vs. Union of India* (2017), 341; *Lily Thomas vs. Union of India & Ors.* (2013), 479–480; *Lok Prahari vs. Election Commission of India* (2018), 330; on manifesto promises, 222; *Mohinder Singh Gill vs. Chief Election Commissioner* (1978), 14, 183, 318–319, 321, 472–473; *National Legal Services Authority vs. Union of India* (2014), 378; *N.P. Ponnuswami vs. Returning Officer, Namakkal Constituency* (1952), 319–320, 471; *People's Union for Civil Liberties (PUCL) vs.*

Union of India & Ors (2003), 228, 478–479, 480; *Ratilal Panchand vs. State of Bombay* (1954), 441; *R.C. Poudyal vs. Union of India* (1993), 474–475; reprimanded ECI on UP elections, 436; *Sadiq and Anr. Vs. Election Commission* (1972), 320, 472; *Shreya Singhal and Ors vs. Union of India* (2015), 409–410; *Shrimanth Balasaheb Patel & Ors vs. Speaker Karnataka Legislative Assembly & Ors* (2019), 104–105, 316; *S.R. Bommai vs. Union of India* (1994), 442–443; *S.R. Chaudhuri vs. State of Punjab and Ors* (2001), 100; *Union of India vs. Association of Democratic Reforms* (2002), 476–477; *Union of India vs. Harbans Singh Jalali* (2001), 320

Suu Kyi, Aung San, 278–280
Swaminathan, T., 485

Taliban women conditions, 367–370
Tamil National Alliance (TNA), 250–251
Tandon, B.B., 34, 36, 84, 486
Tek Fog, 416
Telangana Rashtra Samithi (TRS), 76
Telecom Regulatory Authority (TRAI), 167–168
television rating agencies: INTAM, 165–166; television audience measurement (TAM), 165–167
television (TV) channels/media: Cable Television Network Rules

of 1994, 171; Cable Television Networks (Regulation) Act of 1995, 171; myths and realities, 178–186; National Broadcasting Standards Authority (NBSA), 171–173; need for laws and regulations, 170–173; News Broadcasters Association (NBA), 171–172; Policy Guidelines for Uplinking of Television Channels from India of 2000, 171; television rating point (TRP) scandal, 165–169; sting operation in 2014, 184–185; Supreme Court directives on 2020, 170

Telugu Desam Party, 61, 76

Thackeray, Uddhav, 63, 99–100

Thakur, Anurag, 81–82

Thatcher, Margaret, 360, xvi

Thero, Sobitha, 251–252

Towards Equality - The Report of the Committee on the Status of Women in India, 1975, 450

transgender people (or hijra community) in India: cultural and social significance, 376; and Election Commission, 377–379; HIV among, 378–379; life cycle of, 377; socio-economically marginalized communities, 376–377; Transgender Persons (Protection of Rights) Bill, 2016, 378

Trinamool Congress (TMC), xix, 31–34, 182, 198–199, 213–214, 216, 364; women-centric schemes, 361

Trivedi, R. K., 486

Trump, Donald, 288

T.S. Krishnamurthy, 486

two tied verdicts, 183

Tyagi, Jitendra, 434

Udasin, Mahant Bajrang Muni, 437–438

UN Human Development Index, 224

UN International Day of Democracy, 390

UN International Yoga Day, xvi

United People's Freedom Alliance (UPFA), 251

universal adult suffrage, 4, 10

Uttarakhand Kranti Dal, 54, 65

Vajpayee, Atal Bihari, 214

Varma, Parvesh Sahib Singh, 81–85

vasudhaiva kutumbakam, xvi

vendetta politics, 141

Venugopal, K.K., 138, 319

Verma, J.S., 171, 187

Vidhan Sabha, 71, 100, 121, 123, 130, 155, 194, 209–210, 241, 307

violence, 17, 132, 295, 363, 416, 429, 435; class or community, 436; communal, 278; election-related, 33, 213, 246, 253–256, 279, 292; electoral, 400; gender-based, 365, 377; ghost of, 296–299; mob, 438; post-election, 294; Ram Navami, 438; social media-induced, 413; against women, 382

Viswanathan, K.V., 141

Vivekananda, Swami, 452
voters, 9–11, 14–16, 31, 68–69, 122,
    131, 137, 141, 179, 183, 187,
    189, 199–204, 214, 218–223,
    226–227, 230–231, 236, 251,
    258–259, 272, 274–275, 283,
    286–288, 290–291, 322, 324,
    356–357, 365, 398, 402, 408,
    415, 418, 422, 429, 452–454,
    458; bribing of, 19, 116, 131,
    155, 161, 188; duplicate, 212,
    403; enticement activities, 162;
    floating, 255; identification
    technology, 299; information
    deficit, 17; manipulation, 20;
    migrant, 232–235; minds, 123;
    mobilization, 406; National
    Voter's Day (Matdaata
    Mahotsav), 25–27, 275, 403,
    454; NRI, 239; outreach, 20–21,
    93; proxy, 237; security, 205;
    transgender, 378; turnouts,
    xix–xx, 92, 96, 102, 197, 399;
    women, 4, 372–374
V. S. Sampath, 486

Washington, George, 12
Wen, Tsai-Ing, 363, 385
Wickremesinghe, Ranil, 252,
    254–255
WikiLeaks, 188
women participation and
    representation in politics:
    33 per cent reservation in
    panchayati raj Institutions
    (PRIs), 375; ECI: (decision
    in Uttar Pradesh elections
    in 2012, 356; survey on gaps
    with social categories, 356);
    electoral representation of,
    xix–xx; female participation in
    voting, 372–373; obstacles in
    contesting and getting elected,
    357–358; participation of
    women as candidates, 374–375;
    pre-election surveys, 373–374;
    registration of women voters,
    372; reservation in panchayat
    elections, 355; voter turnout
    among women, 374; women
    out-voted men in state
    assembly elections, 357; women
    politicians, 355; Women's
    Reservation Bill, 358, 364, 458
women status in India vs other
    countries, 359–362
World Association for Public
    Opinion Research (WAPOR),
    186
World Congress on Public Opinion
    Research, 186
World Democracy Day, 385
World Food Programme, 225
World Press Freedom Index, 224
Wylie, Christopher, 401, 418

Yadav, Akhilesh, 60, 62
Yadav, Lalu Prasad, 430
Yadav, Ram Gopal, 31, 62, 216
Yadav, Umlesh, 163
YSR Congress Party (YSRCP),
    215

Zaidi, Nasim, 486
Zhang, Sophie, 415
Zia, Khaleda, 362

Acknowledgements

This rather hefty book that you now hold in your hands is a product of multiple decades of my life. You will find within it essays, reflections, questions and explorations that have kept me occupied all throughout my career, ever since I started as an IAS officer in the early 1970s. It would therefore be an impossibly long and vertiginous effort to name all those that rightfully deserve their mention here. To all the unnamed whose lives have touched and transformed me over the course of these many decades, I bow in gratitude.

However, there are those directly responsible for the production of this book that I must mention here with thankfulness. Firstly, to the editors in whose esteemed publications many of the essays present here first appeared: Shekhar Gupta and Raj Kamal Jha of

The Indian Express, N. Ram of *The Hindu*, Rajesh Ramachandran of *The Tribune* Chandigarh and formerly *Outlook*, Kaushik Mitter of *The Asian Age* and *Deccan Chronicle*, Siddharth Varadarajan of The Wire, and Paresh Nath of *The Caravan*, among many others. Additionally, I am also deeply grateful for all the publications in whose pages many of these essays first appeared: *The Hindustan Times*, *The Quint*,

India Today, India Seminar, *Deccan Herald, Livemint, Business Standard, The Telegraph India* and *The Economic Times*.

My heartfelt thanks also to Abhishek Matta, my energetic and resourceful research associate, who has been present ever since the earliest stages when the book was yet to acquire a concrete form. He compiled and edited all the essays while assisting me with all the necessary research for the book. Likewise, I wish to wholeheartedly thank all my brilliant and highly gifted former research associates whose research work and conversations were integral to all the articles published here: Nikita Singh, Shivanshi Asthana, Ushmayo Bhattacharya, Shruti Slaria and Tripti Jain.

I am deeply grateful to the ever-brilliant Swati Chopra, the associate publisher at HarperCollins, for her diligence, patience and generosity throughout the long and seemingly interminable process of book publication. Kripa Raman and Shreya Mukherjee were keen, astute and ever-vigilant copy editors whose many suggestions improved the book by a large measure. I am grateful to Saurav Das for his brilliant and eye-catching cover design.

Annexure of the book is full of incredibly useful and enlightening tables and data sets concerning the infinite realm of Indian elections. All of them were taken from the magisterial reference book *Election Atlas of India,* edited and directed by Dr R.K. Thukral, for whose efforts our entire nation must be as proud and thankful as I am.

It is with immense gratitude that I extend my sincerest appreciation to Dr Shashi Tharoor, whose exceptional wisdom and eloquence graced the pages of this book with a profound foreword. I am also deeply indebted to all the distinguished personalities whose kind and generous words of advanced praise have not only touched my heart but have also added shining endorsements to this book.

Finally, to Ila, my wife, my first and most unforgiving reader, who vetted every word of every article that I wrote with her long editorial experience and expertise.

About the Author

Dr S.Y. QURAISHI joined the Indian Administrative Service in 1971 and rose to become the seventeenth chief election commissioner of India. He was featured in *The Indian Express*' list of 100 Most Powerful Indians of 2011 and 2012. He introduced a number of electoral reforms, such as the creation of a voter education division, expenditure monitoring division and the India International Institute of Democracy and Election Management, and launched the National Voter's Day. In October 2017, he was appointed the ambassador of democracy by International IDEA (Institute of Democracy and Electoral Assistance), Stockholm, of which he is a board member. He is the author of the two highly acclaimed books, *An Undocumented Wonder: The Making of the Great Indian Election* and *The Population Myth: Islam, Family Planning and Politics in India*. He is also the editor of *The Great March of Democracy: Seven Decades of India's Elections*. He currently resides in New Delhi.